True BASIC™ Primer

William S. Davis
Miami University,
Oxford, Ohio

▲▼▲
ADDISON-WESLEY PUBLISHING COMPANY
Reading, Massachusetts • Menlo Park, California
Don Mills, Ontario • Wokingham, England • Amsterdam
Sydney • Singapore • Tokyo • Mexico City • Bogotá
Santiago • San Juan

To Carl and Jay

Library of Congress Cataloging-in-Publication Data

Davis, William S., 1943—
    True BASIC primer.

  Includes bibliographies and index.
  1. Basic (Computer program language) I. Title.
QA76.73.B3D39 1986   005.13'3   85-15656
ISBN 0-201-03225-2

This Book is in the Addison-Wesley True BASIC™ Series.

True BASIC™ is a trademark of True BASIC, Inc.

Reproduced by Addison-Wesley from camera-ready copy approved by the author.

Copyright © 1986 by Addison-Wesley Publishing Company, Inc.

All rights reserved. No part of this publication may be reproduced, stored in a retrieval system, or transmitted, in any form or by any means, electronic, mechanical, photocopying, or otherwise, without the prior written permission of the publisher. Printed in the United States of America. Published simultaneously in Canada.

ISBN 0-201-03225-2
CDEFGHIJ-HA-89876

Preface

BASIC, the Beginner's All-purpose Symbolic Instruction Code, has been around for quite some time. Developed in 1964 by two Dartmouth College Professors, John Kemeny and Thomas Kurtz, this simple, easy-to-use, non-threatening language is ideal for beginners. Today, it is the world's most popular programming language. IBM has a version. So do Apple, Microsoft, Radio Shack, Atari, and virtually any other microcomputer maker you can name.

Unfortunately, no two BASICs are quite the same. IBM BASIC differs from Apple BASIC, and the version that runs on a Radio Shack computer differs from both of them. A program written in Apple BASIC won't run on an Atari computer, or on an IBM PC®. Moving from one BASIC to another is difficult, as key features are implemented in subtly different ways. There *is* no single language called BASIC. Instead, we have a series of dialects, all derived from the original Dartmouth version.

A great deal has changed since 1964. For one thing, the essential concepts of structured programming have gained wide acceptance. New languages, such as Pascal, have been developed with these structured concepts in mind. Many BASIC dialects have incorporated some of these up-to-date ideas, but, unfortunately, few use the same format. Consequently, the various BASIC dialects have grown even less alike.

Technology has changed, too. Back in 1964, punched card input and printed output were the norms, but today we have graphic terminals, plotters, audio input and output units, and many other devices for communicating with a computer. Most BASIC dialects support at least some of these modern technologies, but, once again, they're all different.

What if Kemeny and Kurtz were to start over? What if they were to redesign their language from the ground up? They'd probably keep the best features of original BASIC: simplicity and ease of use. They would certainly incorporate modern structured, modular programming concepts, and might be expected to add features supporting such up-to-date technologies as graphics and sound. The American National Standards Institute is currently developing an ANS standard BASIC; Kemeny and Kurtz could be expected to follow that standard. The result would be a modern, easy to use, standard BASIC.

Well, they've done it. Their new language, *True BASIC*, incorporates modern structured programming concepts in a simple, elegant, almost obvious way. Independent subroutines are supported. Missing in most BASIC dialects, they are essential to good, modular program design, and they give the programmer access to a vast library of existing subroutines. After having struggled with graphics in another BASIC, I was particularly pleased with *True BASIC*'s graphics support. I am convinced that once you've tried *True BASIC*, you'll never again be satisfied with another version. Like original BASIC in 1964, *True BASIC* promises to set a new standard.

True BASIC Primer has been written to help you learn this new language. It has two primary objectives:

1. To teach a beginner how to analyze a problem and develop a plan for writing a computer program.

2. To teach a beginner or a self-taught programmer how to write well-structured programs in *True BASIC*.

The book assumes no prior programming experience and little or no mathematics beyond high school algebra. It is designed to be used as a textbook or as a self-study guide. Numerous examples and programming exercises are presented; suggested answers to selected exercises can be found in an appendix.

Programming is a two-step process. The programmer begins with a problem and, independent of any language, determines logically the steps needed to solve it. Only after deciding exactly *what* must be done does the programmer begin to write the code that tells the computer *how* to do it. We'll follow that pattern throughout this primer.

Part I, Chapters 1 through 6, introduces the reader both to *True BASIC* and to structured programming; you should read the first six chapters in order. Chapter 1 lays some necessary groundwork. In Chapters 2, 3, and 4, the basic building blocks of any computer program (sequence, decision, repetition) are introduced and illustrated, using *True BASIC* instructions. Subroutines and functions are discussed in Chapter 5. Designing a large program and constructing it from the basic building blocks is the topic of Chapter 6.

Each chapter in Part II (Chapters 7 through 12) presents a single, more advanced *True BASIC* topic. They may be read in any order; for example, if your primary interest is graphics, read Chapters 1 through 6, and then skip ahead to Chapter 9. The material in Chapters 7 through 12 is relatively advanced; read Part I first. The experienced programmer interested in learning *True BASIC* quickly may choose to skim Part I and focus on Part II.

Several brief tutorials on a number of tools and techniques related to *True*

BASIC or to structured programming are collected in Part III (Modules A through E). While important, these tools and techniques are secondary to the primary objectives of the primer; thus it makes sense to separate them from the "mainline." You should find these modules a useful reference.

Each chapter begins with a set of key ideas; they tell you what to look for as you read. When you finish a chapter, go back and reread the key topics. If any seem mysterious, you've probably missed something. Each chapter ends with a summary and a list of the *True BASIC* features introduced in that chapter. Finally, you'll discover the end-of-chapter exercises. Most are programming problems. Do the exercises. You're not going to learn how to program simply by reading about it. The only way to learn to program *is* to program.

The sample programs in this book were written and tested on an IBM PC®. They will run, with little or no change, on any computer for which a *True BASIC* compiler exists. *True BASIC* is the new standard. If you want to learn BASIC, this is the one!

ACKNOWLEDGEMENTS

The author is indebted to the people of True BASIC, Inc., Hanover, New Hampshire. Without their new language, *True BASIC*, there would be no need for this book. Without access to *True BASIC Reference Manual* and *True BASIC User's Guide*, writing it would have been impossible. Throughout the primer, material from these two primary sources is cited and, in some cases, reproduced.

The sample programs in this primer were written on an IBM Personal Computer system. IBM, IBM PC, and PC/DOS are registered trademarks of International Business Machines Corporation. Additionally, IBM provided the photographs that appear as Figs. 1.2 and A.1. Macintosh is a registered trademark of Apple Computer Co., Inc. Radio Shack is a registered trademark of Tandy, Inc.

Many of the sample programs in this primer were photographed directly from an IBM PC display monitor. The photographs were taken by Stephanie Grand of Miami University Audio Visual Services. The author would also like to acknowledge the support of Mark Dalton, Katherine Harutunian, Melinda Grosser, and Peter Gordon, all of Addison-Wesley Publishing Company.

The text was set in Hamilton, Ohio on a Xerox 630 Memorywriter by Venis Torge, who also designed many of the charts and tables that appear throughout the primer. Dr. Allison McCormack copy edited the manuscript, and made many valuable suggestions. Bill Davis helped with the artwork. Finally, the author would like to acknowledge the contributions of three reviewers: George Culp of the University of Texas at Austin, David Haddad of Miami University, and Alan Porter of Huntington Beach, California.

W.S.D.
Oxford, Ohio

Foreword

In 1964 my colleague, Thomas E. Kurtz, and I created a new language to make it easy and pleasant for Dartmouth students to learn programming. We called the new language, "BASIC." We designed it particularly for beginners with little or no technical background, though experienced programmers, too, appreciated its "user-friendliness." We also made it the first interactive programming language. These features gained BASIC popularity not only on the Dartmouth Campus, but well beyond. Over two decades it has become the most widely used computer language in the world.*

BASIC has grown a great deal from its fairly simple first version. It became a language suitable for almost any computer task. As graphical devices became available, highly user-friendly graphics were added to the language. As "structured programmming" became the standard for all better languages, fully structured versions of BASIC began to appear.

When microcomputers became available, it was natural to implement BASIC on them. Unfortunately, the various implementations of BASIC on microcomputers often violated the spirit of the language and failed to keep up with later developments in computer programming. Most of these implementations forced the user to learn the complexities of a particular machine. None of them was fully structured or provided truly user-friendly interfaces. And no two versions of the language were compatible. Tom Kurtz and I, with a group of programmers who shared our concerns about BASIC on microcomputers, decided to do something about this problem. The result is the language we call *True BASIC*®.

After several years of hard work, a committee of the American National Standards Institute, originally chaired by Tom Kurtz, has proposed a standard for BASIC. *True BASIC* closely follows this proposed national standard (ANSI BASIC). It also provides one of the friendliest user-interfaces found in any language. It is our intention to implement the *same* version of the language on various microcomputers, so that programs written in *True BASIC* will run, without change, on a variety of machines. It is our hope that *True BASIC* will not only make it possible for students to learn how to program quickly, but also to program according to the best programming principles.

BASIC was conceived in an educational environment, as a means to bring the extraordinary capabilities of computers into the educational process. That is the idea, too, behind the "Addison-Wesley *True BASIC* Series." This Series, which will include both books and software packages, has four stated goals:

1. To acquaint readers with the *True BASIC* language.

2. To teach structured programming in *True BASIC*.

3. To publish high-quality educational software written in *True BASIC*.

4. To publish textbooks, on any subject, which are enriched by the inclusion of programs written in *True BASIC*.

True BASIC Primer is the first book in this Series to address the first two goals, and I am delighted that Professor Davis has written it. Instructors will now have the opportunity to teach structured programming with the easiest programming language to learn. I hope that they will also conclude that the transition from whatever version of BASIC they are familiar with to the fully structured *True BASIC* is an easy one. And I predict that once the transition has been made, the reader will never return to the messy dialects that are now commonly in use.

Above all, it is my hope that the availability of *True BASIC* will encourage many readers to write first-rate educational software. There is a great need for such software in our colleges and schools. We hope we have created the right tool to make the writing of such software both easy and enjoyable.

John G. Kemeny

*The reader can find the full history of the language in Kemeny and Kurtz, *Back to Basic*, Addison-Wesley, 1985.

Contents

PART I: THE BASICS 1

1. Getting Started.
   Key Ideas   3
   What is a computer?   4
   What is *True BASIC*?   7
   Getting started   8
   The program development process   14
   Summary   14
   References   15
   Exercises   15

2. Sequence.
   Key Ideas   19
   Planning a program's logic   20
   True BASIC   22
   The flow of logic   31
   More *True BASIC*   34
   Another example   38
   Sequential logic   43
   Summary   44

References   45
Exercises   46

3. Decision.
Key Ideas   51
Decision structures   52
Simple IF...THEN logic   54
IF...THEN...ELSE logic   62
Nested IF statements   68
The CASE structure   73
Decision logic   77
Summary   77
References   78
Exercises   79

4. Repetition.
Key Ideas   85
Repetitive logic   86
Count loops   87
FOR...NEXT loops   89
DO loops   95
DO UNTIL   99
DO WHILE loops   101
Nested loops   106
The basic building blocks   110
Summary   100
References   112
Exercises   112

5. Functions and Subroutines.
Key Ideas   117
What are functions and Subroutines?   118
Built-in functions   119
Writing internal functions   122
External functions   126
Subroutines   136
Modular programming   145
Summary   146
References   147
Exercises   147

6. Modular Program Design.
Key Ideas   151
The basic building blocks   152
Complex programs   152

Large programs   153
Planning a large program   160
Functional decomposition   179
A look ahead   182
Summary   182
Exercises   183

PART II: *TRUE BASIC* FEATURES   189

7. **Input and Output.**
   Key Ideas   191
   Data input   193
   READ/DATA statements   199
   Data output   202
   Printer output   208
   Windows   209
   Summary   214
   References   216
   Exercises   217

8. **Arrays.**
   Key Ideas   221
   One-dimensional arrays   222
   Multidimensional arrays   233
   Parallel arrays   237
   Matrix statements   239
   Table manipulation   243
   Arrays as parameters   244
   Matrix arithmetic   246
   Summary   247
   References   248
   Exercises   248

9. **Graphics.**
   Key Ideas   253
   Some basic concepts   254
   Elementary plotting   256
   Color   265
   Plotting areas   266
   The BOX statements   269
   Graphic input   278
   Pictures   179
   Windows   283
   Some final details   284
   Summary   284

References 285
Exercises 286

10. **Strings and Sound.**
Key Ideas 291
String operations 292
String manipulation 293
LINE INPUT statements 300
String functions 304
Making noise 305
Summary 308
References 309
Exercises 310

11. **Files.**
Key Ideas 313
What is a file? 314
Text files 319
Record files 325
Byte files 334
Final comments 334
Summary 334
References 336
Exercises 337

12. **Libraries, Chaining and Recursion.**
Key Ideas 341
Libraries 342
Chaining 350
Recursion 352
Summary 353
References 354
Exercises 354

PART III: TOOLS AND TECHNIQUES 357

A. *True BASIC* **and The IBM PC.** 359
The IBM PC 360
Preparing your *True BASIC* disk 362
Saving and retrieving files 366
Screen modes and colors 369

B. **The** *True BASIC* **Editor.** 371
Creating a program 372
Running the program 378

      Saving the program   379
      Changing the program   382
      Replacing the program   383
      Advanced editing   385

C. Flowcharting. 391
      Program logic flowcharts   392
      References   396

D. Error Handling and Debugging. 399
      Command errors   400
      Syntax errors   400
      Run-time errors   401
      Logical errors   404

E. *True BASIC* and Traditional BASIC. 407
      A brief history of BASIC   408
      Compatibility   409
      Program structure   409
      Converting to *True BASIC*   412

APPENDIX 415

    I. *True BASIC* Instructions. 416
   II. *True BASIC* Functions. 419
  III. *True BASIC* Commands. 425
   IV. Errors and Error Codes. 428
    V. The ASCII Character Set. 431
  VI. Answers to Selected Exercises. 433

INDEX

PART I

The Basics

1. Getting Started

2. Sequence

3. Decision

4. Repetition

5. Functions and Subroutines

6. Modular Program Design

These six chapters are written for the beginner. They assume no prior computer experience. Building on a few basic concepts, simple programs are planned and developed. Step-by-step, the programs become more and more complex, until eventually you'll be dealing with very sophisticated logic. Read these six chapters in order. Take your time; it's important that you understand this material. Don't just read. Do the end-of-chapter exercises; you'll find suggested solutions to some of them in Appendix VI. The only way to learn to program is to program.

1

Getting Started

KEY IDEAS

1. What is a computer?

2. A computer system.

3. The stored program concept.

4. What is True BASIC?

5. Running sample True BASIC programs.

6. The program development process.

WHAT IS A COMPUTER?

A computer is a machine. Its function is to accept data and process them into information. Data are facts or observations, while information is the meaning we attribute to those facts.

Let's use an example to illustrate. A medieval astronomer, Tycho Brahe, spent his entire adult life observing and recording the positions of the planets. He collected data--on a given night, Mars occupied a given position in the sky. When he died, he left his successor, John Kepler, volumes of such data. Kepler sensed a pattern: the orbit of Mars resembled an ellipse. He spent much of his life processing Brahe's data, performing tedious computations and reorganizing the observations in an attempt to verify that pattern. He succeeded, publishing his laws of planetary motion in 1621.

Kepler's laws represent information. Using them, he could understand and predict the motions of the planets. And, using them, modern scientists and engineers were able to land a space craft on Mars. Information has meaning.

Clearly, Kepler's laws were derived from Brahe's data. The raw data, however, were useless without processing. Until they were organized, until the necessary calculations were performed, the data were just unstructured facts, with no clear meaning. Knowing the exact position of Mars on April 1, 1599 might earn an extra move in *Trivial Pursuit®*, but, by itself, that fact is not very useful. Processing data allows human beings to extract their meaning.

A computer is a data processing machine. Data flow into the machine as input *(Fig. 1.1)*. Information flows from the machine as output. The computer processes the data. John Kepler spent twenty years of his life processing data. Today, a college student using a computer can repeat his computations in a few hours!

A Computer System

Consider the computer system pictured in Fig. 1.2. It consists of several components. In the foreground is a keyboard: an input device. Above the keyboard is a display unit: an output device. Output can also be sent to a printer. Programs often enter the system through a diskette drive: secondary storage. The computer

Fig. 1.1: *A computer accepts data as input, processes those data, and generates information as its output.*

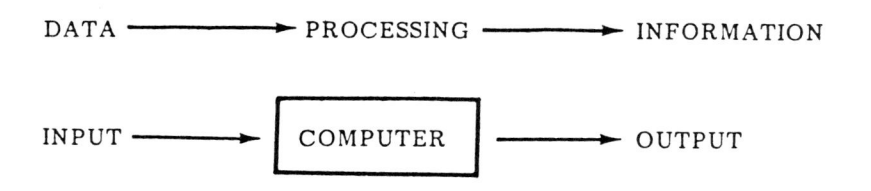

DATA ⟶ PROCESSING ⟶ INFORMATION

INPUT ⟶ | COMPUTER | ⟶ OUTPUT

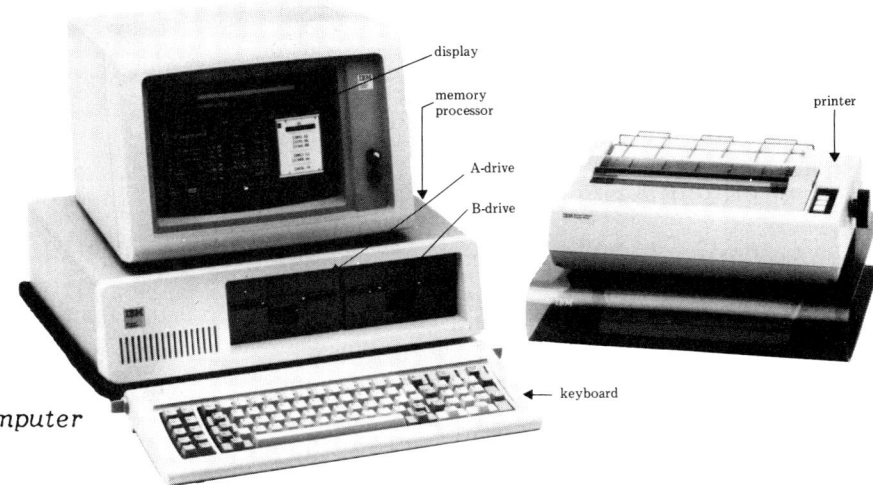

Fig. 1.2: *A typical computer system.*

itself is located in the small cabinet toward the left of the picture.

Located inside the computer are a processor and main memory *(Fig. 1.3)*. Memory holds data; the processor manipulates or processes the data. Most computers can add, subtract, multiply, divide, compare, copy, request input, and request output. So can most pocket calculators. What makes a computer different?

Fig. 1.3: *Inside the computer are two primary components--a processor and main memory. Data are stored in memory; the processor manipulates or processes the data.*

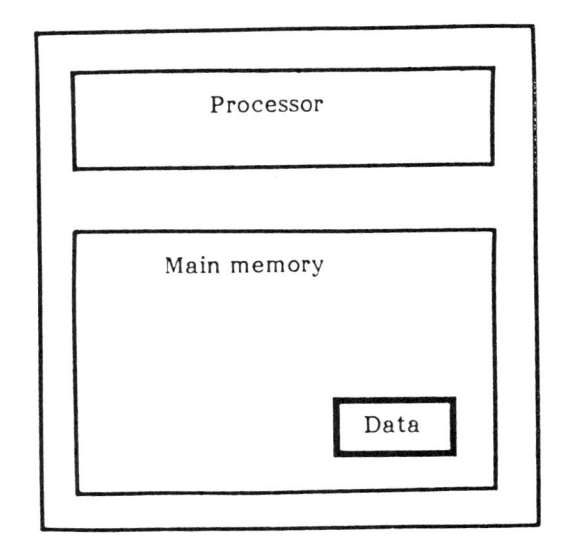

The Stored Program Concept

To add two numbers on a pocket calculator, you:

1. Enter the first number.
2. Press the add (+) button.
3. Enter the second number.
4. Press the result (=) button.
5. Record the sum for future reference.

The calculator processes the data, finding the sum. However, you must provide control, deciding, at each step, what button to push next. A calculator requires direct human intervention at each step.

A computer processes data automatically, with no need for human intervention. Computers are not intelligent, however. They cannot decide independently when to add, subtract, compare, or request input. If a computer is to function without

Fig. 1.4: *A computer is controlled by a program stored in its own main memory.*

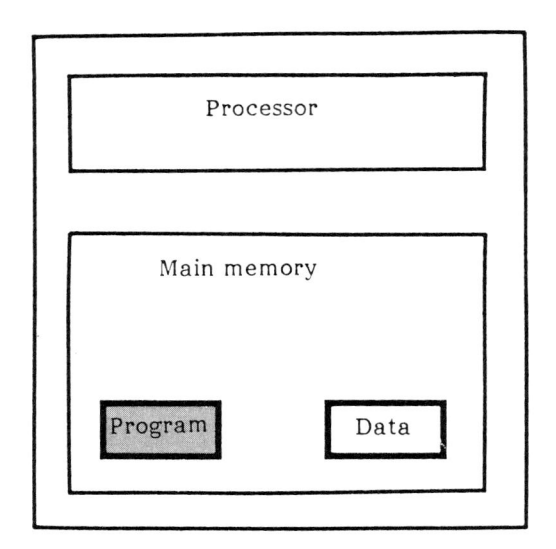

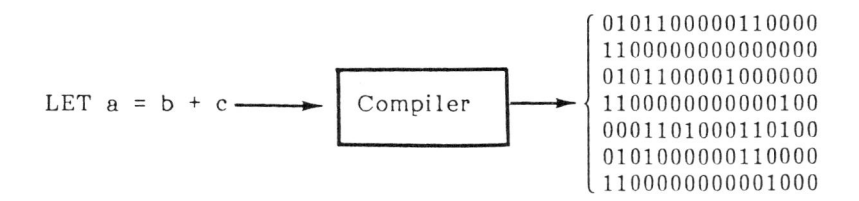

```
                                           ⎧ 0101100000110000
                                           ⎪ 1100000000000000
                                           ⎪ 0101100001000000
LET a = b + c  ⟶   Compiler   ⟶   ⎨ 1100000000000100
                                           ⎪ 0001101000110100
                                           ⎪ 0101000000110000
                                           ⎩ 1100000000001000
```

Fig. 1.5: *A compiler is a program that translates instructions written in a human-like programming language into binary, machine-level instructions.*

direct human control, it must be given a program, a set of instructions that guides the machine, step by step, through a process. The program is physically stored in main memory: a stored program *(Fig. 1.4)*. It is this stored program that distinguishes a computer from a calculator. Let's incorporate this idea into our definition:

Computer: A machine that processes data into information under the control of a stored program.

WHAT IS *TRUE BASIC*?

Programs are written by human beings. Before a computer can attack a problem, someone must carefully define a solution, translate that solution into step by step instructions the computer can understand, and store the resulting program in main memory.

A computer is a binary machine. Its main memory can store only two symbols: 0 and 1. Data and program instructions are represented as combinations of these two binary symbols. The processor follows binary instructions as it manipulates binary data. People don't think in binary. That's where compilers fit in. A compiler is a program that translates instructions written in a humanlike programming language into the binary, machine-level instructions a computer needs *(Fig. 1.5)*.

True BASIC is a compiler language. Derived from the original 1964-vintage Dartmouth BASIC, and based on the pending ANS standard, it retains the simplicity and ease of use of its ancestor. It is not merely a derivative, however. It did not simply evolve over time, with features added or subtracted in response to changing technology. Instead, *True BASIC* is a completely new language, combining the essence of original BASIC, the newer structured concepts, and support for the very latest technology. Like its ancestor, *True BASIC* promises to set a new standard.

GETTING STARTED

A key objective of this primer is to teach you how to write *True BASIC* programs. You should have a *True BASIC* diskette designed for use on your computer system. When you purchased that diskette, you probably purchased a reference manual, too. Reference manuals are written for experienced programmers, and you may have difficulty reading yours. Don't worry. After you've written a few programs, you'll find the reference manual most useful.

Before we begin, we should make a few comments about compatibility. *True BASIC* conforms to the pending ANS BASIC standard. Consequently, a *True BASIC* source program that runs on one computer should work, almost without change, on any other computer that has a *True BASIC* compiler. Compatibility exists only in the *source* code, however. The machine-level, binary instructions that control a Macintosh® are different from those that control an IBM PC®.

The objective of a compiler is to accept source statements and translate them into machine language form. A *True BASIC* compiler written for an IBM PC accepts *True BASIC* statements and translates them to IBM PC machine language. A *True BASIC* compiler written for a Macintosh accepts *True BASIC* statements and translates them to Macintosh machine language. The same source program might be given to both compilers. That's source level compatibility. But the results, the machine-level programs, will be different. If you have an IBM PC, you need a *True BASIC* compiler written for the IBM PC. If you have a Macintosh, you need a *True BASIC* compiler written for a Macintosh. Make sure your compiler matches your machine.

The process of getting your *True BASIC* diskette ready to use varies from computer to computer. You should have received a set of instructions with your *True BASIC* diskette. If you have a User's Guide, the instructions are in there. Follow them before trying any of the exercises suggested in this book. Module A discusses using *True BASIC* on an IBM PC.

Fig. 1.6: *The True BASIC HELLO command is used when you first sign onto the system.*

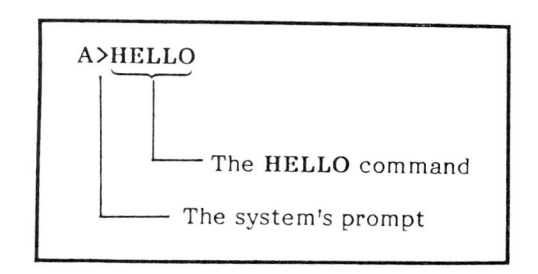

```
A>HELLO
     └─── The HELLO command
  └────── The system's prompt
```

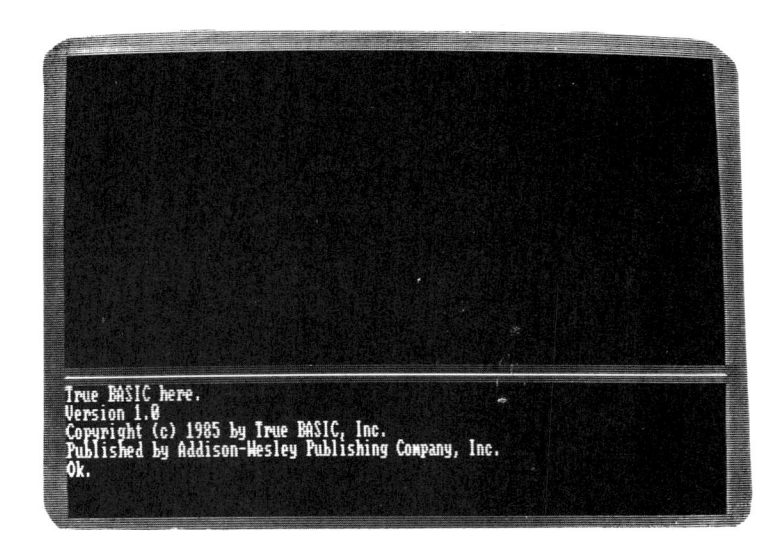

Fig. 1.7: *True BASIC's screen. On top is the editing window where program instructions are written. Below is the history window where commands are issued and results are displayed.*

Starting *True BASIC*

After you've prepared your diskette, load it in your system disk drive and turn on the computer. You may be asked to enter the date and the time--follow the instructions displayed on your screen. Eventually, you'll see a "prompt" followed by the cursor (the little blinking line or box that indicates where the next character typed will appear on the screen). Type **HELLO** *(Fig. 1.6)*. You can use any combination of upper and lower case letters. Then press the enter or return key. A few seconds later, the material shown in Fig. 1.7 will appear on your screen. You're in *True BASIC*.

The screen is divided into two parts called windows *(Fig. 1.7, again)*. On the top is the editing window, where you'll write your *True BASIC* instructions. On the bottom is the history window, where you'll issue commands to *True BASIC*.

What's the difference between a command and an instruction? An instruction is a single step in a program; for example, an instruction might tell the computer to add two numbers. A command tells the computer to execute a set of existing instructions.

Try a command. Type **FILES** *(Fig. 1.8)*, and then press the enter key. You'll see a list of program names displayed in the history window. The logic that read the disk and displayed the list of files already exists. By typing the command **FILES**, you told *True BASIC* to execute that logic. Other commands allow the programmer to begin a new program, read an old or existing program from disk

Fig. 1.8: *The True BASIC FILES command. This command displays in the history window a list of all the programs stored on the diskette.*

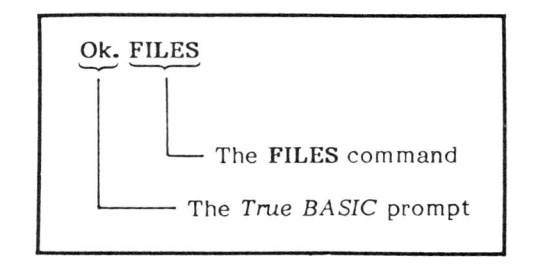

```
Ok. FILES
    │    │
    │    └── The FILES command
    └─────── The True BASIC prompt
```

and load it into main memory, store a program on disk, execute a program, and perform a number of other support functions.

Let's run the program named **TRIVIA**. It asks a series of trivia questions and then grades your responses. The command **OLD** *(Fig. 1.9)* loads an existing (old) program from disk. Using any combination of upper and lower case letters, type

OLD TRIVIA

(We'll show commands in all capitals to make them easy to identify.) Press the enter key. Your disk drive should start working and, in a few seconds, the beginning of the program will appear in your editing window *(Fig. 1.10)*. Don't worry about reading the program just yet--we'll get to that later. For now, let's run it.

To execute the program, simply type the word **RUN** *(Fig. 1.11)* and press the enter key. At first nothing will seem to happen; *True BASIC* is compiling the program, and that takes time. After a few seconds, the first question will appear in the history window *(Fig. 1.12)*. Type your answer and press enter. The program will tell you if your answer is correct and, if it isn't, give you the answer. Then it will ask another question. After you respond to several questions, the program will summarize your performance and give you an opportunity to play

Fig. 1.9: *The True BASIC OLD command. In response to an OLD command, True BASIC locates the named program on diskette and loads a copy into main memory.*

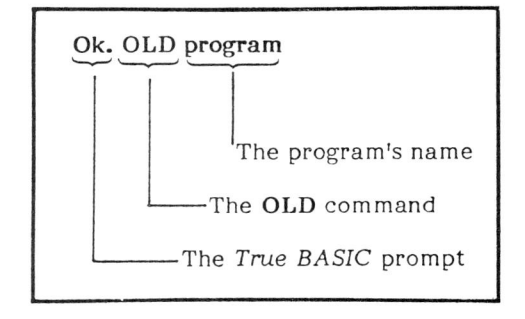

```
Ok. OLD program
    │    │    │
    │    │    └── The program's name
    │    └─────── The OLD command
    └──────────── The True BASIC prompt
```

10

```
! Trivia quiz.
!
READ num_quest                    ! Number of questions

FOR i = 1 to num_quest             ! Read all questions

   READ question$, answer$

   PRINT question$;
   LINE INPUT reply$               ! Get user's guess

   IF reply$ = answer$ then        ! If correct...
      LET right = right + 1        ! count right replies
      PRINT "Correct."             ! and say bravo.
   ELSE
      PRINT "No, the correct answer is "; answer$; "."
   END IF
```

```
True BASIC here.
Version 1.0
Copyright (c) 1985 by True BASIC, Inc.
Published by Addison-Wesley Publishing Company, Inc.
Ok. old trivia
Ok. _
```

Fig. 1.10: *In response to an* **OLD** *command, True BASIC finds the requested program on disk and loads a copy into main memory.*

again. If you want to, type yes; if not, just type no.
   Try another program. Type:

OLD FLAG

(Note: this program requires graphics support. If your computer doesn't have a graphics card, **FLAG** won't work.) Once the program appears in your editing window *(Fig. 1.13)*, type **RUN**. After a few seconds your screen's background color will change, and a picture of the American flag will appear *(Fig. 1.14)*. When you finish looking at the flag, press any key to return to the history window.

Fig. 1.11: *The True BASIC* **RUN** *command. In response to a* **RUN** *command, True BASIC compiles and then executes the program currently stored in main memory.*

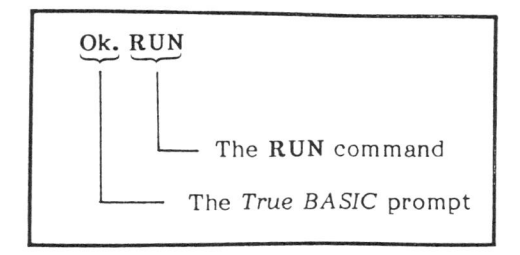

```
Ok. RUN
    |   |
    |   └── The RUN command
    └────── The True BASIC prompt
```

```
! Trivia quiz.
!
READ num_quest              ! Number of questions
!
FOR i = 1 to num_quest      ! Read all questions
!
    READ question$, answer$
!
    PRINT question$;
    LINE INPUT reply$       ! Get user's guess
!
    IF reply$ = answer$ then    ! If correct...
        LET right = right + 1   ! count right replies
        PRINT "Correct."        ! and say bravo.
    ELSE
        PRINT "No, the correct answer is "; answer$; "."
    END IF
```
Copyright (c) 1985 by True BASIC, Inc.
Published by Addison-Wesley Publishing Company, Inc.
Ok. old trivia
Ok. run
What is the capital of Austria? Vienna
Correct.
What year did Franklin Pierce take office? _

Fig. 1.12: The **TRIVIA** program asks a series of trivia questions, accepts your answers, checks your answers, and grades your performance. This slide shows the first question and the author's response.

Fig. 1.13: Following another **OLD** command, another program (this one's called **FLAG**) is copied into main memory.

```
! U. S. Flag
!
! a True BASIC(tm), Inc. product
!
! ABSTRACT
!     Draws the American flag.
!
! Copyright (c) 1985 by True BASIC, Inc.

OPEN #1: screen .06,.94,.18,.85
SET WINDOW 0,27,-.25,13.25
SET BACK 17
DIM a(5), b(5)

LET x0 = 11.2
FOR y = 12 to 0 step -1
    LET delta = .4*y/12 - .25
```
How many years, on average, does a baboon live? 20
Correct.
How about a gray squirrel? 5
Correct.
You got 80 % right.
Ok. old flag
Ok. _

Fig. 1.14: *Executing the program called **FLAG** generates a very interesting graphic output.*

(A common technique in computer graphics is to tell the computer to pause while you look at the displayed output. Pressing any key tells the machine you're finished looking.)

    A number of sample programs are found on your *True BASIC* disk. Several are described in the exercises below. Try them. On some of the simpler programs, try reading the code to see if you can sense what's going on. *True BASIC* programs are remarkably clear.

    When you've finished using the computer, type **BYE** *(Fig. 1.15)*. You should see the original prompt on your screen. Remove your *True BASIC* diskette and put it away. If you want, insert another program diskette and do some word processing or set up a spreadsheet. If you're really finished, just turn off your computer.

Fig. 1.15: *The True BASIC BYE command. Type **BYE** when you are ready to exit True BASIC.*

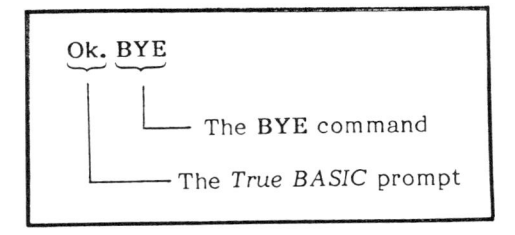

```
Ok. BYE
 |   |
 |   └── The BYE command
 └────── The True BASIC prompt
```

THE PROGRAM DEVELOPMENT PROCESS

So far, you've used some existing *True BASIC* programs. Beginning with Chapter 2, you'll be writing your own. A program is a series of instructions that guides a computer through some process. There is more to programming than just writing instructions, however. If the computer is to generate acceptable results it must be given the *right* instructions in the right order.

A program tells a computer how to perform a certain task. Before writing the program, the programmer must understand that task. Thus, the first step in the program development process is carefully defining and analyzing the task to be performed. Only then can the right instructions be written in the right order.

A computer converts data into information. Programs are written because people want the machine to generate certain information. There's your starting point. Begin by defining, in general terms, exactly what information the program is expected to produce.

Next, ask what functions must be performed to obtain that information. The answer will identify one or more algorithms. An algorithm is a set of rules for arriving at a solution in a finite number of steps. Some algorithms take the form of algebraic expressions, but there are other types, too. For example, a university's admissions algorithm might specify a minimum high school class standing, grade point average, and standardized test score. The tax tables published by the Internal Revenue Service represent yet another type of algorithm.

Once the algorithms are defined, study them. Break them into elementary steps: addition, subtraction, multiplication, division, comparison. Define the order in which the steps must be performed. That sequence of steps represents a plan for writing the program. Given a plan, you can begin writing instructions. In Chapter 2, that's exactly what we'll do.

SUMMARY

A computer is a machine that processes data into information under the control of a stored program. Data flow into the computer through an input device. Along with the program, they are stored in main memory. Following the program's instructions, the processor manipulates or processes the data, placing the results in main memory. Finally, the results flow from main memory to an output device.

The program that controls a computer must be stored in main memory. A computer's main memory can store only combinations of the binary digits 0 and 1, and few programmers are comfortable working in binary. Fortunately, special programs called compilers accept instructions coded in a form convenient to human beings, and translate those instructions into binary, machine-level code.

True BASIC is a compiler that combines the best features of original Dartmouth BASIC with modern structured programming conventions and up-to-date technology. The language follows the pending ANS BASIC standard. The essential purpose of this primer is to teach you how to write *True BASIC* programs.

Although *True BASIC* is designed to be a standard that runs on a variety of computers, certain tasks and functions are machine dependent; for details, check your computer's reference manual, the materials that accompanied your *True BASIC* disk, or (for selected machines) a module in Part III of this book. Assuming that your *True BASIC* disk has been properly prepared, we turned to executing a few existing programs, illustrating the *True BASIC* commands **HELLO, FILES, OLD, RUN,** and **BYE**.

A program guides a computer through some task. Before writing a program, the programmer must understand the task; thus we turned to a brief overview of the program development process before moving on to Chapter 2.

REFERENCES

True BASIC Commands

HELLO	Fig. 1.6, page 8.
FILES	Fig. 1.8, page 10.
OLD program-name	Fig. 1.9, page 10.
RUN	Fig. 1.11, page 11.
BYE	Fig. 1.15, page 13.

EXERCISES

1. What is a computer?

2. What is a stored program? Why is the stored program concept important?

3. *True BASIC* is a compiler. What is a compiler?

4. Why is it so important that your version of *True BASIC* matches your computer system?

5. Briefly explain the steps in the program development process. Why is it so important that the programmer understand the task to be programmed before starting to write the code?

6. Following the instructions that came with your diskette, prepare it for use.

7. Load your *True BASIC* diskette. Start your computer. In response to the prompt, type **HELLO**. Once you're into *True BASIC*, type a **FILES** command. Read the names of the available programs.

8. If you haven't already done so, load (**OLD** command) and start (**RUN** command) the program **TRIVIA**. See how well you can do against the computer.

9. If you haven't already done so, load and run the program **FLAG**. (Note: your computer must support graphics.)

10. Another interesting graphics routine is stored under program name **HANOI**. Load it and run it.

11. Stored under program name **HANGMAN** is a program that plays a familiar game. Load it and play it. Once again, your computer must support graphics, or the program won't work.

12. A simple program named **MPG** computes the miles per gallon for a trip of 320 miles on which 14.3 gallons of gasoline were used. Load it. Read the code; it should make sense. Do the calculation yourself. Now run the program. Note where the data and the answer are displayed. Is the answer right?

13. The program named **SQROOT** prints a table of numbers and their square roots. Load it. Run it and note how the output is displayed.

14. Load the program named **GUESS**. Read the logic in your editing window; try to figure out what it does. Now, run it. When you've finished, load and run another program, **GUESS2**. Compare the two programs.

15. Load the program named **INTEREST**. Read the logic; try to figure out what it does. Now, run it.

16. If your computer supports graphics, load and run the program named **CIRCLE**.

17. If your computer supports graphics, load and run the program **HOUSES**.

18. Load the program named **SMOKY**. Read the code and figure out what it does. Run the program.

19. Load and run the program named **PHONE**.

20. Load and run the program named **KNIGHT**, another program that requires graphics. If you play chess, you may recognize the knight's tour of a chess board.

21. A program named **LISS** generates some very interesting graphics. Load it and run it. The program will ask you to enter values for **x** and **y**. Type 2,5. Then press the enter key. After completing a pattern, the program will pause for a few seconds. Then it will ask for new values for **x** and **y**. Experiment. Type a value for **x**, a comma, a value for **y**, and then press enter. When you've finished using the program, hold down the control [Ctrl] key (it's usually near the left edge of the keyboard) and press break (usually near the upper right). As with the other graphics programs, press any key to get back to the *True BASIC* windows. This time you'll find the cursor in the editing window. If your computer has function keys, press F2 to get back to the history window. Otherwise, use your mouse to select the history window.

2

Sequence

KEY IDEAS

1. Planning a program's logic.
2. The True BASIC **LET** statement.
    a. Constants, variables, and operators.
    b. Expressions.
    c. Writing **LET** statements.
3. The flow of logic through a program.
4. The **INPUT** statement.
5. The **PRINT** statement.
6. The **END** statement.
7. Planning, writing, and executing a True BASIC program.
8. Instruction sequence.

PLANNING A PROGRAM'S LOGIC

Computer programs are written to solve problems, so the first step in writing a program is understanding the problem to be solved. Certain information is needed. To obtain it, certain functions must be performed. Given the necessary data and an understanding of the functions to be performed, you can develop a plan for a program. Given this plan, you can write instructions in a programming language. The idea is simple: figure out what you have to do before you start to do it. That bit of advice seems obvious, but probably the most common error beginners make is starting to write instructions before they really understand the problem.

Perhaps the best way to explain the program development process is through an example. Imagine that we want to compute the area of a circle. The desired information is the area. What must be done to compute it? We all know the formula

$$area = \pi \, radius^2$$

where the Greek letter π (Pi) is a constant equal to roughly 3.1416. The algorithm says to take the circle's radius, square it, and multiply the result by π. We might clarify the problem definition by drawing a simple block diagram *(Fig. 2.1)* showing the necessary input data (radius), the algorithm, and the desired output information (the area).

The next step is to study the algorithm. A useful trick is to imagine explaining its solution to someone who knows absolutely nothing beyond elementary arithmetic. We might suggest the following steps:

1. Start with the value of radius.

2. Square that value (multiply it by itself).

3. Multiply the result by 3.1416.

4. The answer is the circle's area.

Now, given a value for radius, this imaginary person could compute the circle's

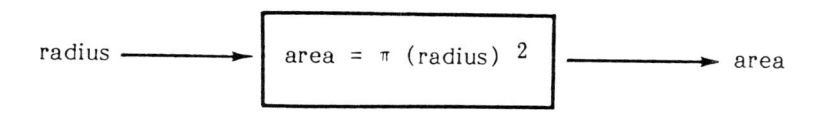

Fig. 2.1: *A block diagram of the "area of a circle" problem.*

radius ⟶ | area = π (radius)² | ⟶ area

Fig. 2.2: *A flowchart of the "area of a circle" problem solution.*

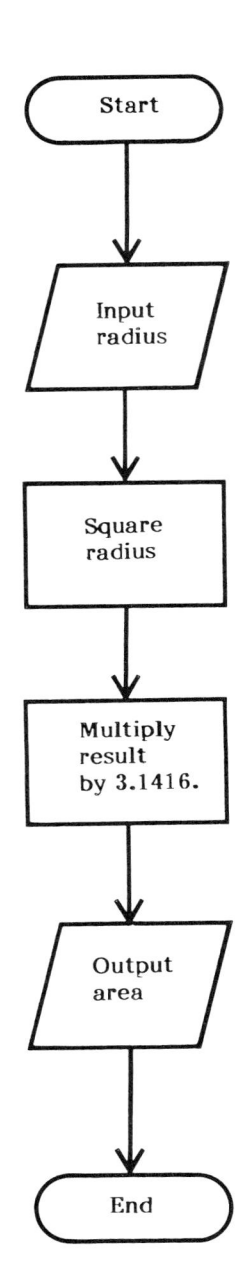

```
            Start
              │
              ▼
          ╱─────────╲
         ╱  Input    ╱
        ╱   radius  ╱
        ╲─────────╱
              │
              ▼
        ┌─────────┐
        │ Square  │
        │ radius  │
        └─────────┘
              │
              ▼
        ┌─────────┐
        │Multiply │
        │ result  │
        │by 3.1416│
        └─────────┘
              │
              ▼
          ╱─────────╲
         ╱  Output   ╱
        ╱    area   ╱
        ╲─────────╱
              │
              ▼
            End
```

area.

You've heard the old saying: A picture is worth a thousand words. A flowchart *(see Module C for a brief introduction)* is a graphic representation of a program. Figure 2.2 shows a flowchart for our solution to the circle problem. Read it. Start at the top and follow the flowlines from top to bottom, relating the logical flow to the steps listed above.

Note that we've defined a series of steps. We must know the radius before computations can begin. The radius must be squared before multiplying. Along with the necessary input and output data *(Fig. 2.1)*, the flowchart represents a plan for writing the program. The task of actually writing the program consists of translating those steps into a language the computer can understand. In this primer, we'll use *True BASIC*.

TRUE BASIC

Constants

Before we can write a *True BASIC* program, we must learn a few things about the language. We'll start with *True BASIC* constants. A constant is an element of data whose value never changes. In *True BASIC*, numeric constants are coded simply by writing their numeric value; several examples are listed in Fig. 2.3. They can be written with or without a decimal point. A sign may precede the constant; if no sign is coded, the number is assumed positive. Note that additional punctuation marks, such as commas or dollar signs, are not allowed, and blank characters cannot be coded in the middle of a numeric constant.

Writing very large and very small numbers can present a problem. For example, the speed of light is roughly 186,000 miles per second, which is 186000 in *True BASIC*. That constant is difficult to read. Scientists use a form of shorthand called scientific notation to represent very large and very small numbers. Using scientific notation, the speed of light can be written as 0.186×10^6. The power of ten indicates how many positions the decimal point should be moved to the right. A *True BASIC* equivalent is 0.186e6, where the "e" represents ten raised to a power. For very small numbers, such as 0.000001, use a negative power of ten: 0.1e-6. A negative exponent indicates how many positions the decimal point should be moved to the left.

The largest and smallest constants that can be coded depend on the computer you are using; following Chapter 5, we'll suggest how you might find the limits on your own computer. Generally, *True BASIC* works to a precision of at least ten digits, and can handle numbers as large as 1e99 or as small as 1e-99.

Computers are not limited to numbers. For example, they can store and manipulate names and addresses, text, letter grades, and many other types of character or string data. String constants *(Fig. 2.4)* are coded by enclosing a series of characters inside a set of quotation marks. Here in Part I, we'll use string constants primarily to identify a program's output. Later, in Chapter 10, we'll consider manipulating string data.

Variables

A variable is a name assigned to an element of data whose value can change. In

Rules for defining numeric constants:

1. Basically, just write the number.

2. A single, optional decimal point may be included.

3. Code a sign (+ or -) in front of the number. If no sign is coded, the number is assumed positive.

4. Except for the sign and the decimal point, other nonnumeric characters are illegal.

5. Embedded blanks are illegal.

6. The maximum number of digits of precision varies with the machine, but *True BASIC* can store and manipulate at least ten.

7. When writing large or small numbers, a form of scientific notation can be used:

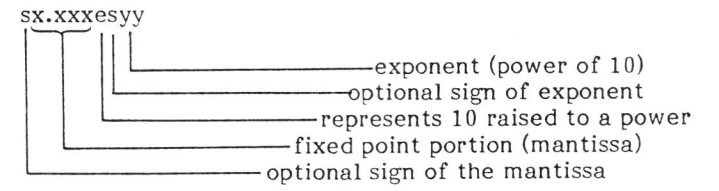

        sx.xxxesyy
                    └────── exponent (power of 10)
                   └─────── optional sign of exponent
              └──────────── represents 10 raised to a power
           └─────────────── fixed point portion (mantissa)
        └────────────────── optional sign of the mantissa

8. Maximum and minimum values vary with the machine, but *True BASIC* can normally handle numbers as big as 1.0E99 and as small as 1.0E-99.

Legal	Illegal	What is wrong?
5		
17356.00	17,356.00	The comma
5.58	$5.58	The dollar sign
-8		
-13.2		
3.1416	3.14 16	The embedded blank
0.01325		
3.258	3.25.8	The extra decimal point
15853	15A53	The embedded letter A.
.5		
0.5		
0.186E06		
-15.32e-5	-15.3a-5	The embedded letter a.

Fig. 2.3: *True BASIC numeric constants.*

Rules for coding string constants:

1. Enclose the string constant in a set of quotation markes (").

2. Any character you can type can be included in a string constant. You get exactly what you type.

3. Because the quotation mark starts and ends a string constant, you must type two of them to get a quotation mark as part of the string. (For example, "a""b".) Suggestion: use the single quote mark or apostrophe (') within the string.

4. Within a string constant, upper case and lower case letters are different. "Area" and "area" are two different constants.

5. String constants may contain as many as 32,000 characters.

6. An empty (null) string is coded as two quotation marks with nothing between them.

Examples	Explanation
"This is a string constant"	
"Area = "	
""	An empty (null) string
" "	Several blanks

Fig. 2.4: *True BASIC string constants.*

the "area of a circle" algorithm, π and 2 are constants, while radius is a variable. Look at it this way. It is possible to compute the area of a circle for any positive radius you can imagine. No matter what the radius may be, however, it is always squared (the constant 2), and π is always 3.1416.

In *True BASIC*, each variable is assigned a name. A numeric variable's name consists of a combination of from 1 to 31 letters, digits, or underline characters. Letters may be typed in upper case, lower case, or both—*True BASIC* doesn't care. The first character in the variable name must be a letter. The underline character or underscore can be used to make the variable name easier to read; for example, **miles_per_gallon** is much clearer than **milespergallon**. Note that blanks are illegal; in effect, the underscore replaces the blank you would normally use to separate words. The rules for defining a string variable name are identical; however, a string variable must end with a dollar sign ($). The dollar sign counts as one of the 31 (maximum) characters. Figure 2.5 shows several valid and invalid variable names, and summarizes the rules for defining them.

Rules for defining variable names:

1. The first character must be a letter of the alphabet.

2. String variables must end with a dollar sign ($).

3. Use any combination of from 1 to 31 letters, digits, and underscore (underline) characters. In a string variable, the dollar sign counts as one of the maximum 31 characters.

4. *True BASIC* does not distinguish between upper and lower case letters. (In other words, a and A are seen as the same character.) Thus you may type any combination of upper and lower case letters.

5. Embedded blanks are illegal.

6. Except for the dollar sign that ends a string variable, other special symbols and punctuation marks are illegal.

Guidelines for selecting variable names:

1. Select a name that makes sense in the context of the program. A variable's name should tell you what the variable represents.

2. Use the underscore character to separate lengthy variable names into recognizable words. For example, use gross_pay instead of grosspay.

3. In this primer, our coding convention will be to use lower case letters for variable names. This convention makes it easy to spot the variables in a *True BASIC* statement.

Legal	Illegal	What is wrong?
A	#A	The # symbol
x		
x5	5x	First character not alphabetic
x_y_z	x.y.z.	The periods (decimal points)
radius	rad&us	The ampersand
radIUS		
gross_pay	gross pay	The embedded blank
GROSS_PAY	GROSS-PAY	The dash or hyphen
MPG	miles/gallon	The slash
FICA_tax	FICA tax	Embedded blank

Fig. 2.5: *True Basic variable names.*

Symbol	Meaning
+	addition
-	subtraction
*	multiplication
/	division
^	exponentiation (raising to a power)

Fig. 2.6: *True BASIC's arithmetic operators.*

Throughout this primer, we will use lower case letters in our variable names. Using lower case letters is not a requirement; it's just a coding convention that helps distinguish the variables from the other parts of a *True BASIC* statement.

The programmer has a great deal of flexibility in defining variable names, but some are better than others. For example, **x** can represent the radius of a circle. However, **r** might be a better choice. An even better choice is **radius**. A good variable name tells you what the variable represents.

Operators

As we look at the algorithm for computing the area of a circle, we see that it consists of a variable (radius) and two constants (3.1416 and 2). In between those constants and variables are the operators that indicate the arithmetic operations to be performed. *True BASIC*'s arithmetic operators are summarized in Fig. 2.6. Other operators, called logical operators, will be explained in Chapter 3.

Expressions

A *True BASIC* expression is composed of variables and constants separated by operators. For example, the algorithm for computing the area of a circle is shown as a *True BASIC* expression in Fig. 2.7. Constants and variables define the data to be manipulated. The operators define the functions to be performed.

Figure 2.8 shows several common formulas written as *True BASIC* expressions. In each example, note that we used blanks to separate the variables, constants, and operators. That is another coding convention; the blanks make the expression easier to read. *True BASIC* does not require the blanks; for example,

```
3.1416*radius^2

3.1416 * radius ^ 2

3.1416      *      radius      ^      2
```

Fig. 2.7: *An expression composed of variables and constants separated by operators.*

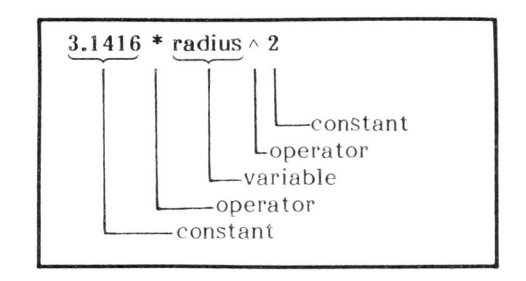

```
3.1416 * radius ^ 2
   │    │   │    │ └─constant
   │    │   │    └─operator
   │    │   └─variable
   │    └─operator
   └─constant
```

are all legal expressions.

The Priority of the Operators

The order in which operations are performed makes no difference in some expressions. In others, however, it does. For example, consider

$$2 + 5 * 3$$

If we do the addition first, we discover that 2 plus 5 is 7, and 7 times 3 is 21. If we do the multiplication first, 5 times 3 is 15, and 15 plus 2 is 17. Obviously, both answers cannot be correct.

If we are to solve such expressions and generate consistent answers, we must have a set of priority rules for the operators. In *True BASIC*, as in most programming languages, the standard rules of algebra are used:

1. Exponentiation (raising a number to a power) is done first.

2. Multiplication and division are done next.

3. Additional and subtraction are done last.

Fig. 2.8: *Some True BASIC expressions.*

Formula	The *True BASIC* version
area of a square	side * side, or side ^ 2
area of a rectangle	width * length
area of a triangle	0.5 * base * height
gross pay	pay_rate * hours_worked
grade point average	grade_points / credit_hours
energy	mass * speed_of_light ^ 2
energy (again)	m * c ^ 2

In the event of "ties" (for example, if an expression contains two or more additions or an addition and a subtraction), the operations are performed from left to right. Thus, in the expression

      4 * 5 / 10

multiplication is done first followed by division.

The standard rules of algebra are not always adequate. For example, consider the expression

      3 + 5 * 4

Multiplication would be done first; the value of this expression is 23. However, what if you wanted to multiply the sum of 3 + 5 by 4? You can change or override the standard rules by using parentheses; for example,

      (3 + 5) * 4

The operations inside the parentheses are performed first.

Fig. 2.9: *Evaluating an expression: an example.*

The expression	(4 * (5 + 3)) / 2
Evaluate parentheses	(4 * (5 + 3)) / 2
Evaluate inner parentheses	(4 * (5 + 3)) / 2
Expression is reduced to	(4 * 8) / 2
Evaluate parentheses	(4 * 8) / 2
Expression is reduced to	32 / 2
Divide	32 / 2
The value of the expression is	16

> A. Evaluate the contents of a set of parentheses first.
>
> B. 1. Exponentiation has top priority.
>   2. Multiplication and division have second priority.
>   3. Addition and subtraction have low priority.
>
> C. In the event of ties (two or more operations with the same priority), proceed from left to right.

Fig. 2.10: *The priority of the arithmetic operators.*

It is possible to "nest" parentheses, coding one set inside another. For example, Fig. 2.9 shows how *True BASIC* would evaluate the expression

$$(4 * (5 + 3)) / 2$$

Take the time to read through this example. *True BASIC*'s arithmetic priority rules are summarized in Fig. 2.10.

Incidentally, parentheses can also be used to clarify an expression. We don't need parentheses in

$$3.1416 * (radius \wedge 2)$$

because the exponentiation will be done first whether we use them or not, but they do make the expression easier to read. When in doubt, use parentheses to clarify your intent.

LET Statements

When we use a calculator to solve an expression, we usually write the answer on a sheet of paper. When we evaluate an expression in *True BASIC*, we record its value in a variable. We tell the computer to do this by coding a **LET** statement (*Fig. 2.11*). For example, the algorithm for computing the area of a circle might

Fig. 2.11: *The True BASIC LET statement.*

> LET variable = expression

be written as

>   LET area = 3.1416 * (radius ^ 2)

The keyword **LET** must be coded; it identifies the statement to *True BASIC*.

What exactly does the **LET** statement mean? Remember that a computer program and its data are stored in main memory. View memory as a series of mail boxes, each one capable of holding a single value *(Fig. 2.12)*. We'll use our labels to identify two of those mail boxes: one is called **area**, another is called **radius**. While we're at it, we'll put a value, 10, into the mail box marked **radius**. (Don't worry about how it got there just yet.) Now, we're ready to execute the **LET** statement.

Focus on the expression first. Take whatever is stored in the box marked **radius** (10) and square it. Next, multiply the result by **3.1416**. The expression has been

Fig. 2.12: *A mailbox analogy can be used to explain what a True BASIC LET statement means.*

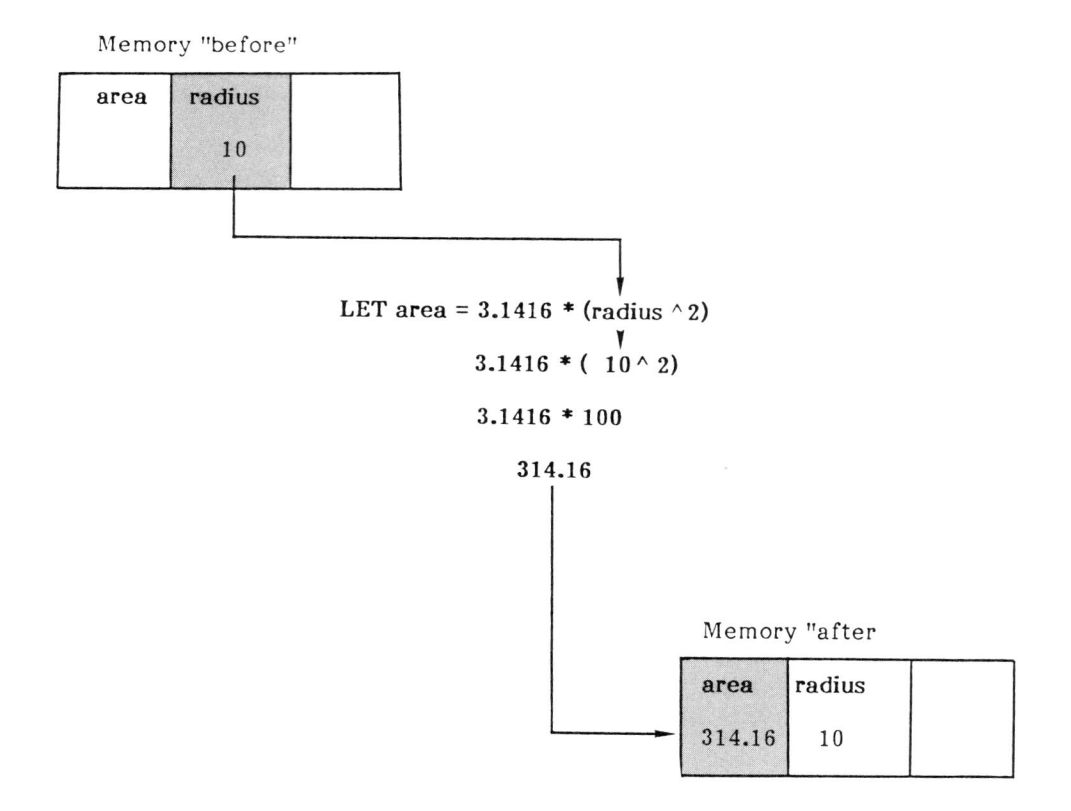

Memory "before"

area	radius	
	10	

LET area = 3.1416 * (radius ^ 2)

3.1416 * (10 ^ 2)

3.1416 * 100

314.16

Memory "after"

area	radius	
314.16	10	

evaluated. Now, we come to the equal sign. In *True BASIC*, an equal sign means "is replaced by." Thus, the current content of the mail box known as **area** is replaced by the value of the expression *(see Fig. 2.12, "after")*.

Note that the equal sign is not an algebraic equal sign. Consider, for example, the statement

    LET count = count + 1

Clearly, the values to the right and to the left of the equal sign cannot possibly be equal; the statement is algebraically illegal. In *True BASIC*, however, the statement says: take whatever is in the memory location called **count**, add 1 to it, and store the answer in the memory location called **count**. For example, imagine that **count** contains the value 3. The statement says to take the current value of **count** (3), add 1 to it, and store the answer (4) back in **count**. It's completely legal (and quite common).

THE FLOW OF LOGIC

In explaining the **LET** statement, we assumed the memory location called **radius** contained a value. What if it didn't? What if we coded:

    LET area = 3.1416 * (radius ^ 2)

and then tried to execute it? The computer would start by getting whatever might be stored in **radius**. What's stored there? We don't know, but the computer wouldn't care. If the value just happened to be zero, it would compute the area of a circle of radius zero. If the value just happened to be 5 million, it would compute the area of a circle of radius 5 million; if the value just happened to be -1, it would compute the area of a circle of radius -1.

We want to compute the area of a circle of radius 10. For the **LET** statement to compute that area, the memory location named **radius** must contain 10. The only way we can be sure **radius** contains 10 is by putting 10 into **radius** before the expression is evaluated. That calls for another instruction:

    LET radius = 10

    LET area = 3.1416 * (radius ^ 2)

The first **LET** statement says "the content of the memory location **radius** is replaced by the value 10." Given the first instruction, the second **LET** statement will compute the area of a circle of radius 10.

Unless they are told to do otherwise, computers execute their instructions in sequence, from the first instruction to the last, from the program's top to its bottom. Consequently, the flow of logic through a program will be from top to bottom. A well-designed, correctly written program mirrors that logical flow.

Let's consider another example. To compute an individual's gross pay, we multiply an hourly pay rate by the number of hours worked. A **LET** statement for this algorithm is

LET gross_pay = pay_rate * hours_worked

If a computer executed that instruction as it stands, the result would be unpredictable. The fact that *you* know the pay rate should be 4.25 and the hours worked should be 20 is beside the point; the computer doesn't know that. The series of instructions

LET pay_rate = 4.25

LET hours_worked = 20

LET gross_pay = pay_rate * hours_worked

would generate the result 85.00 and store it in the memory location known as **gross_pay**.

Reconsider those instructions using the following rule:

> BEFORE EXECUTING A LET INSTRUCTION THE VALUE OF EVERY VARIABLE TO THE RIGHT OF THE EQUAL SIGN MUST BE KNOWN.

Start with the first instruction. To the right of the equal sign is a constant, **4.25**.

A constant's value is known (by definition). There are no variables. Conclusion: the first instruction is legal. Now, focus on the second **LET**. It, too, contains only a constant to the right of the equal sign. The second instruction is legal.

Now look at the **LET** statement that computes **gross_pay**. To the right of the equal sign is a variable, **pay_rate**. Do we know its value? Certainly, it's 4.25. How do we know that? A prior instruction placed that value in the memory location known as **pay_rate**. The other variable is **hours_worked**. Do we know its value? Yes. An earlier instruction stored 20 in **hours_worked**. Since the value of every variable to the right of the equal sign is known, the instruction will produce the expected result.

Look at that series of instructions from yet another perspective. What would happen if we were to change their order? For example, consider

    LET hours_worked = 20

    LET pay_rate = 4.25

    LET gross_pay = pay_rate * hours_worked

This sequence of instructions is legal. How do we know? Read the program from the top, down. Do you ever encounter a variable to the right of an equal sign whose value has not yet been defined? No.

Now, consider a different sequence

    LET pay_rate = 4.25

    LET gross_pay = pay_rate * hours worked

    LET hours_worked = 20

That's wrong. Why? Look at the second **LET** statement. The first variable to the right of the equal sign is **pay_rate**. Look at the instructions that precede this one. Is the value of **pay_rate** known? Sure. So far, so good. Now consider the second variable, **hours_worked**. Look at the instructions that precede this one. Has the value of **hours_worked** been defined yet? No. But, you argue, **hours_worked** does receive a value in the next instruction. Isn't a computer smart enough to look ahead and figure out what I mean? No. Computers execute instructions in sequence. Period. If the sequence of your instructions is wrong, the computer will not get the right answer.

MORE *TRUE BASIC*

Let's return to the area of a circle problem. Figure 2.13 shows a program to compute that area. Each line holds one *True BASIC* statement. The lines beginning with the keywords **INPUT, LET, PRINT,** and **END** hold executable statements that tell the computer to perform one or more of its elementary functions; note that each keyword is a verb, implying that the computer should do something. To the right of the executable statements are comments explaining the program's logic. Before we study the instructions, try reading the program on your own. You should have little trouble following the logic.

Depending on your computer, your display will probably show either 40 or 80 characters per line; thus it would seem that you are limited to 40 or 80 characters per statement. Actually, you're not. What's important in writing a program is not what's displayed on the screen, but what's stored in the computer's memory. Technically, a line starts when you begin typing and ends when you press the enter key. Then, when you resume typing, the next line begins. Using this definition, a *True BASIC* line can hold as many as 32,000 characters. For clarity, however, it's a good idea to live with the 40 or 80 character line limitation. That way, what you see on your screen is what *True BASIC* sees. That avoids confusion.

Fig. 2.13: *The "area of a circle" program in True BASIC.*

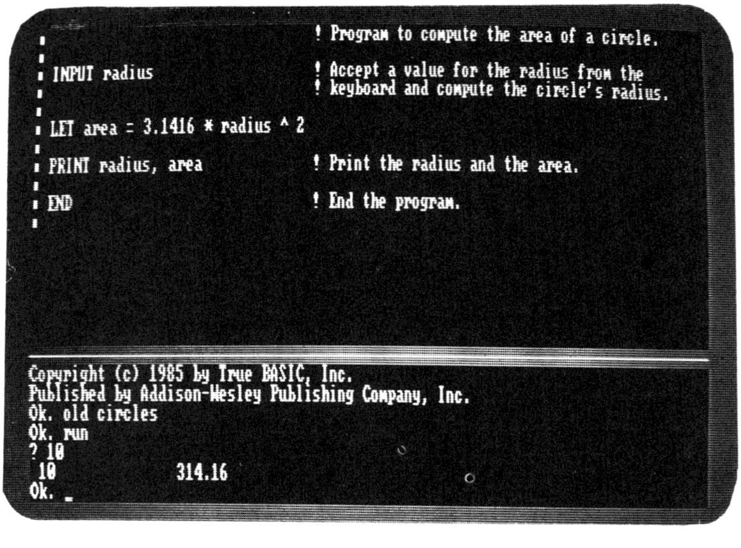

Comments

The English-language descriptions to the right of Fig. 2.13 are comments. Technically, comments are not really part of the program; instead, they explain the program's logic to the reader. Because they make the program easier for people to understand, comments are very valuable.

There are two ways to define *True BASIC* comments. One is to use **REM** (for REMarks) statements. The keyword **REM** is followed by the comment; for example,

REM This is an example of a True BASIC comment.

An exclamation point (!) can also be used to start a comment; see Fig. 2.13 for examples, and note that these comments can be coded on the same line as instructions. We'll use the second form throughout this primer.

The comments in Fig. 2.13 are all coded to the right of the executable statements. Why? Comments are intended to make the program's logic easier to understand. The logic consists of the executable instructions: **INPUT, LET, PRINT,** and **END**. If we aligned the comments and the executable instructions, the instructions would be difficult to find. The purpose of comments is to clarify the logic, not hide it. With the comments moved to the right, they can perform their function without getting in the way.

The INPUT Statement

The first executable statement in our program (Fig. 2.13) is an **INPUT** statement. Its purpose is to get data from an input device, usually the keyboard/display unit. Technically, we don't need an **INPUT** statement in this program. Instead, we could have written

LET radius = 10

LET area = 3.1416 * (radius ^ 2)

and allowed the first **LET** statement to place a value into the main memory location know as **radius**. The statement

INPUT radius

asks the programmer or the person using the computer to provide a value for **radius**.

Fig. 2.14: *The True BASIC* **INPUT** *statement.*

> **INPUT** variable1, variable2, variable3, . . .

A computer executes a program's instructions in sequence, from the top, down. If you were to run this program, the computer would execute the **INPUT** statement first, display a question mark (a prompt) in the history window *(Fig. 2.13),* and wait for you to enter a value. In response, you would be expected to type a number and press the enter key. The value you typed would be stored in the memory location called **radius**. Thus, when the computer reached the **LET** statement, the value of **radius** would be known, and the **area** could be computed.

The general form of the **INPUT** statement is highlighted in Fig. 2.14. A list of variables separated by commas follows the word **INPUT**. When an **INPUT** statement is executed, a prompt is displayed in *True BASIC*'s history window, and the user is expected to provide a value for each variable in the list, typing a series of constants separated by commas. (In Chapter 7, we'll show you how to precede the **INPUT** statement's prompt with a message telling the user exactly what to enter.)

The PRINT Statement

The **PRINT** statement displays in the history window the values of selected expressions. Its general form is highlighted in Fig. 2.15. The keyword **PRINT** is followed by a list of expressions (usually a series of variables and constants) separated by commas. When the **PRINT** statement is executed, each listed expression is evaluated, and its value displayed on the screen.

The screen is divided into five print zones *(Fig. 2.16)*. When a **PRINT** statement is executed, the first expression's value is displayed in the first zone. A comma means "skip to the next print zone," so the second expression's value will appear in the second zone, the third value will appear in the third zone, and so on. Up to five values can be displayed on a single line. If the list of expressions contains more than five items, more than one output line will be needed.

An option is to use semicolons to separate the expressions. A semicolon means that the next value will be displayed immediately following the one just printed. Using semicolons, it is possible to display more than five items on a line.

We'll consider the **PRINT** statement in considerably more detail in Chapter 7.

Fig. 2.15: *The True BASIC* **PRINT** *statement.*

> **PRINT** expression1, expression2, expression3, . . .

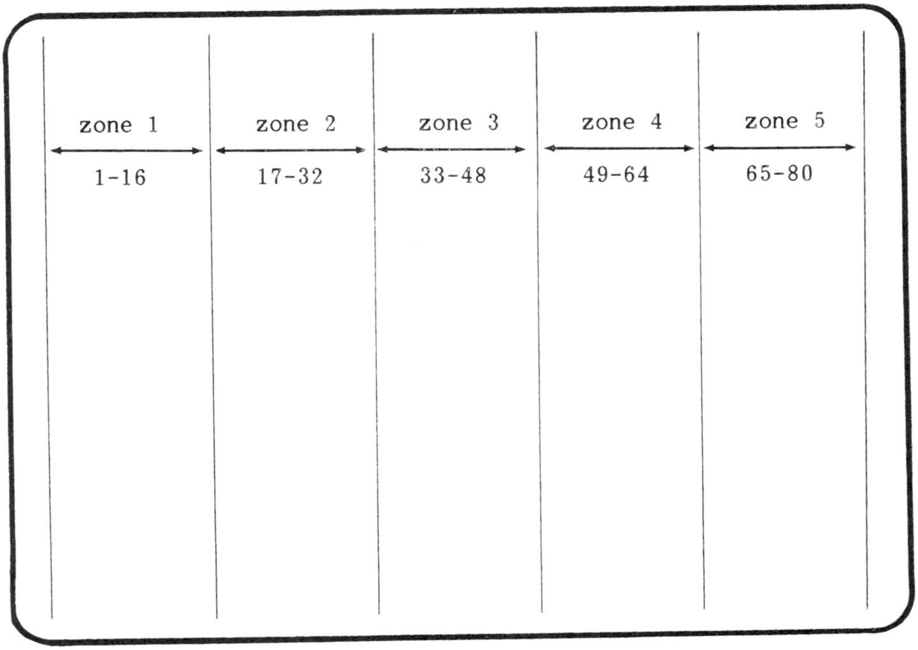

```
┌─────────────┬─────────────┬─────────────┬─────────────┬─────────────┐
│   zone 1    │   zone 2    │   zone 3    │   zone 4    │   zone 5    │
│    1-16     │   17-32     │   33-48     │   49-64     │   65-80     │
```

Fig. 2.16: *The screen is divided into five print zones. When a **PRINT** statement is executed, data values are displayed one per zone.*

The END Statement

Every *True BASIC* program must contain one (and only one) **END** statement *(Fig. 2.17)*. It must be the last statement in the program *(see Fig. 2.13)*. If you fail to provide an **END** statement, *True BASIC* will give you an error message when you try to run the program.

Fig. 2.17: *The True BASIC **END** statement.*

> **END**
>
> Every *True BASIC* program or program unit must contain one, and only one **END** statement. It must be the last statement in the program.

37

ANOTHER EXAMPLE

Let's consider another example. Earlier in this chapter, we used the algorithm for computing gross pay to illustrate the **LET** statement. Anyone who has ever worked knows that gross pay (the product of hours worked and an hourly pay rate) is not take-home pay. To compute take-home pay, often called net pay, you must subtract certain deductions, such as federal tax, state tax, and local tax, from gross pay. We want to write a program to compute net pay.

Let's start by developing a block diagram of the problem. As we begin, we know that the desired output is net pay and that net pay is computed by subtracting deductions from gross pay. What is gross pay? The product of hours worked and an hourly pay rate. We've identified two variables whose values must be input. What do we mean by deductions? Deductions are computed by adding federal tax, state tax, and local tax. We have to compute them, so we need at least three more algorithms. Figure 2.18 shows a complete problem definition with the necessary inputs, algorithms, and outputs.

Note the process we used in developing this problem definition. We started with the desired output: net pay. We identified an algorithm to compute it. Then we studied each of the algorithm's variables, and identified the algorithms needed to compute them. Eventually, we reached an algorithm that could be solved by using constants, input data, or a value computed by another, already known algorithm. When no more unknowns were left, the problem was defined.

Study the algorithms carefully. Start with our objective: net pay. Before computing net pay, we need values for gross pay and deductions. To compute gross pay, we need hours worked and pay rate. Deductions are computed by adding federal tax, state tax, and local tax; thus we need values for federal tax, state tax, and local tax before computing deductions. How do we find federal tax? The algorithm says to take a percentage of gross pay; thus gross pay must be known before we compute federal tax.

Fig. 2.18: *A complete problem definition for the net pay problem.*

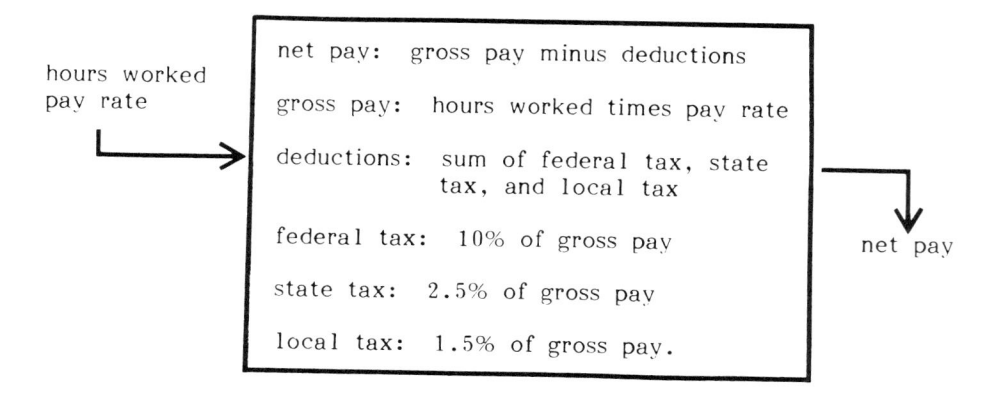

```
hours worked      net pay:     gross pay minus deductions
pay rate
          ───▶    gross pay:   hours worked times pay rate

                  deductions:  sum of federal tax, state
                               tax, and local tax                ───▶  net pay

                  federal tax: 10% of gross pay

                  state tax:   2.5% of gross pay

                  local tax:   1.5% of gross pay.
```

Note how we're analyzing the algorithms. Before a given algorithm can be solved, the value of each of its variables must be known. We can't compute net pay until both gross pay and deductions are known. We can't compute deductions until the values of federal, state, and local taxes are known. We can't compute the taxes until gross pay is known. We can't compute gross pay until hours worked and pay rate are known. Thus, we define the sequence in which our algorithms must be evaluated:

1. Input hours worked and pay rate.

2. Compute gross pay.

3. Compute federal tax.

4. Compute state tax.

5. Compute local tax.

6. Compute deductions.

7. Compute net pay.

8. Print net pay.

The order of steps 3, 4, and 5 could be changed, but, otherwise given the algorithms, the list describes the flow of logic that must be followed in the program we are about to write. Figure 2.19 shows a flowchart for the net pay program. Start at the top, and follow the flowlines from top to bottom; relate the logical flow to the list of steps we prepared above.

Writing the Program in *True BASIC*

The flowchart or the list of steps serves as a blueprint for the program. Once the steps have been defined, the task of translating or converting them to *True BASIC* is essentially mechanical. Start with the first step. It says to input values for hours worked and pay rate. How do we input values in *True BASIC*? Through an **INPUT** statement. Thus, the program's first statement is

>   INPUT hours_worked, pay_rate

Next, our plan tells us to compute gross pay. Thus, our second instruction becomes

Fig. 2.19: *A flowchart for the net pay program.*

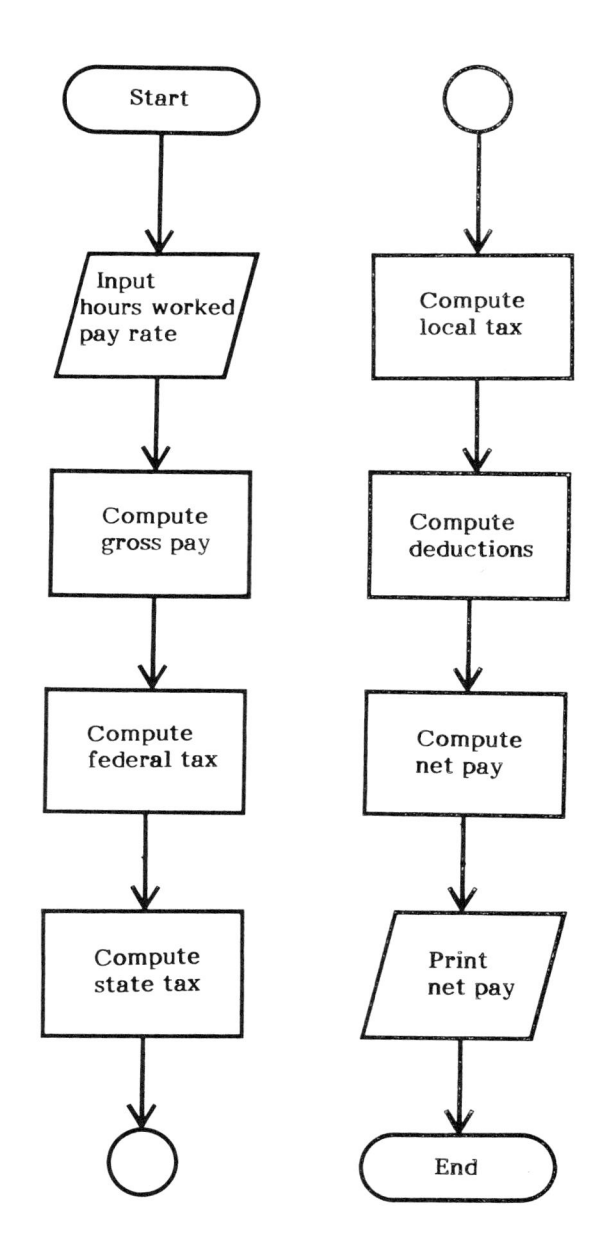

LET gross_pay = hours_worked * pay_rate

One by one, we move through the list of functions as defined by our plan and code the appropriate statement or statements; when we finish, we have a program (Fig. 2.20).

```
                              ! Program to compute an individual's
                              ! net or take-home pay. First, hours
INPUT hours_worked, pay_rate  ! worked and a pay rate are input. Next,
                              ! gross pay is computed.

LET gross_pay = hours_worked * pay_rate

                              ! Given gross pay, it is possible to
                              ! compute the various taxes due.

LET federal_tax = gross_pay * 0.10
LET state_tax = gross_pay * 0.025
LET local_tax = gross_pay * 0.015

                              ! Total deductions are simply the sum
                              ! of all the taxes due.

LET deductions = federal_tax + state_tax + local_tax

                              ! And net pay is computed by subtracting
                              ! deductions from gross pay.

LET net_pay = gross_pay - deductions
PRINT net_pay
END
```

Fig. 2.20: *The net pay program coded in True BASIC. Note, in particular, the sequence of instructions.*

Executing the Program

Let's submit our net pay program to *True BASIC*, compile it, and execute it. Imagine that we've already loaded *True BASIC*. We have to inform the compiler that we're about to enter a new program, so we type a **NEW** command *(Fig. 2.21)* in the history window:

   NEW NETPAY

NETPAY is the program's name.[1] After you type the command and press the enter key, you'll see the cursor move to the top, or editing, window. Now you can type your instructions, one by one, pressing the enter key at the end of each instruction.

[1]The rules for naming programs vary with the computer system; check your system reference manual for details. Throughout this primer, we'll use program names that are legal on most systems.

Fig. 2.21: *The True BASIC **NEW** command. Use a **NEW** command to tell True BASIC that you plan to write a new program.*

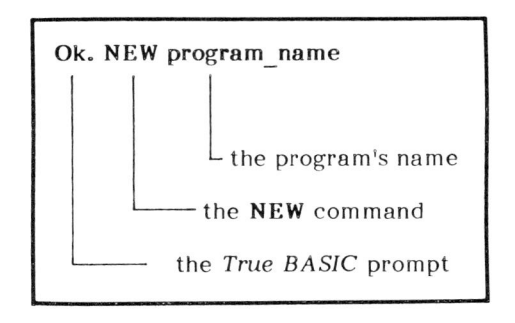

```
Ok. NEW program_name
    |           |
    |           └ the program's name
    |
    |         ── the NEW command
    |
    └──────── the True BASIC prompt
```

As you type the program statements, you will almost certainly make errors. Fortunately, *True BASIC* supports an easy-to-use editor. A brief tutorial and instructions for using the editor are presented in Module B. You might want to take the time to go through the tutorial; it's keyed to the **NETPAY** program.

As you complete the program, the cursor is located in the top editing window. We want to issue a command to run the program. Commands are typed in the lower history window; thus we have to move the cursor back to near the bottom of the screen. If your computer has function keys, pressing F2 moves you from the editing window to the history window. Try it; you'll see the cursor wink off and reappear an instant later in the history window. The F1 key gets you back to the editing window. Press it; you'll see the cursor move back to the top. Press F2 again, and you're back in the history window.

Now let's execute the program. Type **RUN**, and press the enter key. You may have made some typing errors; if so, *True BASIC* will display an error message in the history window and move the cursor to the bad instruction. Correct your errors and type **RUN** again. If you continue to have problems, refer to Module D for some debugging tips.

Eventually your program will be successfully compiled and your instructions will begin executing. You'll see a question mark appear in the history window. Type values for hours worked and pay rate, and press enter. An instant later, the computed net pay will appear in the history window *(Fig. 2.22)*.

If you want to run your program again, type **RUN** again; you can execute it as often as you like. This time, enter different values for hours worked and pay rate. Perhaps when you're finished, you'd like to save the program for future use. Type **SAVE**, and press the enter key. The **SAVE** command *(Fig. 2.23)* copies the program currently stored in main memory to disk. To verify that the program has indeed been saved, try another experiment. Remember the **FILES** command from Chapter 1? Type **FILES**. Displayed in the history window, you should see a list of the programs stored on your diskette. If you look closely, you'll see that a new program named **NETPAY** has been added to the list. We defined **NETPAY** as the program's name in the **NEW** command issued earlier.

Now that your program is on disk, you'll be able to retrieve it whenever you want. As an experiment, turn the computer off, wait several seconds, and turn

Fig. 2.22: *When an **INPUT** statement is executed, a question mark is displayed on the screen in the history window. The user responds by typing values for the requested input variables. The output generated by a **PRINT** statement is also displayed in the history window.*

it on again. After typing the date, the time, and **HELLO,** your *True BASIC* screen will reappear. Type **OLD NETPAY,** and your program will be read back into main memory.

SEQUENTIAL LOGIC

Throughout this chapter, we've concentrated on the simplest of the standard logical structures: sequence. The order in which the instructions are executed controls the computer. If you don't write your instructions in the correct order, the

Fig. 2.23: *The True BASIC **SAVE** command. Use the **SAVE** command to copy the program in main memory to diskette.*

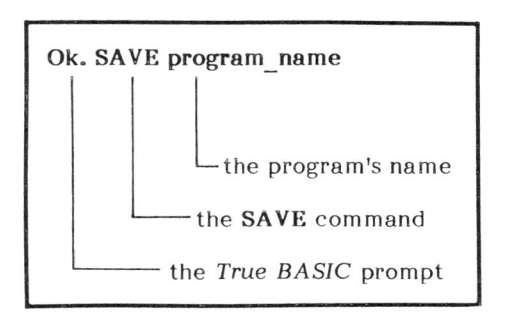

```
Ok. SAVE program_name
              │         │
              │         └─ the program's name
              │
              └─── the SAVE command
         │
         └──── the True BASIC prompt
```

43

computer won't get the correct answer, because computers execute their instructions in sequence. Thus it follows that the flow of logic through your program must be sequential.

Understanding sequential flow is a key to learning how to program. We can state it as a general rule:

> A PROGRAM'S LOGIC FLOWS FROM THE TOP, DOWN.

In Chapters 3 and 4, we'll introduce two other logical structures: decision and repetition. At first glance, they might seem to violate our general rule, but we'll discover that they don't. Sequence, decision, and repetition are the basic building blocks of any computer program. Few programming languages implement these elementary structures better than *True BASIC*.

SUMMARY

Chapter 1 ended with a brief overview of the program development process in which the need for careful planning was emphasized. We began this chapter with a simple example: computing the area of a circle. After defining an algorithm, we analyzed it and developed a plan for a program.

Given that plan, we turned to *True BASIC*. We explained the rules for writing constants, variables, and operators, and explored the priority of the operators. Then, expressions and **LET** statements were introduced, and a *True BASIC* version of the "area of a circle" algorithm written. We incorporated that algorithm in a program, and used it to introduce *True BASIC* comments and the **INPUT, PRINT,** and **END** statements.

After completing the first program, we turned to another example, computing net pay. First, the algorithms were defined. By analyzing the variables needed to solve each algorithm, we were able to develop a list specifying the algorithms' necessary evaluation order. Using this list as a blueprint, we wrote the net pay program and submitted it to *True BASIC*, introducing two new commands, **NEW** and **SAVE**, in the process. The program was written using the facilities of the *True BASIC* editor; a tutorial on the editor can be found in Module B.

The chapter ended with a discussion of the sequential flow of logic through a program. Sequence, decision, and repetition are the basic building blocks of any computer program.

REFERENCES

True BASIC Rules for:

Defining numeric constants	Fig. 2.3, page 23
Defining string constants	Fig. 2.4, page 24
Defining variable names	Fig. 2.5, page 25
Defining arithmetic operators	Fig. 2.6, page 26
Priority of operators	Fig. 2.10, page 29
Writing expressions	pages 26-29
Comments	page 35

True BASIC Statements

LET variable = expression	Fig. 2.11, page 29
INPUT var1, var2, var3, . . .	Fig. 2.14, page 36
PRINT expr1, expr2, expr3, . . .	Fig. 2.15, page 36
END	Fig. 2.17, page 37

True BASIC Commands

NEW program_name	Fig. 2.21, page 42
SAVE program_name	Fig. 2.23, page 43

Support Materials

The *True BASIC* editor	Module B
Flowcharting	Module C
Debugging tips	Module D

EXERCISES

Note: answers to selected exercises can be found in Appendix VI.

1. Several *True BASIC* constants are listed below. Some are valid; some are invalid. Identify the valid ones. What is wrong with the invalid ones?

   a. **15**   b. **197-583**   c. **3,475.92**

   d. **-147**   e. **0.5E8**   f. **$4.98**

   g. **123-45-6789**   h. **-3.5.8**   i. **"string constant"**

   j. **-1.5e-19**   k. **145 382**   l. **"123-45-6789"**

2. A number of variable names are listed below. Indicate the type of each variable (numeric or string). Some are legal; some are not. Identify the legal ones. Suggest corrections for the invalid ones.

   a. **illegal**   b. **2legal**   c. **LENGTH**

   d. **length**   e. **Dollars$**   f. **$dollars**

   g. **net-pay**   h. **net_pay**   i. **cyrkle**

   j. **X**   k. **a&b**   l. **over_31_characters**

3. Write *True BASIC* expressions for the following algorithms.

   a. The area of a square ((side) ^{2}).

   b. The area of a rectangle (length times width).

   c. The area of a triangle (one half times base times height).

   d. The volume of a sphere (π (radius) ^{2} (height)).

   e. A baseball player's batting average (hits divided by times at bat).

f. $(x + y)^3 - (x + y)^2 + 18$

g. $a^3 + a^2b + ab^2 + b^3$

h. $\dfrac{a + b + c}{2}$

i. $\left[\dfrac{a + b + c}{x + y + z}\right]^2$

j. $\dfrac{-b + \sqrt{b^2 - 4ac}}{2a}$

k. $(ab^2)^2$

l. A grade point average.

4. If you have not already done so, turn to Module B and work through the *True BASIC* editor tutorial.

5. If you have not already done so, enter and run the "area of a circle" program we developed in the chapter *(Fig. 2.13)*. Run it several times, typing a different value for the radius each time.

6. If you have not already done so, enter and run the net pay program we developed in the chapter *(Fig. 2.20)*. Run it several times, typing different values for hours worked and pay rate each time.

7. Write a program to input the length of a side of a square, compute the area of the square, and print the computed area.

8. Write a program to input the length and the width of a rectangle, compute the rectangle's area, and print the computed area. *(See Exercise 3,b for the formula.)*

9. Write a program to input a triangle's base and height, compute its area, and print the computed area. *(See Exercise 3,c.)*

10. Write a program to input a cylinder's radius and height, compute its volume, and print the computed volume. *(see Exercise 3,d.)*

11. Write a program to input a baseball player's hits and times at bat, and compute and print a batting average. *(See Exercise 3,e.)*

12. A baseball pitcher's earned-run average is computed by dividing earned runs allowed by the number of equivalent nine-inning games pitched. This involves two computations. First, equivalent nine-inning games are computed by dividing the total number of innings pitched by 9. Next, the earned-run average (ERA) is computed by dividing earned runs allowed by equivalent nine-inning games. Write a program to input innings pitched and earned runs allowed, compute an earned-run average, and print the computed earned-run average.

13. In basketball, each field goal counts two points, and each foul shot counts one. Write a program to input a player's field goals and foul shots, and compute total points scored. Print field goals, foul shots, and total points.

14. The Pythagorean theorem says that, given the lengths of sides "a" and "b", the formula

$$c = \sqrt{a^2 + b^2}$$

can be used to find the length of the third side of a right triangle. Write a program to compute and print "c" given "a" and "b". To find a number's square root, raise it to the 1/2 power.

15. Evaluate the polynomial

$$y = 2x^3 + 3x^2 - 4x + 3$$

for any input value of x. Print x and the answer, y.

16. Write a program to find the surface area of a flat washer given its inner radius and its outer radius. Print the answer.

17. Light travels 186,000 miles per second. Write a program to input a time (expressed in years) and compute how far light travels in that time interval. Print your answer.

18. The area of any triangle can be computed from the formula

$$\text{Area} = \sqrt{S(S-a)(S-b)(S-c)}$$

where: a, b, c are the lengths of the three sides

and:
$$S = \frac{(a+b+c)}{2}$$

Write a program to compute the area of a triangle given the lengths of its three sides.

19. Money in a savings account earns interest. If the interest is left in the account, additional interest is earned on that interest during the next period; this is known as compounding. The formula for computing the future value of a sum of money invested today is

$$F = P(1+i)^n$$

where: F is the future of the investment
P is the present value of the investment
i is the interest rate
n is the compounding period

Write a program to accept an investment amount (P), an interest rate (i), and a number of years (n), and compute the future value of the investment (F). Print your answer.

20. In 1626, a tribe of Indians sold Manhattan Island to the Dutch for roughly $24. If they had invested their money at 8% annual interest, how much would it be worth today? The formula for computing compound interest is explained in Exercise 19.

3

Decision

KEY IDEAS

1. Decision structures.
2. **IF...THEN** logic.
3. **IF...THEN...ELSE** blocks.
4. Nested **IFs**.
5. The **SELECT CASE** structure.

DECISION STRUCTURES

In Chapter 2, we focused on sequential logic, and learned how to develop programs from the top, down. We saw how the computer followed a program's instructions, executing them one by one, in sequence. Every step was completely defined before the program ran. Every instruction we coded was executed.

That's not always desirable. For example, what if a store wanted to offer a discount on large purchases? How could that policy be implemented as part of a program? Using straight sequential logic, it couldn't, because the decision to give a discount can't be made until after the purchase amount is known. A programmer can't possibly know in advance how much each customer entering the store might spend. The discount decision must be made as the program runs.

To cite another example, imagine a mathematical or statistical problem in which one of three different algorithms is selected based on the value (positive, negative, or zero) of a key variable. Again, because the key data value isn't known until the program begins executing, the proper path through the program can't be determined until run time.

We need a mechanism to select a logical path based on events that occur as the program is running. That mechanism is the decision or IF...THEN...ELSE structure *(Fig. 3.1)*.

Follow the steps in the flowchart. The decision structure begins with a condition (the diamond symbol); for example, we might compare two numbers to see if they are equal. The condition is either true or false; no other outcome is possible. If the condition is true, the logic flows down from the decision symbol

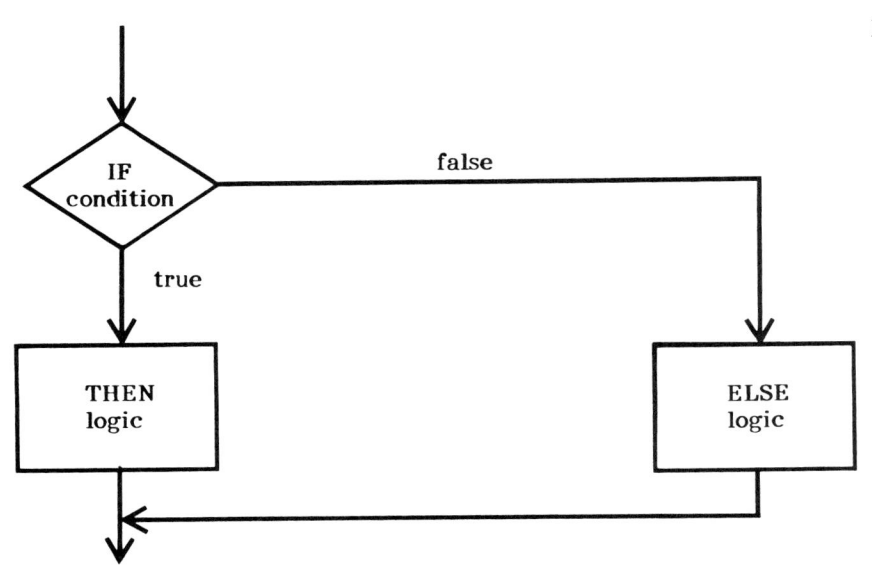

Fig. 3.1: *The general form of a decision structure.*

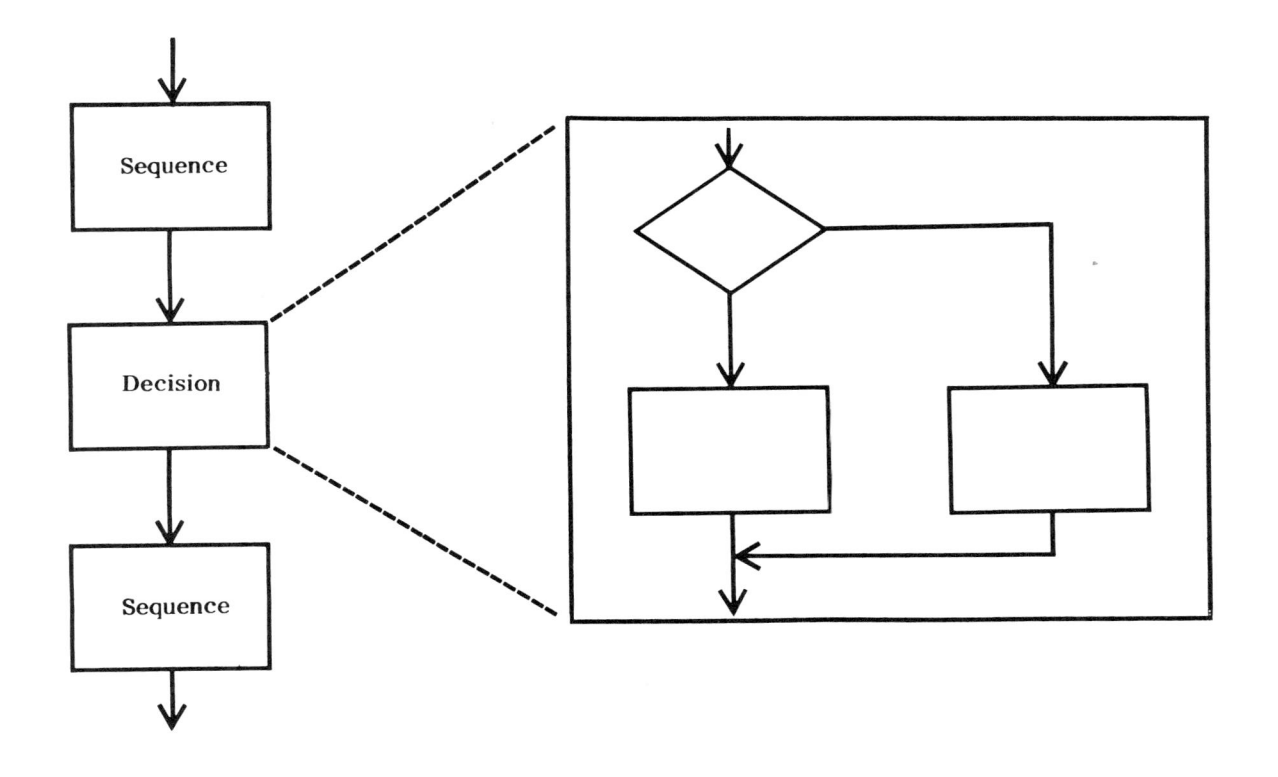

Fig. 3.2: *Viewed as a block, a decision structure is simply one step in a program's sequential logical flow.*

through the sequential block marked THEN. If the condition is false, the flow moves from the decision symbol, to the right, and then down through the block marked ELSE. In either case, after the appropriate instructions have been executed, the logical flow rejoins the main, sequential flowline.

Go through that logic one more time. As you enter the decision structure *(Fig. 3.1)*, you encounter a condition. If the condition is true, you execute the THEN logic and skip the ELSE logic. If the condition is false, you execute the ELSE logic and skip the THEN logic. The actual path through the program is determined at run time.

Note that the primary flow is still sequential. View the decision structure as a single logical block *(Fig. 3.2)*. After executing several instructions, the computer enters the decision block. A test is performed, and a logical path selected. Either the THEN logic or the ELSE logic is executed. When all tasks that depend on the initial condition have been completed, the computer leaves the decision block and moves on to the next sequential block.

SIMPLE IF...THEN LOGIC

Imagine a store that offers a five percent discount on purchases of one hundred dollars or more. The store plans to install a computer-controlled cash register, and wants a program to compute the discount (if any), state sales tax, and the amount due the store. Let's define the problem by sketching a block diagram showing the necessary inputs, outputs, and algorithms *(Fig. 3.3)*. Given the problem definition, we can begin to analyze the algorithms.

Note that the block diagram doesn't quite define everything. For example, consider the sales tax algorithm. Is sales tax computed on the full purchase amount or on the discounted amount? A discussion with the store manager reveals that the tax is applied to the discounted purchase amount, so the discount must be computed before the sales tax. The flowchart in Fig. 3.4 shows the order in which the algorithms must be solved. Given it and the input and output data defined in the block diagram, we can begin to write the program. Before we do, however, let's study the flowchart.

It begins with an input operation. Next comes the decision block. If the input purchase amount is greater than or equal to $100.00, a discount is computed and then subtracted from the purchase amount. If, however, the purchase amount is less than $100.00, nothing happens; the discount logic is bypassed. Based on the value of the purchase amount, a path through the decision block is selected. Following the decision block, sales tax and the amount due are computed and output.

We've highlighted a few things on the flowchart. First, focus on the decision block. Look at it not as individual instructions, but as a block. Note that it represents but one step in an overall sequential flow. Also note the THEN block. It consists of two steps: compute the discount and then compute the discounted amount due. A block of logic can contain any number of steps. Later, as our programs become more complex, the ability to group logic into cohesive blocks will become more and more valuable.

Fig. 3.3: *A block diagram for the purchase discount problem.*

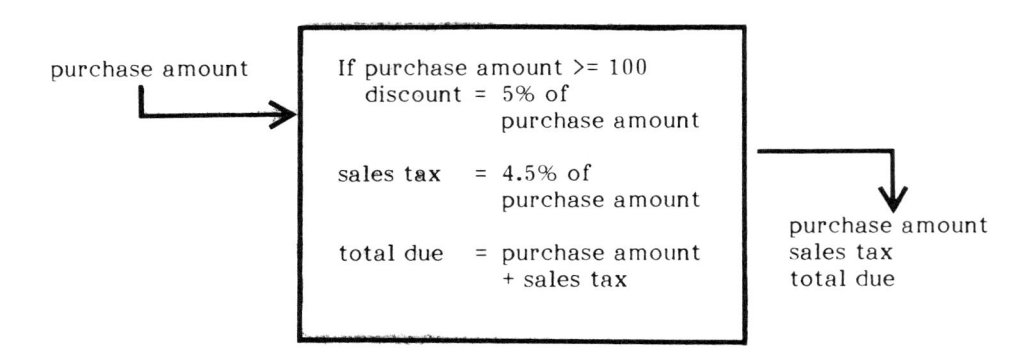

```
purchase amount ──→  ┌─────────────────────────────────┐
                     │ If purchase amount >= 100       │
                     │     discount = 5% of            │
                     │                purchase amount  │
                     │                                 │──→  purchase amount
                     │ sales tax  = 4.5% of            │     sales tax
                     │              purchase amount    │     total due
                     │                                 │
                     │ total due  = purchase amount    │
                     │              + sales tax        │
                     └─────────────────────────────────┘
```

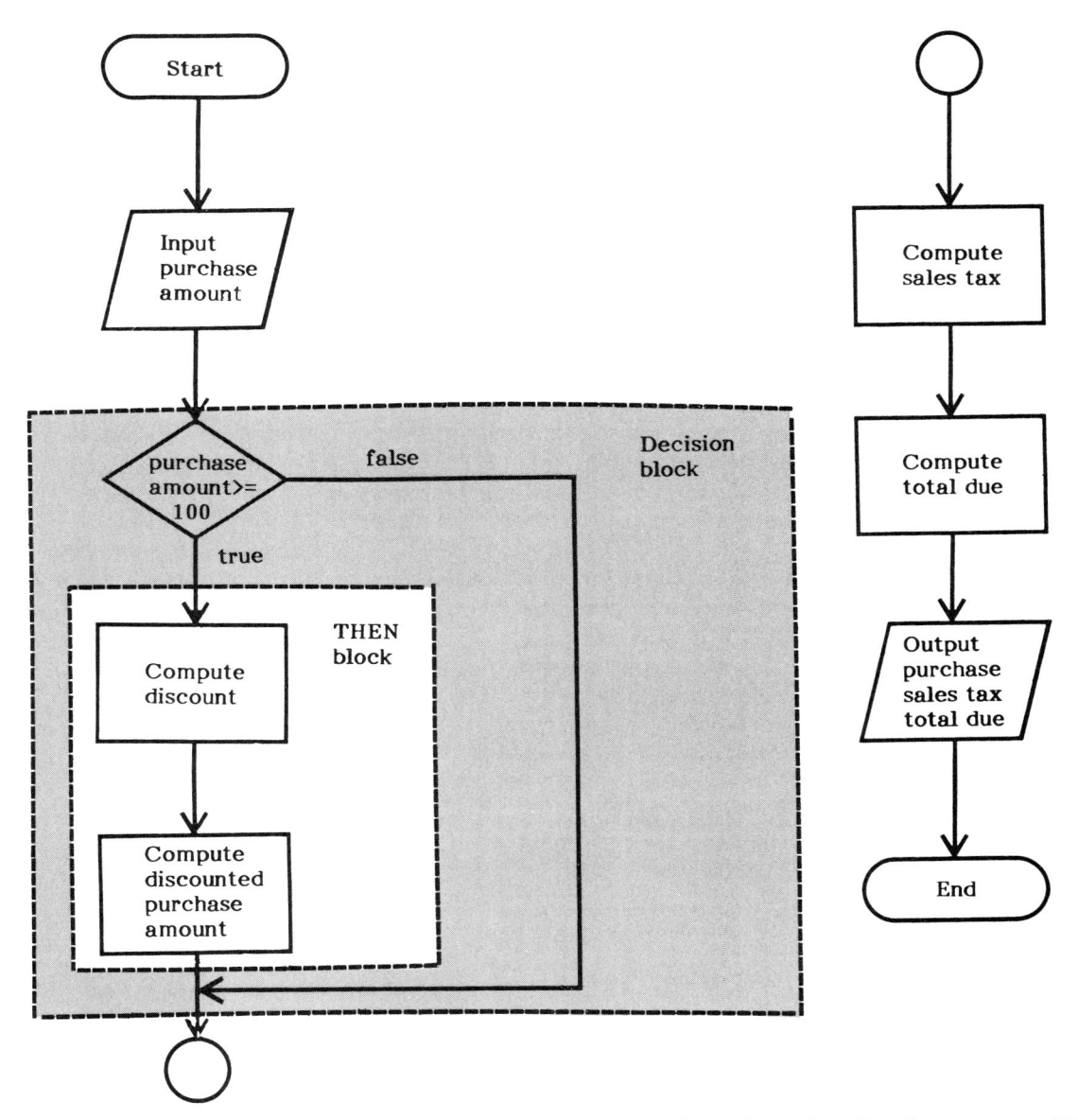

Fig. 3.4: *A flowchart for the discounts problem.*

True BASIC's IF...THEN Structure

The easiest way to implement a decision in *True BASIC* is to use an **IF...THEN** structure. One form is written on a single line *(Fig. 3.5)*. When the **IF** is executed,

55

Fig. 3.5: *A single-line IF...THEN statement.*

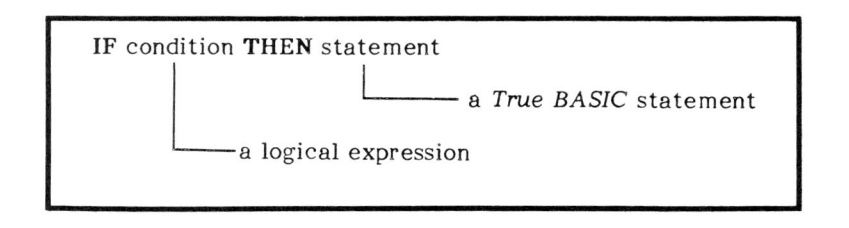

```
IF condition THEN statement
   |                  |
   |                  └── a True BASIC statement
   └── a logical expression
```

the condition, a logical expression, is evaluated. If the condition is true, the statement following **THEN** is executed; if the condition is false, the statement is skipped. The **IF...THEN** block structure *(Fig. 3.6)* is somewhat more flexible. Again, the condition (a logical expression) is evaluated. If it is true, the block of instructions following **THEN** is executed; if the condition is false, the block is skipped. The **END IF**, which must be coded, marks the structure's end. Note that any number of statements can lie between **THEN** and **END IF**.

Logical Expressions

The condition tested in an **IF** statement is a logical expression. Expressions are composed of variables, constants, and operators. In a logical expression we use relational operators and logical operators to compare arithmetic expressions. Note that a single constant or a single variable can form an arithmetic expression.

Let's start with the relational operators *(Fig. 3.7)*. In our example, if the purchase amount is greater than or equal to $100.00, we want to compute a discount. The logical expression

purchase_amount >=100

Fig. 3.6: *An IF...THEN block.*

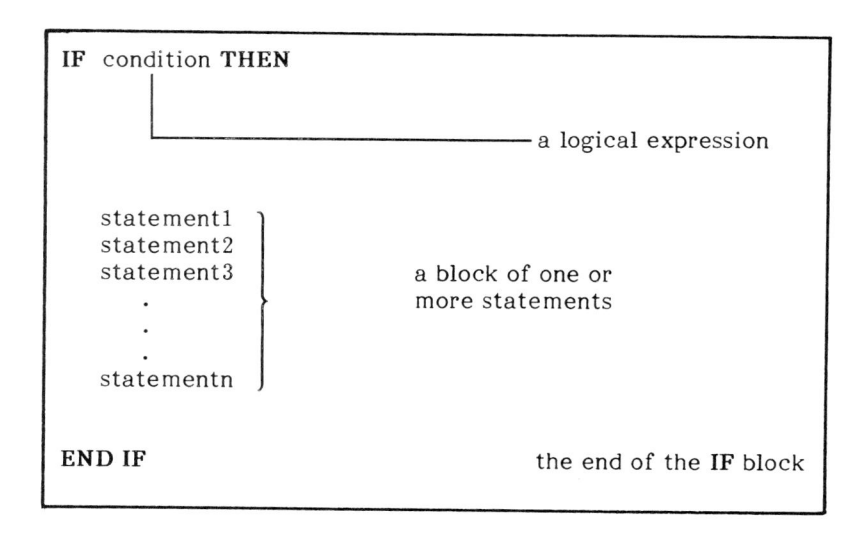

```
IF condition THEN
      |
      └─────────────────── a logical expression

      statement1  ⎫
      statement2  ⎪
      statement3  ⎬  a block of one or
         .        ⎪  more statements
         .        ⎪
         .        ⎭
      statementn

END IF                        the end of the IF block
```

Operator	Meaning
<	less than
<= or =<	less than or equal to
=	equal to
>	greater than
>= or =>	greater than or equal to
<> or ><	not equal to

Some examples:

Expression	is true if:
x < 0	x less than zero (or negative)
x = 0	x equal to zero
x > 0	x greater than zero (or positive)
x <= 100	x less than or equal to 100
x <> 25	x not equal to 25
x = y	x equal to y
x > y + 5	x greater than (y + 5)
(x-3) = (y*2)	(x-3) equal to (y*2)

Fig. 3.7: *True BASIC's relational operators.*

represents this condition. Using this logical expression in an **IF** statement, we get

    IF purchase_amount >= 100 THEN...

When the **IF** statement is executed, the logical expression is evaluated. There are two possibilities: either **purchase_amount** is greater than or equal to 100 (true), or it isn't (false). Based on the result, the computer selects a path through the decision block.

    A logical expression can involve more than one relationship. For example, imagine a bookstore that offers students a discount on art supplies. To qualify for the discount, two conditions are necessary: the total purchase must be for $100 or more, and it must be made in the art department. (Assume it's department 22). After the purchase amount and the department code are input, the statement

IF (purchase_amount >= 100) AND (department = 22) THEN...

allows the program to test for both conditions before granting the discount.

Figure 3.8 lists the logical operators in priority order. Below the operators are several examples illustrating their use. Note that we have consistently used parentheses in these complex logical expressions. While not technically required, the parentheses do help to clarify the expressions.

Writing the Discount Program

Now that you know how to write logical expressions, let's go back to the discounts problem and write a program. We already have a block diagram *(Fig. 3.3)* and a flowchart *(Fig. 3.4)* to guide us.

Focus on the decision block. Should we use a single line **IF...THEN** or should we use the block form? The advantage of the single line form is simplicity; it's an excellent choice for a simple test with a single response. In this case, however, if the logical expression is true, it is necessary to compute both the discount and the discounted purchase amount. Thus we need the block form. A *True BASIC* program for the discount problem is shown in Fig. 3.9.

Follow the logic. First, we'll imagine a $10.00 purchase. Clearly, no discount should be computed. Start with the **INPUT** statement. The **purchase_amount** is $10.00. Mentally execute the **IF** statement. Evaluate the condition

Fig. 3.8: *True BASIC's logical operators, in priority order.*

Operator	Expression is true if:
NOT	the condition is false
AND	both conditions are true
OR	either condition is true

Expression	is true if:
(x=0) AND (y=0)	both x and y equal zero
(x=0) OR (y=0)	either x or y equals zero
NOT (x=0)	x is not equal to zero
(NOT (x=0)) AND (NOT (y=0))	neither x nor y equals zero
(x<a) AND (y=b)	x less than a and y equals b
(NOT (a=b)) OR (a=c)	a is not equal to b or a equals c

```
                                    ! Compute discount and sales tax
                                    ! on a purchase.
        INPUT purchase_amount
                                    ! Discounts of 5% are offered on
                                    ! purchases of $100 or more.

        IF purchase_amount >= 100 THEN
           LET discount = 0.05 * purchase_amount
           LET purchase_amount = purchase_amount - discount
        END IF

                                    ! State sales tax is 4.5%.

        LET sales_tax = 0.045 * purchase_amount

                                    ! Compute and print total due.

        LET total_due = purchase_amount + sales_tax
        PRINT purchase_amount, sales_tax, total_due
        END
```

Fig. 3.9: *A program to compute a discount, sales tax, and a customer's total amount due.*

purchase_amount >= 100

Is it true or false? The purchase amount is $10.00, so the condition is false. Consequently, the logic between **THEN** and **END IF** is bypassed. Sales tax is computed on $10.00. The total amount due is $10.45.

Exercise the program's logic once more. This time, assume the input purchase amount is $100.00. Evaluate the logical expression. Is **purchase_amount** greater than or equal to 100? Certainly. Since the condition is true, the **THEN** block is executed. A discount is computed and subtracted from the purchase amount; the discounted purchase amount is $95.00. The decision block is finished. Sales tax is computed next. Since the purchase amount has been reduced to $95.00, sales tax is computed on $95.00; the total due is $99.28.

"Playing computer" and manually following a program's logic is called desk checking. It's a valuable exercise, well worth the time and effort.

Indentation

Look carefully at the program in Fig. 3.9. Note that the instructions comprising the **THEN** block in our decision structure are indented. That's not a requirement. We could have aligned all the statements *(Fig. 3.10)*. By aligning the code, however, we lose a sense of the relationship between the statements. Look at the same instructions with indentation. Note how the decision block's beginning

```
All statements aligned

    IF purchase_amount >= 100
    LET discount = 0.5 * purchase_amount
    LET purchase_amount = purchase_amount - discount
    END IF
```

```
Statements "belonging to" the structure indented

    IF purchase_amount >= 100
        LET discount = 0.5 * purchase_amount
        LET purchase_amount = purchase_amount - discount
    END IF
```

Fig. 3.10: *When we align the statements in an **IF. . .THEN** structure we lose a sense of the relationships between the component parts. Indenting the statements that "belong to" the decision block makes the logic much easier to understand.*

and end are clearly identified. It is obvious, just by looking at that second set of code, that the two **LET** statements "belong to" the decision block. Indenting the instructions that are part of a logical structure makes a program much easier to understand.

Another Example: Computing a Square Root

Let's consider another example before we move on. Imagine that we want to estimate a number's square root. We'll formalize the problem definition in a block diagram *(Fig. 3.11)*. What if the input value is negative? You can't take the square root of a negative number. Thus, as we plan our program, we'll include a decision structure *(Fig. 3.12)*. If the number is positive or zero, we'll compute and print its square root. If the input number is negative, we'll skip the computation and do nothing. A program to implement this logic is shown in Fig. 3.13. Again, read the program carefully.

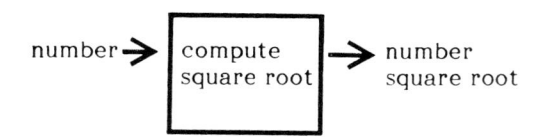

Fig. 3.11: *A block diagram definition of the square root problem.*

Fig. 3.12: *A flowchart showing the logical flow through the square root program.*

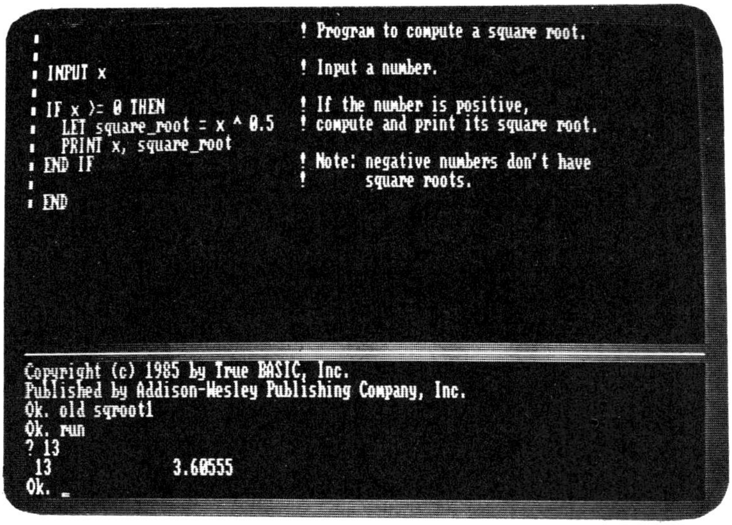

Fig. 3.13: *A program to compute the square root of an input value. The program avoids trying to find the square root of a negative number.*

IF . . . THEN . . . ELSE LOGIC

Something is missing in our square root program. Try desk checking the logic. Input a negative number. What happens? Nothing. Follow the logic. The value is input. Because the number is less than zero, the **THEN** logic is bypassed and the program ends. Running this program would be like making a telephone call and being placed on hold.

Let's change our view of the problem. We're really looking at two possible outcomes. If the input number is positive or zero, we'll compute and print its square root. If, on the other hand, the number is negative, the least we can do is tell the user that we're not going to do anything. A flowchart for the new version of the program is shown in Fig. 3.14.

We're looking at IF. . .THEN. . .ELSE logic. The decision block starts with a test. If the condition tested is true, one set of instructions is executed. A false condition calls for a different set of instructions.

True BASIC's **IF. . .THEN. . .ELSE** logical structures are described in Fig. 3.15. The single-line version is fine for simple tests with simple responses, but the block structure is generally much clearer. In the block structure, the condition, a logical expression, is evaluated. If the condition is true, the statement or statements lying between **THEN** and **ELSE** (block1 in the diagram) are executed, and the rest of the statements in the decision structure are ignored. If the condition is false, the statement or statements between **ELSE** and **END IF** (block2) are evaluated, and the **THEN** logic is skipped.

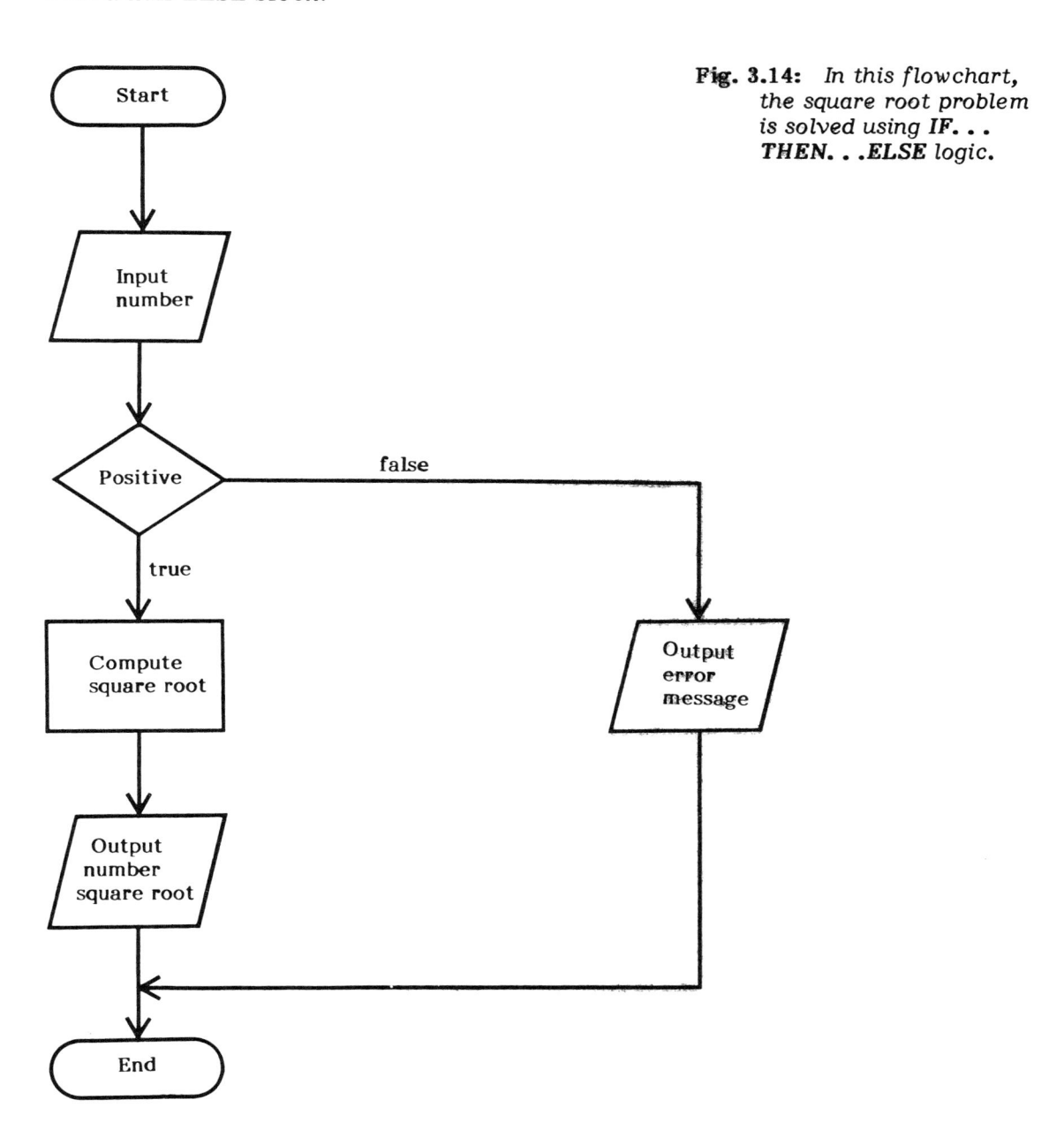

Note that it is legal to code an **IF. . .THEN. . .ELSE** structure with an empty (null) **THEN** block or **ELSE** block. An **IF. . .THEN** is really an **IF. . .THEN. . .ELSE** with a null **ELSE** block.

Fig. 3.14: *In this flowchart, the square root problem is solved using IF. . . THEN. . .ELSE logic.*

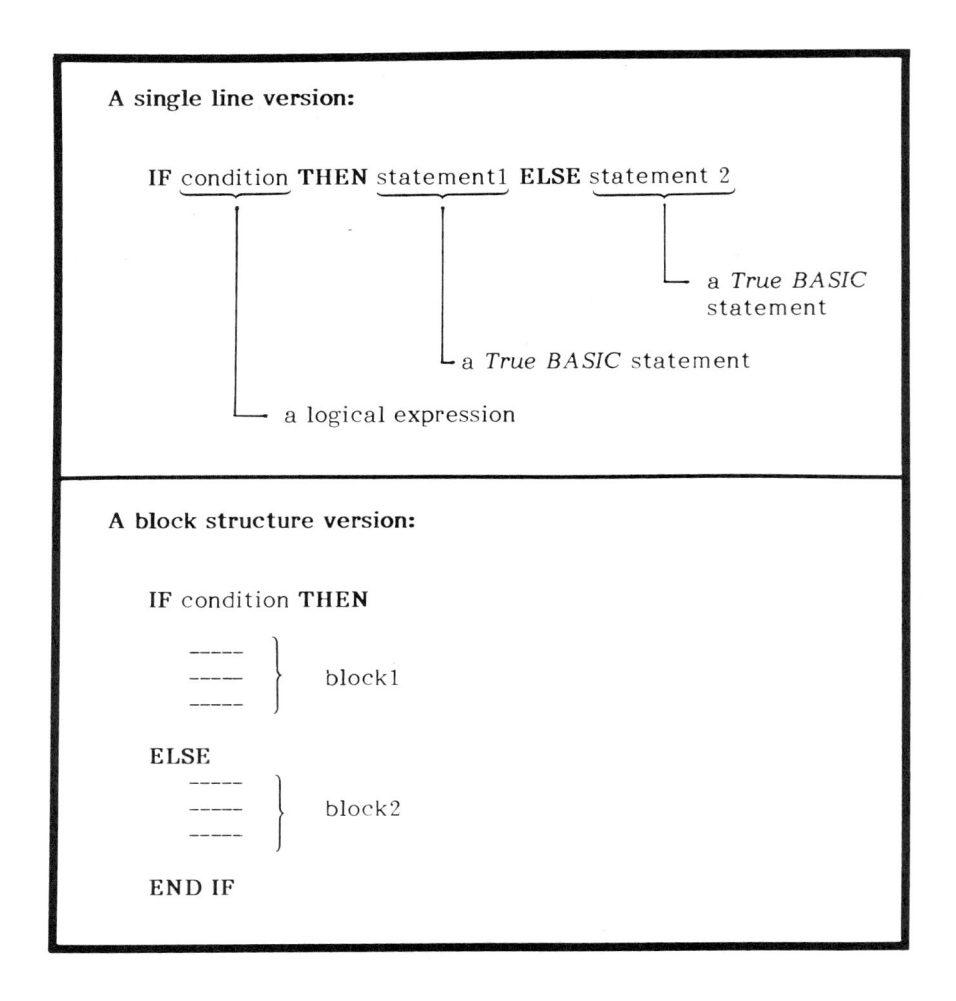

```
A single line version:

    IF condition THEN statement1 ELSE statement 2
         └─────┘      └────────┘      └─────────┘
            │              │               └─ a True BASIC
            │              │                  statement
            │              └─ a True BASIC statement
            └─ a logical expression


A block structure version:

    IF condition THEN
        -----  ⎫
        -----  ⎬  block1
        -----  ⎭
    ELSE
        -----  ⎫
        -----  ⎬  block2
        -----  ⎭
    END IF
```

Fig. 3.15: *True BASIC's **IF...THEN...ELSE** structure.*

Figure 3.16 shows a square root program with an **IF...THEN...ELSE** logical structure. Compare it to our earlier, less elegant version *(Fig. 3.13)*. Generally, it is a good idea to have the computer respond in some way to any possible result of a logical test, especially if that result might be significant to another part of the program or to the user. Even if your response is to do nothing, you should at least say so.

Note also the use of indentation. Do you see how the decision structure, the **THEN** block, and the **ELSE** block are clearly delineated? Something as simple as a few blank spaces or a few blank lines can make a program much easier to read.

```
! Program to compute a square root.
! INPUT x                    ! Input a number.

! IF x >= 0 THEN             ! If the number is positive,
!    LET square_root = x ^ 0.5   ! compute and print its square root.
!    PRINT x, square_root

!  ELSE
!    PRINT "negative number"  ! If the number is negative, print
!                             ! a message.
! END IF

! END
```

```
? 13
 13            3.60555
Ok. old sqroot2
Ok. run
? -5
negative number
Ok. _
```

Fig. 3.16: *This program uses an **IF...THEN...ELSE** structure to avoid computing the square root of a negative number.*

Another Example

Let's consider another example involving decision logic. Often, when computing an individual's gross pay, a premium is paid for time worked in excess of forty hours a week. Usually, this overtime is paid at time and a half. In other words, if an individual's regular pay rate is $8 per hour, overtime is paid at $12 per hour. We want to write a program to compute gross pay, taking overtime into account. Our problem definition is summarized in Fig. 3.17.

Examine the rule for computing gross pay. It says that hours worked in excess of forty are paid at a rate equal to one and a half times the regular pay rate. Sometimes the best way to visualize an algorithm is to do a sample calculation.

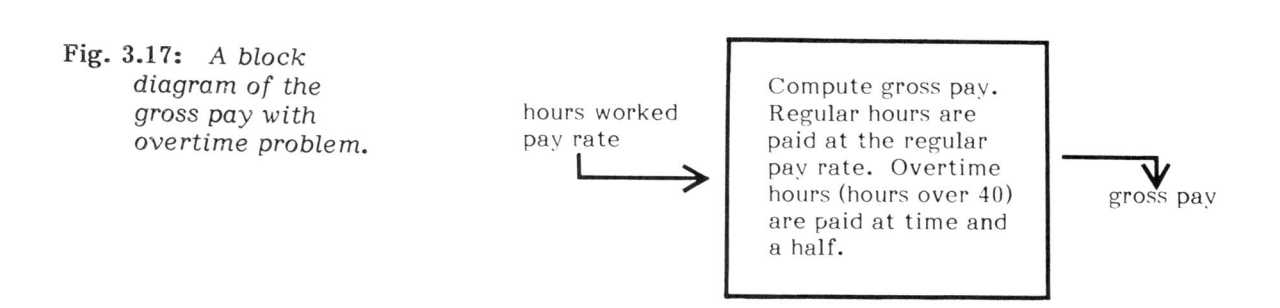

Fig. 3.17: *A block diagram of the gross pay with overtime problem.*

hours worked
pay rate
→
Compute gross pay. Regular hours are paid at the regular pay rate. Overtime hours (hours over 40) are paid at time and a half.
→ gross pay

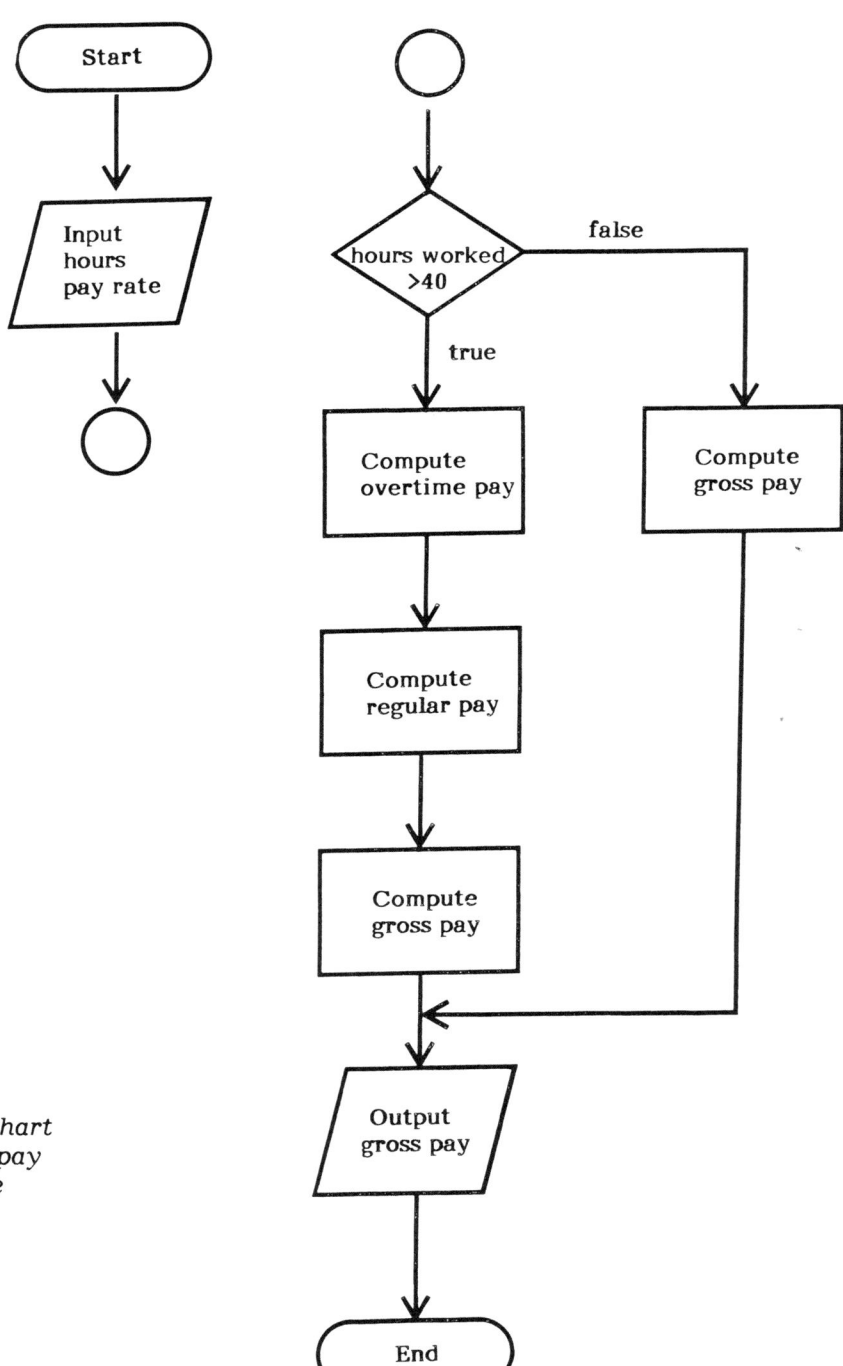

Fig. 3.18: *A flowchart for the gross pay with overtime problem.*

Imagine that an individual works 50 hours at a regular pay rate of $8.00 per hour. How much would this person receive? Hours over 40 are paid at time and a half. That's ten hours at the overtime rate. The overtime rate is $12.00. Those ten hours are worth $120.00. What about the first 40 hours? They're still paid at the regular rate: 40 times $8.00 is $320.00. To get gross pay, we add regular pay and overtime pay: this individual earned $320.00 plus $120.00, or $440.00 for the week.

Review the sample computations and generalize them. First, we computed overtime pay on the hours over 40. Next, we computed regular pay for the first 40 hours. Finally, we added regular pay and overtime pay to get gross pay. We've just defined the steps for computing gross pay with overtime.

What about the person who works 40 or fewer hours? People with no overtime are paid at the regular rate: gross pay is the product of hours worked and the hourly pay rate. We have two rules for computing gross pay.

Which rule do we use? The answer depends on the number of hours worked. When do we know the number of hours worked? At run time, just after hours worked has been input. This problem requires a decision structure. Given our algorithms we can prepare a flowchart *(Fig. 3.18)*. Given the necessary input and output data *(Fig. 3.17)* and the flowchart, we can write the program *(Fig. 3.19)*. Read the program logic carefully.

Fig. 3.19: *A program to compute an employee's gross pay.*

```
                                    ! Compute gross pay with overtime.
INPUT hours_worked, pay_rate

IF hours_worked > 40 THEN           ! Overtime is paid on hours worked over 40.
                                    ! First, overtime pay is computed. Next,
                                    ! regular pay is computed on the first 40
                                    ! hours. Gross pay is the sum of regular
                                    ! pay and overtime pay.

   LET overtime_pay = (hours_worked - 40) * (pay_rate * 1.5)
   LET regular_pay = (pay_rate * 40)
   LET gross_pay = regular_pay + overtime_pay

ELSE                                ! For up to 40 hours worked, gross pay
                                    ! is simply the product of hours worked
                                    ! and the hourly pay rate.

   LET gross_pay = hours_worked * pay_rate

END IF
                                    ! Print the computed gross pay.
PRINT hours_worked, pay_rate, gross_pay
END
```

Fig. 3.20: *Nested IF...THEN...ELSE logic.*

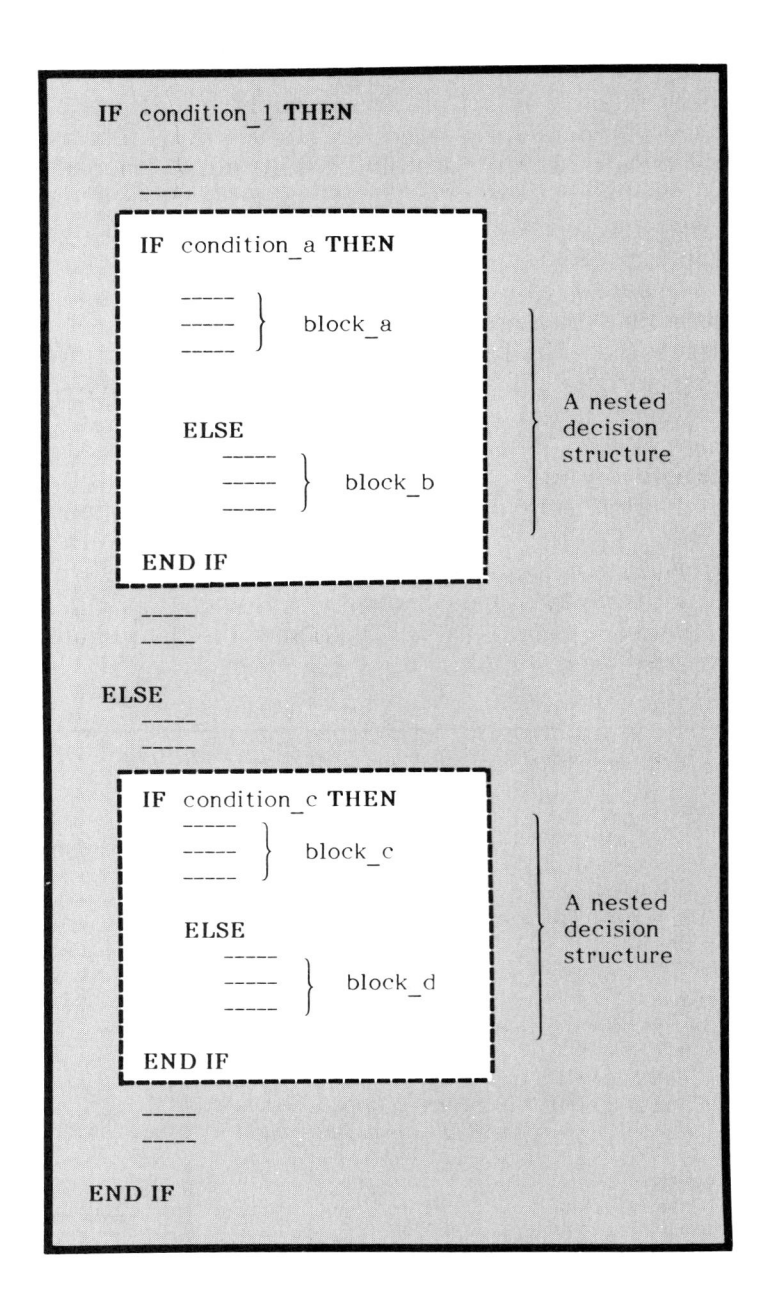

```
IF condition_1 THEN
    -----
    -----
    ┌─────────────────────────────┐
    │ IF condition_a THEN         │
    │     -----                   │
    │     -----  } block_a        │    ⎫
    │     -----                   │    ⎬ A nested
    │ ELSE                        │    ⎭ decision
    │     -----                   │      structure
    │     -----  } block_b        │
    │     -----                   │
    │ END IF                      │
    └─────────────────────────────┘
    -----
    -----
ELSE
    -----
    -----
    ┌─────────────────────────────┐
    │ IF condition_c THEN         │
    │     -----                   │
    │     -----  } block_c        │    ⎫
    │     -----                   │    ⎬ A nested
    │ ELSE                        │    ⎭ decision
    │     -----                   │      structure
    │     -----  } block_d        │
    │     -----                   │
    │ END IF                      │
    └─────────────────────────────┘
    -----
    -----
END IF
```

NESTED IF STATEMENTS

Earlier, we mentioned that a **THEN** block or an **ELSE** block can contain any number of *True BASIC* statements. We also mentioned that if a decision structure is viewed as a block, it is simply one element in a program's general sequential logical flow. In effect, it is reasonable to view a decision structure as just another statement. Clearly, then, an **IF. . .THEN. . .ELSE** structure could be part of another decision structure's **THEN** block or **ELSE** block *(Fig. 3.20)*. This is known as "nesting" **IF** statements.

Note that each **IF. . .THEN. . .ELSE** structure is logically complete, starting with its own **IF** and ending with its own **END IF**. View each structure as a single entity, in effect a single, lengthy statement. Given this viewpoint, it is possible to use an **IF** structure anywhere you can use a simple sequence statement. For example, there is no reason why you can't have an **IF** structure within an **IF** structure within yet another **IF** structure. Be careful, because too many levels of nesting can be confusing, and do carefully indent your code to show the relationships between logical blocks.

The ELSEIF Statement

Many data processing problems call for a series of related logical tests. The first test is performed. If it's true, a block of logic is executed; if it's false, another condition is tested. Several logical tests might be involved; Fig. 3.21 shows a generalized flowchart of this structure. Because a series of related tests is so common, *True BASIC* has a special statement just to handle the **ELSEIF** *(Fig. 3.22)*.

Let's consider an example calling for this kind of logic. Imagine controlling

Fig. 3.21: *ELSEIF logic allows the programmer to code a series of related logical tests.*

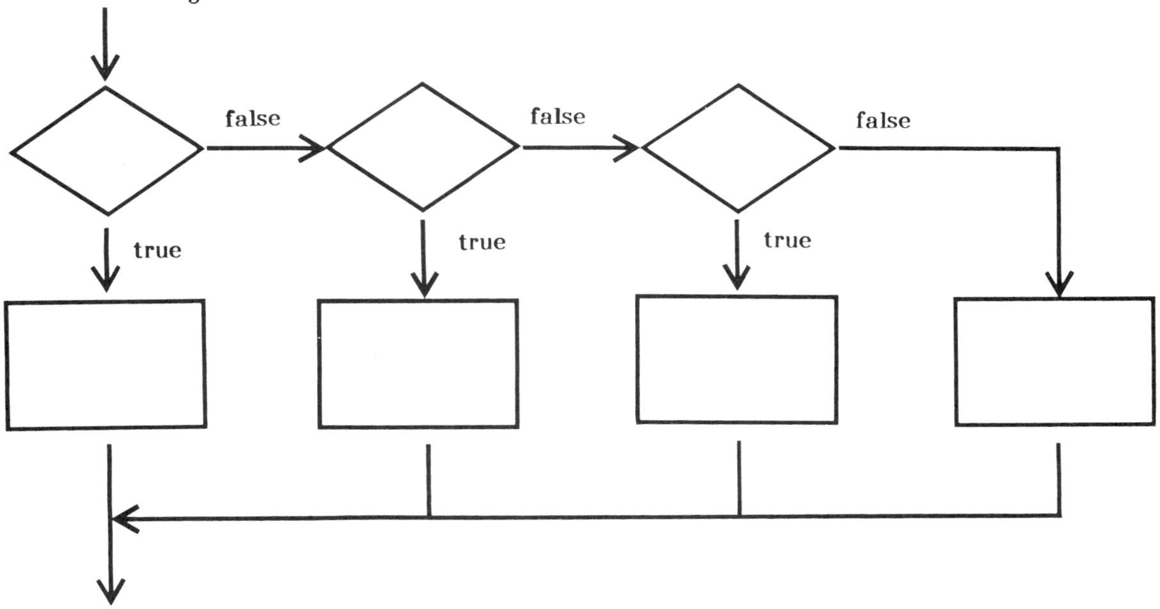

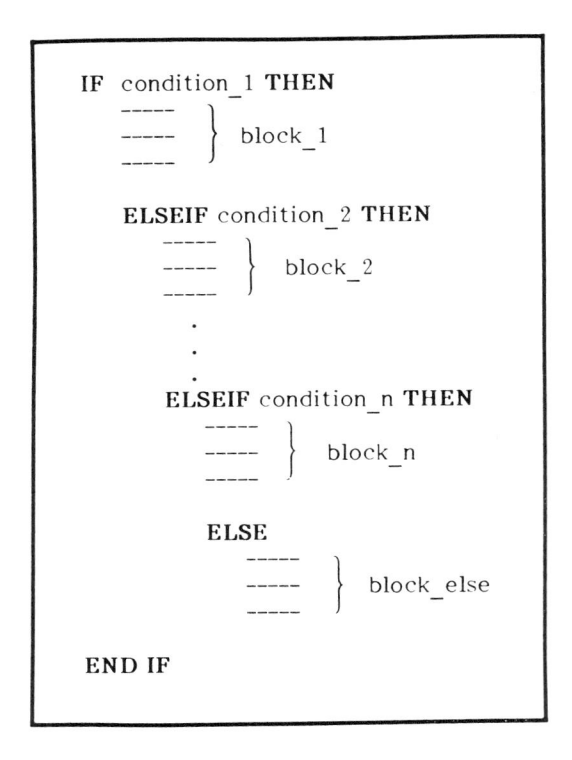

```
IF condition_1 THEN
    -----
    -----  } block_1
    -----

ELSEIF condition_2 THEN
    -----
    -----  } block_2
    -----
        .
        .
        .
ELSEIF condition_n THEN
    -----
    -----  } block_n
    -----

ELSE
    -----
    -----  } block_else
    -----

END IF
```

Fig. 3.22: *The ELSEIF statement.*

an electronic cash register. The purchase amount has been computed and, along with the customer's payment, input to the program. Our objective is to compute and display the change (payment minus purchase amount) to be returned to the customer. Three outputs are possible. If the amount of change is positive, the store owes the customer money. If the payment just matches the purchase amount, no change is due. If the payment is less than the purchase amount, the customer still owes the store money. For each possible outcome we want to display an appropriate message.

The problem definition is summarized in Fig. 3.23; Fig. 3.24 shows a flowchart

Fig. 3.23: *A block diagram definition of the making change problem.*

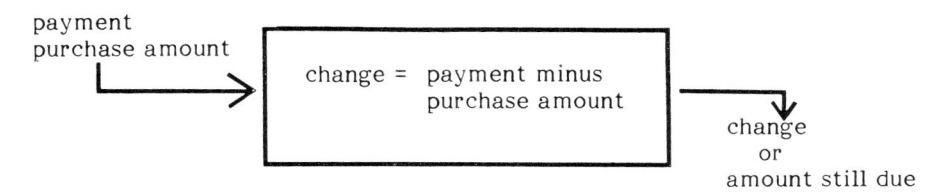

```
payment
purchase amount
      |
      v         ┌──────────────────────────────┐
      ─────────>│ change = payment minus       │─────────>
                │          purchase amount     │    change
                └──────────────────────────────┘      or
                                                   amount still due
```

70

of the logic. Given the problem definition and the flowchart, we can write the program *(Fig. 3.25)*.

Follow the logic carefully. Start with the **IF** statement. If the first condition is true, the store owes the customer money; thus, a "thank you" message and the amount of change due are output. If, however, the condition is false, the

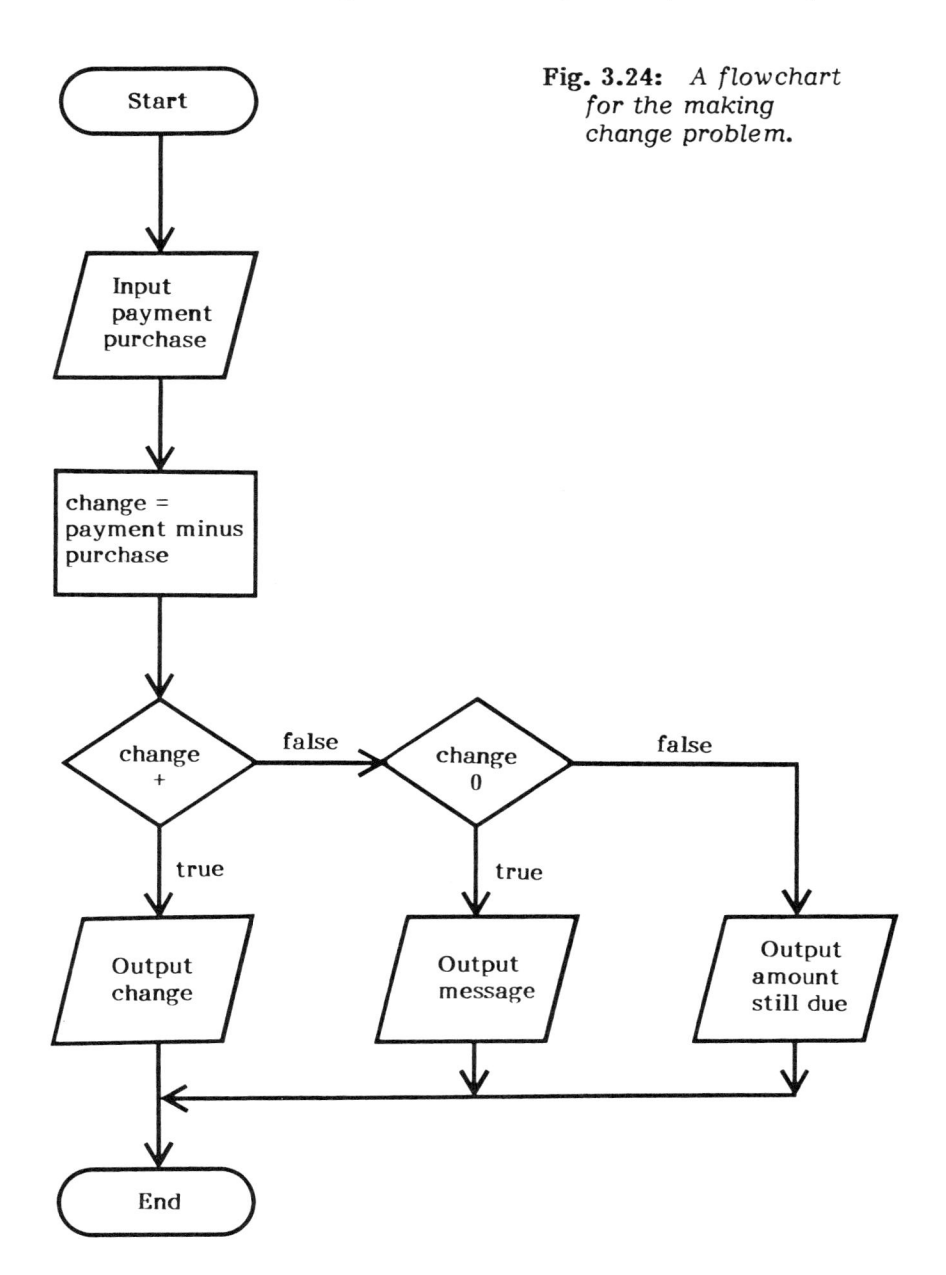

Fig. 3.24: *A flowchart for the making change problem.*

```
                              ! Program to compute the amount of change
                              ! due a customer and print an appropriate
                              ! message. We start by inputting the
                              ! purchase amount and the payment.
INPUT purchase_amount, payment

                              ! The change due is computed.
LET change = payment - purchase_amount

                              ! If the computed change is positive, a
                              ! message is printed, and the change due
                              ! is indicated.
IF change > 0 THEN
   PRINT "Thank you! Your change is ", change

                              ! If no change is due (the customer paid
                              ! the exact amount due), a simple thank
      ELSEIF change = 0 THEN  ! you message is printed.
         PRINT "Thank you!"

                              ! If the customer hasn't paid enough to
                              ! cover the purchase, the "change" is
                              ! converted to a positive number and
                              ! printed along with an appropriate
         ELSE                 ! message.
            LET change = -change
            PRINT "Thank you, but you still owe us ", change
END IF

END
```

Fig. 3.25: *A program to compute the amount of change due on a purchase payment. The program displays an appropriate message depending on whether the change is positive, zero, or negative.*

ELSEIF is executed. A second condition is tested. If it's true, the customer's payment exactly matches the amount due, so a simple "thank you" message is displayed and the program ends. If the second condition is false, the customer must owe more money. Thus the logic following the **ELSE** is executed, and a message is displayed asking for more money.

Generally, as soon as a true condition is encountered, a block of logic is executed and the decision structure ends. As long as the tested condition is false, another **ELSEIF** condition is tested. You can nest as many **ELSEIF** conditions as you want. Following the last **ELSEIF** is an **ELSE** block that is executed if the final condition is false.

THE CASE STRUCTURE

We want to order some diskettes for our personal computer. A single box of ten costs $35.00. If, however, we order between two and five boxes, the price drops to $32.00 per box. An order of from six to ten boxes costs only $29.00 per box, while the price drops to $27.50 for orders of more than ten boxes. We want to write a program to accept as input the number of boxes of diskettes ordered, and output the total cost. The problem definition is summarized in Fig. 3.26; note that the algorithm is expressed in the form of a table. Figure 3.27 shows a flowchart of the necessary logic.

Compare this flowchart to the one we developed for the "making change" problem *(Fig. 3.24)*. They are quite similar. We could certainly use **ELSEIF** statements to write the *True BASIC* code, testing for each breakpoint. There is, however, one problem with the **ELSEIF** statement. It is a form of nested **IF**. Too many levels of nesting can be very confusing. Fortunately, there is an alternative: the **SELECT CASE** structure *(Fig. 3.28)*.

The case structure begins with the keywords **SELECT CASE** and an arithmetic expression or a variable. Under this first line is a series of blocks or cases. Each **CASE** is followed by one or more tests. The tests can be constants, ranges of constants, or partial logical expressions *(Fig. 3.29)*.

When the computer encounters a **CASE** structure, it immediately evaluates the expression. It then goes through the tests in order until it finds one that matches the expression's value. When it does, the instructions in the block following that **CASE** are executed, and control drops to the first instruction after the **END SELECT**. You can have as many tests as you want. It is important that your tests be mutually exclusive; in other words, each test should represent a unique value of the expression. The **CASE ELSE** block is executed if none of the coded tests match the expression; it must be the last block in the list. If you need a **CASE ELSE** and you don't have one, you'll get a run time error.

Perhaps the best way to illustrate the case structure is through an example. Figure 3.30 shows the code for the price breaks problem. Let's go through the logic a few times. We'll start by entering the value 1 in response to the

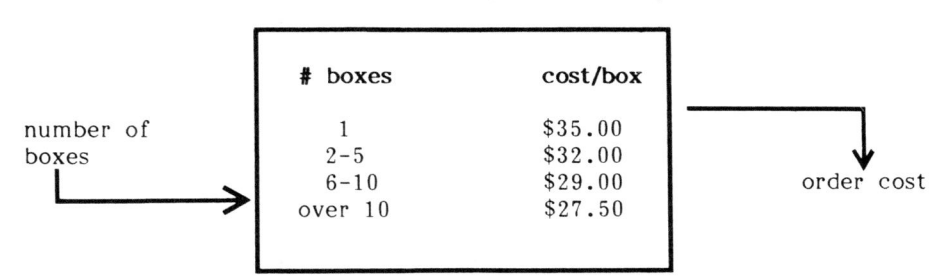

Fig. 3.26: *A block diagram definition for the price breaks problem.*

# boxes	cost/box
1	$35.00
2-5	$32.00
6-10	$29.00
over 10	$27.50

number of boxes → [table] → order cost

```
                              Start
                                │
                                ▼
                         ┌─────────────┐
                         │   Input     │
                         │  number     │
                         │   boxes     │
                         └─────────────┘
```

Fig. 3.27: *A flowchart for the price breaks problem.*

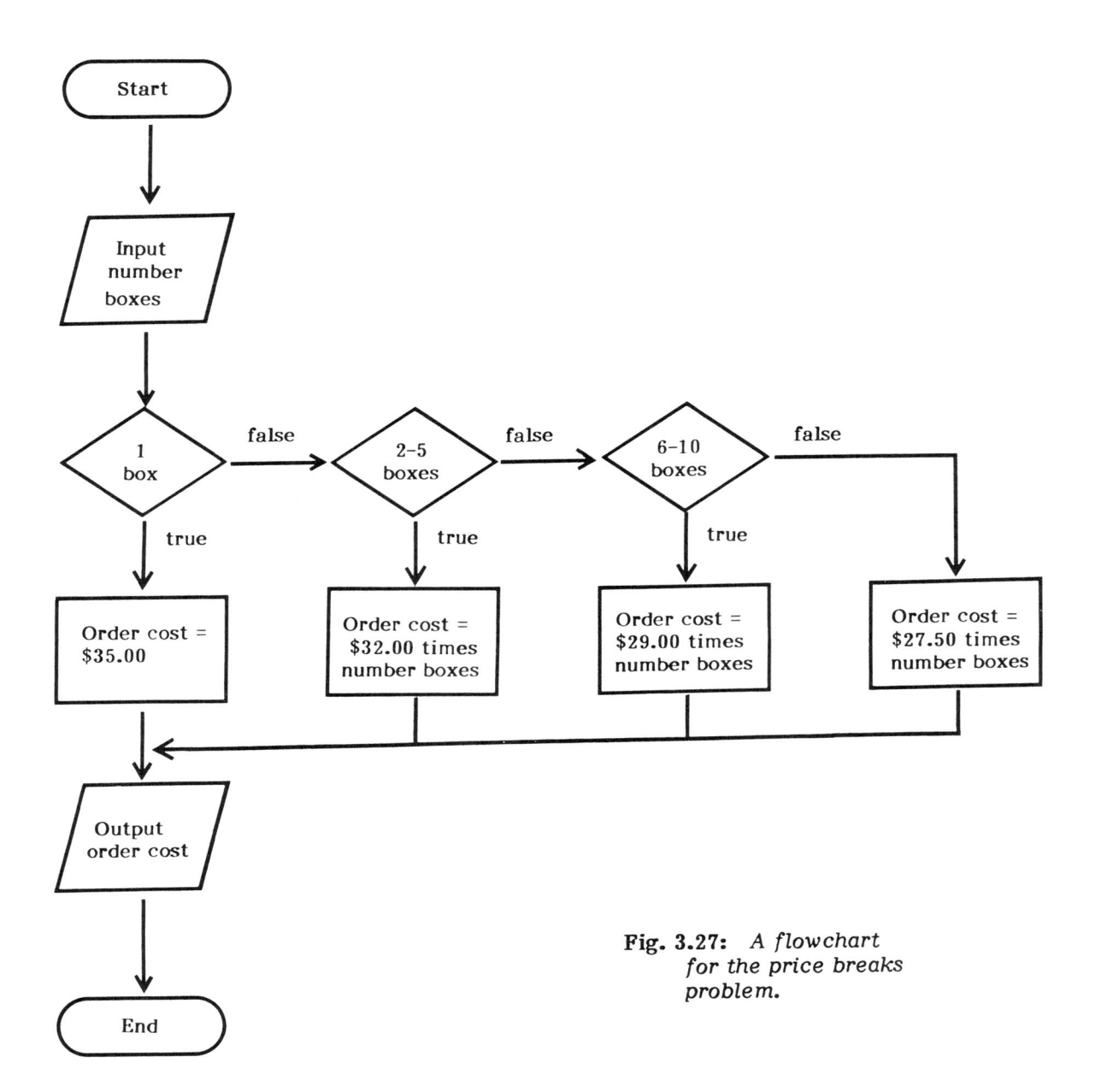

program's request for **number_boxes**. Next comes the **SELECT CASE** structure. The value of the expression **number_boxes** (a single variable is a valid expression) is 1. Now we check the tests, starting with the first **CASE**. Immediately we have a match; the cost of the order is $35.00. The **PRINT** statement, the first instruction following the **END SELECT**, comes next; the output is displayed,

74

```
SELECT CASE expression
    CASE test_1, test_2, ...
        -----
        -----  } block_1
        -----
    CASE test_3, test_4, ...
        -----
        -----  } block_2
        -----
            .
            .
            .
    CASE test_n, test_m, ...
        -----
        -----  } block_n
        -----
    CASE ELSE
        -----
        -----  } block_else
        -----
END SELECT
```

Fig. 3.28: *The SELECT CASE structure.*

Fig. 3.29: *Some SELECT CASE tests.*

Test type	Examples
constant	0 25 3.1416 −306
low **TO** high	2 **TO** 5 3.75 **TO** 5.38 −10 **TO** 0 1e20 **TO** 1e25
IS relation constant	**IS** > 5 **IS** <= 100 **IS** <> −8 **IS** = 1.5e22

```
                                    ! Compute total cost of an order for
                                    ! diskettes. The price per box of 10
                                    ! varies with the number of boxes ordered.
INPUT number_boxes                  ! Start with the number of boxes ordered.
                                    ! Using a case structure, compute the cost
                                    ! of the order.
SELECT CASE number_boxes

                                    ! A single box costs $35.00.
  CASE 1
    LET cost = 35.00
                                    ! If the order is for between 2 and 5
                                    ! boxes, the price is $32.00 per box.
  CASE 2 TO 5
    LET cost = 32.00 * number_boxes

                                    ! If the order is for between 6 and 10
                                    ! boxes, the price is $29.00 per box.
  CASE 6 TO 10
    LET cost = 29.00 * number_boxes

                                    ! For orders of more then 10 boxes, the
                                    ! price is 27.50 per box.
  CASE ELSE
    LET cost = 27.50 * number_boxes

END SELECT
                                    ! Print the number of boxes ordered and
                                    ! the total order cost.
PRINT number_boxes, cost
END
```

Fig. 3.30: *This program computes the total cost of an order for diskettes, taking into account the supplier's price breaks.*

and the program ends.

Let's try the logic again. This time we'll enter 10 boxes. The expression **number_boxes** is equal to 10. Evaluate the tests, moving from the top, down. Is 10 equal to 1? No. Move on to the second case. Does 10 lie between 2 and 5? No. Move on to the third case. Does 10 lie between 6 and 10? Yes. (Note that the end points of a range are included in that range.) The cost is $29.00 times **number_boxes**, or $290.00. Following the computation of cost, the first statement after the **END SELECT** is executed and the result is displayed.

Selecting from several sets of computations depending on the value of an expression or a control variable is quite common in data processing; as you learn to program, you'll have reason to use the **SELECT CASE** structure. Price breaks are one example. Income tax computations often use a different tax rate depending on the computed gross pay, making a case structure a natural choice. In mathematics, we often have to select an algorithm based on whether a number is positive, negative, or zero. Many statistical problems require dividing a series of input values into ranges in order to develop a frequency distribution. You never need the case structure; you can always use a series of **ELSEIF** statements. However, if you need more than two or three tests, the case structure is much clearer.

DECISION LOGIC

In Chapter 2, we concentrated on sequential logic. Our programs consisted of several instructions executed in fixed sequence, from the top, down. Each instruction we coded was executed; there were no exceptions.

In this chapter, we introduced decision logic. A decision block begins with a condition. The path of flow through the decision block depends on the condition; thus, the instructions actually executed are selected at run time. The ability to select a path based on a run time condition is a very powerful skill. It allows a computer to react to changing conditions, giving it a rudimentary "intelligence."

Note, however, that the general logical flow through a program is still sequential, still top, down. View the decision structure as a block. The computer enters the block at the top. All computations that depend on the condition or conditions are performed within the block. Finally, the computer exits from the bottom of the block. The decision block is but one step in the program.

Thus far we have considered two of the three basic building blocks of any program: sequence and decision. In Chapter 4, we'll study the third one: repetition.

SUMMARY

The chapter began with a brief introduction to decision logic. We expressed a need for decisions made at run time. We then illustrated the general form of an If...THEN...ELSE structure, pointing out that the primary logical flow was still sequential.

Next we introduced *True BASIC*'s **IF...THEN** structure. A discounting problem was defined and flowcharted. Both the single line and block forms of **IF...THEN** logic were illustrated, and logical expressions explained. Finally, an **IF...THEN** structure was used to code the discounts program. As another example, we defined, flowcharted, and coded a program to compute a square root, bypassing the computation when a negative number was input.

We then moved to **IF...THEN...ELSE** logic. First we modified the square root program to display a message when a negative value was input, using that simple example to introduce the general form of an **IF...THEN...ELSE** structure. The idea of desk checking a program to verify its correctness was discussed.

We then defined another problem, computing gross pay with overtime, developed a plan, and wrote the code.

It is possible to nest **IF** structures. The **ELSEIF** statement can be used to encode a series of related tests. To illustrate the **ELSEIF** statement, we considered another problem: displaying a cash register message based on the amount of change due the customer. We defined the problem, planned a solution, and wrote the program.

Selecting from several alternative sets of logic based on the value of a single variable or expression is common in data processing. The **SELECT CASE** structure is an excellent choice for solving many such problems. We introduced a price breaks application to illustrate the case structure, carefully defining the problem and then flowcharting a solution. The general form of the **SELECT CASE** structure was introduced and the various types of tests explained. Finally, we wrote the price breaks program and, by desk checking it, illustrated how a **SELECT CASE** structure works.

The chapter ended with a brief review of the basic building blocks of any program: sequence, decision, and repetition.

REFERENCES

True BASIC Statements and Structures

IF...THEN (single line)	Fig. 3.5, page 56
IF...THEN block	Fig. 3.6, page 56
IF...THEN...ELSE	Fig. 3.15, page 64
ELSEIF	Fig. 3.22, page 70
SELECT CASE	Fig. 3.28, page 75

True BASIC Rules for:

Logical expressions	Fig. 3.7, page 57
Logical operators	Fig. 3.8, page 58
SELECT CASE tests	Fig. 3.29, page 75

EXERCISES

1. Write logical expressions to test for the following conditions:

   a. The area of a circle is to be computed only if the radius is positive.

   b. Gross pay is to be computed only if the pay rate is less than $15.50.

   c. A student will receive an A if total grade points are greater than or equal to 90.

   d. A student is named to the Dean's list if his or her grade point average is 3.5 or greater.

   e. For any right triangle, the equation

   $$a^2 = b^2 + c^2$$

   where a is the length of its longest side and b and c are the lengths of the other two sides, is true. Assume that a, b, and c have been input, and check to see if the triangle is a right triangle.

   f. An "overdrawn" notice is to be displayed if a customer's checking account balance drops below zero.

   g. Interest on a savings account is to be computed only if the account balance is $50.00 or greater.

   h. Gross pay is to be computed only if hours worked lie between 20 and 75.

   i. A computation is to be performed if the value of (x + y) lies between 0 and 25.

   j. In a school's student data base, each student is identified by class (1 means freshman, 2 means sophomore, etc.), by sex (1 means female, 2 means male), and by major (the major code for computer science is 317). We want to identify all junior male computer science majors.

2. Early in the chapter, we wrote a program to compute a 5% discount on purchases exceeding $100. Modify the program to compute a 10% discount on purchases exceeding $500.

3. A company uses a three tier structure for computing weekly gross pay. The first 40 hours are paid at the regular pay rate. Hours between 40 and 60 are paid at time and a half. Hours over 60 are paid at double time—twice the regular rate. Modify the gross pay program *(Fig. 3.19)* to reflect this new algorithm.

4. Modify the square root program *(Fig. 3.16)* so that it takes appropriate action when the number input is positive, negative, or zero. Note that the square root of 0 is 0, and we know that without computing it.

5. Our diskette supplier has just announced a price change. The new prices are:

Number of boxes	Price per box
1	$33.50
2-6	$31.00
7-10	$28.50
10-20	$27.00
over 20	$26.00

Modify the price breaks program *(Fig. 3.30)* to reflect the new price structure.

6. Write a program to input two numbers, select the larger number, and display it.

7. Write a program to input three numbers, select the smallest, and display it.

8. Write a program to input a day, a month, and a year and determine if they represent a legitimate date. Hint: How many days in a month? How many months in a year?

9. First class postage rates are 22 cents for the first ounce and 17 cents for each additional ounce up to a maximum of 12. Packages over 12 ounces are sent under a different rate structure. Write a program to input the weight of a letter in ounces and output the proper amount of postage.

10. Interest on a savings account is paid only if the account balance exceeds $50.00. Write a program to accept the account's existing balance, compute 6% interest on that balance, and display the new balance (old balance plus interest), taking into account the minimum balance rule.

11. Write a program to input the lengths of the three sides of a triangle, making sure to enter the largest value first. Use the Pythagorean theorem *(Exercise 1,e)* to determine if the triangle is a right triangle.

12. Because data entry clerks make mistakes, input data are often checked before being used in a computation. Write a program to compute an individual's gross pay (hours worked times pay rate) only if the hours worked lies between 20 and 75 and the pay rate lies between 3.50 and 15.00. If the data fail either validity check, display an appropriate message.

13. The roots of a quadratic equation can be computed by solving the expression

$$\frac{-b \pm \sqrt{b^2 - 4ac}}{2a}$$

where a, b, and c are the coefficients of the equation

$$ax^2 + bx + c = 0$$

Write a program to compute the roots given values for a, b, and c. Note that there are three possible results based on the value of the term under the square root symbol (the discriminant). If the discriminant is positive, there are two real roots. If it's zero, there is one real root. If the discriminate is negative, however, there are no real roots. Depending on the value of the discriminant, your program should output two roots, a single root, or a message explaining that there are no real roots.

14. Monthly electric bills are based on the number of kilowatt hours of electricity used. Imagine that the local electric company uses the following rate structure to compute a customer's bill:

Kilowatt hours used	Amount due	Per hour over
less than 500	$42.00	--
500-1000	$42.00 + 0.055	500
1000-2000	$69.50 + 0.045	1000
2000-5000	$114.50 + 0.04	2000
over 5000	$234.50 + 0.035	5000

Write a program to input kilowatt hours used and output the customer's bill amount.

15. Two automobiles are approaching the same intersection. Car A is exactly two miles from the intersection, traveling west at a rate of 35 miles per hour. Car B is three miles from the intersection, traveling north at 55 miles per hour. Will the two cars collide?

16. To be eligible for retirement, an individual must pass at least one of the following tests:

    a. Any age, with at least 30 years service.

    b. 55 years old, with at least 25 years service.

    c. 60 years old, with at least 5 years of service.

    Retirement is mandatory at age 65. Retirement pay is based on the average amount earned in the individual's three highest income years. The formula for computing the monthly retirement benefit is

    $$\frac{(\text{average income})\,(2\%)\,(\text{years of service})}{12}$$

    Write a program to accept an individual's age, years of service, and three highest annual incomes. Verify that the person is eligible for retirement and compute his or her monthly benefit.

17. An instructor uses the following table to convert a student's total grade points to a letter grade:

Grade points	Grade
90-100	A
80-89	B
70-79	C
60-69	D
under 60	F

Write a program to input grade points and determine the student's grade.

18. During 1985, the rules for withholding federal income tax from an individual's weekly pay were as follows:

If taxable income lies between	the tax is	of excess over
$0 and $ 27	$0.00	
$27 and $ 84	12%	$27
$84 and $185	$6.84 + 15%	$84
$185 and $292	$21.99 + 19%	$185
$292 and $440	$42.32 + 25%	$292
$440 and $556	$79.32 + 30%	$440
$556 and $663	$114.12 + 34%	$556
$663 or above	$150.50 + 37%	$663

Taxable income is defined as gross pay minus $20.00 for each dependent claimed. (Note: taxable income cannot be less than zero.) Write a program to input gross pay and the number of dependents and compute the amount to tax to be withheld.

19. The amount of federal income tax that an individual must pay is based on the total amount of taxable income that he or she earned during the year. For 1985, the following tax table was used for single individuals.

For taxable income between	and	The tax is	of amount over
$0	$2,390	zero	------
2,390	3,540	------ + 11%	$2,390
3,540	4,580	$126.50 + 12%	3,540
4,580	6,760	251.30 + 14%	4,580
6,760	8,850	556.50 + 15%	6,760
8,850	11,240	870.00 + 16%	8,850
11,240	13,430	1,252.40 + 18%	11,240
13,430	15,610	1,646.60 + 20%	13,340
15,610	18,940	2,082.60 + 23%	15,610
18,940	24,460	2,848.50 + 26%	18,940
24,460	29,970	4,283.70 + 30%	24,460
29,970	35,490	5,936.70 + 34%	29,970
35,490	43,190	7,813.50 + 38%	35,490

43,190	57,550	10,739.50 + 42%	43,190
57,550	85,130	16,770.70 + 48%	57,550
85,130	------	30,009.10 + 50%	85,130

Write a program to accept taxable income as input and compute the total federal income tax due.

20. The price per carton of data processing forms depends on how many cartons are ordered. One supplier uses the following price schedule:

	Number of cartons			
Description	1-4	5-9	10-24	over 24
stock paper forms	$47.00	$41.70	$38.60	$32.25

Write a program to input the number of cartons ordered and output both the unit cost and the total order cost.

21. A common technique for verifying input data is computing a check digit. Imagine that each student in a class is assigned a 4-digit computer password. Although the students haven't been told this, the first three digits are taken from their social security numbers. The fourth digit is computed by multiplying the first and third digits, and dividing their product by the second digit. The units portion of the resulting quotient is used as the fourth "check" digit. Write a program to input a four digit identification number, compute the check digit, and then compare the computed check digit to the one actually entered. Depending on the result of the test, display an appropriate message.

4

Repetition

KEY IDEAS

1. *Repetitive logic.*

2. ***FOR...NEXT*** *loops.*

3. *Simple **DO** loops.*

4. ***DO UNTIL*** *loops.*

5. ***DO WHILE*** *loops.*

6. *Nested loops.*

7. *Sequence, decision, and repetition.*

REPETITIVE LOGIC

Think back to the problems we studied in Chapters 2 and 3. Most of them were relatively simple. Consider, for example, computing the area of a circle. Faced with such a problem, you would most likely reach for your calculator. You certainly wouldn't take the time to write a computer program. But what if you needed the areas of several hundred circles? Suddenly, using a calculator seems less appealing.

Computing gross pay is another example. To find one individual's gross pay, a calculator is probably the best choice. But what if a company must compute gross pay for thousands of employees? Using a calculator means that a clerk must control each step manually, pushing the same sequence of buttons over and over again. Using a computer, we can write a program to compute one person's gross pay, and then repeat those instructions thousands--even millions--of times.

A programmer tells a computer to repeat a set of instructions by coding a loop. Two conditions are necessary for a valid loop. First, there must be a set of instructions to execute repetitively. Second, there must be an exit condition--a way out of the loop. A loop without an exit condition is called an endless loop. Unless it is stopped, it will literally execute forever.

A DO WHILE loop *(Fig. 4.1)* begins with a condition. If the condition is true, the instructions in the loop are executed and the condition is tested again. As long as the condition is true, the loop instructions are repeated. As soon as the condition is false, the computer moves on to the first instruction following the loop.

A DO UNTIL loop *(Fig. 4.2)* begins with a block of instructions. After the instructions have been executed, a condition is tested. If the condition is false, control returns to the top of the loop and the instructions are executed again. As long as the exit condition is false, the loop logic repeats. However, as soon as the condition is true, the computer moves on to the first instruction following the loop.

It is possible to design a loop with its exit condition (a logical test, or an IF

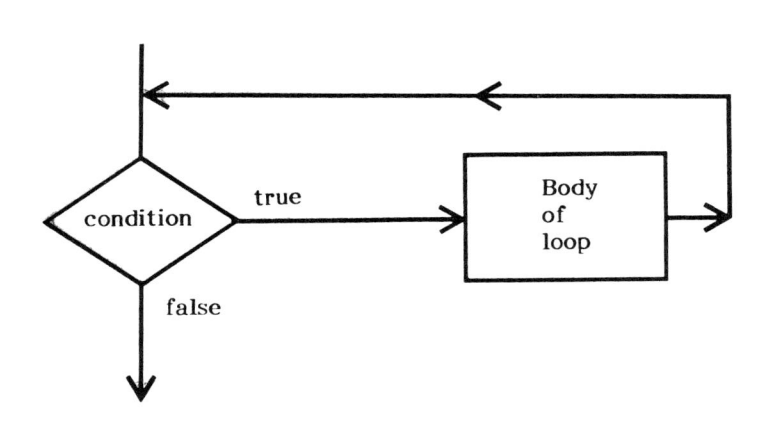

Fig. 4.1: *The general structure of a DO WHILE loop.*

Fig. 4.2: *The structure of a DO UNTIL loop.*

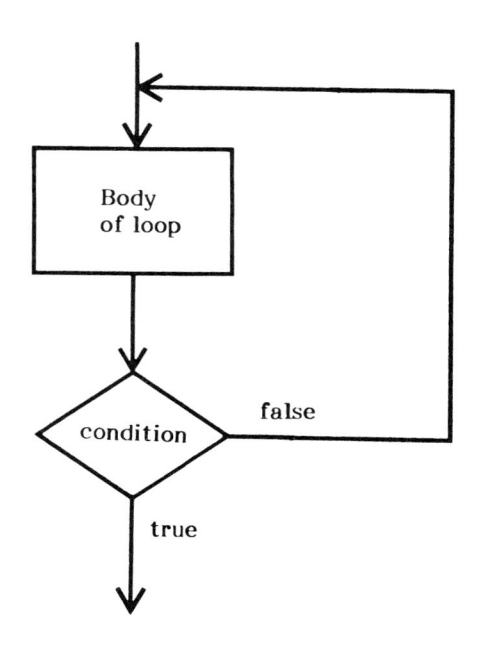

statement) somewhere in the middle. This approach, however, is not recommended, because it is easy to lose sight of an exit condition buried in the middle of a complex loop. Clarity is an important programming objective. Clear, easy-to-follow programs are relatively easy to debug and to maintain. Placing the exit condition near a loop's beginning or end makes the condition easy to find.

Note the overall sequential flow of a repetitive loop structure *(Fig. 4.3)*. We enter the loop at its top. The instructions in the loop execute repetitively until the exit condition is sensed. Then the logical flow leaves the loop at its bottom, rejoining the program's overall sequential, top down flow. View a repetitive structure as a block. The repetitive block is but one sequential step in the program logic.

COUNT LOOPS

A set of instructions often must be repeated a fixed number of times. To illustrate, we'll use an example. We want to compute the sum of the digits from 1 to 100. (There is a formula for computing the sum directly, but we'll ignore it.) As is our practice, we'll formalize a problem definition by drawing a block diagram *(Fig. 4.4)*.

Let's analyze the algorithm. How would you solve this problem? One possibility is to write a very long algebraic expression

$$\text{sum} = 1 + 2 + 3 + 4 + \ldots + 99 + 100$$

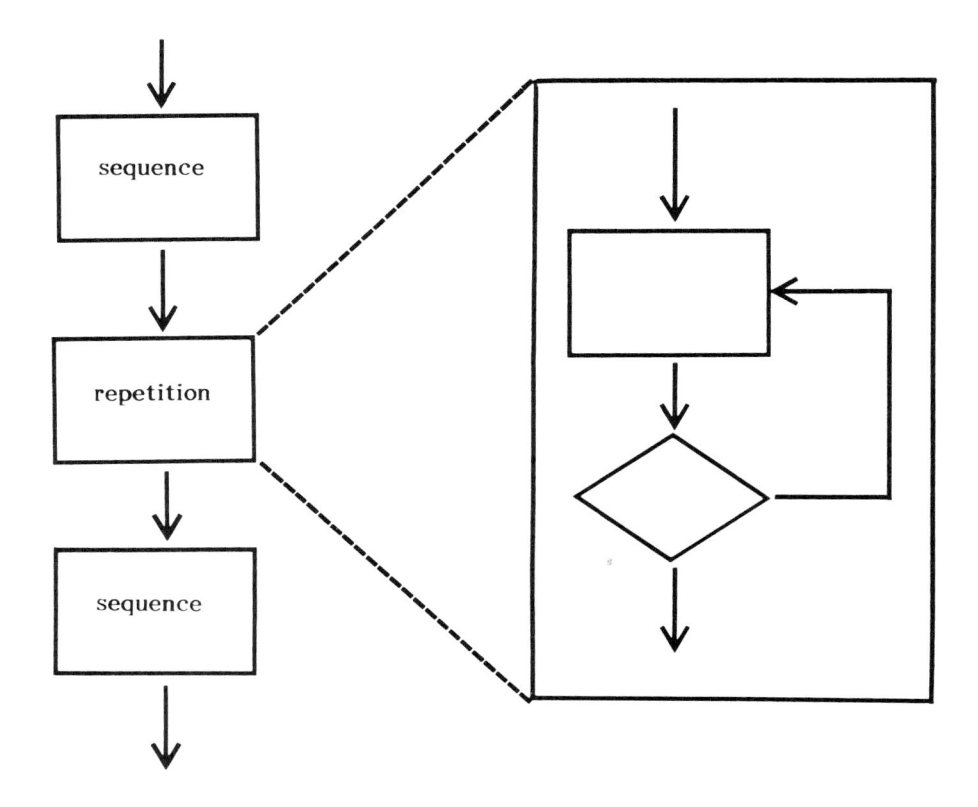

Fig. 4.3: *Viewed as a block, a repetitive structure is but one step in the overall sequential flow through a program.*

and then solve it. Try writing that expression. After you've written the first four or five terms, you will almost certainly be convinced that there must be an easier way.

An alternative is to accumulate the values. The process of accumulation can be visualized by watching the changing value of an automobile's odometer. The odometer indicates how far the car has been driven since it was manufactured. New mileage is simply added to the old total. A similar approach can be used to compute the sum of a series of values.

Try using a calculator. Start with 1. Now compute 1 + 2; the answer, 3, should appear in the calculator's window. Continue counting. The next number is 3. Add it to the sum of the first two: 3 + 3 = 6. Move on to 4: 6 + 4 = 10. Keep going. The process is simple. Count. As you count, add each integer to the previous sum. When you've reached your objective (in our example, 100) stop.

Although a calculator could certainly be used to solve this problem, the task would be time consuming. Additionally, there is a risk of error. What if you forget your count? What if you enter the wrong number? A better choice is to write a computer program.

The process involves counting and accumulating. Generally, we add 1 to our count, and add the count to our accumulator, repeating these instructions while the count is less than or equal to 100. We start counting at 1. Also, we have to initialize the accumulator to zero. The steps in the process can be summarized as:

1. Set accumulator to 0.

2. Set count to 1.

3. If count is less than or equal to 100, then

   a. Add count to accumulator.

   b. Add 1 to count.

   c. Repeat step 3.

4. Output accumulator.

Figure 4.5 shows these steps in flowchart form. Now that we have defined the necessary output *(Fig. 4.4)* and developed a flowchart for the logic, we are ready to write the code. First, however, we'll consider *True BASIC*'s **FOR. . .NEXT** loop structure.

FOR. . .NEXT LOOPS

Repeating a loop a known number of times is a common data processing problem. The solution is to count each time through the loop and exit when the count reaches the target. Because count loops are so common, most programming languages provide the programmer with a simple count loop structure. *True BASIC*, with its **FOR. . .NEXT** structure *(Fig. 4.6)*, is no exception.

The loop begins with a **FOR** statement. Following the keyword **FOR** is the

Fig. 4.4: *A block diagram definition of the sum of digits problem.*

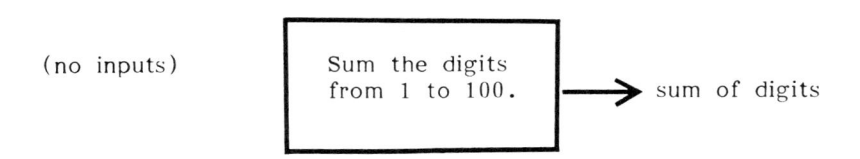

(no inputs) → | Sum the digits from 1 to 100. | → sum of digits

Fig. 4.5: *A flowchart for the sum of digits problem.*

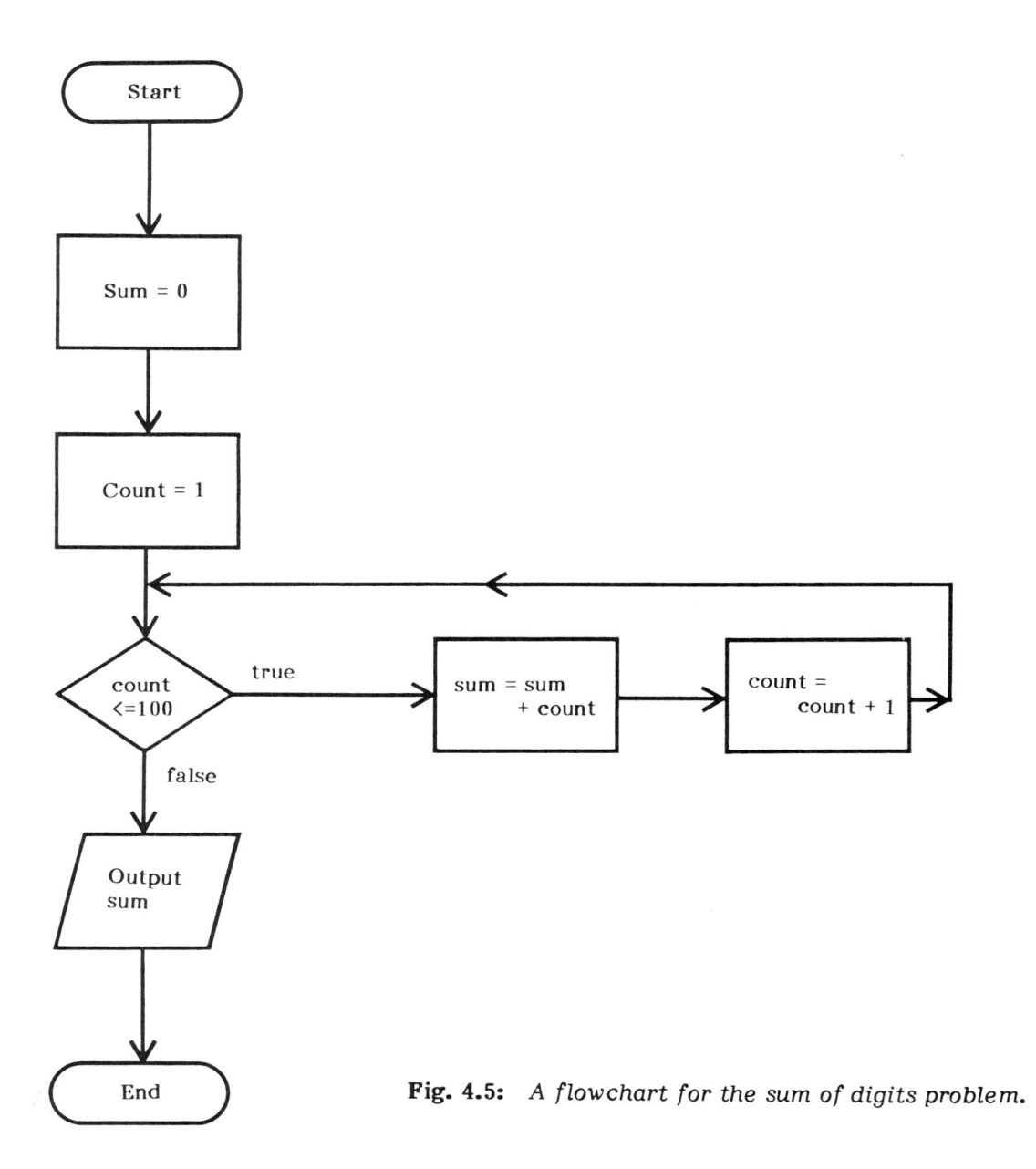

loop's control variable. When the computer encounters a **FOR. . .NEXT** structure, it evaluates the expressions **first, last,** and **increment.** Next, the value of the expression **first** is assigned to **variable.** Following these initialization procedures, the condition

variable <= last

is tested. If the condition is true, the body of the loop is executed. If the condition is false, the loop ends.

The loop's last statement is identified by the keyword **NEXT**. When this statement is encountered, the value of the expression **increment** is added to **variable,** and control returns to the conditional test near the top of the loop. The loop continues executing as long as the condition is true; a **FOR. . .NEXT** loop is a form of **DO WHILE** loop. As soon as the control variable exceeds **last,** the computer exits the loop. The flowchart on the next page *(Fig. 4.6b)* illustrates the loop logic.

The statement

Fig. 4.6 a: *The structure of a FOR. . .NEXT loop.*

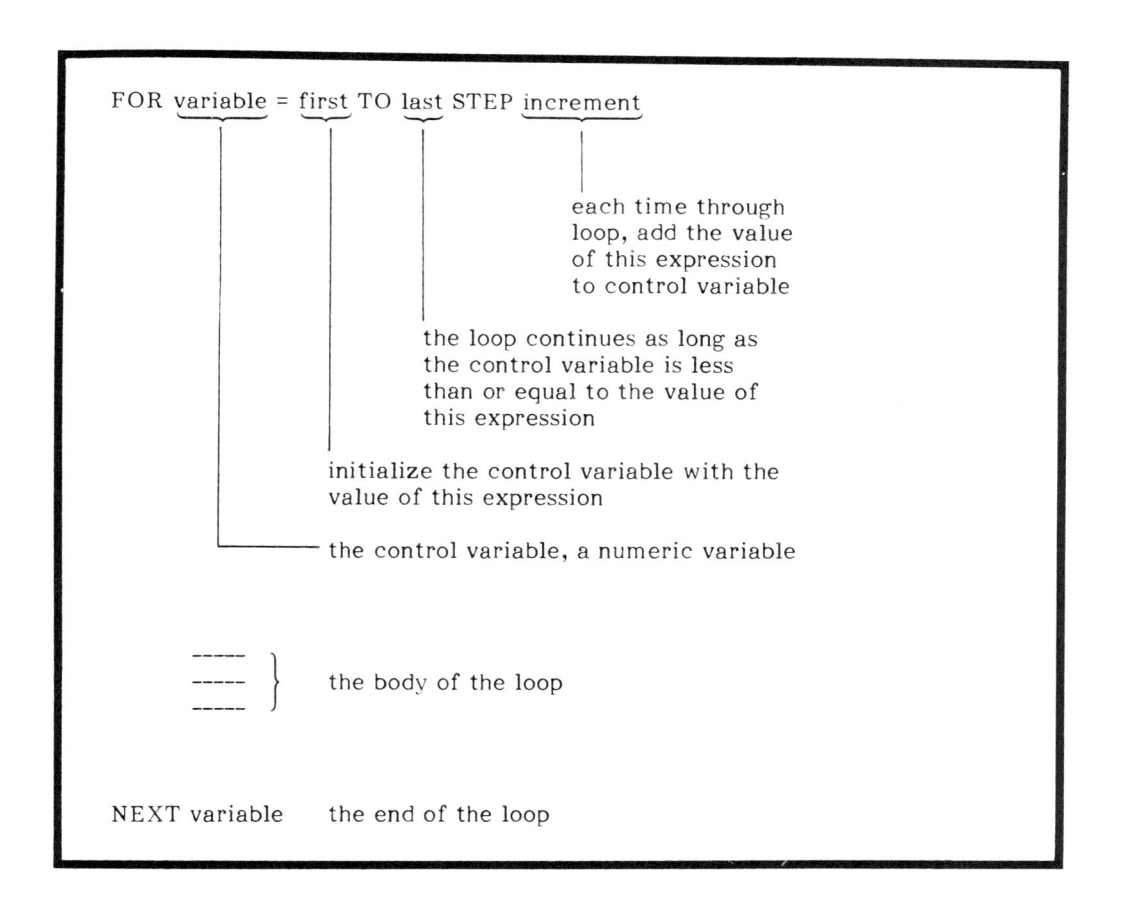

```
FOR variable = first TO last STEP increment
                                    |
                                    each time through
                                    loop, add the value
                                    of this expression
                                    to control variable

                         the loop continues as long as
                         the control variable is less
                         than or equal to the value of
                         this expression

              initialize the control variable with the
              value of this expression

              the control variable, a numeric variable


    -----
    -----  }  the body of the loop
    -----


    NEXT variable    the end of the loop
```

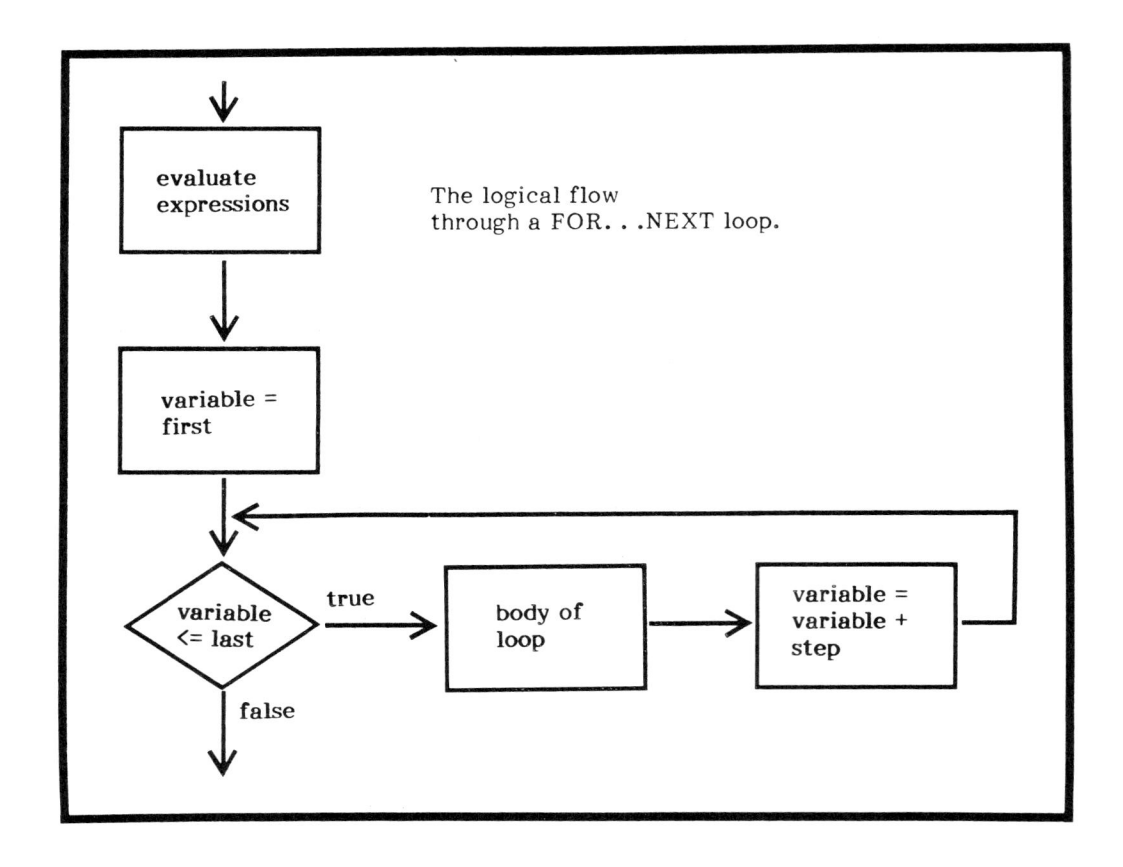

```
           ┌─────────────┐
           │  evaluate   │     The logical flow
           │ expressions │     through a FOR...NEXT loop.
           └─────────────┘
                  │
                  ▼
           ┌─────────────┐
           │ variable =  │
           │   first     │
           └─────────────┘
                  │
                  ▼
              ╱ variable ╲   true    ┌─────────┐      ┌──────────┐
             ╱   <= last   ╲────────▶│ body of │─────▶│variable =│──┐
             ╲             ╱         │  loop   │      │variable +│  │
              ╲           ╱          └─────────┘      │  step    │  │
                  │                                   └──────────┘  │
                 false                                               │
                  ▼                    ◀──────────────────────────────┘
```

Fig. 4.6 b: *The logical flow through a FOR...NEXT loop.*

      FOR count = 1 TO 100 STEP 1

initializes the control variable **count** to 1. Each time through the loop, **count** is incremented by 1. The loop continues as long as **count** is less than or equal to 100. The **STEP** parameter is optional; if it's missing, a step size of 1 is assumed. For example, the statement

      FOR count = 1 TO 100

is equivalent to the one coded a few lines back.
    The step size may be any value. For example, the statement

> **FOR count = 1 TO 100 STEP 3**

would generate count values of 1, 4, 7, 10, and so on until **count** exceeded 100. The step size need not be positive. The statement

> **FOR x = 100 TO 0 STEP –1**

would count backwards, generating values 100, 99, 98, . . . for **x**. With a negative step, the loop's instructions are repeated if the control variable's value is *greater* than or equal to **limit**.

A few final points. If the loop's initial value exceeds **last**, the loop is not executed. This can happen if **first, last,** or both are variables. Also, an **EXIT FOR** statement is available. It allows the programmer to leave a **FOR. . .NEXT** loop from the middle. For example, consider the statement

> **IF x = (y + 2) THEN EXIT FOR**

Imagine that it's halfway between a **FOR** and its associated **NEXT**. If **x** is equal to **(y + 2)**, the **FOR. . .NEXT** loop is immediately terminated, and the instruction following **NEXT** gets control.

Be careful when using an **EXIT FOR** statement. It's easy to overlook an exit condition coded in the middle of a loop, and if you do, you can lose track of the program's logical flow. That, in turn, can lead to debugging and maintenance problems. In fact, some instructors won't let you use an **EXIT FOR** statement.

Coding a FOR. . .NEXT Loop

Let's use a **FOR. . .NEXT** loop to code the sum of digits problem. We have already prepared the problem definition *(Fig. 4.4)* and a flowchart *(Fig. 4.5)*. A finished program is shown in Fig. 4.7. Read the logic carefully. Desk check it for the first few values of **n**. It is important that you take the time to understand what a program is doing.

As we begin, **sum** is set to 0. Enter the loop. The control variable, **n**, is initialized to 1. In the body of the loop, the value of **n**, is added to **sum**; the value of **sum** is now 1. Move on to the **NEXT** statement. It increments **n** by 1. (Why 1?) Go back to the top of the loop. Is **n** less than or equal to 100? Yes. Repeat the loop. The value of **n** (2) is added to **sum** (1), and the result (3) is stored in **sum**. Increment **n**, and return to the top of the loop. Is **n** less than or equal to 100? Yes. Repeat the loop. This time, **n** (3) is added to **sum** (3), and the result (6) is stored in **sum**. Try a few more cycles on your own.

```
                              ! Program to compute the sum of the digits
                              ! from 1 to 100.
!
! LET sum = 0                 ! Initialize accumulator to zero.
!
! FOR n = 1 TO 100            ! Loop counts and accumulates the total.
!     LET sum = sum + n
! NEXT n
!
! PRINT sum                   ! Print the accumulated sum.
! END
!


Version 1.0
Copyright (c) 1985 by True BASIC, Inc.
Published by Addison-Wesley Publishing Company, Inc.
Ok. old sumdig
Ok. run
 5050
Ok. _
```

Fig. 4.7: *A program to compute the sum of the digits from 1 to 100.*

Another Example

Before we move on, let's consider another example of a count controlled loop. Imagine we're planning a trip to Mexico. We're trying to decide what kind of clothing to take, but all the guide books list Mexican temperatures in degrees Celsius rather than in the more familiar Fahrenheit scale. Thus we'd like to develop a conversion table. We know the algorithm

$$\text{Celsius} = (5/9) \, (\text{Fahrenheit} - 32)$$

We'd like our table to show the Celsius equivalent of Fahrenheit temperatures ranging from 100 to 0 in increments of 10 degrees.

We'll begin by formally defining the problem *(Fig. 4.8)*. The logic is simple.

Fig. 4.8: *A block diagram definition of the temperature conversion problem.*

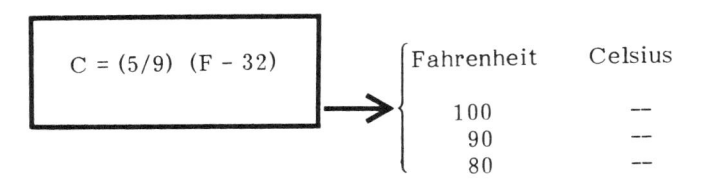

C = (5/9) (F - 32)	Fahrenheit	Celsius
	100	--
	90	--
	80	--

We want to start with 100 degrees Fahrenheit, compute its Celsius equivalent, and display both temperatures. Then, we want to decrease the Fahrenheit temperature by 10 degrees and repeat the process. We want to continue doing this until degrees Fahrenheit drop below 0. A flowchart for this logic is shown in Fig. 4.9. Given the flowchart and the problem definition, we can write the code *(Fig. 4.10)*.

Study the code carefully. Compare it to the sum of digits program *(Fig. 4.7)*. Note that in the former program, the **PRINT** statement was outside the loop, while it's inside the loop in this one. Try to visualize the outputs generated by both programs. The sum of digits program will output a single value. The temperature conversion program will display a set of output values for each pass through the loop. If you can read a program and predict at least the structure of its output, you have a good sense of what the program does.

DO LOOPS

Not all loops are count controlled. Often, a loop will repeat until the input data run out. For example, let's develop a program to compute an arithmetic average.

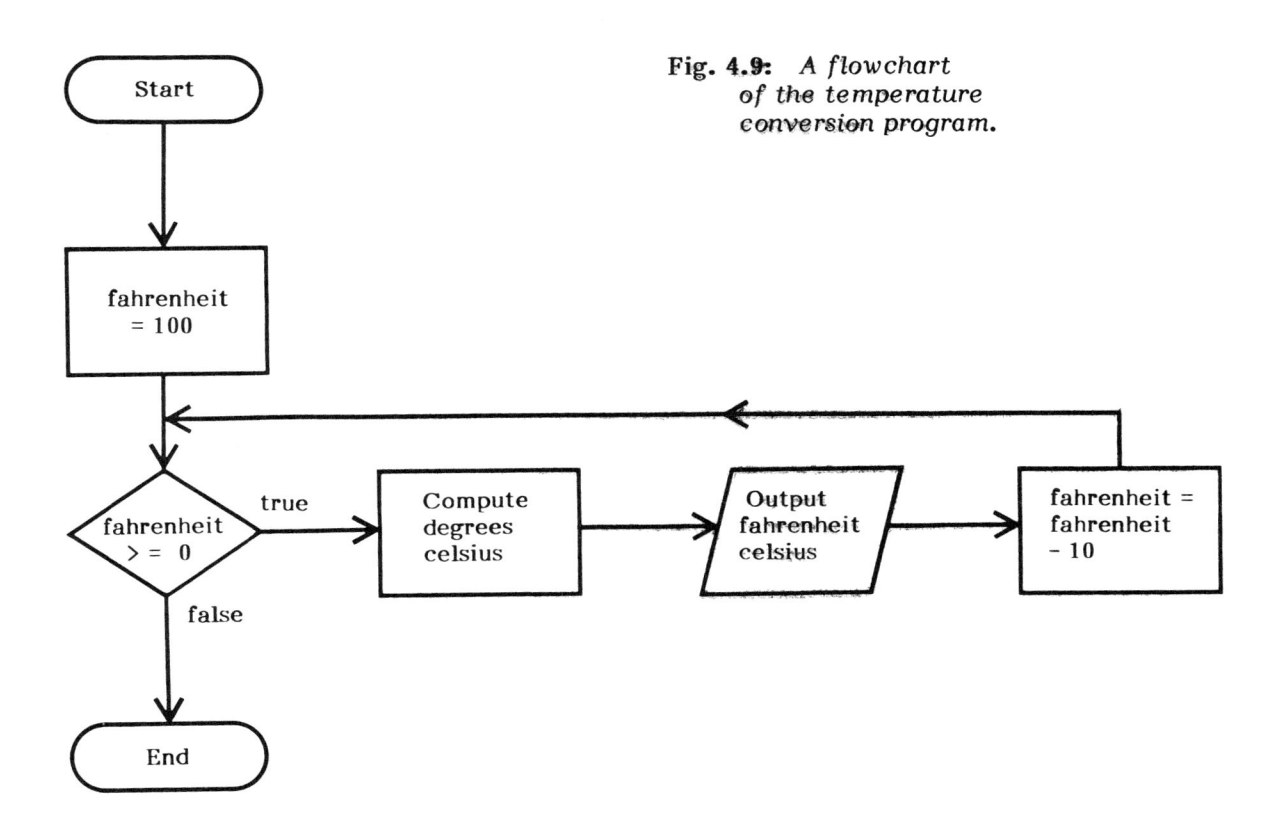

Fig. 4.9: *A flowchart of the temperature conversion program.*

```
! Program to generate and print a Fahrenheit
! to Celsius temperature conversion table.
! The table will show the Celsius equivalents
! to Fahrenheit temperatures ranging from a
! high of 100 degrees to a low of 0 degrees
! in 10 degree increments.

FOR fahrenheit = 100 TO 0 STEP -10

    LET celsius = (5/9) * (fahrenheit - 32)
    PRINT fahrenheit, celsius

NEXT fahrenheit

END
```

```
50        10.
40         4.44444
30        -1.11111
20        -6.66667
10       -12.2222
 0       -17.7778
Ok.
```

Fig. 4.10: *A program to generate a Fahrenheit to Celsius temperature conversion table.*

An instructor, we'll assume, plans to use this program to compute the average grade on an hour exam. It is difficult to predict exactly how many students will take the test, so the instructor has to be prepared for any number.

Let's define our problem. As input, we have a set of student grades *(Fig. 4.11)*. To find the arithmetic average, we sum the grades, count the grades, and divide the sum by the count. Outputs include the sum, the count, and the computed average.

Before we can compute an average, we must sum and count the values to be averaged. For each student's grade, we must

1. Input the grade.
2. Add the grade to an accumulator.
3. Count the grade.

Fig. 4.11: *A block diagram definition of the average problem.*

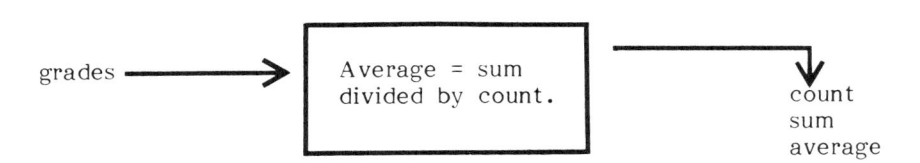

grades ⟶ | Average = sum divided by count. | ⟶ count
                                              sum
                                              average

Because there are many students, we'll repeat these steps many times. We'll need a loop. There is only one thing wrong with the steps we listed above. There is no way out. There is no exit condition.

How many times do we want to repeat the loop instructions? We don't know. There might be twenty-five students in the class. There might be thirty. We won't know until we run the program. We do know, however, that we want to repeat the count/accumulate loop until there are no more grades to be input. There's our exit condition. We want to exit the loop when we run out of input data. How can we signal the program that there are no more data? The answer is by using a sentinel value.

A sentinel value is an out-of-range data value. For example, we plan to input examination scores. If the lowest possible score is zero, a negative number might make a good sentinel value. If the highest possible score is 100, a large number such as 999 might make sense. However, a number like 50 would be a poor choice, because someone in the class might score 50 on the exam.

Once the sentinel value is defined, we can design the program to test for it. In our problem, since scores below zero are impossible, we'll use a negative number. Right after reading a grade, we'll check to see if it's negative. If it is, we'll assume that the user has just signaled "end of data," and exit the loop. Figure 4.12 shows a flowchart of the average problem with an end of data sentinel value test.

Writing a DO Loop

The average program can be coded by using a **DO** loop *(Fig. 4.13)*. The structure begins with the keyword **DO**. It is followed by the statements that form the body of the loop. The keyword **LOOP** marks the structure's end. For example, the loop

    DO

        INPUT x

        LET sum = sum + x

        LET count = count + 1

    LOOP

inputs values of **x**, accumulates them, and counts them. Only one thing is missing: an exit condition. This loop would run forever. We must include a test for the end of data. We'll use a negative value of **x** as a sentinel value, and code

Fig. 4.12: *A flowchart for the average program.*

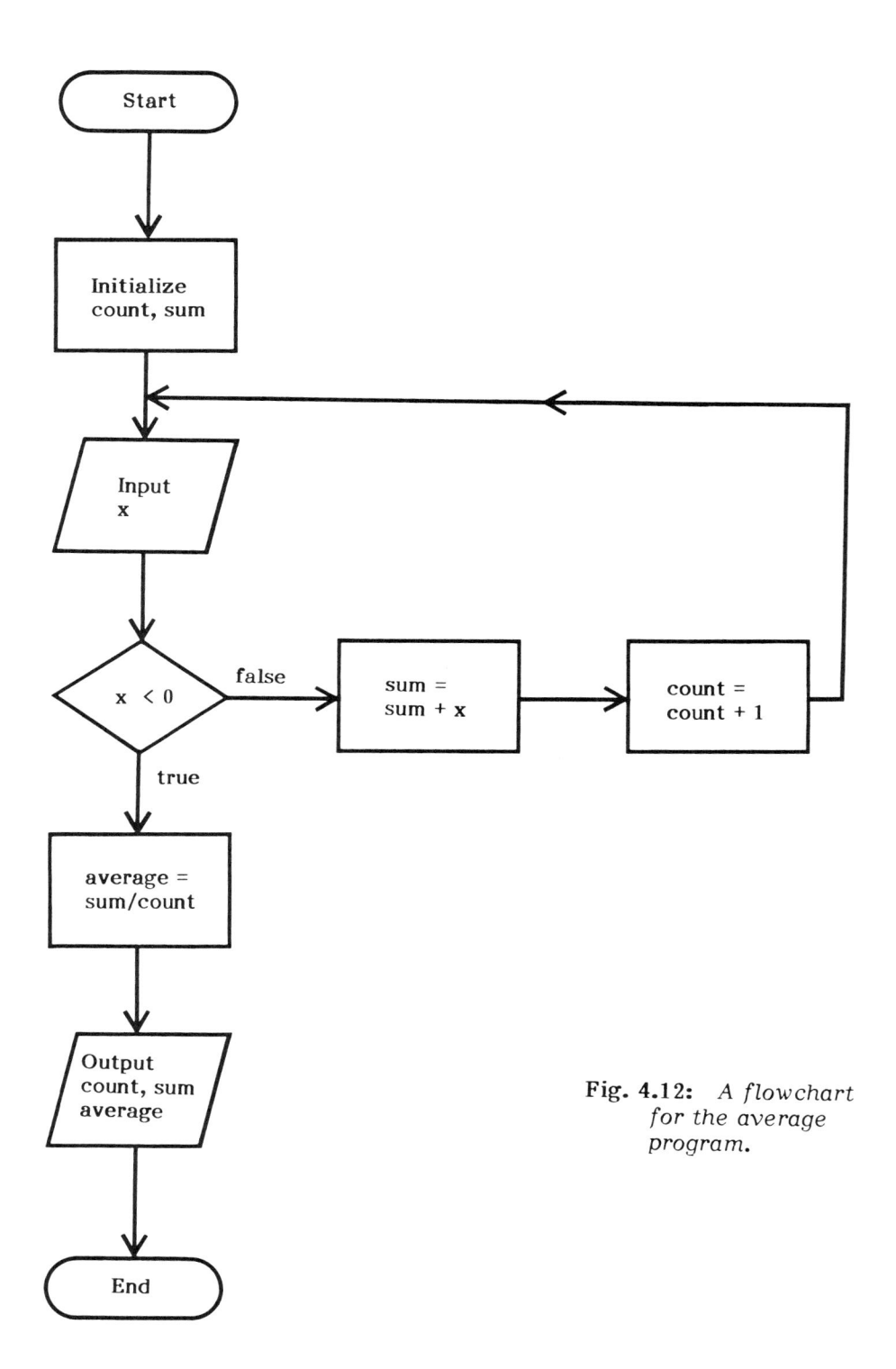

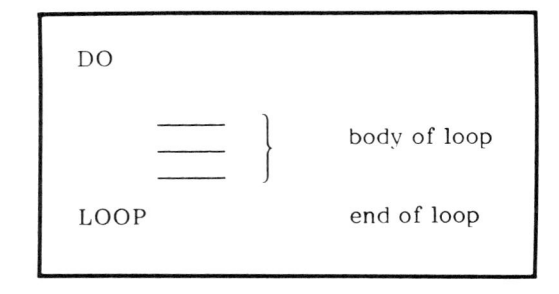

Fig. 4.13: *A True BASIC DO loop.*

```
DO
    INPUT x
        IF x < 0 THEN EXIT DO
    LET sum = sum + x
    LET count = count + 1
LOOP
```

Now we have an exit condition. If the input value is negative, **EXIT DO** causes control to be transferred to the statement immediately following **LOOP**.

Figure 4.14 shows the average program. Once again, read the code carefully.

DO UNTIL

One weakness of the simple **DO** loop described above is the fact that the exit condition is tested inside the loop. The **EXIT DO** statement suffers from the same problem as the **EXIT FOR**: it's easy to overlook. Using an **EXIT DO** was reasonable in the average program because: (1) the loop was relatively short, (2) the exit condition was tested quite close to its beginning, and (3) comments and indentation clearly identified the exit condition. Even so, many programmers (and programming instructors) would prefer that the exit condition always be coded at the loop's beginning (**DO WHILE**) or at its end (**DO UNTIL**). A good program is clear and easy to follow. Coding the exit condition as the loop's first or last statement makes it easy to find, and that, in turn, makes the code much more clear.

Let's modify the average program to use a **DO UNTIL** loop *(Fig. 4.15)*. The loop begins with the keyword **DO**. It ends with the keyword **LOOP**. An **UNTIL** option is attached to the **LOOP** statement. The body of the loop will be repeated until the exit condition is true.

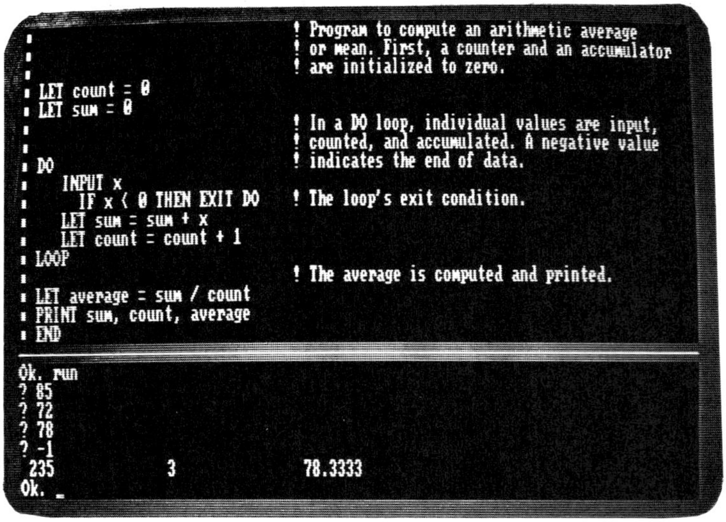

```
    ! Program to compute an arithmetic average
    ! or mean. First, a counter and an accumulator
    ! are initialized to zero.
LET count = 0
LET sum = 0
                    ! In a DO loop, individual values are input,
                    ! counted, and accumulated. A negative value
                    ! indicates the end of data.
DO
    INPUT x
        IF x < 0 THEN EXIT DO   ! The loop's exit condition.
    LET sum = sum + x
    LET count = count + 1
LOOP
                    ! The average is computed and printed.
LET average = sum / count
PRINT sum, count, average
END
```
```
Ok. run
? 85
? 72
? 78
? -1
 235            3            78.3333
Ok. _
```

Fig. 4.14: *A program to compute an arithemtic average using a simple DO loop.*

For example, we might code the following count/accumulate loop:

    DO

        INPUT x

        LET sum = sum + x

        LET count = count + 1

    LOOP UNTIL x < 0

It will accept input values, accumulate them, and count them until the input value is negative. There is one thing wrong with the logic, however. That negative value is a sentinel value--no student could possibly receive a negative score. We don't want to count and accumulate it, but, since the test occurs after the count and accumulate steps, we will. To avoid counting and accumulating the sentinel value, we have to code

```
    INPUT x

    IF x >= 0 THEN

        LET sum = sum + x

        LET count = count + 1

    END IF

LOOP UNTIL x < 0
```

Figure 4.16 shows the average program with a **DO UNTIL** structure. Compare it with the simple **DO** loop version *(Fig. 4.14)*. Clearly, the two programs do the same thing; they are equivalent. The difference lies in the testing of the exit condition. With a simple **DO** loop, the test occurs inside the loop. On a complex loop that can be a problem. In the **DO UNTIL** version, the exit condition was easy to find because it was located at the end of the loop. However, we had to code an extra test to avoid manipulating the sentinel value. On a simple loop, that can be an annoyance. Both techniques work. The choice is a matter of personal preference.

DO WHILE LOOPS

Sometimes it is desirable to test for an exit condition at the top of a loop. Such applications call for a **DO WHILE** structure *(Fig. 4.17)*. Note that the exit condition is tested first. If the condition is true, the loop's instructions are executed. The **LOOP** statement sends control back to the top, where the exit condition is tested

Fig. 4.15: *True BASIC's DO UNTIL structure.*

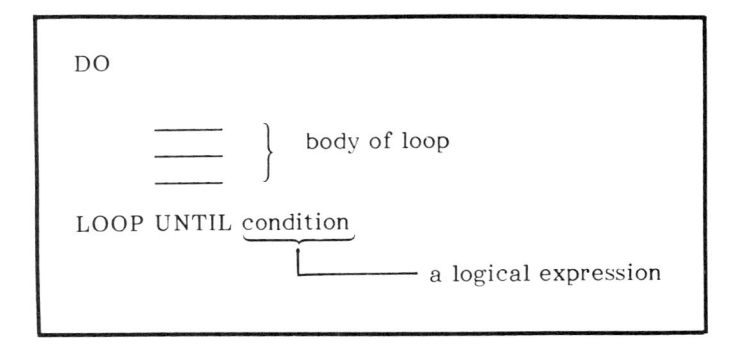

```
DO

    ___  ⎫
    ___  ⎬ body of loop
    ___  ⎭

LOOP UNTIL condition
                └──── a logical expression
```

```
! LET count = 0              ! Program to compute an arithmetic average
! LET sum = 0                 ! or mean. First, a counter and an accumulator
!                             ! are initialized to zero.
!
! DO                          ! In a DO loop, individual values are input,
!                             ! counted, and accumulated. A negative value
!                             ! indicates the end of data.
!    INPUT x
!    IF x >= 0 THEN            ! A negative number means no more data. We
!       LET sum = sum + x      ! do not want to count and accumulate this
!       LET count = count + 1  ! sentinel value.
!    END IF
! LOOP UNTIL x < 0            ! Here is the loop's exit condition.
!
! LET average = sum / count   ! After exiting the loop, the average is
! PRINT sum, count, average   ! computed and printed.
! END

Ok, run
? 112
? 375
? 91
? -1
 578           3           192.667
Ok.
```

Fig. 4.16: *Another version of the average program using a DO UNTIL loop structure.*

again. As long as the condition is true, the loop repeats; as soon as it is false, the loop ends, and control is transferred to the statement immediately following **LOOP**.

Let's use an example to illustrate. In 1983, the population of the United States was estimated at roughly 234 million, while Mexico's was estimated at roughly 76 million. However, Mexico's population was growing at much faster rate than that of the United States. We had almost reached zero population growth, with

Fig. 4.17: *True BASIC's DO WHILE structure.*

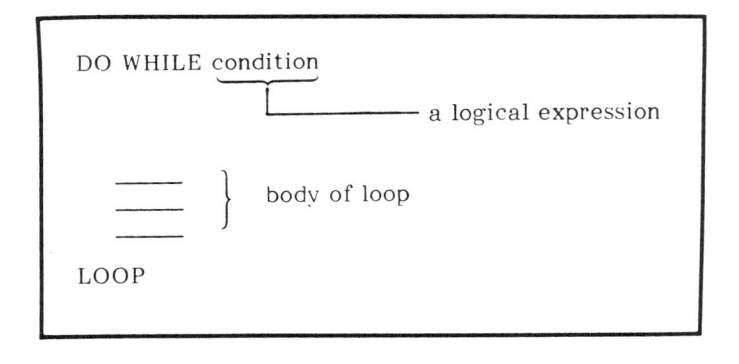

```
DO WHILE condition
         ─────────── a logical expression

    ───
    ───  } body of loop
    ───

LOOP
```

a growth rate of only 0.7 percent. Mexico's population, on the other hand, was growing at an annual rate of 3.3 percent. If these trends continue, Mexico will eventually surpass the United States in population. Assuming the current rates remain valid, when would this happen?

The block diagram in Fig. 4.18 summarizes our problem definition. We have the 1983 populations of both countries. Using the growth rates, we'll compute the estimated 1984 populations and compare them. As long as the population of the United States exceeds that of Mexico, we'll repeat our calculations. The objective is to print the year when that relationship is no longer true.

It's one thing to state our objective in English. It's quite another thing to convert that problem definition into a set of algorithms a computer can solve. Let's use an example to develop the algorithms. Imagine a tiny country with a population of 1000 people and a growth rate of 10 percent. What does that growth rate mean? It means that, in the next year, the country's population is expected to increase by 10 percent. We start with a thousand people. During the next year, babies are born, people die, people move into the country, and others leave. The net change is 10 percent, or 100 people. One year from now, the expected population will be 1100.

What happens in the second year? If the growth rate continues at 10 percent, the new base population, 1100, should increase by 110 new inhabitants. At the end of year two, the population will be 1210. Note that the 100 people added during year 1 contribute to year 2's growth.

Let's generalize. In a given year, a country's population growth is

growth = population * growth rate

At the end of the year, the new population is

population $_{n+1}$ = population $_n$ + growth

which is

population $_{n+1}$ = population $_n$ + (population $_n$ * growth rate)

Fig. 4.18: *A block diagram definition of the population problem.*

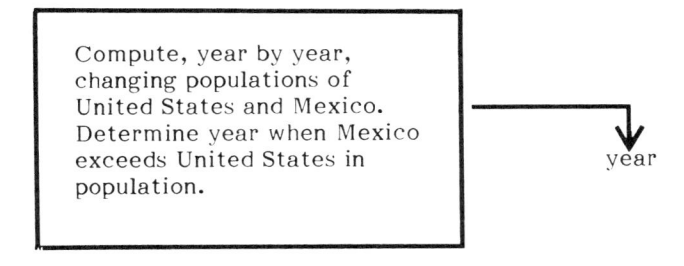

```
Compute, year by year,
changing populations of
United States and Mexico.    ──────▼
Determine year when Mexico        year
exceeds United States in
population.
```

or   population$_{n+1}$ = population$_n$ * (1 + growth rate)

The population at the beginning of year 2 is the same as the population at the end of year 1; thus, to project year 2's population, we use the same formula. If this relationship were placed in a loop and executed repetitively, we could start with an initial population and a growth rate, use the population at time zero to estimate population at the end of one year, use this new number to estimate year 2's population, and so on. If we did the same thing for both the United States and Mexico, we could compare their populations year by year, repeating the loop as long as our population exceeded Mexico's.

The United States' population growth rate is 0.7 percent. Thus, the algorithm for computing an end-of-year population is

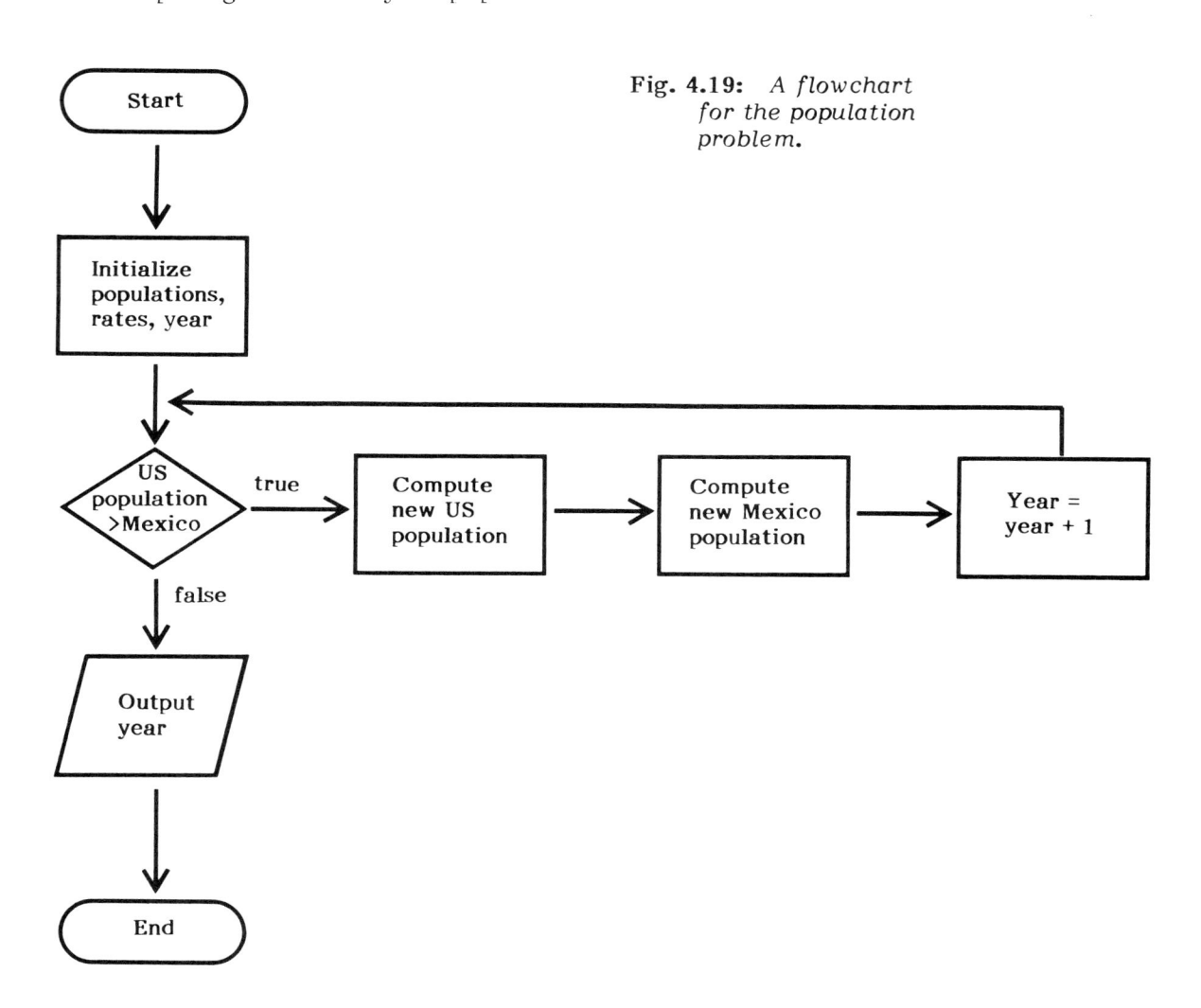

Fig. 4.19: *A flowchart for the population problem.*

```
                                  ! Program to compute the year Mexico's
                                  ! population will exceed that of the
                                  ! U. S., assuming current growth rates.
LET current_year = 1983           ! First, the base year and that year's
LET US_population = 243E6         ! populations and growth rates are
LET US_growth = 0.007             ! initialized.
LET Mexico_population = 76E6
LET Mexico_growth = 0.033
                                  ! Inside the loop, estimated populations
                                  ! for both countries are computed year by
                                  ! year. If the population of the United
                                  ! States exceeds that of Mexico, the loop
                                  ! is repeated.
DO WHILE US_population > Mexico_population

    LET US_population = US_population * (1 + US_growth)
    LET Mexico_population = Mexico_population * (1 + Mexico_growth)
    LET current_year = current_year + 1
LOOP
                                  ! As soon as Mexico's population matches
                                  ! or exceeds that of the U. S., the loop
                                  ! ends and the magic year is printed.
PRINT current_year
END
```

Fig. 4.20: *A program to estimate when the population of Mexico may exceed that of the United States.*

$$\text{population}_{n+1} = \text{population}_n * (1 + 0.007)$$

or

$$\text{population}_{n+1} = \text{population}_n * 1.007$$

Mexico's growth rate is 3.3 percent, so Mexico's algorithm is

$$\text{population}_{n+1} = \text{population}_n * (1 + 0.033)$$

or

$$\text{population}_{n+1} = \text{population}_n * 1.033$$

A flowchart of the logic is shown in Fig. 4.19. Given the problem definition, the algorithms, and the flowchart, we can write the program *(Fig. 4.20)*.

Read the program logic carefully. First, initial conditions are set. Next, we enter the loop, a **DO WHILE**. Within the loop, new populations for both the United States and Mexico are computed, and the year is incremented. The test comparing the two countries' populations is performed at the top of the loop; as long as the

United States population continues to exceed Mexico's, the loop repeats. Eventually, the control condition is not met, and the magic year is printed.

Combining WHILE and UNTIL Tests

A **DO WHILE** loop is simply a **DO** loop with an exit condition attached to its beginning. A **DO UNTIL** loop is a **DO** loop with an exit condition attached to its end. It is possible to use both tests in a single loop; for example,

> **DO WHILE condition1**
>
>   - - - -
>   - - - - } body of loop
>   - - - -
>
> **LOOP UNTIL condition2**

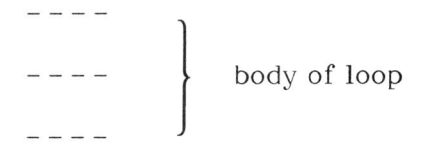

The loop will repeat as long as condition1 is true or until condition2 is false.

NESTED LOOPS

If you live in an area where the winter temperature frequently drops below thirty degrees, you have probably heard of the wind chill factor. As anyone who has been out in the cold knows, the degree of discomfort or the risk of frostbite are not only functions of the temperature. On a windless day, twenty degrees may be quite comfortable, but when a brisk wind is blowing, that same twenty degrees seems intolerable. Just as the summertime combination of heat and humidity is worse than the heat alone, the wintertime combination of cold and wind is far worse than just the cold.

    The wind chill factor is a number used to measure the combined effect of low temperature and wind. By plugging the temperature (in Fahrenheit) and the wind velocity (in miles per hour) into a formula, an "equivalent temperature" is computed. In theory, this temperature (with no wind) is equivalent to the combination of temperature and wind. For example, a day when the temperature is twenty degrees and the wind is blowing at twenty miles per hour will seem as cold as a windless minus six degree day.

    You may be able to find a formula for computing a wind chill factor in a science textbook, a text on meteorology, or an encyclopedia. Generally, however, only wind chill tables are published, so we'll give you the formula:

$$\text{wind chill} = 91.4 - [0.288 \; (\sqrt{\text{wind velocity}}) + 0.450$$

$$-0.019 \, (\text{wind velocity})] \, [91.4 - \text{temperature}]$$

where wind velocity is in miles per hour and temperature is in degrees Fahrenheit.

We want to generate a table of wind chill factors. Temperatures should range from 30 degrees to minus 30 degrees in ten-degree increments. Wind velocities should range from 10 to 40 miles per hour, in 10-mile per-hour increments. A block diagram problem definition can be seen in Fig. 4.21.

Now that we have the algorithm and a sense of the desired output, we can plan a program. The problem is that we have two control variables: temperature and wind velocity. Let's analyze the problem one variable at a time. We'll start with a fixed temperature, 30 degrees, and, given this temperature, develop a plan for computing the wind chill factors for wind velocities ranging from 10 to 40 miles per hour. The flowchart in Fig. 4.22 presents a valid logical flow; you should recognize it as a **DO WHILE** loop or as a **FOR. . .NEXT** loop.

The next step is to make temperature a variable, too. The secret is to increment the temperature just after the wind velocity loop is completed. Then we can check for the upper limit on temperature and loop back to repeat the wind chill loop *(Fig. 4.23)*. Look at the flowchart carefully. What we have is a loop within a loop: nested loops. The outer loop controls the value of temperature. The inner loop, which is part of the outer loop, controls the value of wind velocity.

When loops are nested, the inner loop must be completely inside the outer loop *(Fig. 4.24)*; the loops may not overlap. It is possible to have one loop within another loop, within yet another--multiple levels of nesting. Some versions of BASIC limit the number of levels permitted, but *True BASIC* does not. The only real limit is the programmer's ability to keep track of what is going on.

We're about ready to code the wind chill program, but let's take another look at the algorithm first. It is rather complex. In fact, some people panic when they see an algebraic relationship with so many terms. Lengthy **LET** statements can be difficult to follow, too. When faced with such a complex expression, break it into pieces. For example, we might separate the formula's three key terms:

Fig. 4.21: *A block diagram definition of the wind chill factors problem.*

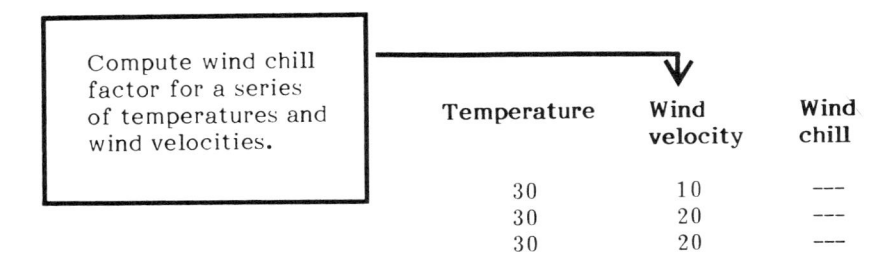

Compute wind chill factor for a series of temperatures and wind velocities.	Temperature	Wind velocity	Wind chill
	30	10	---
	30	20	---
	30	20	---

Fig. 4.22: *A partial flowchart for the wind chill problem. This one shows the logic to compute wind chill factors for several wind velocities with a constant temperature.*

term1 = 0.288 * (wind velocity ^ 0.5)

term2 = 0.019 * wind velocity

term3 = 91.4 - temperature

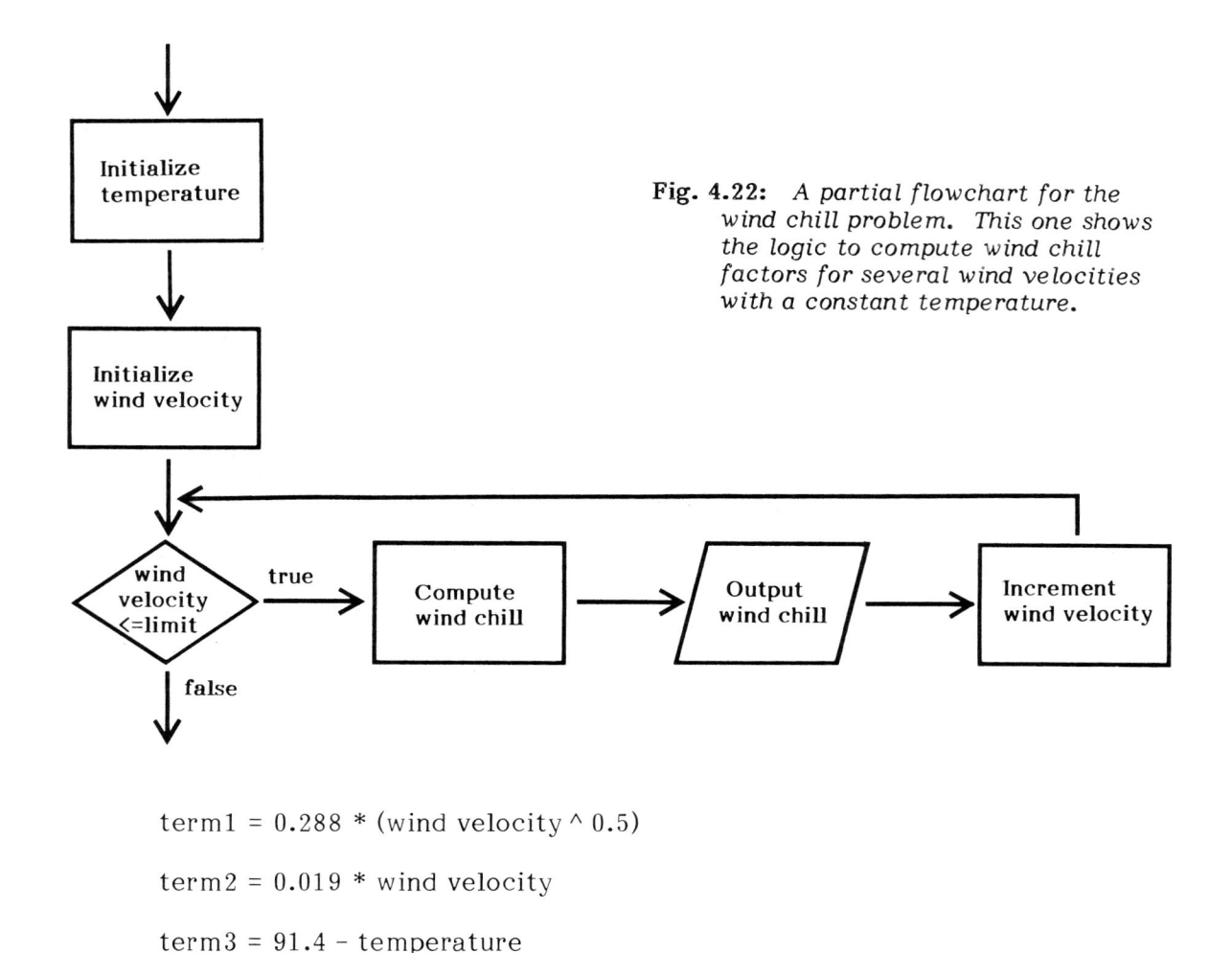

Given these terms, we can combine them.

wind chill = 91.4 - ((term1 + 0.450 - term2) * term3)

The resulting step by step solution of the algorithm is much clearer than a single, lengthy expression.

A program to compute and display a wind chill table is shown in Fig. 4.25. We have highlighted the two loops. Note how the inner loop is completely contained within the outer loop. Read the program carefully. Force yourself to follow the logic. Predict the output. Enter the program on your computer and run it. Make

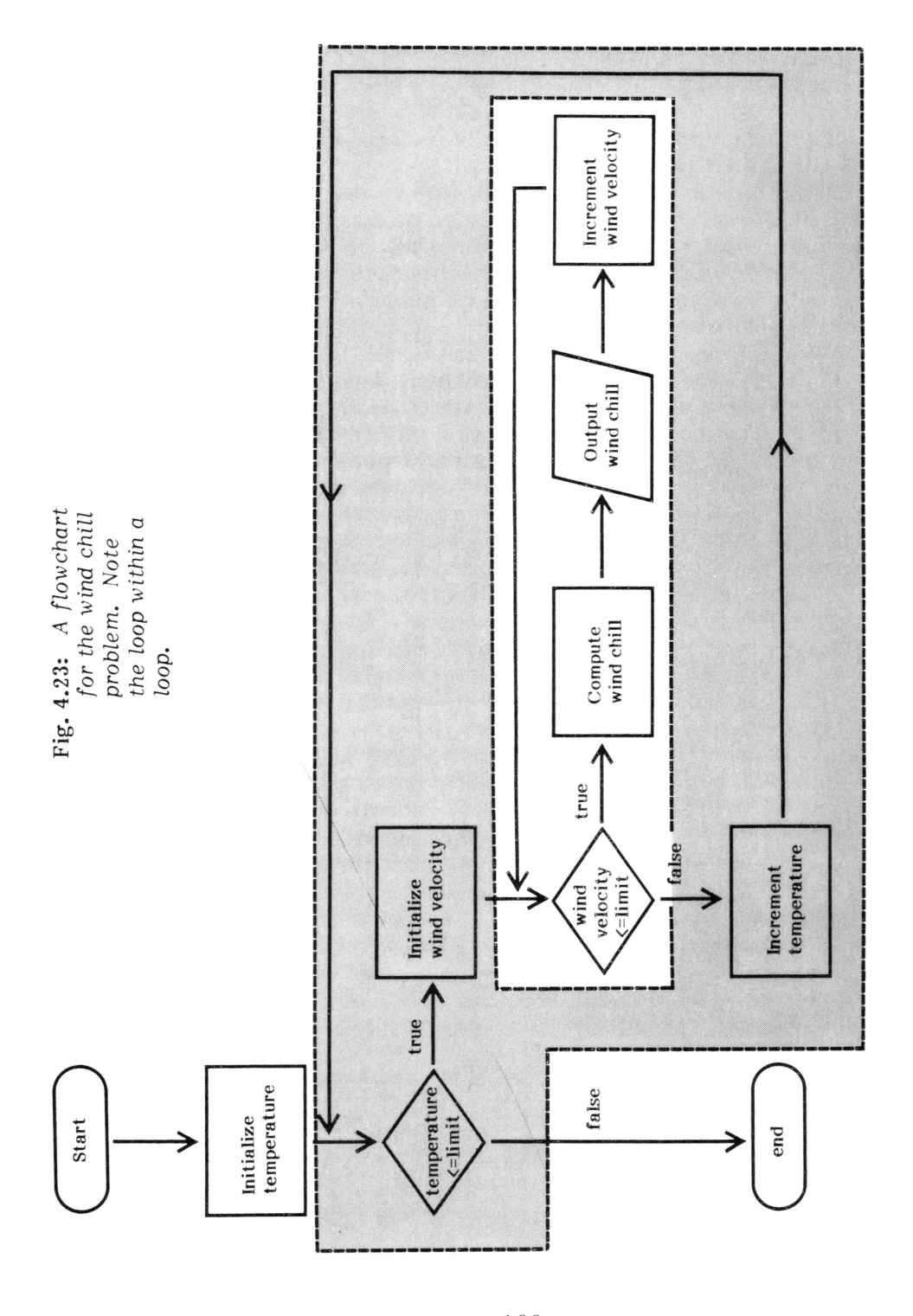

Fig. 4.23: A flowchart for the wind chill problem. Note the loop within a loop.

sure the actual results match (at least in format) your mental picture; if they don't, find out why.

THE BASIC BUILDING BLOCKS

Chapter 2 focused on simple sequence. Its objective was to show that the basic flow of logic through a program is sequential. In Chapter 3, we introduced the decision structure, showing how the path through a program can be determined at run time. The overall flow through a decision block is still sequential, however. Control enters at the top. Control exits at the bottom. The decision block is but one step in the program.

In this chapter, we introduced repetition. The basic idea is that a block of code can be repeated, again and again, until an exit condition occurs, or as long as a control condition holds. Like a decision block, the overall flow of logic through a repetitive block is still sequential. Control enters the block at the top. When the exit condition is met, control leaves the block at the bottom. Like a decision block, a repetitive block is but one step in a program.

Sequence, decision, and repetition are the three elementary building blocks of any program. In the next two chapters, we'll study how a programmer might combine sequence, decision, and repetition blocks to form a complex, realistic program.

SUMMARY

The chapter began with a brief discussion of the need for repetitive logic. Repetition allows the computer to execute the same set of instructions over and over again. A loop is a block of logic that executes repetitively. Every loop must have an exit condition. We considered the general forms of DO WHILE and DO UNTIL loops, and showed that the overall flow through a loop is still sequential; a repetitive block is but one step in a program.

Fig. 4.24: *Loops can be nested. However, the inner loop must be completely inside the outer loop, and the loop structures may not overlap.*

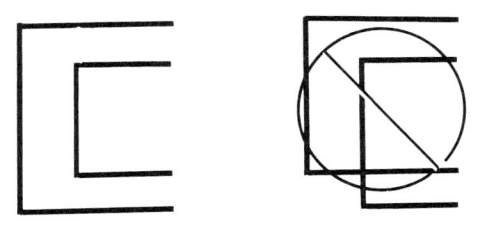

```
                                    ! Program to compute and print a table of
                                    ! wind chill factors. The wind chill is a
                                    ! function of both temperature and wind
                                    ! velocity. The table will list tempera-
                                    ! tures from -30 degrees to +30 degrees in
                                    ! 10 degree increments. For each tempera-
                                    ! ture, wind chill factors will be comput-
                                    ! ed for wind velocities ranging from 10
                                    ! to 50 miles per hour in increments of 10
                                    ! miles per hour.

                                    ! The control variable for the outer loop
                                    ! is temperature.
FOR temperature = -30 TO 30 STEP 10
                                    ! The control variable for the inner loop
                                    ! is wind velocity. Because the formula
                                    ! for computing a wind chill factor is
                                    ! complex, we'll break it into steps.
   FOR wind_velocity = 10 TO 50 STEP 10

      LET term1 = 0.288 * (wind_velocity ^ 0.5)
      LET term2 = 0.019 * wind_velocity
      LET term3 = 91.4 - temperature
      LET wind_chill = 91.4 - ((term1 + 0.450 - term2) * term3)
      PRINT temperature, wind_velocity, wind_chill

   NEXT wind_velocity

   PRINT                            ! Print a blank line to separate
                                    ! temperatures.
NEXT temperature
END
```

Fig. 4.25: *The wind chill factors program. Note how the nested loops are highlighted.*

The task of summing the digits between 1 and 100 was used to illustrate count control loops. We defined the problem, flowcharted a solution, and then introduced the **FOR. . .NEXT** loop structure. A second example, converting Fahrenheit temperatures to Celsius, allowed us to illustrate a negative loop increment.

Simple **DO** loops were covered next. We developed a program to compute an arithmetic average, accumulating and counting a series of input values within a loop. A sentinel value (a negative number) was used as an exit condition. We tested for the sentinel value after the **INPUT** statement, within the loop, using the **EXIT DO** statement as our way out. The average program was then modified to illustrate the **DO UNTIL** structure.

We then turned to another problem, writing a program to determine when the population of Mexico would exceed that of the United States. We used a **DO WHILE** structure to solve that problem.

It is possible to nest loops, coding one inside another. To illustrate nesting, we defined a problem to develop a wind chill table. Using flowcharts, we planned a solution and then coded it. When loops are nested, the inner loop must be completely inside the outer loop.

Sequence, decision, and repetition are the basic building blocks of any program. In the next two chapters, we'll consider how these basic building blocks can be combined to form a complex program.

REFERENCES

True BASIC Statements and Structures

FOR...NEXT	Fig. 4.6, page 91
EXIT FOR	page 93
DO loops	Fig. 4.13, page 99
EXIT DO	page 99
DO UNTIL	Fig. 4.15, page 101
DO WHILE	Fig. 4.17, page 102

EXERCISES

1. Modify the sum of digits program *(Fig. 4.7)* to compute the sum of the odd digits between 1 and n. Input n.

2. The base of the absolute temperature scale is absolute zero, which is -273 Celsius. To convert a Celsius temperature to an absolute temperature, simply add 273. Modify the temperature conversion program *(Fig. 4.10)* to output equivalent Fahrenheit, Celsius, and absolute temperatures for Fahrenheit temperatures ranging from 100 down to 0 degrees in five-degree increments.

3. On a true-false/multiple choice test, the instructor can factor in a penalty for wrong answers. With a penalty, a negative score is possible. Given

the possibility of a negative score, we can't use a negative value as a sentinel value. (Why not?) Modify the average program *(Fig. 4.14 or Fig. 4.16)* to use a different sentinel value (you pick it).

4. Modify the population problem *(Fig. 4.20)* to use a DO UNTIL structure.

5. The wind chill program *(Fig. 4.25)* develops a wind chill table using temperature as the control variable for the outer loop. Modify the program so that wind velocity is the control variable for the outer loop.

6. Write a program to develop a table of the squares and square roots of the integers from 1 to 25.

7. One mile is equivalent to 5280 feet, 1760 yards, and 1.609344 kilometers. Write a program to generate a conversion table for distances ranging from 1 to 25 miles. Each time through the loop, display the equivalent miles, feet, yards, and kilometers.

8. Read an input value, x. Write a program to sum the integers starting with 1 until the sum is greater than or equal to x. Output x and the last integer summed.

9. The factorial of a number is the product of all positive integers less than or equal to it; for example, 5! or five factorial is 5*4*3*2*1. Write a program to input a number and compute its factorial.

10. A series of positive and negative numbers is to be input to a program. Separately sum and count the positive and negative values. Use zero as a sentinel value. When all values have been counted and accumulated, compute separate averages for the positive and negative values.

11. A series of numbers between 0 and 100 are input to a program. Divide the numbers into quartiles; in other words, count the number of values lying between 0 and 25, the number of values lying between 25 and 50, and so on. Display your counts.

12. Using whatever rules are applied in your school, write a program to compute your grade point average.

13. Write a program to generate a loan repayment table. For example, assume a $1000 loan is to be paid back in a series of $50 monthly payments. Interest is 18% per year or 1.5% per month on the unpaid balance. The first few payments might be summarized as follows:

Beginning balance	Payment	Interest	Principle	Ending balance
1000.00	50.00	15.00	35.00	965.00
965.00	50.00	14.48	35.52	929.48
929.48	50.00	13.94	36.06	893.42

Note that the beginning balance for any given month is the same as the ending balance for the prior month. The interest due is the product of the beginning balance and the monthly interest rate. The principal paid is the total payment (in our example, $50) minus the interest due. The ending balance is the beginning balance minus the principal paid.

You might begin by writing a program to solve the example problem presented above. When you finish, generalize your solution to accept any loan amount, any monthly interest rate, and any monthly payment amount as input, and use the input data to generate the table. Your generalized program should check to be sure that the payment amount is at least sufficient to cover the first month's interest. If it isn't, don't even bother generating the table.

Table values should be generated until the ending balance reaches zero. Note that the final payment could be for an amount less than the regular monthly payment. You may want to include a count control too; if your payment is close to the first month's interest, this program could run for quite some time.

14. One thousand dollars is invested in a savings account earning eight percent annual interest. How long will it take for the initial investment to double?

15. One technique for estimating a square root is Newton's method. The idea is to start with an initial "guess" and then gradually refine the guess until the answer is close enough. The key to the method is a formula

$$X_{n+1} = 0.5 \left[X_n + \frac{number}{X_n} \right]$$

where: x_n is the prior estimate (initially, the first guess)

x_{n+1} is the new estimate

and number is the value whose square root you wish to find.

Write a program to input a number and an initial guess of its square root.

Plug the initial guess into the formula and compute a new, better estimate. Then plug the new estimate into the formula to produce an even better estimate. Continue until your answer is good enough. How can the proggram tell when the "good enough" condition is met? If the value of

$$\frac{x_n - x_{n+1}}{x_n}$$

is less than a very small value selected by the programmer (0.001, for example), the degree of error in the estimate is acceptably small. Note that the expression can be negative, so be careful when you test it.

16. One technique for finding the area under a curve is dividing the area into a series of rectangles, computing the areas of the rectangles, and summing them. Assume a curve such as

    $$y = x^2 + 5$$

    Find the area under the curve between $x = 0$ and $x = 4$. Start with a single rectangle with base 4. Solve the equation for $y = (16 + 5) = 21$, and compute the area of a rectangle with base 4 and height 21. Now divide the area into two rectangles, each with base 2. Solve the equation for $x = 2$, and compute the area of a rectangle with base 2 and the solution as its height. Now, solve the equation for $x = 4$, and compute the area of the second rectangle. Sum the areas. Now break the area into three rectangles, then four, then five, and so on. Continue until the answer is good enough.

    The "good enough" condition occurs when the difference between the prior estimate and a new estimate is acceptably small, for example, when it's less than 0.001. To give you a sense of what is happening, display each new estimate. If you have taken calculus, integrate the function and compare the result with your answer.

    As a variation, try dividing the area into two, four, eight, sixteen, . . . rectangles. You'll converge to an answer much more quickly. Another variation is to use a triangle on top of a rectangle to estimate the area under each slice of the curve.

17. Using combinations of half-dollars, quarters, dimes, nickels, and pennies, how many different ways can one make change for a dollar?

18. Write a program to make change. Read the amount of a purchase and the amount paid; the difference is the change due the customer. (Be careful,

it might be negative.) Output the total amount of change due and list the composition of the change; in other words, how many dollars, half dollars, quarters, dimes, nickels, and pennies should be given to the customer?

19. Write a program to generate a sales tax table for purchase amounts between one cent and one dollar. Use a sales tax rate of 5.5 percent. The rule for computing the amount of tax due is to "round up;" in other words, as soon as the computed tax due exceeds one cent, even if it's only 1.0001 cent, the tax becomes two cents.

20. The sine of a number is defined by the formula

$$\sin(x) = x - (x^3/3!) + (x^5/5!) - (x^7/7!) \ldots$$

where 3! is 3 factorial *(see exercise 9)*. Write a program to input x and estimate its sine. An acceptable answer is one for which the error is less than 0.01 percent.

21. "It's not the heat, it's the humidity." This common summertime complaint recognizes that the discomfort an individual feels is due to the humidity as well as the temperature. In fact there's a measure of this degree of discomfort analogous to the wind chill factor. The discomfort index is computed from the equation

$$\text{discomfort} = \text{temperature} - (0.55 - 0.55*\text{humidity}) * (\text{temperature} - 58)$$

where the temperature is in degrees Fahrenheit and the humidity is expressed in decimal terms (60% humidity is 0.60). Write a program to generate discomfort indexes for temperatures ranging from 70 to 110 degrees and humidities ranging from 60 percent to 100 percent. Use increments of 5.

22. Fibonacci numbers are defined as follows:

$$F_0 = 0, \quad F_1 = 1, \quad F_{n+2} = F_{n+1} + F_n$$

For example, the first several Fibonacci numbers are: 0, 1, 1, 2, 3, 5, 8, 13, ... Write a program to generate the first fifty Fibonacci numbers.

5

Functions and Subroutines

KEY IDEAS

1. *What are functions and subroutines?*

2. *Built-in functions.*

3. *Internal functions.*

4. *External functions.*

    a. *Module independence.*

    b. *Local and global data.*

5. *Subroutines.*

6. *Modular programming.*

WHAT ARE FUNCTIONS AND SUBROUTINES?

Sequential, decision, and repetitive structures are the basic building blocks of any program. A program's logical flow moves from top to bottom, block by block, through a series of sequential, decision, and repetitive structures.

Sometimes, it is useful to remove portions of the code from this main sequential flow. Routines to perform standard or common computations may have already been written, so why reinvent the wheel? Instead, pick up the existing code and link it to a new program. In other cases, a set of logic may appear several times in the same program. Why not write the instructions once and simply reference them when needed? Finally, there is the problem of program complexity. Lengthy programs can be difficult to read, debug, and maintain. It's better to break the logic into modules. Functions and subroutines allow the programmer to achieve these objectives.

Fig. 5.1: *Functions and subroutines can be viewed as black boxes. When they are referenced, the program's logical flow leaves the mainline and enters the function or subroutine. Using input parameters, computations are performed and a value or values returned to the main program. Control then returns to the mainline, where the primary sequential flow is continued.*

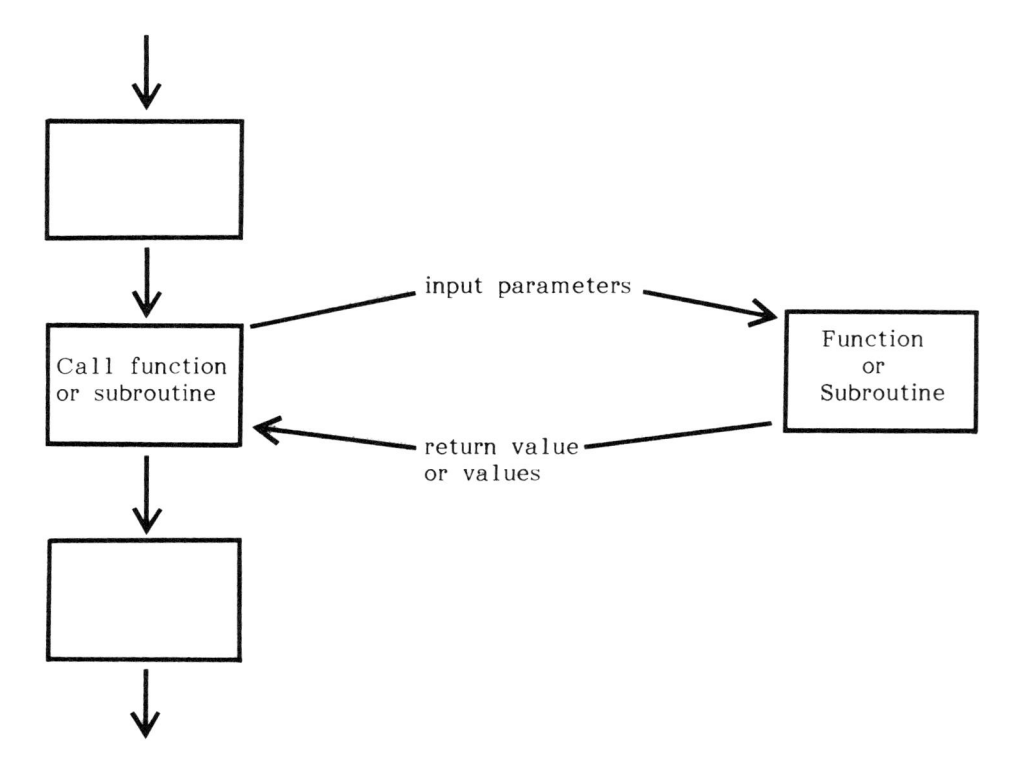

```
LET variable = Function_name (expression1,expression2,...) + ...
```
                         └─ the function's name
                                        └─ parameters list

When the function is referenced,

1. the expressions in the parameters list are evaluated,
2. control is transferred to the function,
3. the parameter values are copied to the function,
4. the function's instructions are executed,
5. a single value is returned to the main program, replacing the function reference,
6. the balance of the main program expression is evaluated, using the value returned by the function as one term.

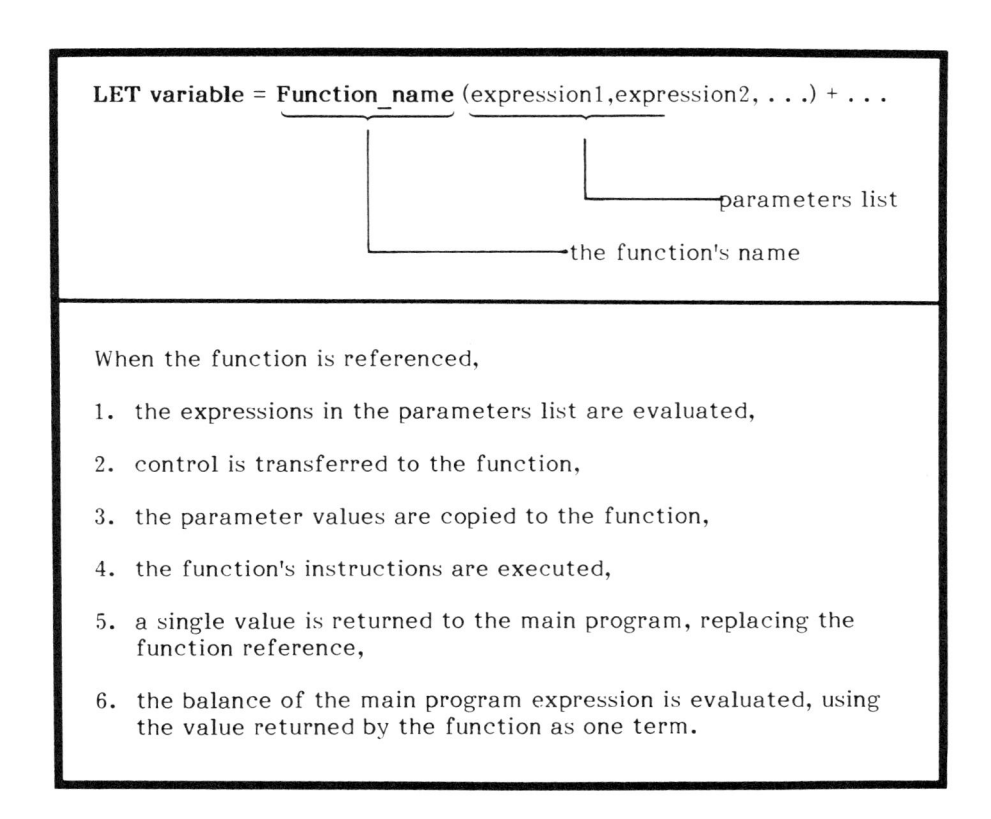

Fig. 5.2: *Referencing a built-in function.*

Imagine a program's logic flowing sequentially through its mainline. View the function or subroutine as a black box *(Fig. 5.1)*. The main program transfers control to the function or subroutine, passing it certain values called parameters. The function or subroutine returns one or more values to the mainline. Now the program continues its primary sequential flow. Functions and subroutines allow the programmer to detour temporarily from a program's main sequential flow, execute a block of logic, and then rejoin the main flow. Functions and subroutines allow the programmer to access already existing logic, reuse the same block of logic several times, or break a complex program into smaller, easier to understand modules. They are very valuable tools.

BUILT-IN FUNCTIONS

Certain mathematical, trigonometric, and other logical functions are used so frequently that it makes little sense to write original instructions for each new program. Instead, the programmer references built-in functions *(Fig. 5.2)*. A

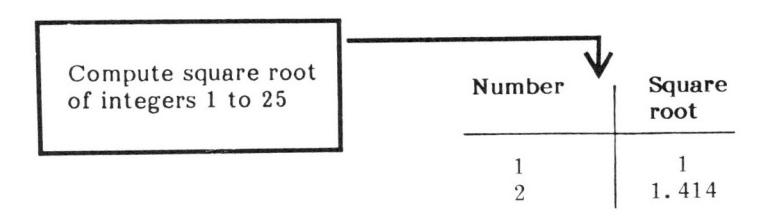

Fig. 5.3: *A block diagram definition of the square roots table problem.*

function is referenced simply by coding it in an expression. When the computer evaluates that expression, it transfers control to the function, passing it one or more parameters. The function returns a single value that effectively replaces the function reference in the original expression. Now, the main program regains control, using the function's value as one term in the expression.

Let's use an example to illustrate built-in functions. Imagine we want to develop a table of the square roots of the numbers from 1 to 25. The problem definition is simple *(Fig. 5.3)*. We want to generate a table, so we'll need a loop. Figure 5.4 shows a flowchart for the program.

How would you find the square root of 13? Since it lies between 9 and 16,

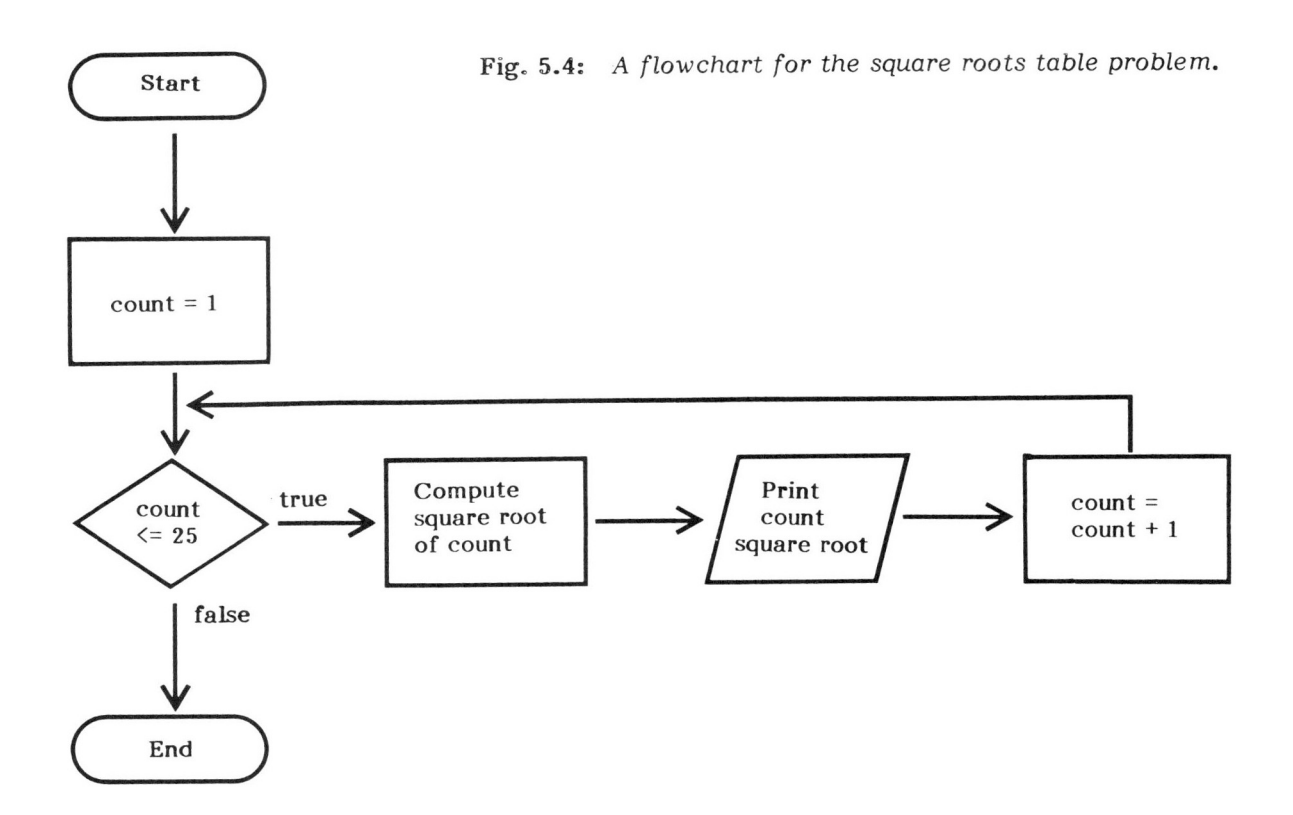

Fig. 5.4: *A flowchart for the square roots table problem.*

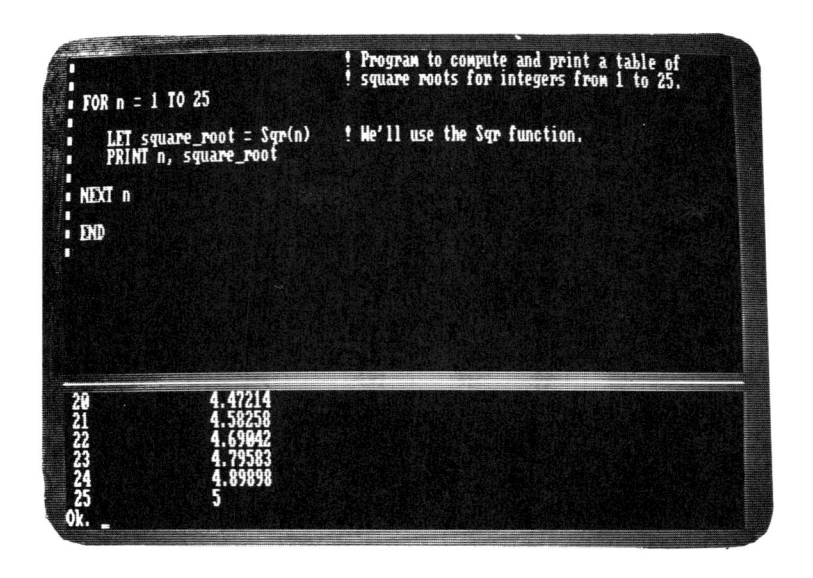

```
FOR n = 1 TO 25                ! Program to compute and print a table of
                               ! square roots for integers from 1 to 25.

    LET square_root = Sqr(n)   ! We'll use the Sqr function.
    PRINT n, square_root

NEXT n

END
```

```
20      4.47214
21      4.58258
22      4.69042
23      4.79583
24      4.89898
25      5
Ok.
```

Fig. 5.5: *The square root program.*

you know its square root must lie between 3 and 4, so you start with "3 point something." Then you refine your estimate, adding decimal positions until the answer is "good enough." Square roots aren't computed, they're estimated.

When you raise a number to the 1/2 power, *True BASIC* estimates its square root. Raise a number to the 1/3 power, and *True BASIC* estimates its cube root. For square roots, there is a better estimating technique. The instructions are found in a built-in function named **Sqr**. Using the **Sqr** function instead of raising the number to the 1/2 power produces a better estimate in less time.

Let's write the square root program *(Fig. 5.5)*. Focus on the statement containing the **Sqr** function. When that instruction is executed, the current value of the parameter, **n**, is copied to the **Sqr** function. The function estimates **n**'s square root. The value of the square root is then copied back to the main program, replacing the function reference in the **LET** statement. Finally, the square root of **n** is stored in **square_root**.

Appendix II summarizes *True BASIC*'s built-in functions. Mathematical functions are available to return an absolute value, an integer value, a logarithm, a minimum or maximum value, a remainder, a random number, a square root, and a variety of other values. Trigonometric functions can be used to return sines, cosines, tangents, and other trigonometric values. Other functions return string values; we'll consider them in Chapter 10.

In an expression, a function is used much as a variable. The function returns a single value. If the value is numeric, it can participate in addition, subtraction, or any of the other arithmetic operations. String functions return string values that call for string operators. A function's type is important. The name of a string function must end in a dollar sign ($). Numeric function names must not.

One function reference can be another function's parameter. For example, in the statement

   LET answer = Sqr (Sin(x)) + 2

the function **Sin(x)** would be evaluated first. It would return the sine of variable **x** in radians. Next, the square root of the sine of **x** would be estimated, replacing the **Sqr** reference. Finally, the square root would be added to 2, and the answer stored in **answer**.

A function can also reference itself. We'll study this technique, called recursion, in Chapter 12. Logical and matrix functions will be covered in subsequent chapters, too.

WRITING INTERNAL FUNCTIONS

Built-in functions are useful, but they cover only a limited number of fairly universal tasks. You may be able to identify additional tasks common to your business, hobby, or interest. If so, you can write your own functions. For example, imagine that your hobby is writing programs to play games. In one game, you want the computer to select a random number between 1 and 10 and then give the player three chances to guess it. As output, the program will tell the player if a guess is correct or incorrect and, if it's wrong, whether it's high or low. Figure 5.6 shows a block diagram definition of the game. A flowchart of the necessary logic *(Fig. 5.7)* shows a loop with a series of tests to evaluate the player's guesses. We want the computer to pick a number between 1 and 10. The **Rnd** function returns a "pseudo-random" number between 0 and 1 which can be converted to a number between 1 and 10. When the computer evaluates the expression

Fig. 5.6: *A block diagram definition of the guessing game problem.*

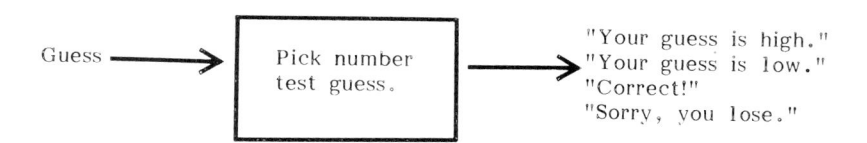

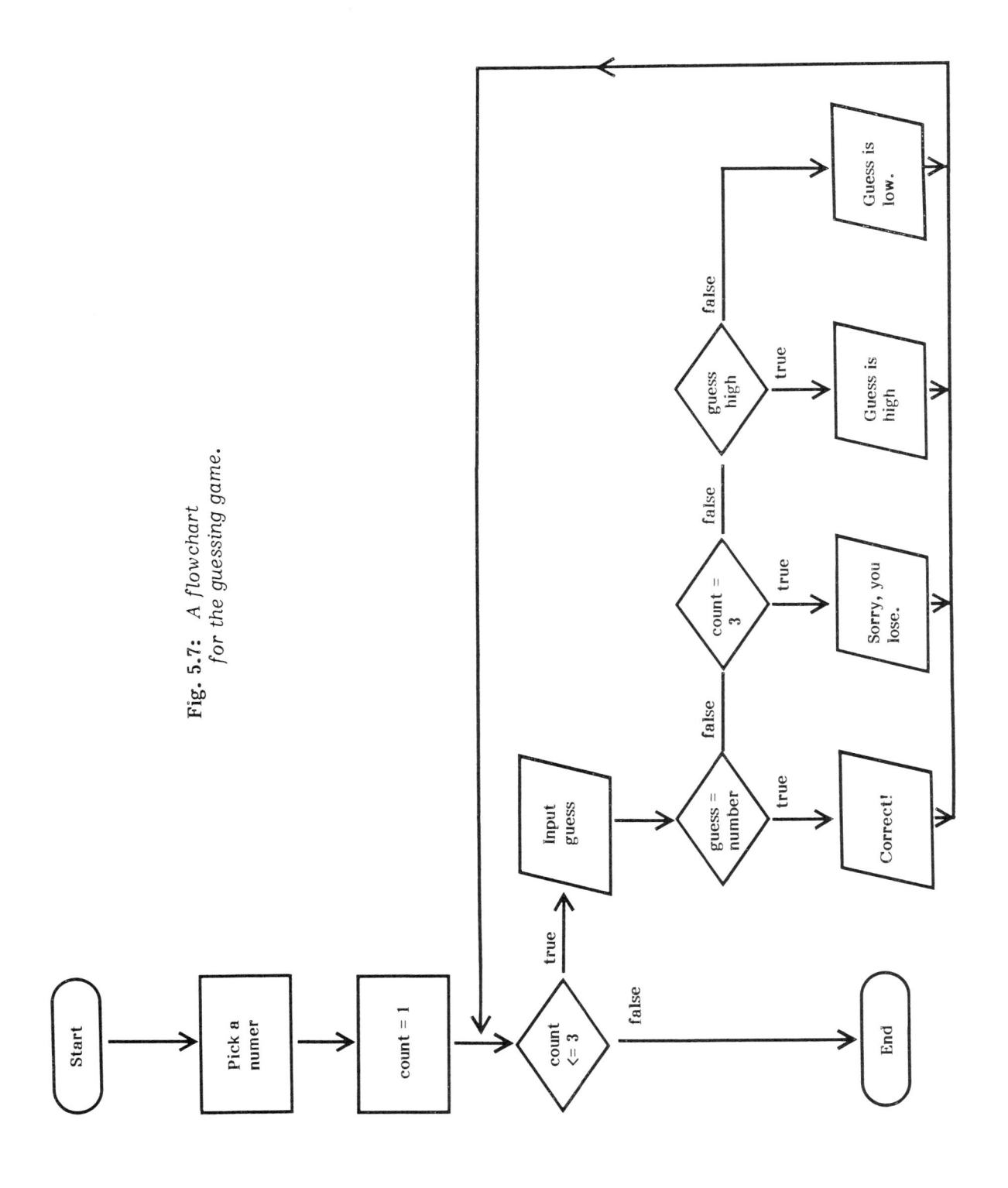

Fig. 5.7: A flowchart for the guessing game.

> **Rnd * 10 + 1**

the function name, **Rnd,** is replaced by a random number greater than 0 but less than 1. Multiplying that value by 10 gives us a product greater than 0 but less than 10. By adding 1, we get a random number greater than 1 but less than 11.

We want a number between 1 and 10; more specifically, we want one of the integers: 1, 2, 3, 4, 5, 6, 7, 8, 9, 10. We can get an integer by using another function

> **Int(Rnd * 10 + 1)**

When the computer encounters this expression, it will find a value for **Rnd,** multiply the value by 10, and add 1 to the product, yielding a random number larger than 1 and less than 11. This random number is then passed to the **Int** function, which returns the greatest integer less than or equal to the parameter it receives. Since the random number must be greater than 1 and less than 11, its integer portion must lie between 1 and 10.

We could simply incorporate the expression developed above in our program, coding

> **LET random number = Int(Rnd * 10 + 1)**

Imagine, however, that selecting a random number between 1 and some upper limit is a common problem. Rather than writing that complex expression each time you need a random integer, it might make sense to define a function.

A function can be defined as a single line or as a block *(Fig. 5.8)*. The function's name must be a legal variable name; to distinguish them visually from variables, we'll capitalize the first letter in a function name. A function's type is important; thus, string function names must end with a dollar sign and numeric function names cannot. Note that we have used built-in functions in our definition. That's legal, though not necessary. Once the function is defined, we can use it in a program *(Fig. 5.9.)*. Note that the definition must come before the function is used.

The function is referenced in the statement

> **LET random_number = The _number(10)**

The value 10 is passed to the function, which returns a random integer between

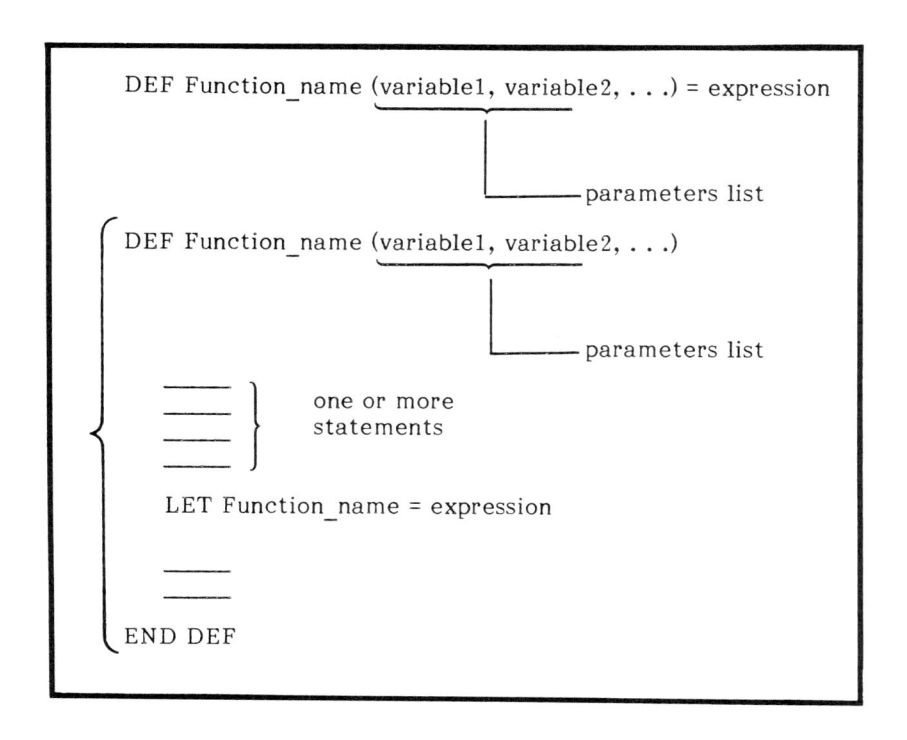

```
DEF Function_name (variable1, variable2, ...) = expression
                   └─────────┬──────────────┘
                             └── parameters list

⎧ DEF Function_name (variable1, variable2, ...)
⎪                    └─────────┬──────────────┘
⎪                              └── parameters list
⎪
⎨      ═══
⎪      ═══ } one or more
⎪      ═══   statements
⎪      ═══
⎪   LET Function_name = expression
⎪      ───
⎪      ───
⎩   END DEF
```

Fig. 5.8: *A function is defined by coding a DEF statement.*

1 and 10. In another program, we might reference **The_number** with a different parameter. Our function will return a random integer between 1 and whatever upper limit we provide.

The function definition is the first instruction in the program. Won't the computer try to execute the function first? No. Functions and subroutines are not like other instructions. They are executed only when they are referenced.

What's the point of writing that function? It would be almost as easy to write an expression to generate a random number. But what if we wrote the function and then stored it on disk? (We might even store it in a library, one of the topics of Chapter 12.) Then, by using an **INCLUDE** command *(Fig. 5.10)*, we could use the same function in dozens of different programs. Why reinvent the wheel? Solve a problem once and use the solution over and over again.

The built-in function **Rnd** returns a pseudo-random number. If you run the program more than once, you'll discover that it always returns the same sequence of random numbers. This is fine for debugging a program or repeating an experiment, but it may be desirable to introduce unpredictability. Simply precede the first reference to the **Rnd** function with a **RANDOMIZE** statement *(Fig. 5.11)*. You can code the **RANDOMIZE** statement in the main program, or make it part of a block structure function.

```
                              ! A guessing game. A function is defined
                              ! to select a random number between 1 and
                              ! some upper limit, n.
DEF The_number(n) = Int(Rnd * n + 1)

                              ! Referencing the function, the computer
                              ! selects a random number between 1 and 10.
LET random_number = The_number(10)

                              ! The user inputs as many as three guesses.
FOR count = 1 TO 3
    INPUT guess
                              ! If the guess is correct, a message is
                              ! displayed and the loop is exited.

    IF guess = random_number THEN
        PRINT "Correct! You win!"
        EXIT FOR                      ! Note exit condition.

                              ! If the guess is wrong and it's the third
                              ! guess, the player loses.

    ELSEIF count = 3 THEN
        PRINT "You lose. The number is", random_number

                              ! Following an incorrect first or second
                              ! guess, the player is told if the guess
                              ! is high or low.

        ELSEIF guess > random_number THEN
            PRINT "Your guess is high."
        ELSE
            PRINT "Your guess is low."
    END IF
NEXT count

END
```

Fig. 5.9: *The guessing game program.*

EXTERNAL FUNCTIONS

Module Independence

Our function **The_number** was an internal function coded near the beginning of the main program. An external function comes after the main program's **END** statement. Why bother writing external functions? For several reasons. We

```
        INCLUDE file_name
                └────┬────┘
                     │
                     └── the name under which the
                         previously written instructions
                         were saved on disk.
```

To use an INCLUDE command:

1. In the editing window, leave the cursor on the line below which you want the saved instructions to be added.

2. Return to the history window (the F2 key).

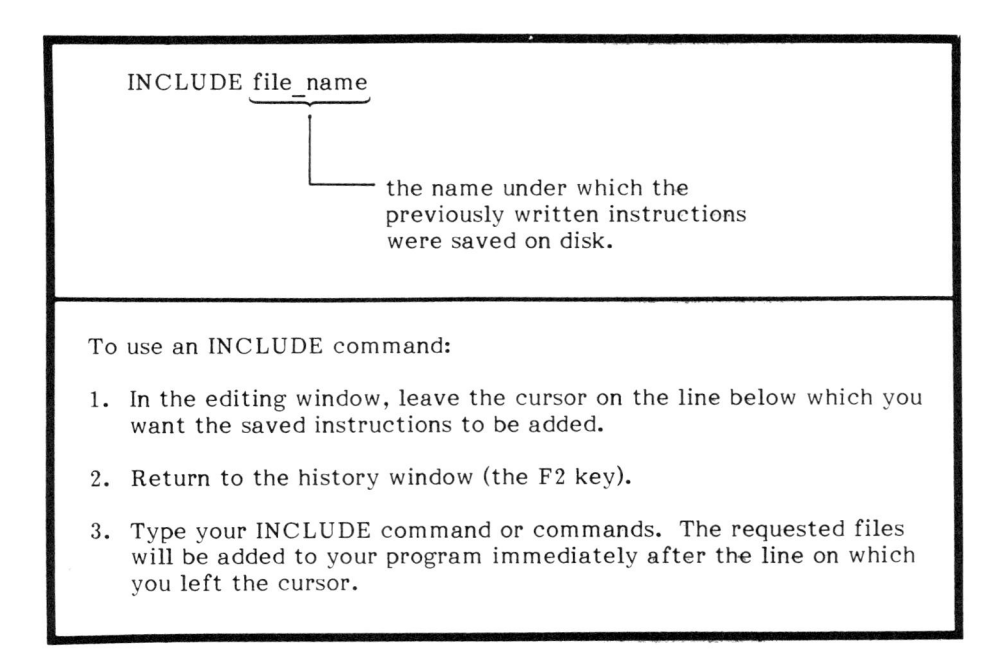

3. Type your INCLUDE command or commands. The requested files will be added to your program immediately after the line on which you left the cursor.

Fig. 5.10: *The INCLUDE command can be used to include in a new program instructions previously coded and saved on disk.*

might have numerous functions stored on disk. After writing a new main program, we can leave the cursor just after the **END** statement, return to the history window (F2 key), and type one or more **INCLUDE** commands, adding the functions to the end of the program. That's a bit easier than inserting them into the code.

The most significant advantage of using external functions, however, is module independence. Ideally, a function should be viewed as a black box. Give it a set of input values (the parameters), and it returns a single result. How it arrives at that result is irrelevant. External functions are independent. Internal functions are not.

Fig. 5.11: *The RANDOMIZE statement.*

```
RANDOMIZE




Use before referencing the Rnd function if you
want Rnd to return unanticipated values.
```

What do we mean when we say that a module is independent? Simply that computations taking place within the module cannot affect the rest of the program. Let's use an example to illustrate a *lack* of module independence *(Fig. 5.12)*. As the computer executes the statement

> LET x = 10

a memory location is assigned the name **x** and the value 10 is stored there. Next comes the statement

> LET product = Sum(2,4) * x

Obviously, we want the function to compute 2+4 and return the answer (6) so that we can multiply it by whatever is stored in the memory location called **x**. The value of **x** should, of course, be 10, but as we'll see, it won't be.

Look at the function. Its parameters are **a** and **b**, so two memory locations named **a** and **b** are set aside. When the function is referenced, the values of the parameters are copied into these memory locations: **a** will hold 2 and **b** will hold 4. Next, the statement

> LET x = a + b

is executed. The contents of location **a** are added to the contents of location **b**, and the result is stored at **x**. Location **x** has already been defined. It held

Fig. 5.12: *In an internal function, all variables are global. Thus the internal function is not independent.*

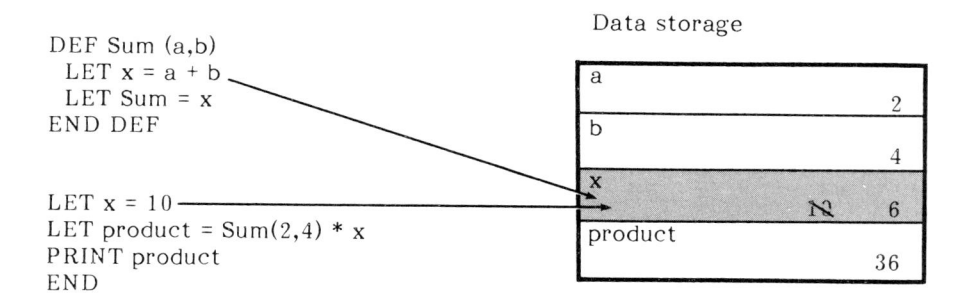

```
DEF Sum (a,b)
   LET x = a + b
   LET Sum = x
END DEF


LET x = 10
LET product = Sum(2,4) * x
PRINT product
END
```

Data storage

a	2
b	4
x	6
product	36

```
DECLARE DEF Sum
LET x = 10
LET product = Sum(2,4) * x
PRINT product
END

DEF Sum (a,b)
    LET x = a + b
    LET sum = x
END DEF
```

Main program's storage

x	
	10
Sum	
	6
product	
	60

Function's storage

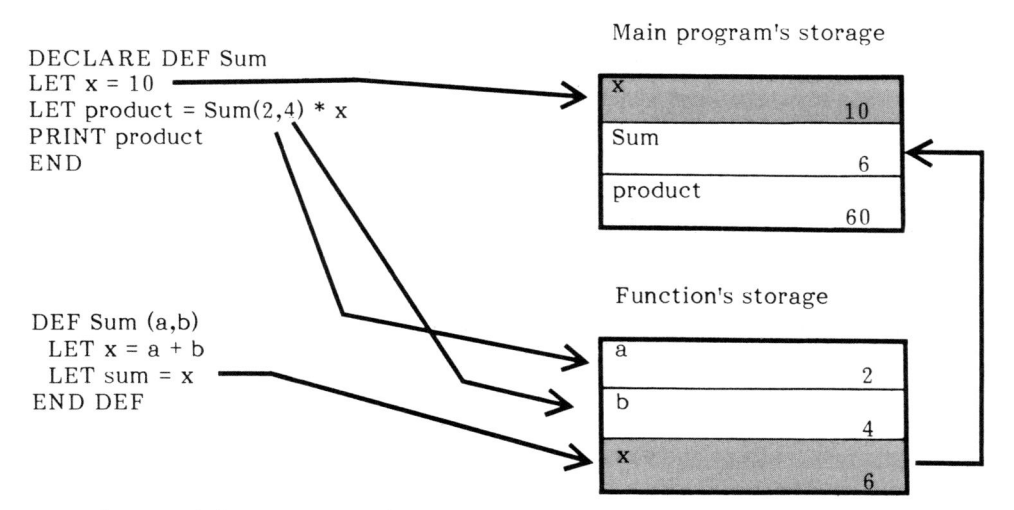

a	
	2
b	
	4
x	
	6

Fig. 5.13: *External functions are independent; their variables are local.*

the value 10. After this **LET** statement is executed, however, it won't. Instead, it will hold the sum, 6. The next statement

   LET sum = x

assigns the sum to the function name; when we return to the mainline, **Sum(2,4)** is replaced by the value 6.

What happens next? Whatever replaces **Sum(2,4)** in the original expression is to be multiplied by the contents of memory location **x**. We expected **x** to contain the value 10, but it doesn't. Why? Because the function changed the value stored in **x**. We'll get the wrong answer, 36. We expected the product to be 60, not 36. The internal function, **Sum,** modified the contents of one of the main program's variables. Consequently, the main program computed the wrong answer. Internal functions are not independent.

Local and Global Data

The problem is that all the variables in our program are *global*. A variable is simply a name assigned to a memory location. Global variables are names that are known to two or more modules. In this example, both the main program and the function shared the same memory space. The variable **x** referred to a memory location. To both the function and the main program, **x** referred to the *same* memory location.

Now, consider **Sum** as an *external* function *(Fig. 5.13)*. External functions are independent of the main program because each external function has its own *local* data storage. In the main program, memory locations are assigned names **x** and **product**. In the function, separate memory locations are assigned names **a, b,** and **x**. Note that the variable name **x** represents one memory location in the main program, and a *different* memory location in the function. The main program's variables are *local*, known only to it. The function's variables are local, known only to it. The main program doesn't know the function's variable names. The function doesn't know the main program's variable names. The two modules are independent.

But won't we have two memory locations with the same name? Yes. Won't that confuse the computer? No. Two independent variables with the same name confuses a computer no more than having two friends named Bill or Sue confuses you. A variable name represents a memory location. Within the main program, **x** is the name assigned to a location in the main program's storage area. Within the function, **x** is the name assigned to a location in the function's storage area.

What happens when the program is executed? First, the main program assigns the value 10 to *its* memory location **x**. Next comes the **LET** statement. The function **Sum** must be evaluated. Two parameters are coded. The constant 2 is copied to the function's memory location **a**; the constant 4 is copied to the function's location **b**. Now the function gets control. The contents of its locations **a** and **b** are summed, and the result is stored in its location **x**. Note that the main program's location **x** is not affected. Finally, the sum is returned to the main program. The multiplication produces the correct answer: 60.

The problem with internal functions is that the same memory locations are shared by two or more modules; in other words, all variables are global. Every module that has access to a memory location can change its contents. In simple applications, that's not a problem. When computations become complex, however, intermediate work variables are often needed. Those work variables are global, too. If by chance the programmer developing the function chooses the same variable names as the programmer coding the main program, the results can be unpredictable. If the main programmer expects a variable to hold a count, and the function changes the contents of that variable, the main program might not work. With internal functions, it is essential that the main programmer know the variable names used inside the function. An internal function is not a simple black box, because you can't use it without knowing its contents.

External functions are different. To use one, the programmer need know only the parameters to be passed. All intermediate results are stored in the function's own local storage area. A single value is returned. There are no surprises; an external function can be used without knowing its contents.

Why is this important? When a single programmer writes a simple program using simple functions, it isn't. But what if you want to use a function written by someone else? If you include it as an internal function, you'll have to read through the code and make sure you don't use the same variable names. If you include it as an external function, you can ignore the other programmer's code. What if several programmers are assigned to write portions of a large, complex program? If their modules are independent, each one can ignore the details of the others' code, focusing only on the parameters. That simplifies programming.

External Functions: an Example

Let's develop a program that uses an external function. Imagine an instructor has a class of thirty students. A project calls for dividing the class into teams of five students each. The instructor wants to know how many different combinations of thirty students taken five at a time are possible. The formula for computing the number of possible combinations of n things taken r at a time is

$$\text{combination} = \frac{n!}{r!\,(n-r)!}$$

where n! is the factorial of n. The factorial of a number is the product of all the positive integers up to and including that number; for example, 5! is 5*4*3*2*1.

The problem is defined in Fig. 5.14. Figure 5.15 shows the necessary logic. Note that three different factorials must be computed. When the same computation is needed more than once, it makes sense to use a function.

Focus on the logic to compute a factorial. Let's use an example and then generalize it. We know that 5! is 5*4*3*2*1. Given the value 5, how would you compute its factorial? The key would seem to be a count loop. Start the count at 1. Each time through the loop, multiply the developing product by the count. Continue as long as the count is less than or equal to 5. We need an initial value for that product. Zero will not do. (Why?) We'll use 1. A flowchart for the factorial logic is shown in Fig. 5.16.

By definition, the factorial of zero (0!) is 1. Factorials do not exist for negative numbers. Given these definitions and our flowchart, we can write a factorial function *(the shaded part of Fig. 5.17)*. Read the logic carefully. Note the initial check for a negative number; we'll return the value -1 when we encounter one. Note also that the loop's initial count is 2. Why? What happens if **n** is 1 as the loop begins? Remember that the test in a **FOR. . .NEXT** loop occurs at the top of the structure. If the initial count exceeds **n**, the loop is skipped. The value of product remains 1. What is the factorial of 1?

We can use the factorial function to compute the number of possible student combinations simply by adding it to the end of the program *(Fig. 5.17)*. Because

Fig. 5.14: *A block diagram definition of the combinations problem.*

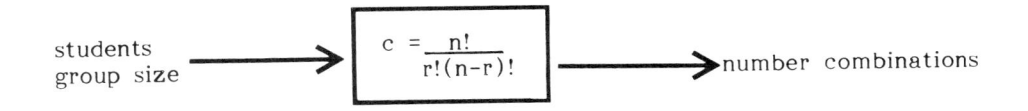

students, group size → $c = \dfrac{n!}{r!(n-r)!}$ → number combinations

```
Start
  ↓
Initialize n, r
  ↓
Compute n!
  ↓
Compute r!
  ↓
Compute (n-r)!
  ↓
  ○

  ○
  ↓
Compute combinations
  ↓
Output combinations
  ↓
End
```

n = number students in class
r = group size

Fig. 5.15: *A flowchart for the combinations problem.*

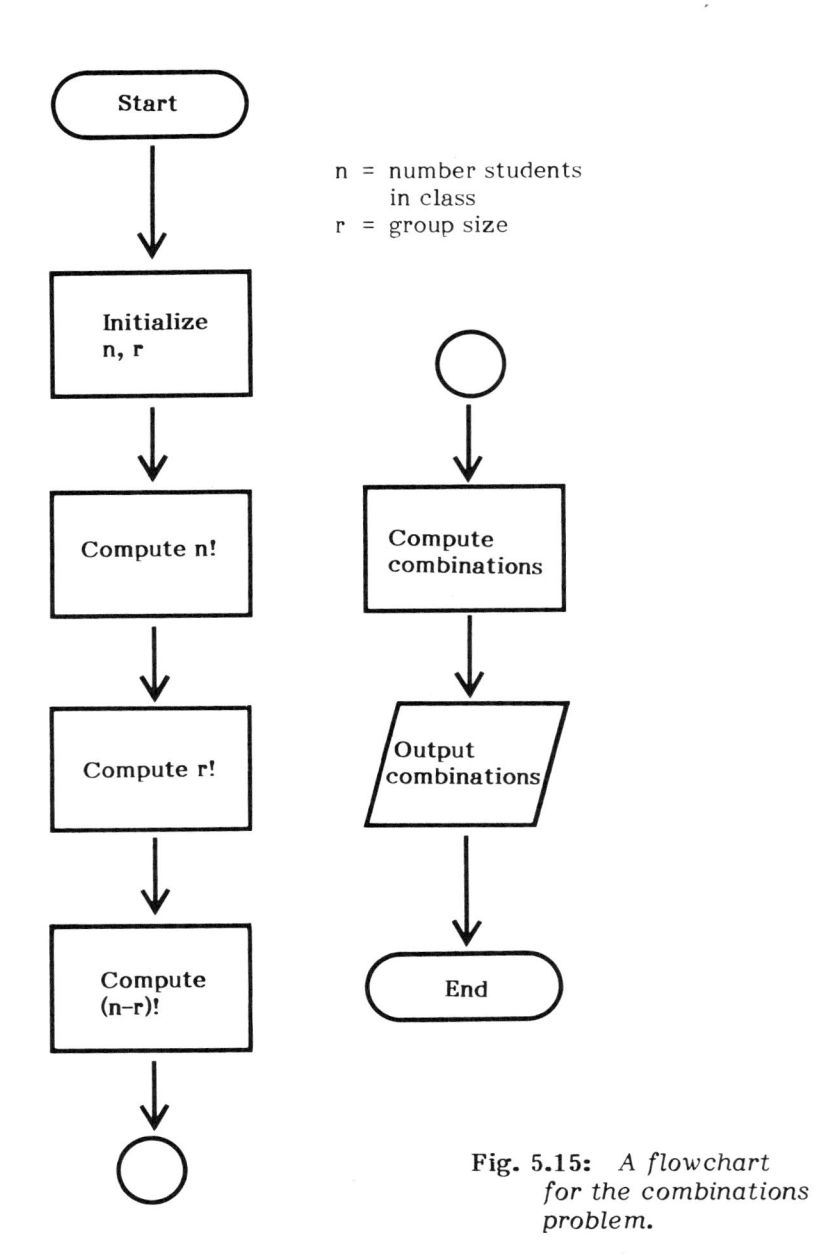

Fig. 5.16: *A flowchart for computing a factorial.*

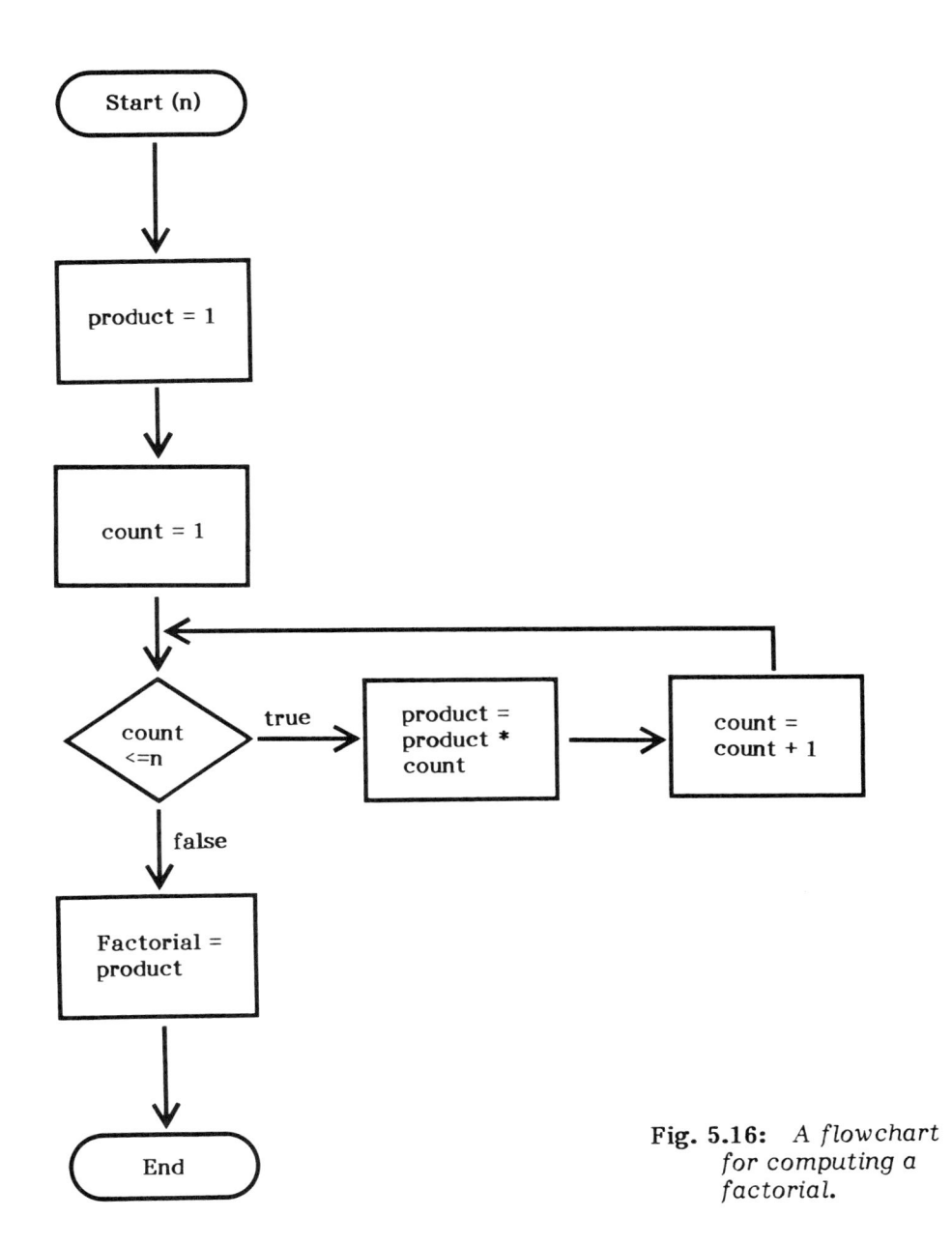

```
DECLARE DEF Factorial          ! Program to compute the number of
                               ! possible groups of r students in a
                               ! class of n students. We begin by
                               ! declaring an external function.

                               ! Next, values for the number of students
                               ! in the class and the planned group size
                               ! are input.
INPUT students, group_size
                               ! The formula for computing the number of
                               ! combinations of n things taken r at a
                               ! time is: [n! / (r! * (n-r)!)]
                               ! We begin by invoking the external
                               ! function to compute the factorials
LET nfactorial = Factorial(students)
LET rfactorial = Factorial(group_size)
LET difference = Factorial(students - group_size)

                               ! Next we use the factorials to compute
                               ! the number of possible combinations.
LET combinations = nfactorial / (rfactorial * difference)

                               ! Finally, we output the computed
                               ! number of combinations.
PRINT students, group_size, combinations
END
```

Fig. 5.17: *A program to compute the number of possible combinations of 30 students taken 5 at a time. The function Factorial is shaded.*

the function is external, we don't have to worry about how it computes a factorial. Instead, we can treat it as a black box, giving it a value and expecting it to return the value's factorial. Incidentally, our factorial function could also be used by other programs.

The main program *(Fig. 5.17)* begins with a **DECLARE** statement *(Fig. 5.18)*. Why is it necessary? A function reference looks like a subscripted variable (the subject of Chapter 8). If we just coded a function name, *True BASIC* would have no way of telling if it referred to a function or to a variable. That's why, when an *internal* function is used, the **DEF** statement must precede any reference to the function. That's why *external* function names must be listed in a **DECLARE** statement. **DEF** and **DECLARE** statements tell *True BASIC* that certain names are to be interpreted as function names. It's a good idea to code them at the beginning of the program.

Note that the main program and the function were planned and flowcharted independently. That's another advantage of using functions and subroutines.

```
DEF factorial (n)                   ! External function to compute the
                                    ! factorial of n.

   LET product = 1                  ! The variable product is a work field.

                                    ! Since factorials are not defined for
                                    ! negative numbers, if n is negative,
                                    ! the value -1 is returned.
   IF n < 0 THEN
      LET product = -1

                                    ! A factorial is computed only for posi-
                                    ! tive integers exceeding zero. Since the
                                    ! factorial of both 0 and 1 is 1,
                                    ! product remains 1 if n is 0 or 1.
   ELSEIF n > 0 THEN
      FOR count = 2 to n
         LET product = product * count
      NEXT count
   ELSE
   END IF
                                    ! Finally, the value of product is assign-
                                    ! ed to the function's name (Factorial),
                                    ! and the result is returned.
   LET Factorial = product
END DEF
```

Fig. 5.17, *continued*.

Fig. 5.18: *When external subroutines are used they must be identified in a DECLARE statement before they are referenced.*

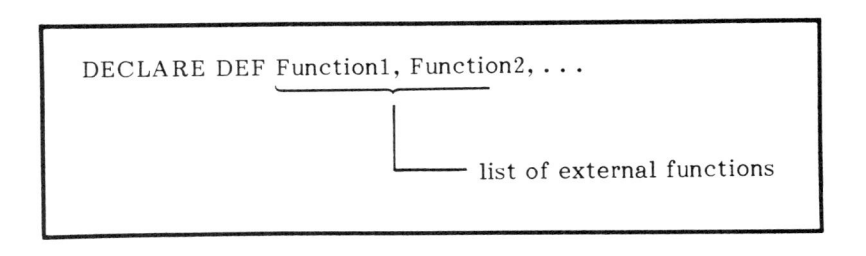

```
DECLARE DEF Function1, Function2, . . .
                     └──── list of external functions
```

Instead of solving one big problem, we broke it into two little ones--compute a factorial and compute the number of combinations. The idea is simple: divide and conquer. Small problems are easier to solve than big ones. By dividing a large problem into a number of small ones and attacking the small problems separately, we can greatly simplify the task of writing a computer program. We'll examine this idea in detail in Chapter 6.

True BASIC follows the pending ANS BASIC standard. In that standard, the keyword **FUNCTION** is used instead of the keyword **DEF**. *True BASIC* will accept either **FUNCTION** or **DEF**.

SUBROUTINES

Subroutines and Functions

There are some problems with functions. For one thing, they return only a single value. Another limitation has to do with the way parameters are passed. When a function is referenced, the values of each of the parameters are physically copied into the function's storage space. That means duplicate space for each parameter. Finally, functions are referenced in expressions. That's fine for computing square roots, factorials, and other intermediate values, but it's a bit annoying to have to set up a phoney expression when a final result is required. As long as a task calls for a single, intermediate result with relatively few parameters, a function is a good choice. Otherwise, a subroutine may be a better alternative.

When a subroutine is called, its parameters are passed by reference, not by value. They are not copied. Instead, the subroutine is given the address or memory location where each value is stored, and it manipulates the data in the main program's storage area. If four parameters are passed to a subroutine, as many as four new values can be sent back to the calling routine. Subroutines are not limited to returning single values.

As with functions, a subroutine can be internal or external. An internal subroutine is coded within a main program; it must be defined before it is referenced. Internal subroutines share their variables with the main program. Because all variables are global, an internal subroutine is not independent.

An external subroutine follows the main program's **END** statement. External subroutines are independent, sharing only their parameters with the main program. While the parameters are global, any other variables used within the subroutine are local. As we'll see in Chapter 6, this independence can be very important.

If internal subroutines are not independent, why use them? One reason is simply to remove a lengthy block of logic from a program's mainline. For example, many real-world programs contain elaborate data output routines designed to display data in a clear, easy-to-read format. Dozens of instructions might be involved. Reading through all those instructions can be distracting. The program can be greatly simplified if these instructions are shifted to an internal subroutine.

A single function, data output, is performed. Moving the details away from the mainline allows a reader to skip over those details and focus on the essential logical flow.

Why choose an internal subroutine, though? Why not an external subroutine? An external subroutine's primary advantage is its independence; its work variables are local. External subroutines do, however, share their parameters with the main program; the parameters are global. An output routine, such as the one described above, performs few if any computations, and thus uses few if any work variables. Instead, it may output dozens of global variables. If an external subroutine is used, all these parameters must be passed to it; the parameters list may not fit on a single line. With an internal subroutine, all variables are global. Thus the subroutine can be called with no parameters, and simply access the main program's variables by name.

When a subroutine houses a significant computation involving intermediate work variables, however, it should be external. The problem is the work variables. If the subroutine were internal, a programmer using it would have to know the work variables. With an external subroutine, the work variables can be ignored.

In the next section, we'll illustrate an external subroutine. An internal subroutine will be used in Chapter 6.

A Subroutine to Compute an Average

Computer science majors, business data processing majors, and students studying a variety of other disciplines take an introduction to computers course. They have just finished an examination, and the instructor would like to compare the performances of these various groups. Four different averages are needed: one for computer science majors, one for business data processing majors, one for other majors, and one for all students. Figure 5.19 shows a block diagram problem definition.

We've already written a program to compute an average *(see Figs. 4.14 and*

Fig. 5.19: *A block diagram definition of the grade averages problem.*

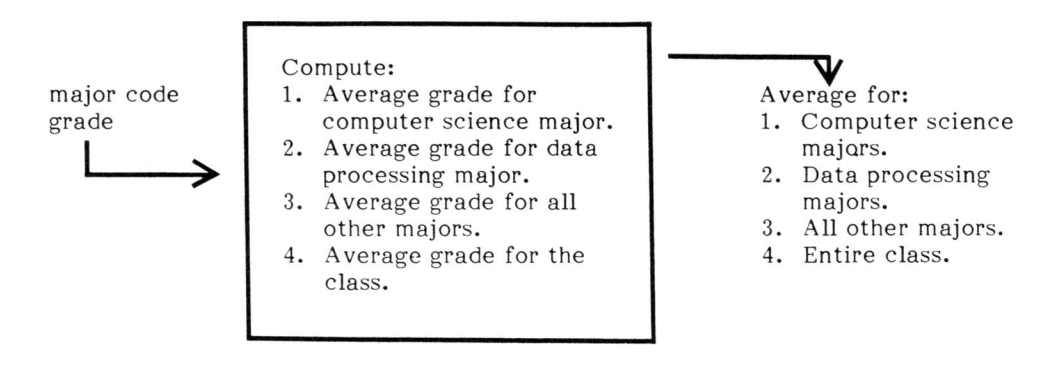

```
major code       Compute:                              Average for:
grade            1. Average grade for                  1. Computer science
                    computer science major.               majors.
          ───▶  2. Average grade for data              2. Data processing
                    processing major.                     majors.
                 3. Average grade for all              3. All other majors.
                    other majors.                      4. Entire class.
                 4. Average grade for the
                    class.
```

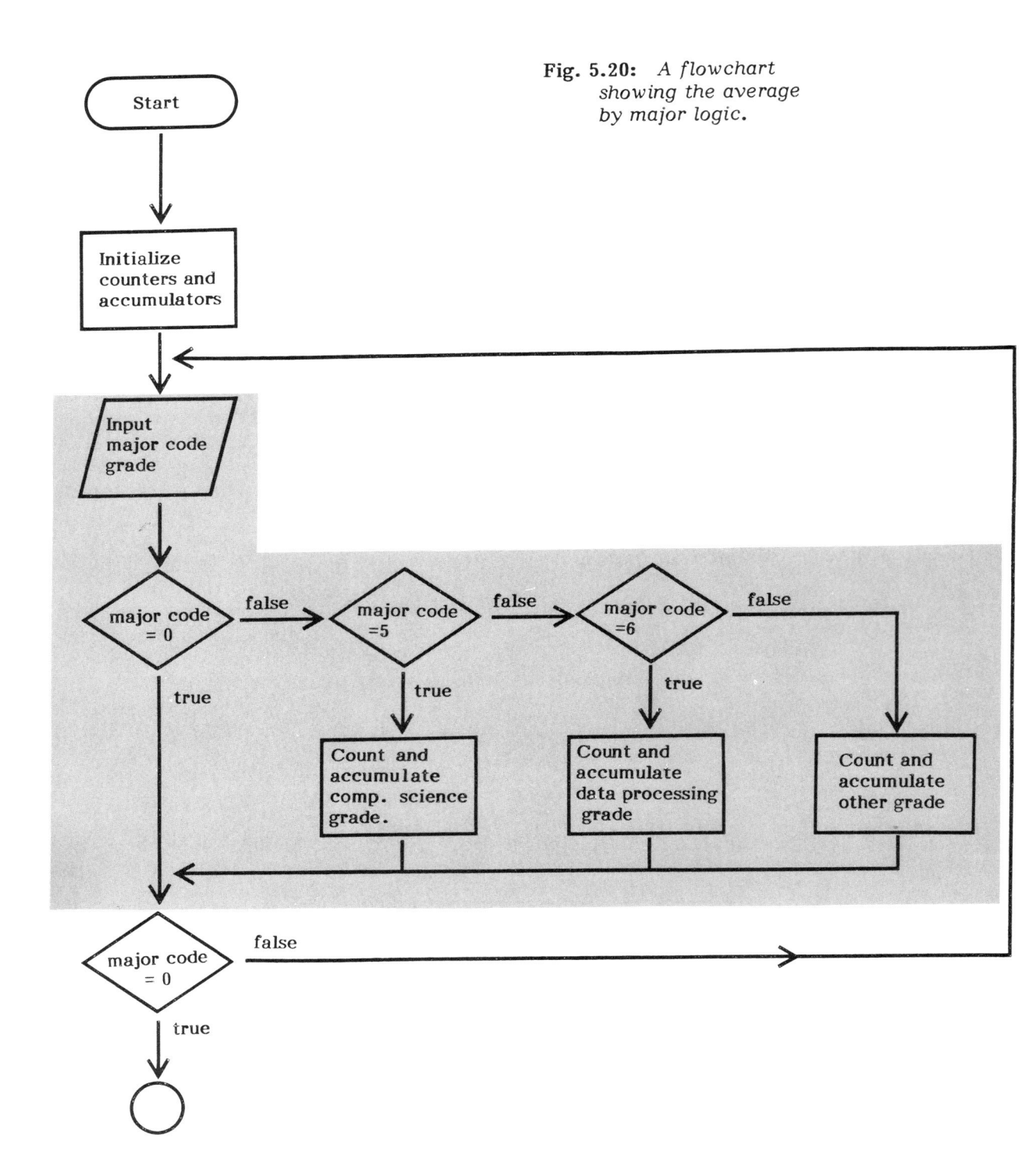

Fig. 5.20: *A flowchart showing the average by major logic.*

Fig. 5.20, *continued*.

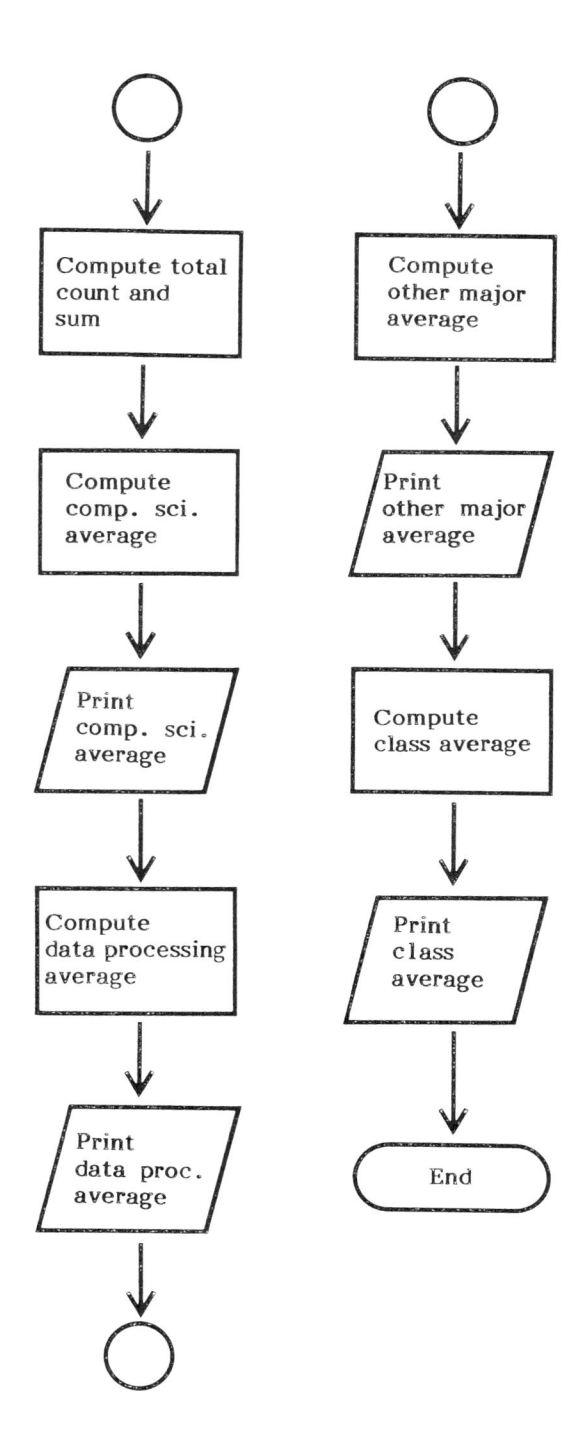

4.16). The basic idea is simple. We input a value, count it, and accumulate it. Then we go back and input another value. A sentinel value signals the end-of-data condition. We can exit the loop by using an **EXIT DO** or by defining a **DO UNTIL** structure. Finally, the average is computed by dividing the accumulated sum by the count.

This problem is a bit more complex, however. We need four different averages. To compute the computer science majors' average, we must count and sum *their* grades. To compute the data processing majors' average, we must count and sum their grades. The instructor's grade book is kept in alphabetical order, so we can't expect all the computer science majors' grades to be entered first. Before we plan the count and accumulate loop, let's focus on a single student's data and determine exactly what we might do with it.

We start with the input of a student's major code and examination grade *(shaded portion of Fig. 5.20).* We'll use a zero major code as our sentinel value. We don't want to count and accumulate the sentinel value, so we do nothing if the major code is 0. If the student is a computer science major (major code 5), we'll count and accumulate the grade. If the student is a data processing major (major code 6), we'll count and accumulate the grade under different variable names. If the major code is neither 5 nor 6, the student must be some other major, so we'll use the "other major" counter and accumulator.

This basic logic must be repeated for each student's input data, so we'll need a loop. A DO UNTIL structure with an end-of-loop sentinel value test seems reasonable *(Fig. 5.20).* After exiting the loop, the count and sum for the entire class can be found by adding the computer science, data processing, and other-major counts and sums. Finally, the four averages can be computed and output.

We need four averages. Since the same computation must be repeated four times, it makes sense to write a function or a subroutine. Because the average is the desired end result rather than just an intermediate step, we'll choose a subroutine.

Writing a Subroutine

Treat a subroutine as a small program in its own right. Begin by defining the problem with a block diagram *(Fig. 5.21).* The objective is an arithmetic average or mean. To compute it, we divide an accumulated sum by a count. Thus, a sum and a count must be input to the subroutine.

Fig. 5.21: *A block diagram definition of the average subroutine.*

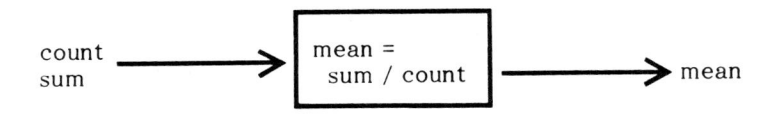

count, sum → | mean = sum / count | → mean

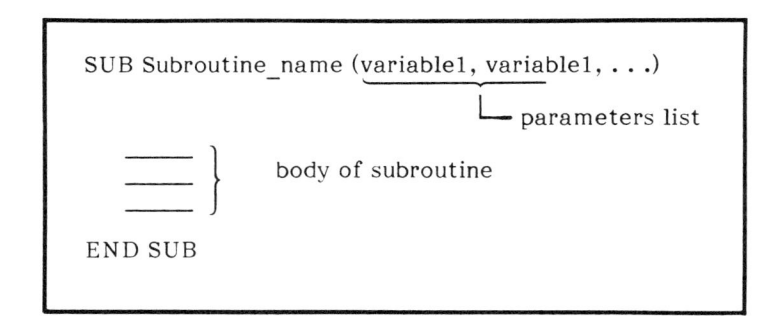

```
SUB Subroutine_name (variable1, variable1, ...)
                              └─ parameters list

───┐
───├ body of subroutine
───┘
END SUB
```

Fig. 5.22: *A subroutine is defined by coding a SUB statement.*

View the block diagram as a black box, ignoring its contents. We want to pass to the subroutine values for count and sum and get back a value for the mean. Those "inputs and outputs" are the subroutine's parameters. Any program that calls this subroutine should be concerned only with the parameters. How it computes the average is beside the point.

Next move inside the subroutine and plan its logic. In our example, the logic is straightforward. Given values for count and sum, an average is computed. That's about it. There is no need to prepare a flowchart.

A subroutine is defined by a **SUB** statement *(Fig. 5.22)*. The keyword **SUB** is followed by the subroutine's name, which must be a valid variable name. Because functions are used much as variables, we had to pay attention to the function's type. That's not necessary with subroutines. In fact, subroutine names may not end in a dollar sign.

Following the subroutine name is a list of variables separated by commas--the parameters. Numeric parameters require numeric variable names; string parameters require string variable names. As we'll see shortly, the order in which the parameters are coded must match their order in an associated **CALL** statement. Otherwise, parameters can be coded in any sequence. In this primer, we'll code input variables first and output variables last. A completed subroutine to compute an arithmetic average is shown in Fig. 5.23.

Calling the subroutine

We have a subroutine to compute an average. We'll give it a name and save it for later use. Now we can turn our attention to the main program *(Fig. 5.20)*.

Look at the logical flow. Clearly the main loop is a **DO UNTIL** structure. Within the loop, we select a counter and an accumulator based on the value of a major code. A series of **ELSEIF** statements or a **SELECT CASE** structure could be used; we'll choose the latter. Given these structures, we can write the code *(Fig. 5.24)*.

Focus on the last several statements--they're shaded. The **IF** statements

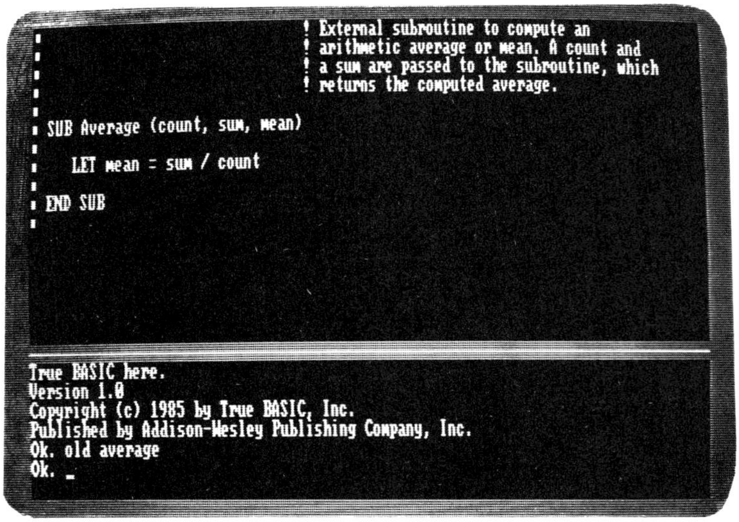

```
! External subroutine to compute an
! arithmetic average or mean. A count and
! a sum are passed to the subroutine, which
! returns the computed average.

SUB Average (count, sum, mean)
    LET mean = sum / count
END SUB
```

True BASIC here.
Version 1.0
Copyright (c) 1985 by True BASIC, Inc.
Published by Addison-Wesley Publishing Company, Inc.
Ok. old average
Ok. _

Fig. 5.23: *A subroutine to compute an arithmetic average or mean.*

allow us to avoid calling the subroutine if the number of students in a particular major is zero. It's the **CALL** statements we're really interested in, though. A subroutine is referenced by a **CALL** statement *(Fig. 5.25)*. Following the keyword **CALL** is a subroutine name and a series of expressions separated by commas. Those expressions, the parameters, can be constants, variables, or more complex expressions.

When a **CALL** statement is executed *(Fig. 5.26)*, the computer evaluates the expressions in the parameters list, reducing each one to a single number or string. Then it looks for a **SUB** statement with a subroutine name matching the one in the **CALL** statement. Once the subroutine is located, the parameters are passed.

In a way, it's a bit misleading to say that parameters are passed to a subroutine, because the parameter values aren't really copied. Back in Chapter 2, we talked about how each variable is assigned space in main memory. The variable name is simply a label that identifies the space. In our example *(Fig. 5.26)*, all our parameters are variables. When the subroutine is called, its parameters and the **CALL** statement's parameters are matched up in order--first parameter to first parameter, second to second, and so on.

For example, focus on the first parameters: **cs_count** and **count**. The variable **cs_count** is defined in the main program. Space has been set aside and labeled **cs_count**. The value stored in this memory location is not copied to the subroutine. Instead, its address is given to the subroutine. In effect, **count** becomes a different

```
                                  ! This program accepts the input
                                  ! of examination grades paired with
                                  ! major codes. It then computes averages
                                  ! for computer science majors, data pro-
                                  ! cessing majors, all other majors, and
                                  ! the class as a whole.

LET cs_sum = 0                    ! First, the various counters and
LET cs_count = 0                  ! accumulators are set to zero.
LET dp_sum = 0
LET dp_count = 0
LET other_sum = 0
LET other_count = 0

DO                                ! Data are read until a zero major code
   INPUT major_code, grade        ! is entered. As long as the major code
                                  ! is positive, it is used to select a
                                  ! counter and an accumulator for the grade.

   SELECT CASE major_code         ! Selecting input records by major code is
                                  ! a case structure

     CASE 0                       ! Major code 0 is the sentinel value.

     CASE 5                       ! Computer science is major code 5.

        LET cs_sum = cs_sum + grade
        LET cs_count = cs_count + 1

     CASE 6                       ! Data processing is major code 6.

        LET dp_sum = dp_sum + grade
        LET dp_count = dp_count + 1

     CASE ELSE                    ! Other codes fall into the other category.

        LET other_sum = other_sum + grade
        LET other_count = other_count + 1

   END SELECT

LOOP UNTIL major_code = 0
                                  ! Adding the group totals and group counts
                                  ! yields the class total and class count.

LET total_count = cs_count + dp_count + other_count
LET total_sum = cs_sum + dp_sum + other_sum
```

Fig. 5.24: *A program to compute a series of averages using a subroutine. continued on next page.*

```
                                  ! Assuming that one or more scores have
                                  ! been entered in each category, the
                                  ! averages are computed and printed.

IF cs_count > 0 THEN
   CALL Average (cs_count, cs_sum, cs_mean)
   PRINT "comp. science", cs_count, cs_mean
END IF

IF dp_count > 0 THEN
   CALL Average (dp_count, dp_sum, dp_mean)
   PRINT "data processing", dp_count, dp_mean
END IF

IF other_count > 0 THEN
   CALL Average (other_count, other_sum, other_mean)
   PRINT "other", other_count, other_mean
END IF

IF total_count > 0 THEN
   CALL Average (total_count, total_sum, total_mean)
   PRINT "class totals", total_count, total_mean
END IF

END

                                  ! External subroutine to compute an
                                  ! arithmetic average or mean. A count
                                  ! and a sum are passed to the subroutine,
                                  ! which returns the computed average.

SUB Average (count, sum, mean)
   LET mean = sum / count
END SUB
```

Fig. 5.24, *continued.*

Fig. 5.25: *A subroutine is referenced through a CALL statement.*

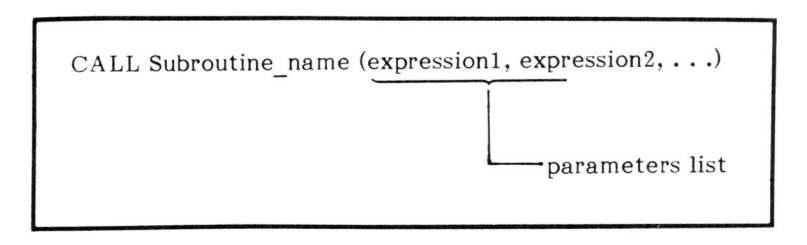

```
CALL Subroutine_name (expression1, expression2, ...)
                                   └──── parameters list
```

                CALL Average (cs_count, cs_sum, cs_mean)

                SUB Average (count, sum, mean)

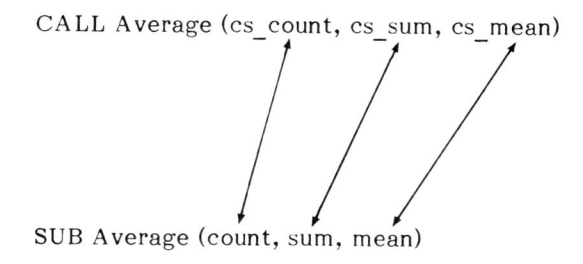

Fig. 5.26: *When a CALL statement is executed, its parameters are matched with the subroutine's parameters. The parameter values are not copied, however. Instead, the main program and the subroutine share the same data.*

label attached to the same space. Variables **cs_count** and **count** refer to the same memory location and, hence, to the same value. The main program and the subroutine share the memory location. The same rule holds for the other variables: **cs_sum** and **sum** and **cs_mean** and **mean** are simply different names for the same memory locations.

The main program placed a value in **cs_sum**. The subroutine manipulates that value, calling it **sum**. The subroutine computes an average and stores it in the memory location it calls **mean**. When the main program regains control, it picks up the value the subroutine stored by referring to variable **cs_mean**. The parameters are not copied. Instead, the two program units share the same data.

When the main program executes the first **CALL** statement, **cs_count**, **cs_sum**, and **cs_mean** are made available to the subroutine. Control is transferred to **Average**. The subroutine computes the average and stores it in the location the main program calls **cs_mean**. Now, control returns to the main program.

A few instructions later, a second **CALL** is executed. This time, values of **dp_count**, **dp_sum**, and **dp_mean** are made available to **Average**. The subroutine gets control. This time, however, its variable **sum** refers to the memory location the main program calls **dp_sum**, and not to location **cs_sum**. Consequently, the subroutine accesses different data, storing **mean** in the location the main program calls **dp_mean**. Do you see how the same subroutine can be used over and over again with different sets of data?

One final point before we move on. Note that **Average** is an external subroutine--it comes after the **END**. With external functions we needed a **DECLARE** statement. It is not necessary to declare subroutines because they are referenced through **CALL** statements. If a name appears in a **CALL** statement, it must be a subroutine name.

MODULAR PROGRAMMING

In the example we just completed, defining a subroutine saved us the trouble of coding the same instructions four times. While that's a valid reason for using subroutines, it isn't the most important one.

As a beginner, you are, quite reasonably, starting with relatively simple programs. As your skill increases, you are going to want to tackle more difficult assignments. The secret to writing a large program is to break the task into a series of small steps and then attack them one by one. The most effective way to accomplish that objective is to use subroutines, writing one for each independent module. It's an approach used by professional programmers, and it makes a great deal of sense. We'll study this modular programming concept in Chapter 6.

SUMMARY

Some computations are common to a variety of applications. Occasionally, a set of logic is repeated several times in the same program. More generally, when a program becomes lengthy and complex, it makes sense to break it into smaller modules. Functions and subroutines allow the programmer to solve all three problems.

True BASIC has built-in functions to perform common mathematical and trigonometric computations. Other built-in functions will be explained in later chapters. We used a square root problem to illustrate the use of one built-in function: **Sqr**.

Next we turned to writing internal functions. We started with a guessing game problem and developed a function to select a random number between 1 and 10. We introduced the **DEF** and **END DEF** statements, and defined the rules for selecting a function's name. We used the built-in functions **Rnd** and **Int** to solve this problem, and introduced the **RANDOMIZE** statement.

Internal functions are part of the main program. They are not independent, sharing all their variables with the mainline (global data). This can cause problems. Often, a better choice is to define the function after the **END** statement, making it an external function. External functions are independent, with their own local data. Data independence means that a function can be viewed as a black box.

To illustrate an external function, we introduced a problem to compute a number of combinations. The formula called for several factorials. Since the same computation occurred a number of times, it made sense to develop a function. We explained how parameters are copied to the function, and how the function returns a single value to the main program. We also showed how an **INCLUDE** command can be used to add a previously saved function or subroutine to a program.

Functions are fine for relatively simple computations using a few parameters and returning a single value. Subroutines are better for more complex computations calling for more parameters, or when more than a single result is required. Functions are used much like variables, and are fine for returning intermediate values as part of a larger computation. Subroutines are a better choice for returning final, ready to be output values.

In a subroutine, parameters are passed by reference. We used an example, computing a set of averages by major, to illustrate subroutines. After analyzing the problem and developing a solution, we turned to the average subroutine and planned it. A subroutine is defined by a **SUB** statement; it ends with an **END SUB** statement. In the main program, a **CALL** statement is used to reference the subroutine. We used a **CALL** statement and the subroutine **Average** to illustrate how parameters are passed.

In the next chapter, we'll consider how functions and subroutines can be used to break a large, complex program into smaller, easier to write modules.

REFERENCES

True BASIC Statements

DEF, END DEF	Fig. 5.8, page 125
RANDOMIZE	Fig. 5.11, page 127
DECLARE	Fig. 5.18, page 135
SUB, END SUB	Fig. 5.22, page 141
CALL	Fig. 5.25, page 144

True BASIC Commands

INCLUDE file_name	Fig. 5.10, page 127

Other References

Built-in functions	Appendix II

EXERCISES

1. In Chapter 2, we indicated that one of the exercises at the end of Chapter 5 would tell you how to find the largest and smallest numbers supported on your computer. The built-in function **Maxnum** returns the largest number, while **Eps(0)** returns the smallest value. Using these two functions, write a short program to find and display the largest and smallest numbers supported on your computer.

2. In the last chapter, Exercise 13 asked you to generate a loan repayment table. Using the **Round** built-in function to round all values to the nearest cent, modify the program.

3. In earlier chapters, we raised a number to the 1/2 power in order to compute its square root. Modify the program of Fig. 5.4 to generate three outputs for each table entry: the number, its square root as estimated by the **Sqr** function, and its square root as estimated by raising it to the 1/2 (or 0.5) power. Compare the results. If they differ, which one is more accurate?

4. Write a program to generate a table of the sines and cosines of the angles ranging from 1 to 2π radians in increments of 0.5 radians.

5. Write a program to generate a table of the sines and cosines of the angles ranging from 10 to 360 degrees in 10 degree increments. Hint: use an **OPTION ANGLE DEGREES** statement.

6. Write a program to display the current date and time.

7. Use the **Rnd** function to simulate rolling a die. The key is to generate random numbers between 1 and 6. Write a loop to generate and print ten such numbers. Try running the program both with and without a **RANDOMIZE** statement, and note the difference.

8. Write a module to select a single card from a deck of 52. A good approach is to identify the suit by using **Rnd** to select a random number between 1 and 4, and then to select another random number between 1 and 13 to identify the card.

9. Earlier, we used a factorial function to compute a number of combinations *(Fig. 5.17)*. The formula for computing a related statistic, the number of permutations, is

$$\frac{n!}{(n-r)!}$$

Add a permutations computation to the program.

10. In the card game "high/low" or "acey/ducey," a player is dealt two cards. The player then bets on whether a third card will lie between the first two. Write an external function to select a card at random. Suits don't count in this game, so just generate a random number between 1 (ace) and 13 (king). Display the two cards (by number). Allow the player to place a bet; a bet amount of 0.00 is no bet. If the player bets, use the

function to select a third card. If it lies between the first two, the player wins; if not, the player loses. Note that ties (two 8s, for example) lose. Winning players collect twice their bet; losing players collect nothing.

11. Write a program to generate electric bills using one of the following rate structures:

Code	Rate is	plus	or each kilowatt hour over
1	$20.00	$0.055	0
	$22.75	$0.050	50
	$25.25	$0.045	150
	$29.75	$0.040	250
2	$25.25	$0.040	150
	$29.25	$0.035	250
	$38.00	$0.030	500
3	$50.00	$0.025	1000
	$150.00	$0.020	5000
	$230.00	$0.018	10000

   Rate code 1 is available to anyone. Code 2 is for total electric homes, while code 3 is for large industrial users. Write a program to input a rate code and the number of kilowatt hours used, and generate the customer's bill. Write subroutines or functions for each of the rate structures.

12. Write a subroutine to simulate rolling a set of dice. Return the individual die values and their sum. Write a main program to call this subroutine and display all three parameters.

13. Chapter 4, Exercise 12, asked you to write a program to compute a grade point average using your school's rules. Write a subroutine to compute a grade point average. Write a simple main program to call the subroutine and display the grade point average.

14. Three sailors are lost on a desert island. During their first day on shore, they work to collect coconuts. As it grows dark, they agree to divide the coconuts into three equal piles in the morning. Not really trusting his friends, one sailor wakes up early, sneaks over to the coconuts, and divides them into three equal piles. One coconut is left over, so he gives it to a monkey, hides his pile, and pushes the remaining two piles back into one.

A bit later a second sailor arises and does the same thing, dividing the remaining coconuts into three equal piles and hiding his share. Again he has one left over. He gives it to the monkey, and mixes the remaining two piles back into one.

Finally, the third sailor wakes up and repeats the process. Once again, the remaining pile is divided into three. One left-over coconut is given to the monkey. One pile is hidden. The remaining two are mixed back together.

How many coconuts were in the original pile? (There are several correct answers.) Hint: use the **Remainder** built-in function.

15. In a common experiment, a mouse is dropped into a maze and allowed to wander at will until, hopefully, it finds the exit and earns a reward. Performance is measured by observing the number of moves or the elapsed time between a given mouse's entrance and exit. A consistent improvement in performance is taken as evidence of learning.

    A major problem in designing such experiments is setting standards. An untrained mouse could be expected to escape the maze simply by wandering at random until it stumbled across the exit. How long would this take? Given a chance success to use as a base, a set of performance standards can be established.

    Of course, a standard can be set by turning thousands of mice loose, one by one, in the maze. Their average performance could then be used to design the experiment. Unfortunately, this approach is time-consuming and very expensive. A better technique is to use the computer to simulate a mouse's moves.

    View the maze as a simple 5x5 matrix--almost a small checkerboard. Define one position (3 across, 1 up, for example) as the entrance, and another (perhaps 5 across and 4 up) as the exit. Drop the mouse into the entrance. Assume that the animal has no reason to prefer one direction over another; in other words, assume that it will wander at random. Use the **Rnd** function (inside an external function that you write) to select random numbers between 1 and 4, and use the random number it returns to select a direction--up, down, left, right. Compute the mouse's new position by adding to or subtracting from the old horizontal or vertical position; remember that the mouse cannot move beyond the edge of the maze. If the mouse should accidentally stumble on the block you have designated as the exit, it's out. Count the number of moves the mouse needs to escape. Do that for thousands of simulated mice, and you have a benchmark. If a mouse stumbling at random can escape in "n" moves, a smart mouse should be able to do considerably better.

    For this experiment, run 25 simulated mice through the maze. Compute the average number of moves required. Note that some mice might conceivably never escape; you may want to limit each mouse to perhaps 100 moves.

6

Modular Program Design

KEY IDEAS

1. *The basic building blocks.*
2. *Complex programs.*
3. *Large programs.*
    a. *Modularization.*
    b. *Documentation.*
4. *Planning a large program.*
    a. *The skeleton program.*
    b. *Adding modules.*
5. *Functional decomposition.*

THE BASIC BUILDING BLOCKS

Sequence, decision, and repetition are the basic building blocks of any computer program. No matter how complex a program might be, its logic still consists of combinations of these three elementary structures. Subroutines and functions allow the programmer to group portions of the code, but even they are constructed from sequence, decision, and repetitive blocks. If you can use the basic building blocks, you can write a program.

Not that developing a large or complex program is easy! We learned in Chapters 2 through 5 that, within an elementary logical block, the right instructions must be combined in the right order. Within a large or more complex program, the right elementary *blocks* must be combined in the right order. In this chapter, we'll consider how to combine the basic building blocks to form a program. Our approach might be termed "divide and conquer." The basic idea is to break a large problem into a series of small problems, and then attack them one by one.

COMPLEX PROGRAMS

Perhaps the best way to grasp this divide and conquer idea is through an example. Let's develop a program to simulate playing a game of dice, or craps *(Fig. 6.1)*. The rules are somewhat complex. A player throws a set of dice. If the sum of the dice is 7 or 11, he wins. A 2, 3, or 12 loses. If anything else (4, 5, 6, 8, 9, 10) is rolled, that first roll becomes the "point." The player rolls again. If the "point" comes up, he wins; if a 7 comes up, he loses. If the dice show anything else, he rolls yet again, and he keeps on rolling until he gets either the "point" or a 7. Those rules represent our algorithm. Let's analyze them.

Start with the first roll of the dice. Three outcomes are possible *(Fig. 6.2)*. If the first roll is 7 or 11, the player wins; if the first roll is 2, 3, or 12, he loses. Those two outcomes are quite clear. The complexity arises with the third possible outcome. Let's study it in more detail. Figure 6.3 shows the logical flow if the first roll is 4, 5, 6, 8, 9, or 10. Note the repetitive nature of the process. The player will continue to roll the dice until either the "point" or a 7 appears.

Note what we've done. Faced with a relatively complex problem, we broke it into three simple ones. We then studied the smaller problems one by one, developing partial solutions. Now we're ready to combine our partial solutions *(Fig. 6.4)*.

Fig. 6.1: *A block diagram definition for a program to simulate a game of craps.*

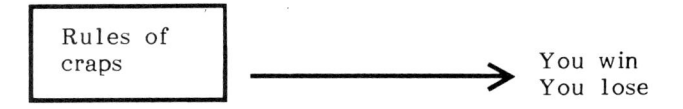

```
                    ┌──────────────┐
                    │  First roll  │
                    └──────┬───────┘
              ┌────────────┼────────────┐
      ┌───────┴──┐  ┌──────┴──┐  ┌──────┴──────┐
      │  7, 11   │  │ 2, 3, 12│  │ Anything else.│
      │  wins    │  │ loses   │  │ Roll again    │
      │          │  │         │  │ until 7 or    │
      │          │  │         │  │ point.        │
      └──────────┘  └─────────┘  └───────────────┘
```

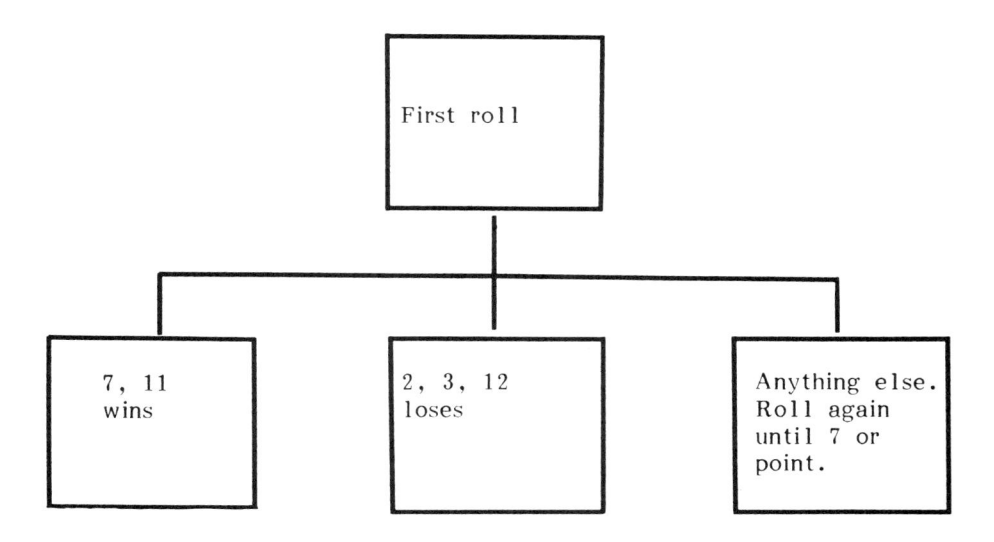

Fig. 6.2: *Based on the results of the first roll, three possible outcomes can be identified.*

We have a plan for writing a program. Look at the flowchart. The block marked "roll dice" appears twice. It might make sense to write a function or a subroutine to simulate rolling the dice. We'll use a subroutine *(Fig. 6.5)*.

The key to the program is selecting one of the three primary outcomes. We'll use a **SELECT CASE** structure to code it. If the first roll is 4, 5, 6, 8, 9, or 10, the logic calls for a repetitive structure. A **DO UNTIL** loop seems a reasonable choice. Given these decisions, we can write the program *(Fig. 6.6)*.

Read the code carefully. It represents a clear, concise statement of the rules of craps. (In fact, you may find it easier to follow than the English version we started with.) Recall how we developed the program. We started by dividing the problem into smaller problems. Then we solved the smaller problems and combined the partial solutions. Studying the resulting flowchart, we identified logical patterns and, based on our experience with the elementary building blocks, decided how to code them. Finally, we wrote the program.

LARGE PROGRAMS

Although complex, the craps program was relatively brief. How does a programmer develop a really large program? Even the biggest program can ultimately be broken into individual sequence, decision, and repetitive blocks, but the problem is the sheer number of such blocks. Large programs create special problems requiring special solutions.

For example, consider keeping track of a program's variables. A small program might contain half a dozen, and that's no problem at all. Large programs, however,

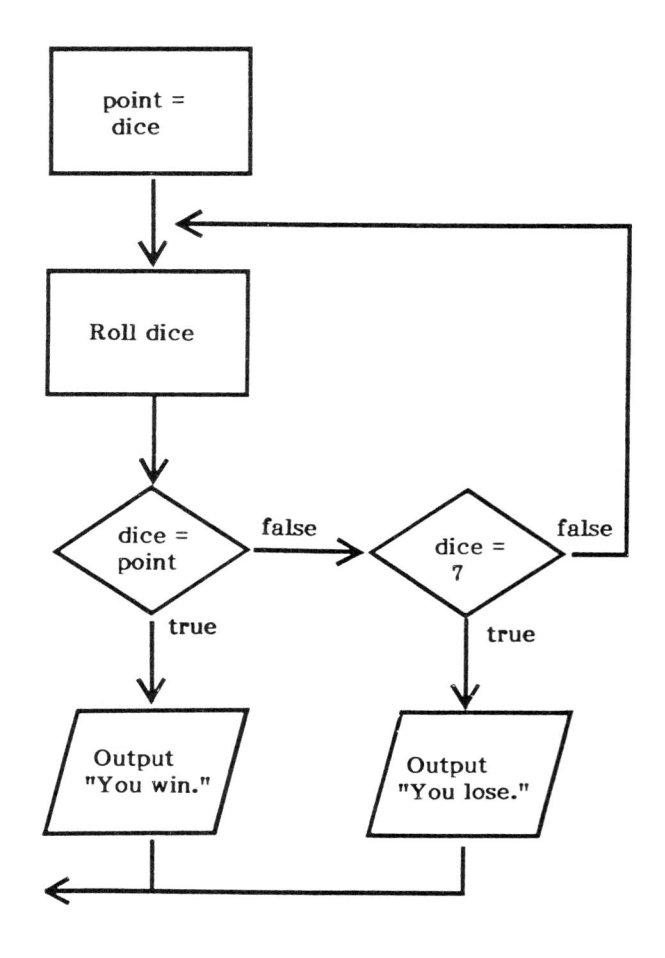

Fig. 6.3: *The rules become complicated when the first roll of the dice yields something other than 7, 11 or 2, 3, 12. Thus the next step is to focus on that third outcome.*

might contain hundreds, even thousands. Human beings have trouble keeping track of large numbers of variables. Studies have consistently shown that the average person can manipulate about seven; problems calling for more almost inevitably lead to confusion and error.

Another problem with a large program is that it's often difficult to follow the logical flow. A small program might fit on a single screen or a single sheet of paper. On the other hand, a large program might cover hundreds of screens or hundreds of sheets of paper, and it's easy to lose your way as you work through

Fig. 6.4: *A flowchart for the craps program.*

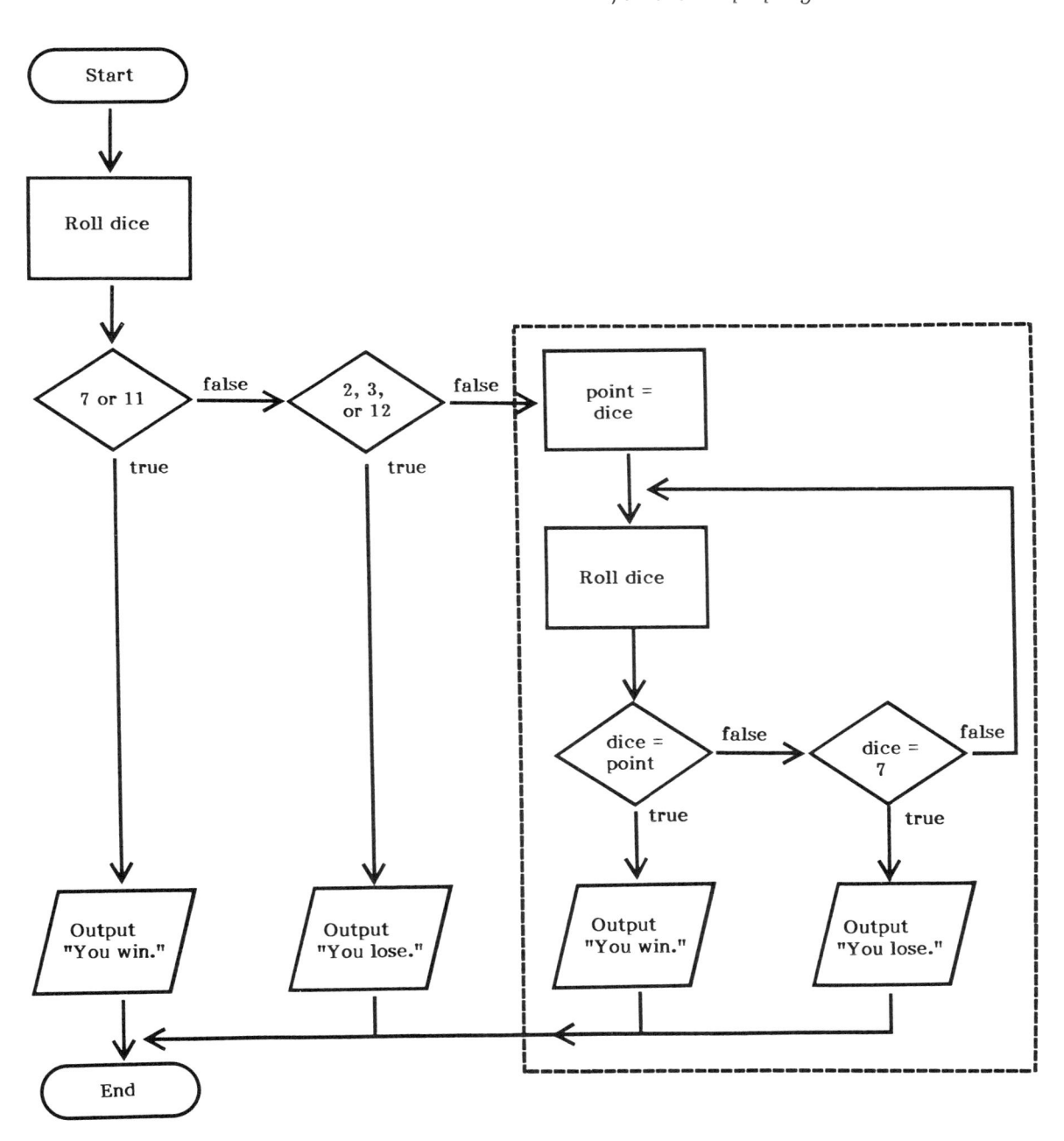

```
! Subroutine to simulate rolling a pair
! of dice. No parameters are passed to
! the subroutine. The subroutine returns
! the values of both die and their sum.

SUB Roll_dice (die1, die2, dice)

    LET die1 = Int(Rnd * 6 + 1)
    LET die2 = Int(Rnd * 6 + 1)
    LET dice = die1 + die2

END SUB
```

```
True BASIC here.
Version 1.0
Copyright (c) 1985 by True BASIC, Inc.
Published by Addison-Wesley Publishing Company, Inc.
Ok. old rolldice
Ok. _
```

Fig. 6.5: *A subroutine to roll a pair of dice.*

all that logic. Tracking logical or repetitive structures is particularly difficult, especially if the individual logical blocks are themselves lengthy. This complexity can lead to significant problems in program debug and maintenance.

Very large programs are often written by programmer teams. How is the work divided? How can the partial programs written by different people be integrated to form a single program? Anytime two or more people are involved, communication difficulties are certain to arise. Two programmers may use the same variable names for quite different values. They may interpret a portion of a plan quite differently, thus generating incompatible code. Any time a team is asked to attack a problem, careful planning and communication are essential.

Modularization: Divide and Conquer

Once again, the solution is: divide and conquer. The objective is to break the big problem into a series of smaller ones. Smaller problems involve fewer variables and less logic. Such small modules are relatively easy to code, debug, and maintain.

Mechanically, the easiest way to combine a series of small modules to form a single large program is to write each module as a subroutine or a function. Subroutines and functions differ from regular code; their instructions are executed only when they are called or referenced. Thus we need a control structure to link them.

```
                          ! Program to simulate a game of craps.

RANDOMIZE                 ! Without the RANDOMIZE statement, the Rnd
                          ! function will return the same series of
                          ! values each time the program is run.

                          ! The game begins with a roll of the dice.

  Call Roll_dice (die1, die2, dice)

  PRINT dice              ! The value of the first roll is printed.
                          ! This first roll now becomes the basis
                          ! for deciding if the player has won or
                          ! lost, or must roll again.

  SELECT CASE dice
    CASE 7, 11            ! If the dice read 7 or 11, player wins.
      PRINT "You win!"

    CASE 2, 3, 12         ! If the dice read 2, 3, or 12, the
      PRINT "You lose."   ! player loses.

    CASE else             ! If the dice read anything else, that
      LET point = dice    ! value is the "point." The player rolls
                          ! again, and continues to roll until
                          ! either a 7 or the "point" comes up.
      DO
        CALL Roll_dice (die1, die2, dice)
        PRINT dice
      LOOP UNTIL (dice = 7) OR (dice = point)

                          ! If a 7 comes up first, the player loses.
                          ! If the "point" comes up first, the
                          ! player wins.

      IF dice = point THEN
        PRINT "You win!"
      ELSE
        PRINT "You lose."
      END IF

  END SELECT

END
```

Fig. 6.6: *A program to simulate a game of craps. The "dice" subroutine (Fig. 6.5) comes after the **END** statement.*

Figure 6.7 illustrates just such a control structure. Note that the program begins with several internal subroutines. Internal subroutines, remember, must be defined before they are referenced. Following the main program's **END** statement are several external subroutines. Focus on the mainline (it's shaded). It consists of a loop; the mainline will repeat until a terminal condition occurs. Inside the loop are several **CALL** statements. The mainline is a control module. It does no actual work. The detailed computations are performed in the subroutines. The mainline controls the order in which the subroutines are called.

This control structure/subroutine approach is strongly recommended for developing large programs. Essentially, it allows the programmer to focus on one subroutine at a time, thus minimizing both the number of variables to be manipulated and the amount of logic to be understood. As a result, coding, debugging, and maintaining the program are greatly simplified. Also, if a programmer team is involved, subroutines suggest an obvious division of the work.

Documenting Large Programs

We're about to consider an example of modular program development. Before we do, however, we should briefly describe the special documentation needs of a large program. To this point, we haven't paid a great deal of attention to documentation, because the small programs of Chapters 1 through 5 were "personal" programs, written and used by the same individual. Large programs require substantial documentation.

As we planned our programs, we developed block diagrams and flowcharts for each one. A large program might require a block diagram and a separate flowchart for each of its modules. However, block diagrams and flowcharts are as much planning tools as documentation tools. By themselves, they aren't enough.

The key to program documentation is often the code itself. Start with clear, meaningful variable names. Use the standard structures: sequence, decision, and repetition. Modularize, breaking the logic into small, cohesive, independent units. Aim at writing clear, easy-to-follow code; avoid shortcuts and tricky logic. A well written program is almost self documenting.

The other key is to comment heavily. Precede each module with a documentation section. Use comments to name the module, identify its programmer, and indicate the date it was written. Dating a module is essential if the programmer is to be certain that the very latest version is used in the program.

Additional comments should clearly identify the input, output, and local variables. The module's function should be explained in English. If appropriate, additional comments might show the algorithm, or at least identify its source. The idea is to clearly explain what the module does. The code will show how the module does it.

Our standard will be to precede each program module with a detailed set of comments. We'll use **REM** statements to identify these pre-module comments, and asterisks (*) to highlight them visually. Within a module, we'll continue to

```
┌─────────────────────────────────────────┐
│ First_internal_subroutine (. . .)       │
│                                         │
└─────────────────────────────────────────┘

┌─────────────────────────────────────────┐
│ Second_internal_subroutine (. . .)      │
│                                         │
└─────────────────────────────────────────┘


┌─────────────────────────────────────────┐
│ DO                                      │
│     CALL First_internal_subroutine (. . .)   │
│     CALL First_external_subroutine (. . .)   │
│     CALL Second_internal_subroutine (. . .)  │
│     CALL Second_external_subroutine (. . .)  │
│         .                               │
│         .                               │
│         .                               │
│ UNTIL exit_condition                    │
│ END                                     │
└─────────────────────────────────────────┘

                                  } Program mainline

┌─────────────────────────────────────────┐
│ First_external_subroutine (. . .)       │
└─────────────────────────────────────────┘

┌─────────────────────────────────────────┐
│ Second_external_subroutine (. . .)      │
└─────────────────────────────────────────┘
```

Fig. 6.7: *A typical control structure. The program's mainline calls a series of internal and/or external subroutines in order.*

use exclamation points to identify comments. You'll see numerous examples throughout the remainder of this chapter.

PLANNING A LARGE PROGRAM

High-level Planning

Everyone who has ever worked knows how to compute payroll *(Fig. 6.8)*. On the surface, the problem is simple. Complications arise when we begin to analyze the various algorithms. Consider, for example, gross pay. The basic rule is to multiply hours worked by an hourly pay rate. Hours over forty may be paid at a special overtime rate, however. Sunday and holiday hours may be paid at double time. A shift premium may be paid to second and third shift workers. Occasionally, bonuses reward outstanding performance. Even after listing all these extras, we've just begun to scratch the surface. Some people are paid a salary. Others earn a commission. In some cases, the hourly rate is based on how well an employee performs relative to some standard. Occasionally, an employee will work on different tasks paying different hourly wages. A programmer could easily write hundreds of lines of code just to implement the gross pay "algorithm."

Next, consider federal income tax. The key to computing federal income tax is taxable income. Taxable income is computed by subtracting twenty dollars from gross pay for each dependent (spouse, child) claimed. The number of dependents must come from somewhere; we've identified an input variable. Given taxable income, the amount of tax is computed from one of two tables, one for single and the other for married taxpayers. We need a way to distinguish single and married people. That calls for yet another input variable.

Look at gross pay, federal tax, local tax, or any of the algorithms. Planning a solution and writing the necessary instructions for any one of them is at least as complex as planning and writing any of the problems we considered in Chapters

Fig. 6.8: *A block diagram definition of the payroll problem.*

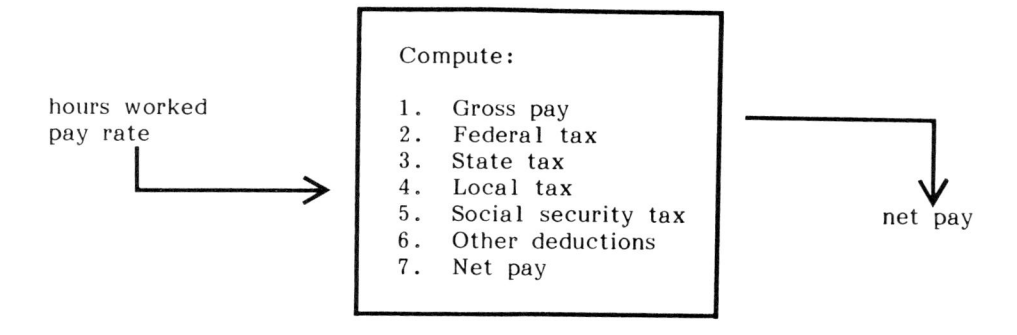

```
                              ┌─────────────────────────────┐
                              │  Compute:                   │
         hours worked         │  1.  Gross pay              │
         pay rate             │  2.  Federal tax            │
         ─────────────▶       │  3.  State tax              │──────┐
                              │  4.  Local tax              │      │
                              │  5.  Social security tax    │      ▼
                              │  6.  Other deductions       │    net pay
                              │  7.  Net pay                │
                              └─────────────────────────────┘
```

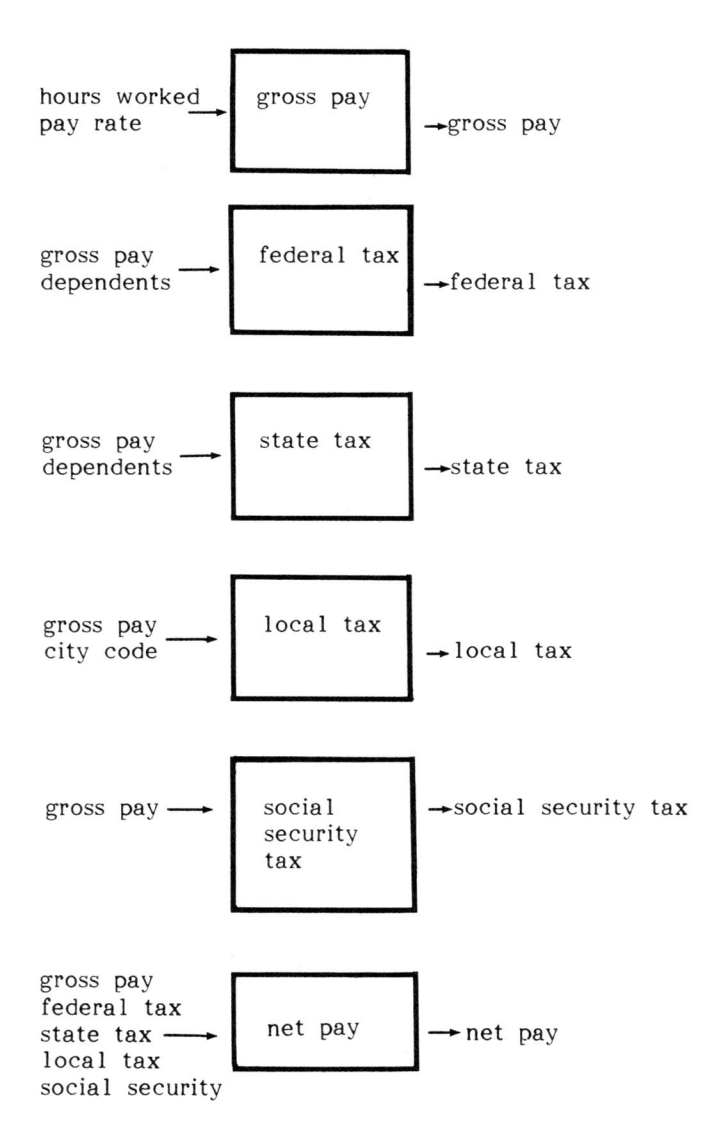

```
hours worked ──→ ┌─────────┐
pay rate         │gross pay│ ──→ gross pay
                 └─────────┘

gross pay    ──→ ┌──────────┐
dependents       │federal tax│ ──→ federal tax
                 └──────────┘

gross pay    ──→ ┌─────────┐
dependents       │state tax│ ──→ state tax
                 └─────────┘

gross pay    ──→ ┌─────────┐
city code        │local tax│ ──→ local tax
                 └─────────┘

gross pay    ──→ ┌────────┐
                 │social  │
                 │security│ ──→ social security tax
                 │tax     │
                 └────────┘

gross pay
federal tax
state tax    ──→ ┌───────┐
local tax        │net pay│ ──→ net pay
social security  └───────┘
```

Fig. 6.9: *Each of the payroll problem's algorithms can be represented as a block diagram.*

1 through 5. Combining the logic for all the algorithms will yield a very large, complex program. We can't just sit down and write it. Careful planning is essential.

The objective is to divide the problem into a series of relatively small modules. The individual algorithms represent a reasonable starting point. Let's describe each one as a black box *(Fig. 6.9)*. Focus on the data, not on the algorithms themselves. At this stage, we have not yet considered how a particular algorithm might be implemented.

Look carefully at those algorithm descriptions. Flowing into and out from the black boxes are several variables. They are the parameters, and are, for the most part, global. Let's compile a list of the global variables *(Fig. 6.10)*. The block diagrams yield additional information, too. We can determine their rough order by looking at them. Clearly, since several require the input of gross pay, computing gross pay must be one of the program's first steps. Since net pay is the desired final output, computing it will come near the program's end. Sequencing the algorithms allows us to define a preliminary control structure. We can illustrate the control structure by drawing a hierarchy chart *(Fig. 6.11)*.

The hierarchy chart shows the relationships between the program's major modules. Our plan is to implement each module as a subroutine. Look at the control structure. On top is the main control module, **Payroll**. Its function is to call or invoke the lower level modules in the proper order. For example, its first step will be to call the data input module. In turn, this module will get the input data and return them to the main control module. Next, **Payroll** will call the gross pay module, passing it necessary parameters. The gross pay module will return a value for gross pay. Subsequently, the modules computing federal tax, state tax, local tax, and net pay will be called. Finally, the results will be output by yet another module.

The Skeleton Program

A good way to visualize the control structure is to follow the logical flow through a preliminary, skeleton version of the program *(Fig. 6.12)*. The listing begins with a set of remarks describing the program's overall function. Next come internal subroutines to get input data and compute net pay. Because they are internal, they must be defined before they are called. The program's mainline comes next (it's shaded). The mainline is a repetitive structure (a **DO UNTIL** loop) containing a series of **CALL** statements. External subroutines to compute gross pay, federal

Fig. 6.10: *From the high-level algorithm descriptions, we can compile a list of global variables.*

Input variables	Output variables
hours_worked	gross_pay
pay_rate	federal_tax
shift_code	state_tax
dependents	local_tax
filing_status	social_security_tax
city_code	net_pay

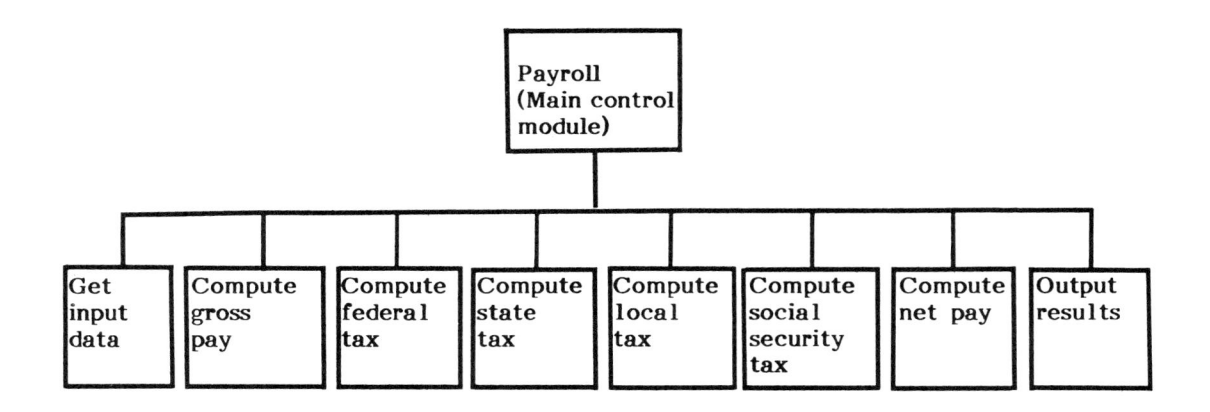

Fig. 6.11: *Using the block diagram algorithms and taking into account the order in which they must be evaluated, we can develop a preliminary control structure for a payroll program. The control structure can be graphically represented by drawing a hierarchy chart.*

tax, state tax, and local tax follow the mainline's **END** statement.

The subroutines are written at a "stub" level. They don't do much. For example, the data input subroutine contains only two **INPUT** statements. **Compute_gross_pay** is composed of a single **LET** statement. The program is, however, logically complete. We can run it. By running it, we can test the control structure.

The skeleton program is the first step in writing the payroll program. The subroutines or stubs are clearly incomplete, with simple computations replacing the more complex logic we know will be required. We have, however, created a control structure. Each of the program's major tasks--compute gross pay, compute federal tax, and so on--is implemented as a subroutine. The parameters are in place. How the gross pay subroutine computes gross pay is of no concern to any other module. Given this control structure, we can attack the individual modules one at a time.

Before we move on, note the detailed documentation shown in Fig. 6.12. Is there any question what each module does?

Planning a Module's Logic

How do we go about planning a module's logic? The same way we've been planning a *program's* logic. We have a block diagram and an algorithm for each module. We'll select a function, analyze the algorithm, and break it into logical steps. Finally, we'll write the instructions and replace the stub-level subroutine with the new version.

```
REM ************************************************************************
REM * PROGRAM NAME: Payroll                                                *
REM * WRITTEN BY:   W.S. Davis            DATE: July 26, 1985              *
REM *                                                                      *
REM * This program computes an individual's net pay (take-home pay).       *
REM * Following data input, gross pay is computed. Given gross pay,        *
REM * federal, state, local, and social security taxes are computed.       *
REM * Finally, the various taxes are subtracted from gross pay to get      *
REM * net pay, and the results are output. The program's mainline          *
REM * repeats until there are no more input data.                          *
REM *                                                                      *
REM *                       GLOBAL DATA                                    *
REM *                                                                      *
REM *      INPUT VARIABLES              OUTPUT VARIABLES                   *
REM *        hours_worked                 gross_pay                        *
REM *        pay_rate                     federal_tax                      *
REM *        shift_code                   state_tax                        *
REM *        dependents                   local_tax                        *
REM *        filing_status                social_security_tax              *
REM *        city_code                    net_pay                          *
REM *                                                                      *
REM *      OTHER GLOBAL VARIABLES                                          *
REM *        deductions                                                    *
REM *                                                                      *
REM * The program begins with three internal subroutines:                  *
REM *                                                                      *
REM *      Get_input_data                                                  *
REM *      Compute_net_pay                                                 *
REM *      Output_payroll                                                  *
REM *                                                                      *
REM * The program's mainline follows the internal subroutines. After       *
REM * the mainline are five external subroutines:                          *
REM *                                                                      *
REM *      Compute_gross_pay                                               *
REM *      Compute_federal_tax                                             *
REM *      Compute_state_tax                                               *
REM *      Compute_local_tax                                               *
REM *      Compute_social_security                                         *
REM *                                                                      *
REM ************************************************************************
```

Fig. 6.12: *A skeleton version of the payroll program. Note how each function has its own subroutine. Note how the mainline controls access to the subroutines.*

```
REM       ***************************************************************
REM       * MODULE:    Get_input_data                                   *
REM       * WRITTEN BY: W.S. Davis          DATE: July 26, 1985         *
REM       *                                                             *
REM       * This internal subroutine inputs and verifies all data.      *
REM       * All variables are global; hence no parameters are           *
REM       * listed in the subroutine definition or in the CALL          *
REM       * statement. This module gets values for:                     *
REM       *    hours_worked           pay_rate                          *
REM       *    shift_code             dependents                        *
REM       *    filing_status          city_code                         *
REM       *                                                             *
REM       ***************************************************************

   SUB Get_input_data
      INPUT hours_worked, pay_rate, shift_code, dependents
      INPUT filing_status, city_code
   END SUB

REM       ***************************************************************
REM       * MODULE:    Compute_net_pay                                  *
REM       * WRITTEN BY: W.S. Davis          DATE: July 26, 1985         *
REM       *                                                             *
REM       * This internal subroutine computes net pay. All              *
REM       * parameters are global; thus none are listed in the          *
REM       * subroutine definition or in the CALL statement.             *
REM       *                                                             *
REM       *  INPUT PARAMETERS    OUTPUT PARAMETERS    LOCAL DATA        *
REM       *  gross_pay           net_pay              deductions        *
REM       *  federal_tax                                                *
REM       *  state_tax                                                  *
REM       *  local_tax                                                  *
REM       *  social_security_tax                                        *
REM       *                                                             *
REM       ***************************************************************

   SUB Compute_net_pay
      LET deductions = federal_tax + state_tax + local_tax
      LET deductions = deductions + social_security_tax
      LET net_pay = gross_pay - deductions
   END SUB
```

Fig. 6.12, *continued.*

```
REM         ****************************************************************
REM         * MODULE:    Output_payroll                                    *
REM         * WRITTEN BY: W.S. Davis            DATE: July 26, 1985        *
REM         *                                                              *
REM         * This internal subroutine outputs the results of the          *
REM         * various payroll computations. All parameters are             *
REM         * global; thus none are listed in the subroutine               *
REM         * definition or in the CALL statement.                         *
REM         *                                                              *
REM         *   INPUT PARAMETERS          OUTPUT PARAMETERS                *
REM         *    gross_pay                 all input parameters            *
REM         *    federal_tax                                               *
REM         *    state_tax                                                 *
REM         *    local_tax                                                 *
REM         *    social_security_tax                                       *
REM         *    net_pay                                                   *
REM         *                                                              *
REM         ****************************************************************
   SUB Output_payroll
      PRINT gross_pay, federal_tax, state_tax
      PRINT local_tax, social_security_tax, net_pay
   END SUB

REM ********************************************************************
REM *                                                                  *
REM * The program's mainline begins here. The main control module is a *
REM * DO loop repeated until no more input data remain. The sentinel   *
REM * value identifying the end-of-data condition is a negative hours  *
REM * worked. Assuming valid data, the mainline calls the various      *
REM * detailed subroutines in order.                                   *
REM *                                                                  *
REM ********************************************************************
DO

   CALL Get_input_data

   IF hours_worked >= 0 THEN
      CALL Compute_gross_pay (hours_worked,pay_rate,shift_code,gross_pay)
      CALL Compute_federal_tax (gross_pay,dependents,filing_status,federal_tax)
      CALL Compute_state_tax (gross_pay, dependents, state_tax)
      CALL Compute_local_tax (gross_pay, city_code, local_tax)
      CALL Compute_social_security (gross_pay, social_security_tax)
      CALL Compute_net_pay
      CALL Output_payroll
   END IF

LOOP UNTIL hours_worked < 0

END
```

Fig. 6.12, *continued.*

```
REM   **************************************************************
REM   * MODULE:     Compute_gross_pay                              *
REM   * WRITTEN BY: W.S. Davis          DATE: July 26, 1985        *
REM   *                                                            *
REM   * This external subroutine computes gross pay.               *
REM   *                                                            *
REM   *  INPUT PARAMETERS    OUTPUT PARAMETERS    LOCAL DATA       *
REM   *   hours_worked        gross_pay                            *
REM   *   pay_rate                                                 *
REM   *   shift_code                                               *
REM   *                                                            *
REM   **************************************************************
   SUB Compute_gross_pay (hours_worked, pay_rate, shift_code, gross_pay)
      LET gross_pay = hours_worked * pay_rate
   END SUB

REM   **************************************************************
REM   * MODULE:     Compute_federal_tax                            *
REM   * WRITTEN BY: W.S. Davis          DATE: July 26, 1985        *
REM   *                                                            *
REM   * This external subroutine computes federal income tax.      *
REM   *                                                            *
REM   *  INPUT PARAMETERS    OUTPUT PARAMETERS    LOCAL DATA       *
REM   *   gross_pay           federal_tax                          *
REM   *   dependents                                               *
REM   *   filing_status                                            *
REM   *                                                            *
REM   **************************************************************
   SUB Compute_federal_tax (gross_pay,dependents,filing_status,federal_tax)
         LET federal_tax = 0.10 * gross_pay
   END SUB

REM   **************************************************************
REM   * MODULE:     Compute_state_tax                              *
REM   * WRITTEN BY: W.S. Davis          DATE: July 26, 1985        *
REM   *                                                            *
REM   * This external subroutine computes state income tax.        *
REM   *                                                            *
REM   *  INPUT PARAMETERS    OUTPUT PARAMETERS    LOCAL DATA       *
REM   *   gross_pay           state_tax                            *
REM   *   dependents                                               *
REM   *                                                            *
REM   **************************************************************
   SUB Compute_state_tax (gross_pay, dependents, state_tax)
      LET state_tax = 0.03 * gross_pay
   END SUB
```

Fig. 6.12, *continued.*

```
REM      **************************************************************
REM      * MODULE:     Compute_local_tax                               *
REM      * WRITTEN BY: W.S. Davis            DATE: July 26, 1985       *
REM      *                                                             *
REM      * This external subroutine computes local income tax.         *
REM      *                                                             *
REM      *  INPUT PARAMETERS    OUTPUT PARAMETERS     LOCAL DATA       *
REM      *   gross_pay           local_tax                             *
REM      *   city_code                                                 *
REM      *                                                             *
REM      **************************************************************
   SUB Compute_local_tax (gross_pay, city_code, local_tax)
       LET local_tax = 0.01 * gross_pay
   END SUB

REM      **************************************************************
REM      * MODULE:     Compute_social_security                         *
REM      * WRITTEN BY: W.S. Davis            DATE: July 26, 1985       *
REM      *                                                             *
REM      * This external subroutine computes federal social            *
REM      * security tax (or FICA tax) due.                             *
REM      *                                                             *
REM      *  INPUT PARAMETERS    OUTPUT PARAMETERS     LOCAL DATA       *
REM      *   gross_pay           social_security_tax                   *
REM      *                                                             *
REM      **************************************************************
   SUB Compute_social_security (gross_pay, social_security_tax)
       LET social_security_tax = 0.0705 * gross_pay
   END SUB
```

Fig. 6.12, *continued.*

```
hours worked
pay rate         ──▶  [Compute gross pay]  ──▶  gross pay
shift code
```

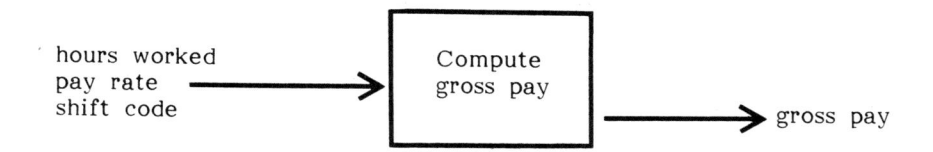

Fig. 6.13: *A block diagram representation of the gross pay algorithm.*

Let's select an algorithm and develop it. We'll choose gross pay *(Fig. 6.13)*. The input and output data define the routine's parameters. We'll assume computing gross pay involves three intermediate computations: regular pay, overtime pay, and a shift premium. Regular pay is simply hours worked times a pay rate. Hours over forty, overtime hours, are paid at one and one half times the regular rate. Finally, employees working the second shift are paid a five percent premium, while third shift workers receive a ten percent premium. The shift premium is paid on the employee's regular pay; no premium is paid on overtime.

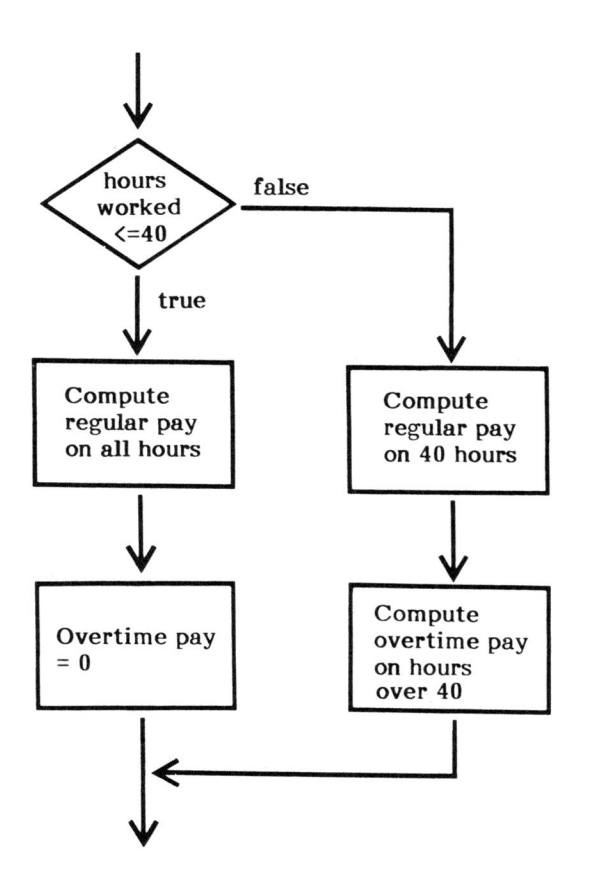

Fig. 6.14: *A simple decision structure can be used to control the regular pay and overtime pay computations.*

```
           │
           ▼
      ╱hours ╲  false
     ╱ worked ╲──────────┐
     ╲ <=40   ╱          │
      ╲      ╱           │
        │ true           │
        ▼                ▼
  ┌──────────┐    ┌──────────┐
  │ Compute  │    │ Compute  │
  │regular pay│   │regular pay│
  │on all hours│  │on 40 hours│
  └──────────┘    └──────────┘
        │                │
        ▼                ▼
  ┌──────────┐    ┌──────────┐
  │Overtime pay│  │ Compute  │
  │  = 0      │   │overtime pay│
  │           │   │on hours    │
  │           │   │over 40     │
  └──────────┘    └──────────┘
        │                │
        └───────◀────────┘
                │
                ▼
```

Computing gross pay involves computing regular pay, overtime pay, and a shift premium. The key to overtime pay is hours worked. We can use a simple decision structure to find regular pay and overtime pay *(Fig. 6.14)*. Next we turn to the shift premium. The shift code can be either 1, 2, or 3. If it's 1, there is no premium. If it's 2, the premium is five percent of regular pay, while a shift code of 3 calls for a ten percent premium. Again, we can use a decision structure *(Fig. 6.15)*. Note that no premium is paid if the shift code is not 1, 2, or 3.

Adding the First Subroutine

Given these plans, we can write the gross pay subroutine. Read the logic carefully. Note that the last statement adds regular pay, overtime pay, and the shift premium to get gross pay.

The next step is to add the new subroutine to our program. We do this by replacing the old "stub-level" subroutine with the new version. Note that the main program's **CALL** statement has not been changed; as far as the main program is concerned, it still passes **Compute_gross_pay** certain parameters, and expects a value for **gross_pay** in return. To the main program, nothing has changed. The only thing that has changed is the new subroutine.

Let's test the program by running it. We'll input some test data, perhaps the

Fig. 6.15: *Another decision structure can be used to control computing the shift premium.*

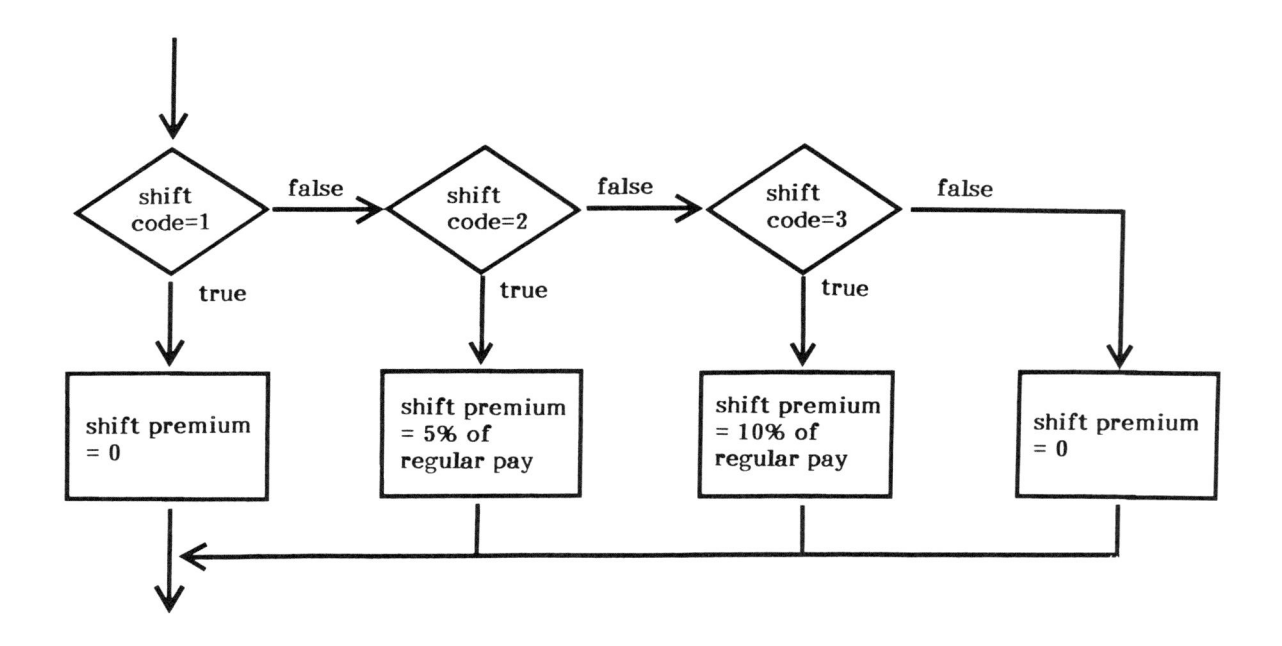

```
REM        *************************************************************
REM        * MODULE:     Compute_gross_pay                              *
REM        * WRITTEN BY: W.S. Davis           DATE: July 26, 1985       *
REM        *                                                            *
REM        * This external subroutine computes gross pay.               *
REM        *                                                            *
REM        *  INPUT PARAMETERS    OUTPUT PARAMETERS    LOCAL DATA       *
REM        *   hours_worked         gross_pay           regular_pay     *
REM        *   pay_rate                                 overtime_pay    *
REM        *   shift_code                               shift_premium   *
REM        *                                                            *
REM        * Regular pay is simply the product of hours worked and      *
REM        * the hourly pay rate. Hours over 40 are paid at 1.5         *
REM        * times the regular rate, yielding overtime pay. A 5%        *
REM        * shift premium is paid to second shift workers; a 10%       *
REM        * premium is paid to third shift workers. The shift          *
REM        * premium is paid on regular earnings only. Gross pay is     *
REM        * the sum of regular pay, overtime pay, and the shift        *
REM        * premium.                                                   *
REM        *                                                            *
REM        *************************************************************

   SUB Compute_gross_pay (hours_worked, pay_rate, shift_code, gross_pay)

                             ! Hours worked determines if overtime pay
                             ! should be computed.

      IF hours_worked <= 40 THEN

                             ! If hours worked is less than or equal to
                             ! 40, overtime pay is zero.

         LET regular_pay = hours_worked * pay_rate
         LET overtime_pay = 0

      ELSE                   ! If hours worked exceeds 40, regular pay
                             ! is computed on the first 40 hours, and
                             ! overtime pay is computed on hours over 40.

         LET regular_pay = 40.0 * pay_rate
         LET overtime_pay = (hours_worked - 40) * pay_rate * 1.5
      END IF
```

Fig. 6.16: *This complete gross pay subroutine replaces the stub version in the skeleton mainline (Fig. 6.12). The logic is continued on the next page.*

```
                              ! If the shift code = 1 (first shift),
                              ! no shift premium is paid.
   IF shift_code = 1 THEN
      LET shift_premium = 0
                              ! If the shift code = 2 (second shift),
                              ! a 5% premium is paid on regular earnings.
   ELSEIF shift_code = 2 THEN
      LET shift_premium = 0.05 * regular_pay
                              ! If the shift_code = 3 (third shift), a 10%
                              ! premium is paid on regular earnings.
   ELSEIF shift_code = 3 THEN
      LET shift_premium = 0.10 * regular_pay
                              ! Any other shift code is an error. No
                              ! shift premium is paid.
      ELSE
         LET shift_premium = 0
   END IF
   LET gross_pay = regular_pay + overtime_pay + shift_premium
END SUB
```

Fig. 6.16, *continued.*

---

same test data used to exercise the skeleton version of the program. If the results are correct, the new subroutine is probably correct. If the results are wrong, the error probably lies in the new subroutine, because nothing else has changed.

We added **Compute_gross_pay** as an *external* subroutine. Why? Basically because it is a computational subroutine that uses intermediate work variables. If **Compute_gross_pay** were an internal subroutine, those work variables would be global. That could cause problems in some other part of the program. We want the subroutine to be independent so that we can ignore its contents when writing the other modules. In the next section, we'll add an internal subroutine.

The Data Input Subroutine

In writing **Compute_gross_pay**, we assumed the input data were correct. Because the data's validity is not the responsibility of the gross pay subroutine, that was a reasonable assumption. The responsibility for verifying the input data rests with **Get_input_data** *(Fig. 6.17).*

What do we mean by "verifying" the input data? Have you ever made a typing error? Everyone has. The input data that drive our payroll program will be entered

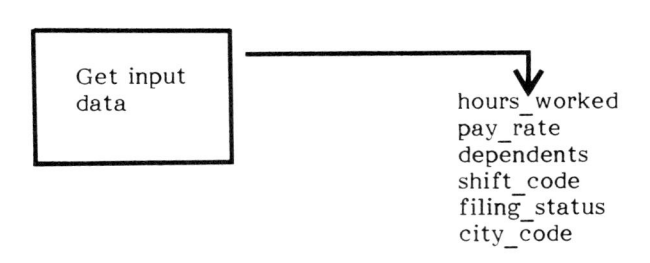

```
                              ┌──────────────┐        ───────────┐
                              │ Get input    │                   │
                              │ data         │                   ▼
                              │              │          hours_worked
                              └──────────────┘          pay_rate
                                                        dependents
                                                        shift_code
                                                        filing_status
                                                        city_code
```

Fig. 6.17: *A block diagram for the Get_input_data subroutine.*

by human beings, and thus are subject to error. Given bad input data, the computer will generate wrong answers. Printing a check for the wrong amount can have serious consequences. It makes sense to check the data as they are input, before they are used.

Of course, no computer can catch a one-tenth hour error in a particular employee's hours worked. It is possible, however, to catch more substantial "out of range" errors such as 0.4 rather than 40.4 hours. Start by defining a series of reasonable values or ranges for each input variable *(Fig. 6.18)*. Then, after the data are input, check to see that each value lies within its range. If it does, accept the value; if it doesn't, ask for verification. By checking the input data as they are input, we can assure that the other modules receive correct (or at least reasonable) data.

Let's study one of the tests and decide how we might implement it. Hours worked must lie between 15 and 75. If a clerk enters 40 hours, that's reasonable. However, 4 or 400 are clearly out-of-range. The basic idea is simple. Input a value for hours worked. If it lies within the range, take it. If, however, the input value is less than 15 or greater than 75, ask the clerk to enter it again. Hopefully, the initial input error will be corrected.

Out-of-range values are not necessarily errors, however. For example, imagine an employee who really did work eighty hours in a given week. The correct value for hours worked would be 80; we don't want to refuse it. Thus, we'll set up a test for hours worked. If the initial value lies within the normal range, we'll accept it. If not, we'll ask for the value to be reentered. If the clerk reenters the same,

Fig. 6.18: *A reasonable range can be established for each of the input variables.*

$$15 \leq \text{hours worked} \leq 75$$
$$3.50 \leq \text{pay rate} \leq 15.50$$
$$0 \leq \text{dependents} \leq 12$$
$$\text{shift code} = 1, 2, \text{ or } 3$$
$$\text{filing status} = 1 \text{ or } 2$$
$$\text{city} = 1, 2, 3, 4, 5, \text{ or } 6$$

out-of-range value, we'll accept it as correct. If the clerk enters a different value, we'll check to be sure that it lies within range before accepting it. Note that we could require several input values before accepting one. We're talking about a loop structure with tests at both ends *(Fig. 6.19)*. Given a plan, we can write the code to implement it (shaded portion of Fig. 6.20).

Read the instructions. Imagine that a value for **hours_worked** has been input. Look at the **DO WHILE** loop. If **hours_worked** lie between 15 and 75, the loop is skipped. We accept the value. Assume hours worked are out of range. Enter the loop. It begins by displaying a series of messages that identify the out-of-range condition. The clerk is asked to try again. The initial value of **hours_worked** is saved so that it can be compared to the new value, and a second **INPUT** statement is expected. In response, the clerk enters a new value.

Move on to the **UNTIL** option. If the newly entered value matches the original value, the loop ends; if a human clerk enters the same out-of-range value twice, the program assumes he or she meant to, and accepts the value as correct. Otherwise, control returns to the top of the loop, where the initial range check is repeated. The loop continues until the clerk enters a value that lies within range, or until the clerk enters the same out-of-range value twice in succession.

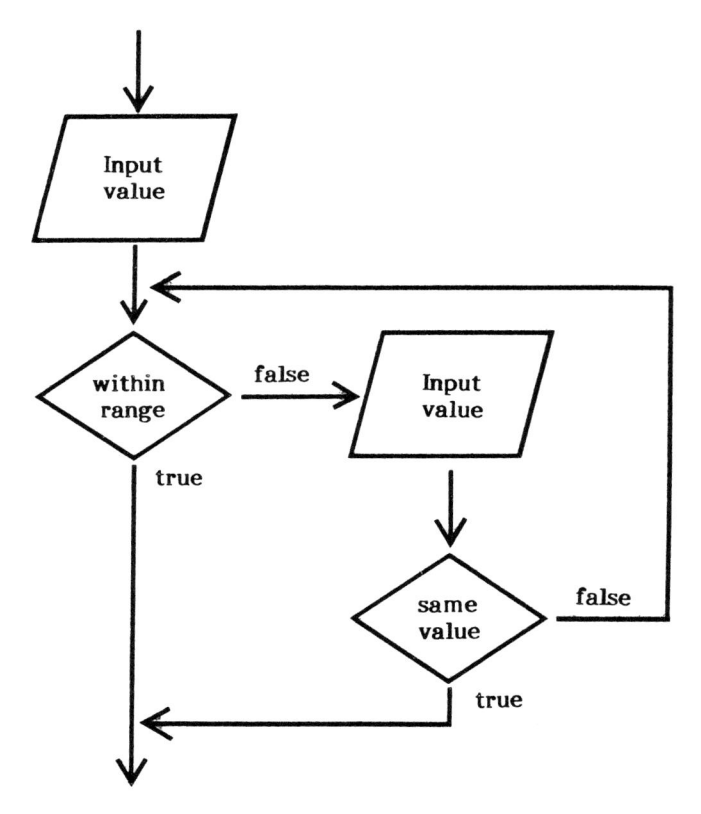

Fig. 6.19: *After an input value is read, it is checked against its range. If the value is out of range, a new value is input. At the end of the loop, we check for a repeated value.*

```
REM       ***************************************************************
REM       *  MODULE:      Get_input_data                                 *
REM       *  WRITTEN BY:  W.S. Davis           DATE: July 26, 1985       *
REM       *                                                              *
REM       *  This internal subroutine inputs and verifies all data.      *
REM       *  Most variables are global; hence no parameters are          *
REM       *  listed in the subroutine definition or in the CALL          *
REM       *  statement.  This module gets values for:                    *
REM       *      hours_worked              pay_rate                      *
REM       *      shift_code                dependents                    *
REM       *      filing_status             city_code                     *
REM       *                                                              *
REM       *  LOCAL VARIABLES: test_value                                 *
REM       *                                                              *
REM       ***************************************************************

   SUB Get_input_data
                              ! First, values are accepted for all
                              ! input variables.

      INPUT hours_worked, pay_rate, shift_code
      INPUT dependents, filing_status, city_code

                              ! A negative hours worked is the
                              ! sentinel value.  If hours worked is
                              ! negative, the subroutine ends.

      IF hours_worked < 0 THEN EXIT SUB     ! Note exit condition.

                              ! One by one, input values are verified.

                              ! Hours worked must lie between 15 and 75.
                              ! If hours worked is out of range, a clerk
                              ! is asked to correct or to verify it.  If
                              ! hours worked is within range, the loop is
                              ! bypassed.

      DO WHILE (hours_worked < 15) OR (hours_worked > 75)

                              ! A series of messages explaining the error
                              ! are displayed.

         PRINT "Hours worked normally lie between 15 and 75."
         PRINT "You entered:", hours_worked
         PRINT "Please correct or verify."
```

Fig. 6.20: *The Get_input_data subroutine. The logic is continued on the next two pages.*

```
                        ! The clerk is expected to input a new,
                        ! corrected value. If the same value is
                        ! input again, it is assumed correct. New
                        ! values will be checked against the
                        ! range before being accepted.

   LET test_value = hours_worked
   INPUT hours_worked
LOOP UNTIL hours_worked = test_value
```

```
                        ! The pay rate must lie between 3.50 and
                        ! 15.50 dollars per hour. The structure
                        ! of this test matches hours worked.

DO WHILE (pay_rate < 3.50) OR (pay_rate > 15.50)

                        ! Messages identify the error.

   PRINT "Pay rate normally lies between 3.50 and 15.50."
   PRINT "You entered:", pay_rate
   PRINT "Please correct or verify."

                        ! A new value is input. If it matches the
                        ! first value, the loop ends. If not, the
                        ! new value is compared against the range.

   LET test_value = pay_rate
   INPUT pay_rate
LOOP UNTIL pay_rate = input_value

                        ! The number of dependents must range
                        ! between 0 and 12. The pattern of this
                        ! test matches the first two.

DO WHILE (dependents < 0) OR (dependents > 12)

   PRINT "dependents normally range between 0 and 12."
   PRINT "You entered:", dependents
   PRINT "Please correct or verify."

   LET test_value = dependents
   INPUT dependents
LOOP UNTIL dependents = test_value
```

Fig. 6.20, *continued.*

```
                              ! The shift code must be 1, 2, or 3. In
                              ! this case, out-of-range values cannot
                              ! be accepted.

   DO WHILE (shift_code < 1) OR (shift_code > 3)

      PRINT "The shift code must be 1, 2, or 3."
      PRINT "You entered: ", shift_code
      PRINT "Please correct."

      INPUT shift_code

   LOOP

                              ! The filing status must be 1 or 2. Out-
                              ! of-range values cannot be accepted.

   DO WHILE (filing_status < 1) OR (filing_status > 2)

      PRINT "The filing status must be 1 or 2."
      PRINT "You entered: ", filing_status
      PRINT "Please correct."

      INPUT filing_status

   LOOP

                              ! The city code must lie between 1 and 6.
                              ! Out-of-range values cannot be accepted.

   DO WHILE (city_code < 1) OR (city_code > 6)

      PRINT "The city code must be 1, 2, 3, 4, 5, or 6."
      PRINT "You entered: ", city_code
      PRINT "Please correct."

      INPUT city_code

   LOOP

END SUB
```

Fig. 6.20, *continued.*

We can do the same thing for each of the input data elements *(Fig. 6.20)*. Note that the subroutine starts with an **INPUT** statement listing all the variables. It then tests for the sentinel value, a negative **hours_worked**; if the sentinel value is sensed, the subroutine ends. Assuming we have not yet sensed end-of-data, the individual values are checked, one by one. If every one lies within range, they are all accepted; none of the **DO** loops is entered. If any value lies outside its range, an acceptable value is obtained before the program moves on. This way, input data are verified before other modules use them. Consequently, the other modules can ignore the possibility of out-of-range data.

Note that not all the **DO** loops have both **WHILE** and **UNTIL** conditions. In the case of **filing_status**, for example, the input value must be 1 or 2, and out-of-range values cannot be accepted. Generally, however, the logic involved in verifying each data element is similar to the **hours_worked** example. You should have little trouble following the subroutine.

What next? We return to our original program and replace the stublevel data input subroutine with our new, more complete version. Then we run the program again. This time, we'll intentionally enter out-of-range values just to make sure that the subroutine catches them. We generated correct answers before. If the answers are still correct, we can assume **Get_input_data** must be correct. If not, since only the new subroutine has changed, it must be wrong. The first step in fixing an error is finding it. Adding subroutines one by one helps to quickly isolate the probable location of an error.

Note that **Get_input_data** is an *internal* subroutine. Why? Consider what it does. It gets input values for each of six global variables. No computations are performed. Except for **test_value**, no local variables are used. The advantage of an external subroutine is its independence. Its work variables are local. But its parameters are global. Most of **Get_input_data's** variables are global; we would gain very little from making it external.

Do we gain anything from making it internal? Yes. Try coding a **CALL** statement listing all six parameters. It won't fit on a single line. If **Get_input_data** were external, we'd have to list all its parameters. Because it's internal, however, we don't have to list any. Internal subroutines share all their variables with the mainline. Thus, when **Get_input_data** reads values for the six variables, the mainline can access them by referencing the same variable names.

Let's generalize. A subroutine's parameters are shared with the mainline. Thus, a subroutine with a large number of parameters cannot really be independent. Unless it performs substantial computations utilizing numerous work variables, there is little point to making it external. Defining it as an internal subroutine allows us to move its logic away from the mainline. Shifting detailed logic into an internal subroutine makes the program easier to understand, simply because it removes "clutter" from the primary logical flow.

Adding the Other Modules

Before our payroll program is complete, we must add modules to compute federal tax, state tax, local tax, deductions, and net pay. We'll follow the same procedure, treating each module as an independent problem to be solved. Problem definition comes first. Based on an analysis of the algorithm or algorithms, we'll plan the module's logic. Finally, we'll write a subroutine. Replacing the initial stub-level subroutine with the new version, we'll test the program. If the test yields valid results, the new subroutine is assumed accurate. Because only the new subroutine has changed, any errors encountered can almost certainly be traced to it. Given errors, we'll debug the new subroutine and try again.

One by one, detailed computational subroutines will be added to the developing payroll program. By the time we finish, the program will be quite lengthy and quite complex. Because we were able to focus on the individual modules one at a time, however, we won't sense that complexity. Instead of one, big, complex program, we'll see several, relatively simple, small ones. To solve a big problem, divide and conquer. Using subroutines allows us to achieve that objective.

FUNCTIONAL DECOMPOSITION

The steps in our gross pay subroutine were relatively simple. Were we to list this subroutine, it would fit on a single sheet of paper. That's reasonable. However, what if one or more of our algorithms had been more complex? What if the subroutine had required hundreds of lines of code? We might have implemented it as a series of lower level subroutines. **Compute_gross_pay** might look like Fig. 6.21 and consist of a series of calls to still lower-level subroutines. If other modules required decomposition, the program's control structure could come to resemble Fig. 6.22.

We decided not to write the lower-level subroutines because **Compute_gross_pay** was relatively brief and easy to follow without further decomposition. Sometimes it makes sense to break a module down. Sometimes it doesn't. How can you decide?

A good module performs a single, complete function. For example, consider our gross pay subroutine. It incorporated all the logic needed to compute just one value: gross pay. If we were to break it into lower-level modules, we might have one for regular pay, another for overtime pay, and a third for the shift

Fig. 6.21: *If the rules for computing regular pay, overtime pay, and the shift premium had been more complex, we might have moved each computation into its own lower-level subroutine. Compute_gross_pay would have then become a control structure, calling the three detailed computational routines.*

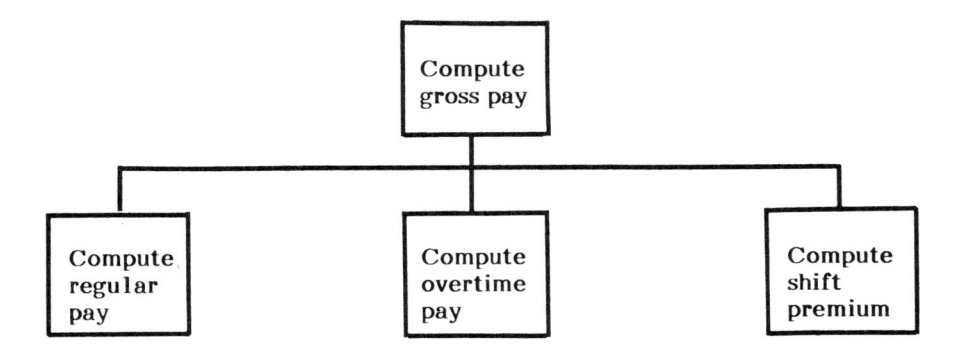

Fig. 6.22: Several of the first-level subroutines might call their own lower-level subroutines, giving the program a more complex control structure. Again, we can use a hierarchy chart to graphically illustrate that control structure.

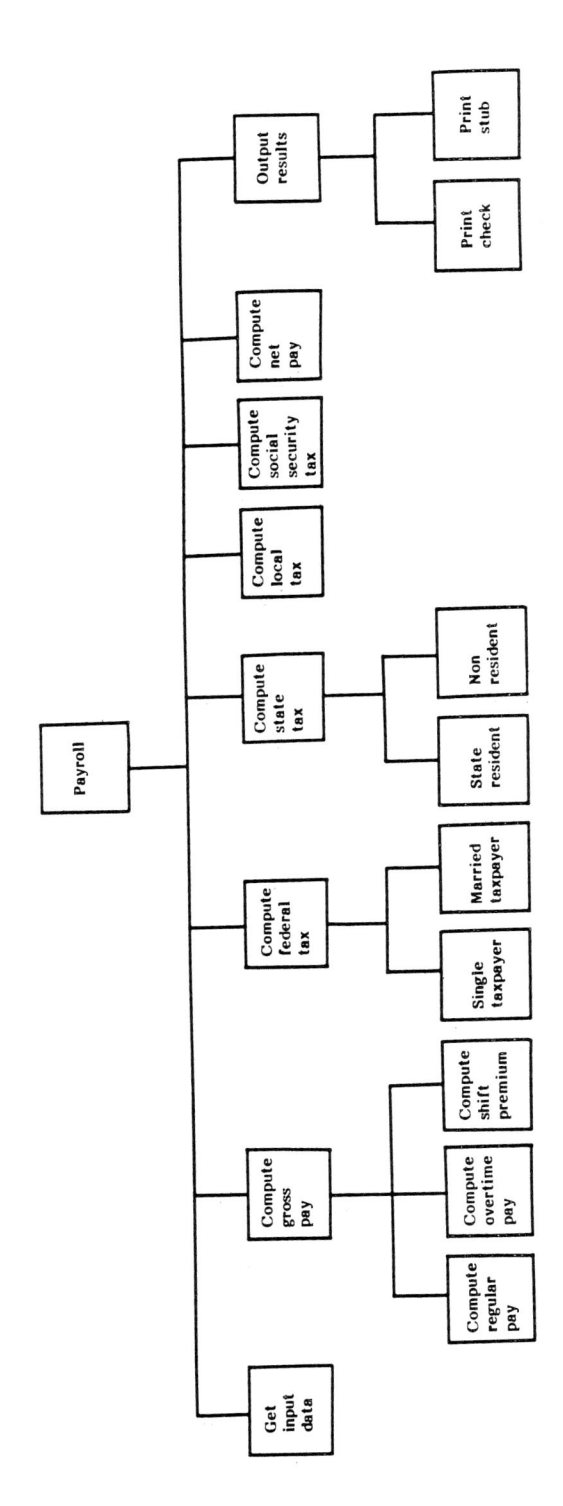

premium. It would be a mistake, however, to have one module compute a part of regular pay, and another compute a different part of regular pay. Why?

The problem would occur during program debug. Imagine that, following a test, regular pay is wrong. If all the computations related to regular pay are concentrated in a single module, finding and removing the error should be easy. If, however, several different modules are involved, the problem might lie in any one of them, or in any combination of two or more of them. That needlessly complicates debugging. A good module performs a single, complete function. Such modules are said to be cohesive.

Another characteristic of a good module is independence. An independent module is one that can be viewed as a black box. We pass it certain parameters; it returns certain results. How it gets those results is beside the point.

Independent modules have their own local data storage. Global data detract from the module's independence. For example, in the payroll program, the first module computed gross pay, and this global value was eventually passed to several other subroutines. If **Compute_gross_pay** were to return an incorrect value, those other subroutines would return incorrect values, too. To this extent, the gross pay module was not independent.

With external subroutines, only the parameters are global. It is only through its parameters that one external subroutine can affect another. It follows, therefore, that the more parameters a subroutine has, the less independent it is. Thus we have one measure of a module's independence. Ideally, a module should have relatively few parameters. Those with numerous parameters may be trying to accomplish too much. That's a good sign that the module should be further decomposed.

Let's pull these ideas together. When planning a large program, we want to divide the logic into small modules that can be planned and implemented one by one. Ideally each module should perform a single, complete function. Also, each module should be as independent as possible, with as few parameters as possible.

Breaking a program into small, independent, single-function, modules is called functional decomposition. A few guidelines can be suggested. A good module will involve a single screen or, at most, a single page of code. If your gross pay subroutine begins to exceed a full screen, think about shifting one of the intermediate computations to a lower-level subroutine. If a low-level subroutine consists of only a handful of instructions, think about moving its code back up.

A good approach is to keep breaking a problem down until you reach the point where the next subdivision would get you to individual instructions. For example, consider payroll again. Clearly, computing gross pay is one key function. To find gross pay, we identified three different computations: regular pay, overtime pay, and shift premium. Each could be an independent module, a lower-level subroutine. The main program could call the gross pay module which could, in turn, call the regular pay, overtime pay, and shift premium subroutines.

What about regular pay? Should its computation be broken into still lower-level modules? Study the algorithm. When you try to decompose it, you almost naturally begin to think about the product of hours worked and an hourly pay rate. That's an instruction. We don't want to decompose the regular pay module; we've taken it far enough.

The secret to learning how to decompose a problem is practice. You can't just read about it. You have to do it. Try the exercises at the end of this chapter. Try writing the programs and the subroutines. If you can learn how to functionally decompose a problem and then attack the pieces individually, you'll really know how to program.

A LOOK AHEAD

Part I of this primer has focused on the basic building blocks of any program: sequence, decision, and repetition. You learned how to group the basic structures to form subroutines and functions. In this chapter, you learned how to develop a large program as a group of independent subroutines linked by a control structure. Given a sense of how the basic building blocks can be combined to form a complex program, you are ready to write such programs. If you really understand the material in Chapters 1 through 6, there is no programming task that is beyond you.

There are, of course, techniques that you have not yet learned. Your input and output can be made much more clear. You should learn to manipulate data in the form of a table or an array. You probably want to learn how to generate graphic output, manipulate string data, and have your computer produce sound. Accessing data in external files is an important skill, as is using program libraries. You have the background to learn these individual skills. They are the subject of Part II.

Chapters 7 through 12 present a number of more advanced topics. They can be read in any order. If you'd like to learn more about input and output, read Chapter 7 next. If your real interest is graphics, skip directly to Chapter 9. Good luck!

SUMMARY

Any program, no matter how large or complex, can ultimately be broken down into combinations of the basic building blocks: sequence, decision, and repetition. The subject of this chapter was combining the basic building blocks to build large or complex programs.

We started with a complex program to simulate a game of craps. The rules of the game represented our algorithm. By studying the rules, we were able to break the problem into three smaller problems. We then planned three partial solutions and combined them. Finally, recognizing the decision and repetitive structures in the flowchart, we wrote a program. Next, we considered a general plan of attack for a large program. The basic idea was: divide and conquer. If a large problem is divided into several smaller problems, the smaller problems can be attacked one by one, which simplifies coding, debugging, and program maintenance. A way to implement our plan of attack is to write each partial solution as a subroutine, and then to provide a mainline control module to call the various subroutines in order. We also considered the special documentation requirements of a large program.

We used a payroll system as an example of a large program. Although apparently a simple application, payroll becomes quite complex when you consider all its algorithms. The algorithms gave us a basis for initially subdividing the logic. After defining them at a block diagram level, we wrote a skeleton version of the program, with a stub-level subroutine for each algorithm. Then we planned and coded the gross pay subroutine. Our new version replaced the stub version in the skeleton program, and we tested our logic. The data input subroutine was added next. One by one, the detailed computational subroutines replaced the stub-level subroutines until the complete program was tested and implemented.

The chapter ended with a brief discussion of functional decomposition. The objective is to break a program into a series of independent, single-function modules linked by a control structure.

EXERCISES

1. Start with the craps program *(Fig. 6.6)*. Enter it into your system. Now, modify it. Add the logic to allow a player to play against the computer. Give the player an initial amount of money, perhaps $100. Before the dice are rolled, allow the player to bet. If he or she wins, add the amount of the bet to the player's bankroll. If the computer wins, subtract the bet. Before each new roll, give the player a chance to cash out. The game automatically ends when the bankroll reaches zero.

    Don't try to just write the code. Think about it. How will you keep track of a player's bankroll? When will you add to it or subtract from it? How will you allow the player to cash out? When? Develop a plan first. Then write the program.

2. Start by entering the skeleton gross pay program *(Fig. 6.12)* into your system. Then:

    a. Add the gross pay subroutine *(Fig. 6.16)*, and test the program.

    b. Add the data input subroutine *(Fig. 6.20)* and test the program.

    c. Chapter 3, Exercise 18 *(page 83)* presented a table for computing the amount of federal income tax to be withheld from an employee's weekly pay. Using that table, plan and code a subroutine to compute federal income tax, and add it to the payroll program.

d. Assume that the rules for withholding state income tax are defined by the following table:

Gross pay between	and	tax is	of excess over
$0.00	$25.00	zero	
25.00	50.00	0.00 + 1%	$25.00
50.00	100.00	0.25 + 2%	50.00
100.00	200.00	2.15 + 3%	100.00
200.00	500.00	4.25 + 4%	200.00
500.00	and up	16.25 + 5%	500.00

Using the table, plan and write a subroutine to compute state tax, and add it to the payroll program.

e. Local income tax is charged at several different rates. The following tax rates are used in our area:

City code	Tax rate
1	1%
2	1.25%
3	1.5%
4	2%
5	2.25%
6	2.5%

The city code is an input value. Write a subroutine to compute city tax, and add it to the payroll program.

f. Social security tax is 7.05% of gross pay. Add this computation to the payroll program. Would you add it as a subroutine or as a simple computation? Why?

g. Add to the payroll program the logic to output gross pay, federal tax, state tax, local tax, social security tax, and net pay. In Chapter 7, we'll consider ways in which you might format your output data to make them easier to read. Anticipate an end-of-chapter exercise; keep the data output function in a subroutine.

3. Another game easily simulated by a computer is blackjack or "21." A player is dealt two cards. Face cards count 10; numbered cards (2 through 10) count their face values; aces count either 1 or 11 (player's choice). The objective is to come as close to 21 as possible without going over, or exceeding, 21. After the first two cards are dealt, a player may stay with them or accept another card. As long as the total value of all cards does not exceed 21, the player can keep taking cards.

   A player wins by beating the dealer (in our case, the computer). Blackjack or 21 (an ace and a face card) wins automatically. Players who exceed 21 lose. Otherwise, if the player's total points exceed the dealer's total points, the player wins. The dealer wins all ties (that's the house's edge). The dealer (the computer) gets two cards, and must keep taking additional cards until his or her hand is worth at least 16. The dealer is not allowed to take another card if his or her hand totals 17 or more.

   Write a program to play blackjack against the computer. Give the player an initial $100. Accept bets before a hand is dealt. If the player wins, add the amount of the bet to his or her bankroll. If the player loses, subtract the amount of the bet. The game ends when the player decides to quit or when the bankroll reaches zero.

4. Loan officers in a bank often find it necessary to do interest computations. Among the questions they must answer are:

   a. If I invest P dollars today at i% interest, how much will I have after n years? The formula is:

   $$F = P (1 + i)^n$$

   b. I need F dollars n years from now. How much must I invest at i% interest? The formula is:

   $$F = P / (1 + i)^n$$

c. If I deposit R dollars per year at i% interest, how much will I have after n years? The formula is:

$$F = R\left[\frac{(1 + i)^n - 1}{i}\right]$$

d. I need F dollars in n years. How much must I invest each year at i% interest? The formula is:

$$R = F\left[\frac{i}{(1 + i)^n - 1}\right]$$

e. If I borrow P dollars today for n years, how much must I repay each year at i% interest? The formula is:

$$R = P\left[\frac{i(1 + i)^n}{(1 + i)^n - 1}\right]$$

f. How much is a promise to pay R dollars per year for n years at i% interest worth today? The formula is:

$$P = R\left[\frac{(1 + i)^n - 1}{i(1 + i)^n}\right]$$

Write a program that allows the loan officer to select a computation and enter the appropriate parameters. Display the result.

5. "Take away" games are popular programming exercises. A simple example starts with a pile of twenty-three matches. A player and the computer (or two players) take turns removing 1, 2, or 3 matches. The objective is to avoid taking the last match. Write a program to play the game against the computer. "Flip a coin" to determine who goes first.

There is a strategy to this game; it can effectively be won on the first move. Figure out the strategy--try starting with the last move and working backwards. Program the computer to follow your strategy. Given the first move your program should always win. Given the second move, your program should "pounce" on a player's mistake and follow a winning strategy.

6. A bank offers three types of checking accounts. Type-A accounts are charged ten cents per transaction (check or deposit). There is no minimum balance or additional charge. Type-B accounts are charged a flat $10.00 per month, with an additional five cents per transaction if the number of transactions exceeds 100 in a given month. There is no monthly charge for Type-C accounts as long as the minimum balance remains above $500. If the minimum balance drops below $500, a Type-C account reverts to a Type-A account. Interest is paid on Type-B and Type-C accounts as long as the minimum balance for the month exceeds $500. The interest rate of 0.75% per month is paid on the actual minimum balance minus $500.

   Write a program to update a single checking account. Start by entering the account type (A, B, or C) and the old, beginning-of-month balance. One by one, enter check amounts and deposit amounts in time sequence; your program must be able to distinguish checks from deposits. Check amounts are to be subtracted from the account balance; deposit amounts are to be added to it. Be sure to track the running balance, as the minimum balance must be known for Type-B and Type-C accounts. After the last transaction is processed, compute monthly charges and/or interest earned, and adjust the balance accordingly. Output the old balance, the number of checks written, the total value of all checks, the number of deposits, the total value of all deposits, any charges, any interest earned, and the end-of-month balance.

PART II

True BASIC Features

7. Input and Output

8. Arrays

9. Graphics

10. Strings and Sound

11. Files

12. Libraries, Chaining, and Recursion

Each of the six chapters in Part II presents, in depth, a single, advanced *True BASIC* feature. These chapters assume that you have read and understood the material in Part I, or that you are an experienced programmer. Instead of guiding you through the process of planning and implementing a complete program, they focus on specific techniques that can be used to improve a program. They are designed to be a reference as well as an introduction, and can be read in any order.

7

Input and Output

KEY IDEAS

1. *Data input.*

    a. **INPUT** *with* **PROMPT.**

    b. **KEY INPUT.**

    c. *Lengthy input lists.*

    d. *Input errors.*

2. **READ, DATA, RESTORE.**

3. *Data output.*

    a. *The* **PRINT** *statement.*

    b. **PRINT USING.**

4. *Printer output.*

5. *Windows.*

```
                              ! A guessing game. A function is defined
                              ! to select a random number between 1 and
                              ! some upper limit, n.
DEF The_number(n) = Int(Rnd * n + 1)

                              ! First we'll print a brief explanation of
                              ! the game so the player knows what to do.
PRINT "The computer is about to select a number between 1 and 10."
PRINT "You'll have three chances to guess the number. After each of"
PRINT "your first two guesses, the computer will tell you if your"
PRINT "guess was high or low. Good luck!"
RANDOMIZE                     ! We want unexpected numbers.

                              ! Referencing the function, the computer
                              ! selects a random number between 1 and 10.
  LET random_number = The_number(10)

                              ! The user inputs up to three guesses.
  FOR count = 1 TO 3
    INPUT PROMPT "Enter a number between 1 and 10: ": guess

                              ! If the guess is correct, a message is
                              ! displayed and the loop is exited.
    IF guess = random_number THEN
       PRINT "Correct! You win!"
       EXIT FOR               ! Note exit condition.

                              ! If the guess is wrong and it's the third
                              ! guess, the player loses.
    ELSEIF count = 3 THEN
        PRINT "You lose. The number is", random_number

                              ! Following an incorrect first or second
                              ! guess, the player is told if the guess
                              ! is high or low.
       ELSEIF guess > random_number THEN
           PRINT "Your guess is high."
           ELSE
               PRINT "Your guess is low."
     END IF
NEXT count

END
```

Fig. 7.1: *The guessing game program can be improved by adding start-of-program instructions and input prompts.*

DATA INPUT

Prompting Input

When an **INPUT** statement is executed, a question mark is displayed in the history window. The user responds by typing a value for each listed variable. Unfortunately, the standard prompt neither identifies the values to be entered, nor suggests how many. You have probably learned to check the **INPUT** statement in the editing window before entering data, but checking the code won't work on a large program, or on a program written by someone else. A well-written program displays instructions and prompts to tell the user exactly what to do.

In Chapter 5 we developed a program to play a number guessing game. Let's add a series of **PRINT** statements to explain how the game is played *(Fig. 7.1)*. Such directions clarify the program's function, but, by themselves, are not enough. Because the standard question mark prompt can confuse an unsophisticated user, it's better to display explicit prompts; for example,

> PRINT "Enter a number between 1 and 10: ";
>
> **INPUT guess**

The **PRINT** statement tells the user exactly what to do. It ends with a semicolon, which means "don't move the cursor." Thus, when the statements are executed, the message is printed, a question mark is displayed on the same line, and the value is entered.

Instead of coding both a **PRINT** and an **INPUT** statement, the *True BASIC* programmer can use an **INPUT** with **PROMPT** *(Fig. 7.2)*. Refer once again to the guessing game program *(Fig. 7.1)*. Find the **INPUT PROMPT** statement. When executed, the expression "Enter a number between 1 and 10:" replaces

Fig. 7.2: *The INPUT with PROMPT statement.*

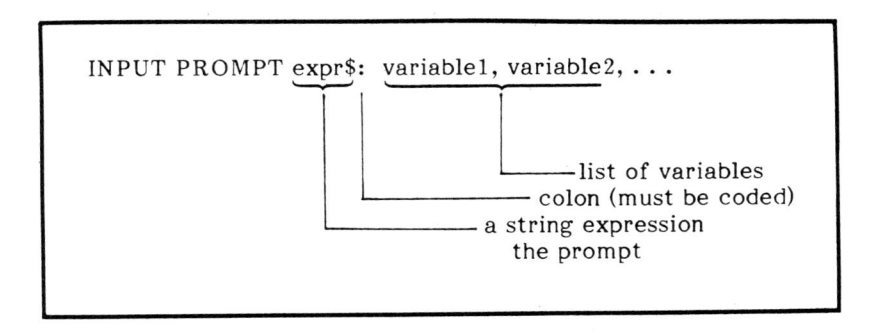

```
INPUT PROMPT expr$:  variable1, variable2, . . .
            |        |
            |        |————— list of variables
            |        ——————— colon (must be coded)
            ————————————————  a string expression
                              the prompt
```

the usual question mark prompt. Check the history window in Fig. 7.3 to see the new output. Compare this new version to the one we wrote in Chapter 5. Try playing both versions. Note how much the directions and the prompt add to the game.

Key Input

The only way to play the guessing game program repetitively is to issue a series of **RUN** commands, and that's inconvenient. Let's revise it once more. We'll use a **DO WHILE** loop as the basic control structure. When a game ends, we'll ask the user if he or she wants to play again, and input the response. For example, near the loop's end, we might code

> **PRINT "Do you want to play again? Type yes or no.";**
>
> **INPUT response$**

and repeat the loop as long as the response is "yes."
   An option is to use a **GET KEY** statement *(Fig. 7.4)*. When a **GET KEY**

Fig. 7.3: *Printed instructions and the input prompt add a great deal to the guessing game program.*

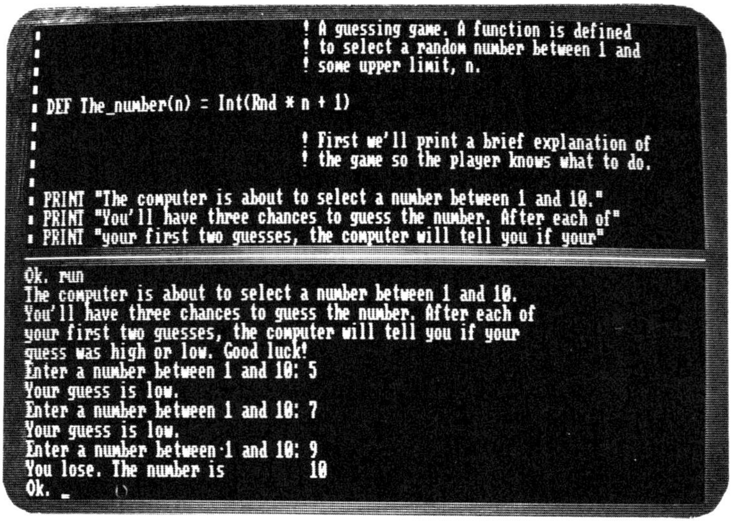

```
          ┌─────────────────────────────────────────────────┐
          │   GET KEY variable                              │
          │           └──┬──┘                               │
          │              │                                  │
          │              └──── the value of the next key pressed
          │                    is stored in this variable.  │
          │                                                 │
          └─────────────────────────────────────────────────┘
```

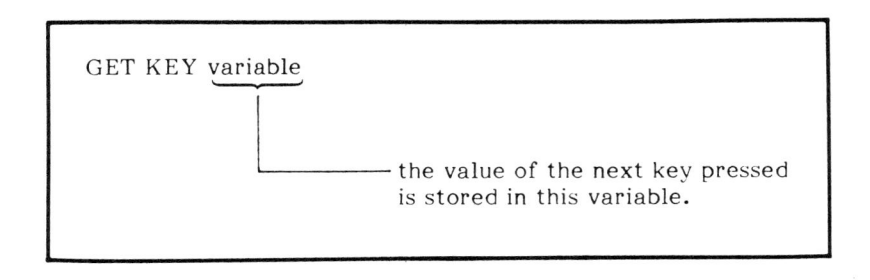

Fig. 7.4: *The GET KEY statement returns the value of the next key pressed by the user. The key values are listed in Appendix V.*

statement is executed, the value of the next key pressed by the user is stored in the designated variable. What do we mean by a key's "value?" Pressing a key sends a single character into main memory. Characters are stored as binary codes. Each character has its own unique code; for example, an upper case A is stored as 01000001. The decimal and hexadecimal equivalents of the various characters as represented in the ASCII (American Standard Code for Information Interchange) code are shown in Appendix V. A character's value is its code value. For example, a capital A is (in decimal) 065, while a lower case a is 097.

Now let's change the guessing game program *(Fig. 7.5)*. Start near the **END** with the "play again" prompt and the **GET KEY** statement. Following execution of the **GET KEY** statement, the numeric value of the first key pressed is stored in **reply**. Move to the top of the loop. A capital Y has the value 89; a lower case y is 121. If **reply** holds 89 or 121, the loop repeats; if not, it ends. To make sure the loop executes the first time through, we set **reply** to 89 before we started.

Lengthy Input Lists

The guessing game program required very little input. If a problem calls for several input data items, the list of variables can become quite lengthy. One option is coding a separate **INPUT** statement for each variable. There are several advantages to this approach. An input prompt can be attached to each statement, clearly identifying the value to be entered. Correcting input errors (our next topic) is greatly simplified. However, item-by-item input is slow. In repetitive applications, a user quickly learns the input data pattern, and generally prefers to enter a complete set of data on a single line.

Single line input brings us back to the original problem. Given the clear, meaningful variable names that we certainly should use, we may not be able to fit the **INPUT** statement and all its variables on a single 80-character line. Fortunately, there is a solution.

Consider the statements

```
    INPUT employee_number, hours_worked, pay_rate,

    INPUT shift_code, dependents, marital_status,

    INPUT city_code
```

Note that the first two end with commas. The comma means "more to come." In effect, *True BASIC* combines the statements. In response to the first input prompt, the user enters values for all seven variables. The complete list flows into the computer. The first three values are assigned to the first **INPUT** statement's variables, the second three to the second **INPUT** statement's variables, and so on. Because there is no comma following **city_code**, it marks the end of the input operation.

On programs that repeat only a few times, code a separate **INPUT** statement for each variable. Because the user must enter values only once or twice, the relative slowness of the one-at-a-time approach isn't a factor. On repetitive programs, however, it makes sense to allow the user to enter the data unprompted.

Fig. 7.5: *To allow for repetitive playing of the guessing game program, we'll add a GET KEY statement, and use the player's response to control a DO WHILE loop.*

```
                        ! A guessing game. A function is defined
                        ! to select a random number between 1 and
                        ! some upper limit, n.
DEF The_number(n) = Int(Rnd * n + 1)

                        ! First we'll print a brief explanation of
                        ! the game so the player knows what to do.
PRINT "The computer is about to select a number between 1 and 10."
PRINT "You'll have three chances to guess the number. After each of"
PRINT "your first two guesses, the computer will tell you if your"
PRINT "guess was high or low. Good luck!"

                        ! At the end of the program, the player
                        ! will be given an option to play again.
                        ! As long as the player presses a capital
                        ! Y (key 89) or a lower case y (key 121),
                        ! the program continues. When the player
                        ! presses any other key, the program ends.
                        ! The key value (reply) is initialized to
                        ! an upper case Y to start the program.
RANDOMIZE               ! We want unexpected numbers.
```

```
LET reply = 89
DO WHILE (reply = 89) OR (reply = 121)
                              ! Referencing the function, the computer
                              ! selects a random number between 1 and 10.
  LET random_number = The_number(10)
                              ! The user inputs up to three guesses.
  FOR count = 1 TO 3
     INPUT PROMPT "Enter a number between 1 and 3: ": guess
                              ! If the guess is correct, a message is
                              ! displayed and the loop is exited.
     IF guess = random_number THEN
        PRINT "Correct! You win!"
        EXIT FOR              ! Note exit condition.
                              ! If the guess is wrong and it's the third
                              ! guess, the player loses.
     ELSEIF count = 3 THEN
          PRINT "You lose. The number is", random_number
                              ! Following an incorrect first or second
                              ! guess, the player is told if the guess
                              ! is high or low.
          ELSEIF guess > random_number THEN
              PRINT "Your guess is high."
          ELSE
              PRINT "Your guess is low."
     END IF
  NEXT count
                              ! Next, we determine if the player would
                              ! like to play again.
  PRINT "Would you like to play again? If yes, press Y;"
  PRINT "if no, press any other key."

  GET KEY reply               ! This instruction inputs a single key.
LOOP

END
```

Fig. 7.5, *continued.*

Start with a pattern; for example,

> **PRINT "In response to each prompt (?), enter values for:"**
>
> **PRINT "employee number, hours worked, pay rate, shift"**
>
> **PRINT "code, dependents, marital status, and city code."**
>
> **PRINT "Use commas to separate values."**

Display it before the first **INPUT** statement is executed. Display it again only if the user makes an error.

Input Errors

True BASIC is designed to catch certain input errors. Figure 7.6 shows a simple

Fig. 7.6: *Note the error messages in the history window as this simple program is run. They illustrate the three types of input error messages True BASIC generates.*

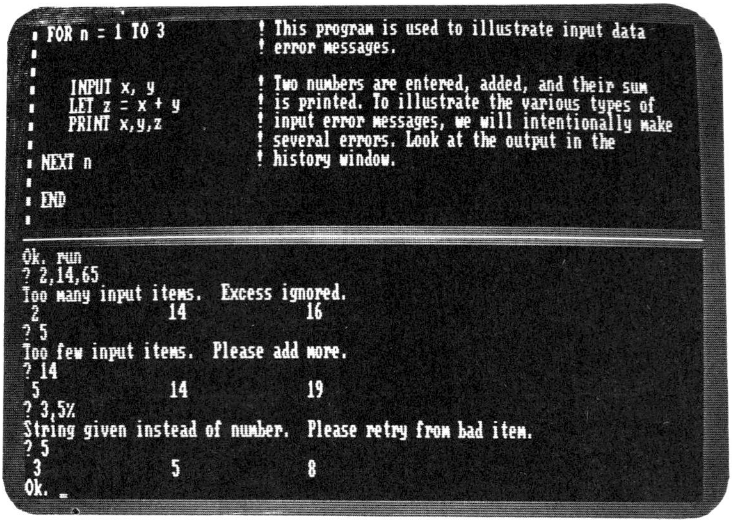

```
FOR n = 1 TO 3                  ! This program is used to illustrate input data
                                ! error messages.
    INPUT x, y                  ! Two numbers are entered, added, and their sum
    LET z = x + y               ! is printed. To illustrate the various types of
    PRINT x,y,z                 ! input error messages, we will intentionally make
                                ! several errors. Look at the output in the
NEXT n                          ! history window.

END
```

```
Ok. run
? 2,14,65
Too many input items. Excess ignored.
 2              14              16
? 5
Too few input items. Please add more.
? 14
 5              14              19
? 3,5%
String given instead of number. Please retry from bad item.
? 5
 3              5               8
Ok.
```

```
READ variable1, variable2, . . .
           ⎵
           └──────── list of variables
```

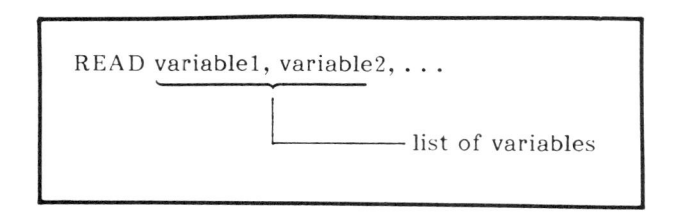

Fig. 7.7: *A READ statement resembles an INPUT statement.*

program illustrating, in the history window, the three basic types. Enter too few values, and you'll be asked for more. Enter too many, and the excess values are ignored. In either case, the proper response is obvious.

The third type occurs when an illegal value (for example, a number containing a non-numeric character) is entered. When this happens, the message "Please retry from bad item." is displayed. This message is potentially confusing, particularly to a nontechnical user. Imagine, for example, a list of five input values. If the second one is entered incorrectly, items 2, 3, 4, and 5 must be retyped. If only the last item is wrong, however, only the last item must be reentered. The proper response depends on which value is wrong. To avoid confusion, ask for one value at a time, unless, of course, the application demands a lengthy list of input values. When faced with such an application, consider using **LINE INPUT** statements *(see Chapter 10).*

True BASIC can catch only obvious errors. It does not guarantee the data's accuracy. If you want to verify your data, you must write your own routines.

READ/DATA STATEMENTS

When an **INPUT** statement is executed, the user is expected to enter data. An alternative is to use **READ** *(Fig. 7.7)* and **DATA** *(Fig. 7.8)* statements. For

Fig. 7.8: *DATA statements define a series of values. When the program is run, these values are collected to form a data pool. When a READ statement is executed, the next value (or values) is selected from the pool and assigned to the READ statement's variable (or variables).*

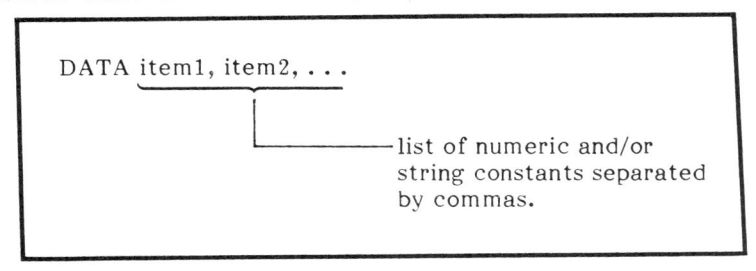

```
DATA item1, item2, . . .
         ⎵
         └──────── list of numeric and/or
                   string constants separated
                   by commas.
```

example, consider a program to compute an arithmetic average, or mean. We wrote such a program in Chapter 4; let's modify it *(Fig. 7.9)*.

We'll start by coding several **DATA** statements; they're grouped right before **END**. Actually, they can be placed anywhere; we stuck them at the program's end to get them out of the way. When the program is run, all its **DATA** statements are collected and combined to form a single data pool. A pointer holds the address of the first value in the list.

The **READ** statement looks much like an **INPUT** statement. When the **READ** is executed, the next available value is taken from the data pool and stored in the designated variable. As each value is assigned, the pointer moves to the next value; thus the data items in the pool are assigned in sequential order. Data types must match; for example, an error occurs if a string value is assigned to a numeric variable. With **INPUT** statements, you enter data as the program runs. With **READ** and **DATA** statements, you effectively enter the data before the program runs.

READ/DATA statements are valuable in a number of applications. One is program testing or debug. The objective is to find and correct errors. A common approach is to enter test data until something goes wrong, correct the error, and then enter the test data again. This cycle continues until no more errors are found. Instead of repeatedly entering the same test data, simply define a

---

Fig. 7.9: *In this version of the average program, READ and DATA statements replace the INPUT statement.*

```
                                    ! Program to compute an arithmetic average
                                    ! or mean. First, a counter and an
LET count = 0                       ! accumulator are initialized to zero.
LET sum = 0

                                    ! In a DO loop, individual values are read,
                                    ! counted, and accumulated. A negative
DO                                  ! value indicates the end of data.
   READ x
   IF x >= 0 THEN                   ! A negative number means no more data. We
      LET sum = sum + x             ! do not want to count and accumulate this
      LET count = count + 1         ! sentinal value.
   END IF
LOOP UNTIL x < 0                    ! Here is the loop's exit condition.

LET average = sum / count           ! After exiting the loop, the average is
PRINT sum, count, average           ! computed and printed.

                                    ! The program's DATA statements are
                                    ! grouped here, just before the END.
DATA 52,63,57,83,65,89,84,87,60,59,68,96,71,88,85,83,87,98,-1
END
```

Fig. 7.10: *A RESTORE statement moves the pointer back to the beginning of the data pool, and thus allows the DATA statements' values to be reused.*

```
RESTORE
```

series of **DATA** statements, and replace your **INPUT**s with **READ**s. After testing is complete, put the **INPUT** statements back.

Another application involves data that change only occasionally. For example, consider payroll. Data such as hours worked and pay rate vary with each employee, but the various tax rates change annually, at most. We could, of course, code the tax rates as constants, but they *can* change, and rewriting a subroutine to reflect a new rate structure can introduce bugs to a program. Instead, define each rate structure as a set of variables (perhaps as a table or an array, see Chapter 8) to be input each time the program runs. Given variable tax rates, a new rate structure would require only that input data, and not program logic, be changed.

Using **INPUT** statements to enter tax rates is inefficient and risky (people do make errors). It's far better to store the rates in a file *(see Chapter 11)*, and copy them from disk as the program begins. An option is to define them as a series of **DATA** statements, and to use **READ** statements to initialize the rate variables. Incidentally, **DATA** statements are local to their program unit (mainline, external function, or external subroutine), so the data to initialize rates can be defined entirely within the subroutine that uses them.

In other applications, the same data are used over and over again. Storing the values in an array *(see Chapter 8)* is one solution; using **READ/DATA** statements is another. For example, when computing a statistical value called a standard deviation, a series of input values are read, accumulated, and counted, and then their average or mean is computed. Next, the average is subtracted from each input value, and the differences are squared. The standard deviation is computed from the sum of these squares.

The data are used twice. With **INPUT** statements, every value must be entered once to compute the average, and then again to compute the standard deviation. With **READ** and **DATA** statements, the values can be reused. When a program is run, all its **DATA** statements are collected and combined to form a single data pool. Each **READ** statement gets the "next" value or values from the pool. A pointer keeps track of the next value. A **RESTORE** statement *(Fig. 7.10)* moves the pointer back to the first item in the pool.

When data are **INPUT**, it is necessary to define a sentinel value to signal the end-of-data condition. With **READ/DATA** statements, a programmer can take advantage of the **MORE DATA** and **END DATA** logical conditions. Since the **DATA** statements are already in the computer, the computer knows how many items it has. The **MORE DATA** condition is true if there are more data. The **END DATA** condition is true if there are no more data. **MORE DATA** and **END DATA** can be tested in an **IF** statement, a **WHILE** option, or an **UNTIL** option.

DATA OUTPUT

The PRINT Statement

The essentials of the **PRINT** statement were covered in Chapter 2, and we've used it in almost every program developed since then. A **PRINT** statement, when executed, displays output in the history window. On most computers, the screen's right edge *(Fig. 7.11)*, called the margin, is set at 80, meaning that each line holds up to eighty characters. The lines are divided into five print zones, each sixteen characters wide. Not all computers follow this standard, however; if you don't know your monitor's zone width, code

   ASK ZONEWIDTH variable

   PRINT variable

The current number of characters per zone will be stored in the specified variable,

Fig. 7.11: *On most computers, each screen line can hold 80 characters. The line is divided into five print zones, each 16 characters wide.*

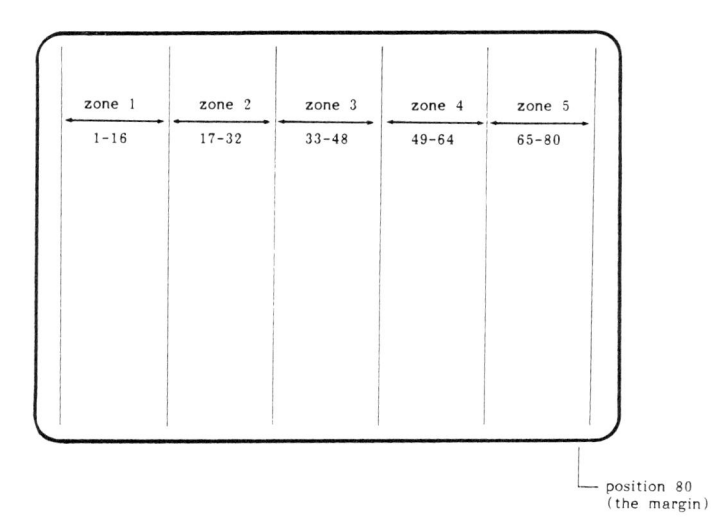

```
          zone 1    zone 2    zone 3    zone 4    zone 5
          1-16      17-32     33-48     49-64     65-80
```

position 80 (the margin)

202

and then displayed.

In a **PRINT** statement, a list of expressions follows the keyword **PRINT**. Normally, the expressions are separated by commas. A comma means "skip to the next zone." Thus, the value of the first expression is displayed in zone 1; the second expression's value is displayed in zone 2, and so on. If the list contains more than five expressions, more than one line will be needed to display all the values. If a string variable or a string constant is more than 16 characters long, it will cover two or more zones. For example, when

    PRINT "01234567890123456789", x

is executed, the string constant will cover zone 1 and part of zone 2. The comma means "skip to the next zone," so the value of **x** will be displayed in zone 3.

Semicolons can be used to separate the expressions in a **PRINT** list. A semicolon means "don't move the cursor." In the statement

    PRINT a; b

the value of **b** will be displayed immediately after **a**'s value. Commas and semicolons can be mixed in a single **PRINT** statement.

You can directly control both the line width and the zone width. The statement

    SET MARGIN expression

sets the margin, while

    SET ZONEWIDTH expression

sets the zone width. Later in this chapter, we'll consider how a programmer can define windows for displaying output. The margin and zone width are important considerations when windows narrower than a full screen are used.

Closer control over the spacing of your output can be achieved by using the **TAB** function. In Chapter 4, we wrote a program to generate a temperature conversion table; Fig. 7.12 shows a new version with a **TAB** function controlling the output. When a **TAB** is encountered, the cursor moves to the specified location on the print line. If a comma follows the **TAB**, the cursor moves from there to the start of the next zone before displaying the next expression's value. If

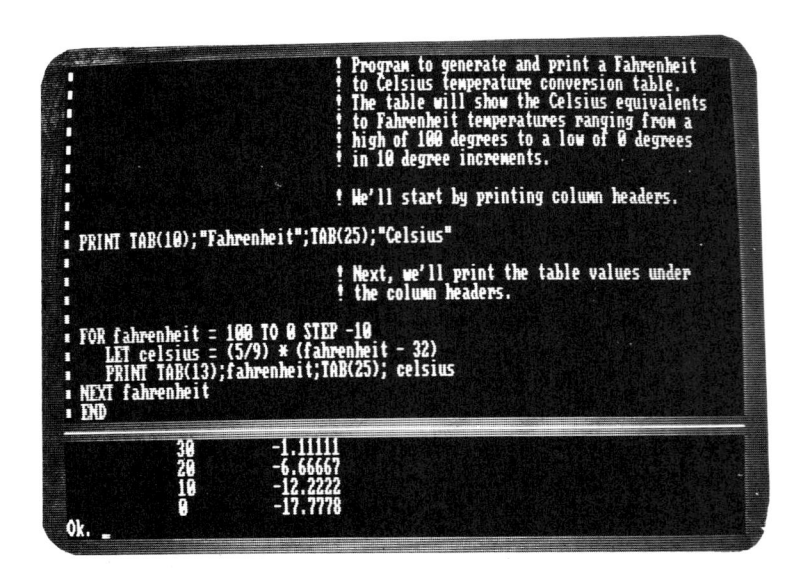

```
! Program to generate and print a Fahrenheit
! to Celsius temperature conversion table.
! The table will show the Celsius equivalents
! to Fahrenheit temperatures ranging from a
! high of 100 degrees to a low of 0 degrees
! in 10 degree increments.

! We'll start by printing column headers.

PRINT TAB(10);"Fahrenheit";TAB(25);"Celsius"

! Next, we'll print the table values under
! the column headers.

FOR fahrenheit = 100 TO 0 STEP -10
    LET celsius = (5/9) * (fahrenheit - 32)
    PRINT TAB(13);fahrenheit;TAB(25); celsius
NEXT fahrenheit
END
```

```
            30       -1.11111
            20       -6.66667
            10      -12.2222
             0      -17.7778
Ok.
```

Fig. 7.12: *In this version of the temperature conversion program, TAB functions are used to control the output format.*

the **TAB** is followed by a semicolon, the cursor does not move before the next expression's value is displayed.

PRINT USING

For many applications, commas, semicolons, and **TAB** functions are fine. However, more precise control over printed output is sometimes required. The **PRINT USING** statement *(Fig. 7.13)* ignores the standard print zones, allowing the programmer to specify a format for each output value.

A string expression composed of format characters and message characters follows the keyword **USING**. Message characters (blanks or explanatory notes) are printed exactly as they are coded. The format characters are used to build patterns for printing output values; they are summarized in Fig. 7.14. A sign (+ or -) or a dollar sign can be placed in front of a number. The number itself can be printed with leading blanks (#), leading zeros (%), or leading asterisks (*). Any of the digit characters (#, %, or *) can be used to form a pattern for string output. Commas and a decimal point can be added to a number; a comma is printed only if significant digits lie to its left. A floating point number's exponential part can be printed. Finally, a character string can be right justified (>) or left justified (<) in its field.

```
PRINT USING format$: item1, item2, ...
```
- a list of expressions or output values
- a colon (must be coded)
- a string expression composed of format and message characters

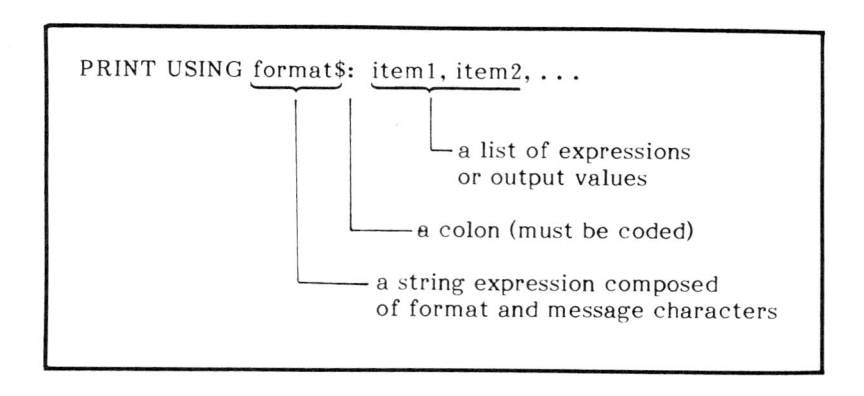

Fig. 7.13: *The PRINT USING statement allows the programmer to control the format of output data.*

A colon (:) separates the format string from the data list. Typically, each item in the list has its own format pattern. Message characters (blanks, for example) separate the individual patterns. If not enough format patterns are defined, they are reused from the start as often as necessary. Excess patterns are ignored. If a value is too big to be printed within its format pattern, a string of asterisks is printed instead. Any character that is not a format character is a message character. Message characters are printed as coded.

Let's use the temperature conversion program to illustrate. Start with a

Fig. 7.14: *A summary of True BASIC's format characters.*

Character	Meaning
+	Print leading + or -.
-	Print leading space or -.
$	Print leading dollar sign.
*	Print leading zeros as asterisks.
%	Print leading zeros as zeros
#	Print leading zeros as blanks.
,	Insert comma in number (if appropriate).
.	Align and print decimal point.
^	Print exponent field.
<	Left-justify character field.
>	Right-justify character field.

Note: *, %, or # can be used to define a pattern for a string value.

Fig. 7.15: *The first step in defining format patterns is planning a dummy version of the desired output.*

```
Fahrenheit     Celsius
   100          37.8
   xx           xx.x
   xx           xx,x

    0          -17.8
```

sheet of paper, and plan exactly how the output should look *(Fig. 7.15)*. We want the words "Fahrenheit" and "Celsius" on the first line. Subsequent lines should contain a Fahrenheit temperature and the equivalent Celsius temperature, nicely aligned and centered under the column headers. Because the Fahrenheit temperatures range from a high of 100 to a low of 0, we'll never need more than a 3-digit integer to display them. To get a sense of how many digits we'll need for the Celsius temperatures, we'll compute the extreme values: 0 degrees Fahrenheit is -17.8 degrees Celsius, and 100 degrees Fahrenheit is 37.8 degrees on the Celsius scale. We'll need a sign, too.

Given a dummy layout, we can plan our format strings. Let's start with the column headers. String data can be printed using any numeric format characters—the # sign is a good choice. The word Fahrenheit is 10 characters long; Celsius is 7. We want 2 blank spaces between the words. Thus our format string is

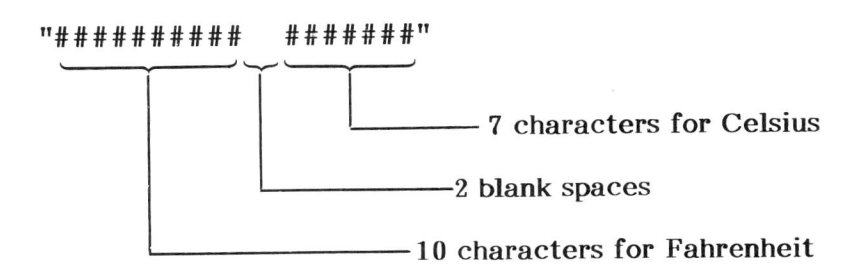

"########## #######"
           │   │
           │   └── 7 characters for Celsius
           └── 2 blank spaces
    └── 10 characters for Fahrenheit

The statement that prints the header is highlighted in Fig. 7.16.

Next, we'll plan patterns for the temperature values. Start with the Fahrenheit temperature. We need three digits. How do we want to handle leading zeros? We can print them, replace them with asterisks, or replace them with blanks. In this case, replacing leading zeros with blanks makes the most sense, so we'll use ###. Celsius temperatures require a sign, a decimal point, and three digits. We'll use -##.#. Finally, we'll add spaces to align the numbers with their column headers. We need 4 blanks at the beginning of the line, and 6 blanks to separate the temperatures, giving us

```
"    ###      -##.#"
 └┬┘ └┬┘ └┬┘   └─┬─┘
  │   │   │     └───── the Celsius temperature
  │   │   └─────────── six (6) blanks
  │   └─────────────── the Fahrenheit temperature
  └─────────────────── four (4) blanks
```

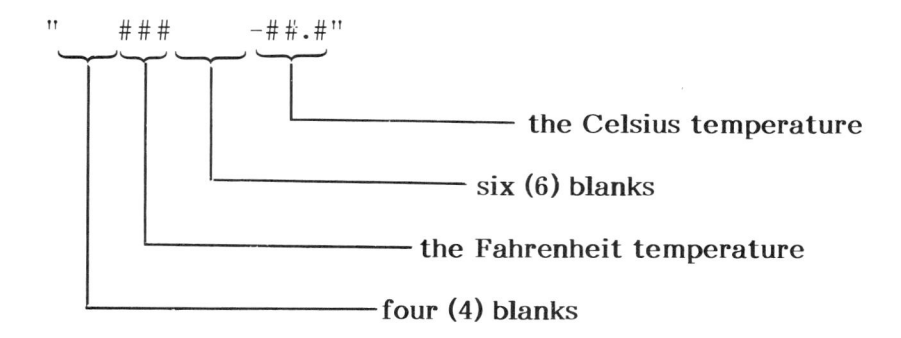

A **PRINT USING** statement containing this format string is highlighted in Fig. 7.16.

Designing format patterns is not difficult. Work on the output variables one by one. Start by writing the largest possible value. Add necessary punctuation—signs, commas, a decimal point. If appropriate, add a leading dollar sign. Now decide how you want leading zeros treated. If you want to replace them with asterisks, code an asterisk (*) for each digit in the number. If leading

---

Fig. 7.16: *In this version of the temperature conversion program, format patterns attached to PRINT USING statements control the output.*

```
                        ! Program to generate and print a Fahrenheit
                        ! to Celsius temperature conversion table.
                        ! The table will show the Celsius equivalents
                        ! to Fahrenheit temperatures ranging from a
                        ! high of 100 degrees to a low of 0 degrees
                        ! in 10 degree increments.

                        ! We'll start by printing column headers.
PRINT USING "##########   #######": "Fahrenheit", "CELSIUS"

                        ! Next, we'll generate the table.
FOR fahrenheit = 100 TO 0 STEP -10

   LET celsius = (5/9) * (fahrenheit - 32)

                        ! The PRINT USING option allows us to control
                        ! the format of the output.
   PRINT USING "    ###      -##.#": fahrenheit, celsius

NEXT fahrenheit
END
```

zeros are to be printed, use a percent sign (%). Leading blanks call for a # symbol. Add punctuation marks and a sign, and you have the pattern for that item. Develop patterns for each output item, and then combine them to form a single string, using appropriate message characters (blanks or words) to separate them.

Figure 7.17 shows several examples of format strings. Note that *True BASIC* rounds to the number of decimal positions specified by the format pattern.

A **PRINT USING** statement with a format string and a list of variables can become quite lengthy, easily exceeding an 80-character line. When that happens, code a series of **PRINT USING** statements, ending all but the last one with a semicolon. The semicolon means "don't move the cursor." Thus, the output generated by the second **PRINT** statement will appear on the same line as that generated by the first.

Patterns for string data can be formed from any numeric format characters; we'll use the # symbol. If the format pattern defines more characters than the data contains, the value is centered in the field and padded to the right and left with blanks. Use a less than symbol (<) to left justify the value; for example,

"<####"

defines a 5-character, left-justified string. Use a greater than symbol (>) to right justify the field.

In a **PRINT USING** statement, commas separate the items in the output list. Semicolons and **TAB** functions are not legal. A semicolon can, however, appear at the end of the list.

PRINTER OUTPUT

One problem with displaying output data on a screen is that the display unit isn't portable. For example, it makes no sense to carry a computer and a display

Fig. 7.17: *Some examples of output format patterns.*

Dummy value	Format string	Data value	Output
$99.99	"$**.**"	3.98	$*3.98
10,000	"##,###"	2745	2,745
-99	"-##"	-3	- 3
x = 99	"### ##"	"x =",35	x = 35
9999	"%%%%"	22	0022
+1,500,000	"+#,###,###"	-356012	- 356,012
-0.1999	"-%.%%%"	-0.03	-0.0300
1.385e15	"%.%%%^^"	1.6e2	1.6e+2

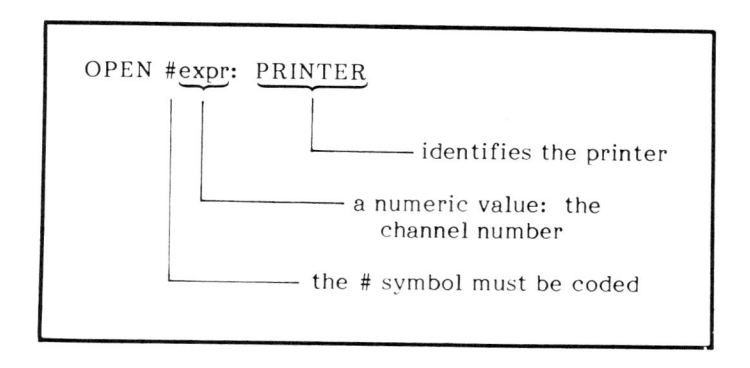

```
OPEN #expr:  PRINTER
         │        │
         │        └─── identifies the printer
         │
         └──── a numeric value: the
               channel number
         
         └──── the # symbol must be coded
```

Fig. 7.18: *Before data can be sent to the printer, a channel must be opened.*

on your vacation just so you can refer to a temperatuare conversion table. Sometimes, printed output is much more convenient.

Each device on your computer system is accessed via an electrical connection that *True BASIC* calls a channel. The keyboard and display are on channel #0. Other devices must be assigned a channel number and opened before they can be used. To access the printer, start by referencing it in an **OPEN** statement *(Fig. 7.18)*; for example,

> **OPEN #1: PRINTER**

This **OPEN** statement assigns channel #1 to the printer. Once it is executed, you can send your output to the printer by coding

> **PRINT #1: expr1, expr2, . . .**

Figure 7.19 shows the temperature conversion table program with printer output. Note, just before the **END** statement, that channel #1 is closed (the **CLOSE** statement, see Fig. 7.20). The sequence is always: **OPEN** a channel, **PRINT** to it (or **INPUT** from it), and then **CLOSE** the channel when you're finished.

WINDOWS

When you print to the screen, your output is displayed in the history window. If only a few lines are printed, that's fine. In fact, when you were learning how to program, seeing the output in the history window was useful, because you

```
                        ! Program to generate and print a
                        ! temperature conversion table. The table
                        ! will show the Celsius equivalents to
                        ! Fahrenheit temperatures ranging from a
                        ! high of 100 degrees to a low of 0
                        ! degrees in 10 degree increments.

OPEN #1: PRINTER        ! Since we want our output to go to the
                        ! printer, we must open the printer.

                        ! We'll start by printing column headers.

PRINT #1, USING "#########   #######": "Fahrenheit", "CELSIUS"

                        ! Next, we'll generate the table.

FOR fahrenheit = 100 TO 0 STEP -10

   LET celsius = (5/9) * (fahrenheit - 32)

                        ! The PRINT USING option allows us to
                        ! control the format of the output.

   PRINT #1, USING "      ###        -##.#": fahrenheit, celsius

NEXT fahrenheit

CLOSE #1                ! Since we opened the printer,
                        ! we must close it.
END
```

Fig. 7.19: *In this version of the temperature conversion program, the output is sent to the printer.*

Fig. 7.20: *The general form of a CLOSE statement.*

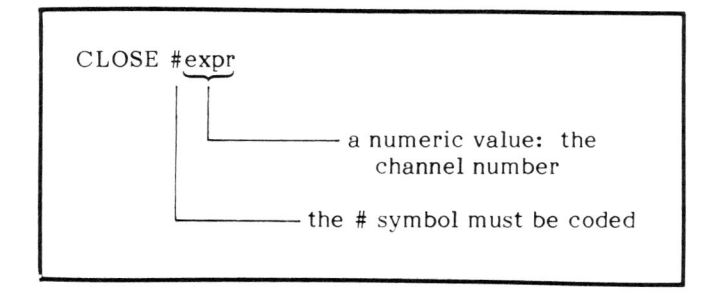

```
CLOSE #expr
         │ └──── a numeric value: the
         │           channel number
         └────── the # symbol must be coded
```

could look to the editing window and compare the results with the instructions that generated them.

As your programming skills improve, however, you'll find the history window limiting. Not much data can be displayed in seven lines. Also, while the editing window may be useful for program debugging, it adds unnecessary clutter when a fully debugged program is running. On some computers you can change the window size by using a **SPLIT** command; check your *User's Guide* for details.

A more general solution is to open a new window. A window is a portion of the screen. Think of the screen as a standard x-y coordinate system *(Fig. 7.21)*. The origin (0,0) is at the lower left. The screen is one unit across and one unit high. Thus the upper left corner is position (0,1), the lower right corner is (1,0), and the upper right corner is (1,1).

To define a window, you **OPEN** it *(Fig. 7.21)*. Each window is assigned a channel number; code it after the keyword **OPEN**. After the channel number, type a colon (:), followed by the keyword **SCREEN** and the minimum and maximum coordinates for the window's x axis and y axis, respectively.

Figure 7.22 shows the temperature conversion program with its output going to a full-screen window. The **OPEN** statement defines the window; when it is executed, the history and editing windows disappear, and the full screen becomes the current window. **PRINT** statements always send their output to the current window. At the end of the program, the window should be closed; if you forget the **CLOSE** statement, the **END** takes care of it.

Note the **DO** loop near the end of the program. It contains only a **PAUSE** statement *(Fig. 7.23)*. When a window is closed, *True BASIC* automatically reverts to its standard editing and history windows (channel 0), and you may not have time to read the output before it disappears. The **PAUSE** statement holds the display for the specified number of seconds before the next instruction is executed.

The loop's exit condition is

LOOP UNTIL KEY INPUT

The condition **KEY INPUT** is true if any key has been pressed since the last **INPUT** statement was executed, and false otherwise. This loop will repeat, holding the full screen output, until the user presses a key (any key). Thus the user controls how long the output is displayed.

A full screen can be used for data input, too. Like the **PRINT** statement, the **INPUT** statement always works with the current window. When a window is opened, the cursor is set at its top left corner. As **INPUT** and **PRINT** statements are executed, the cursor moves down the window, just as it moves down the history window, line by line.

Full screen input is particularly valuable on applications calling for the entry of a great deal of data. For example, in a payroll program the input data for an individual can all be entered on the first line. As the values are checked,

OPEN #n: SCREEN 0,0.5, 0.5,1   OPEN #n: SCREEN 0.5,1, 0.5,1

0,1   1,1

0,0   0,1

OPEN #n: SCREEN 0, 0.5, 0,0.5   OPEN #n: SCREEN 0.5,1, 0,0.5

Full screen:

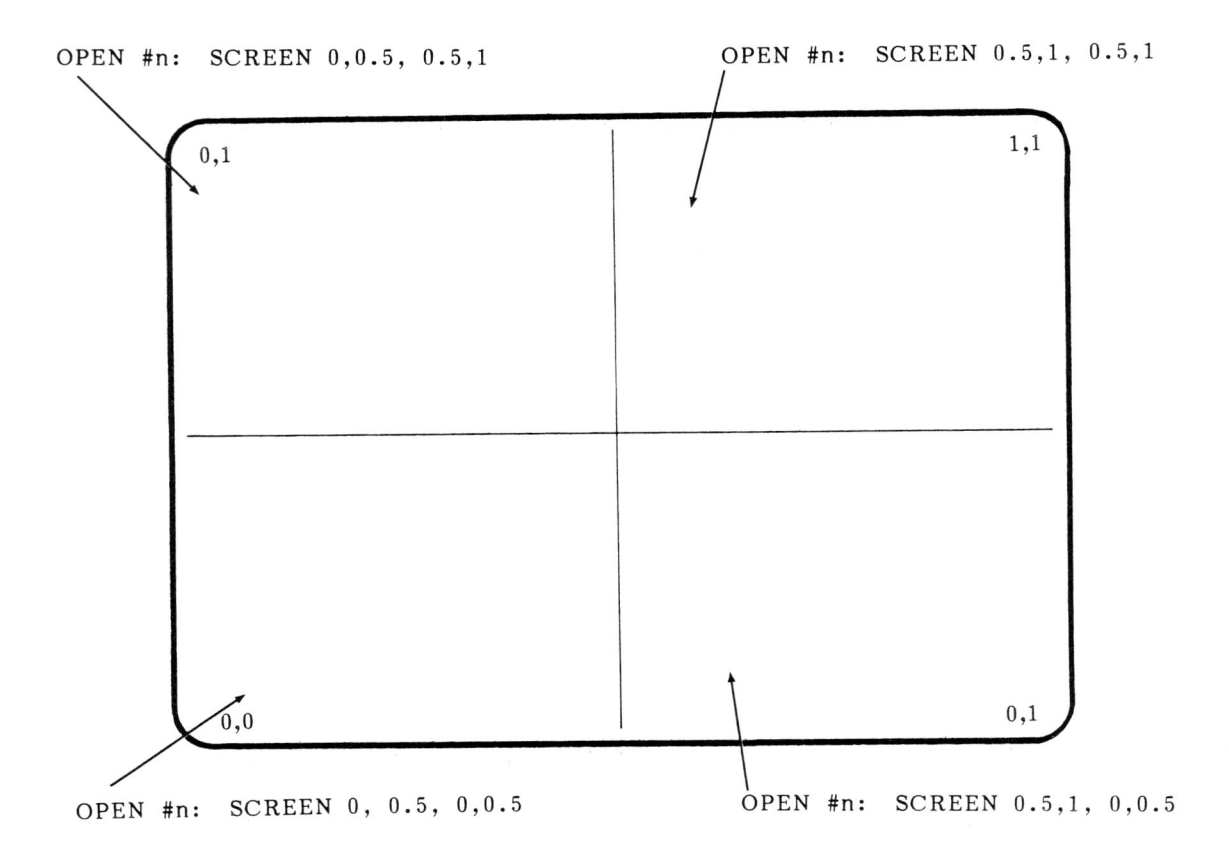

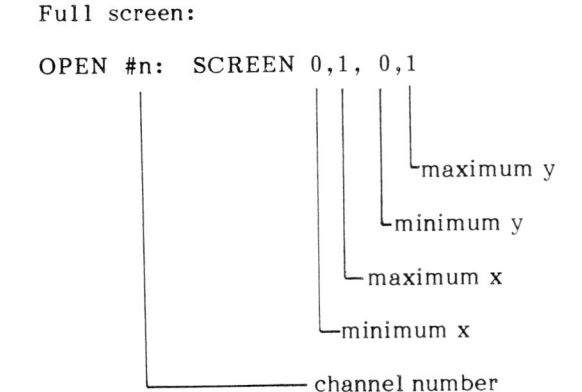

OPEN #n: SCREEN 0,1, 0,1
                                          └─ maximum y
                                  └─ minimum y
                           └─ maximum x
                    └─ minimum x
        └─────────── channel number

Fig. 7.21: *To understand windows, view the screen as an x-y coordinate system. You can OPEN a window simply by specifying its maximum x and y values.*

```
                              ! Program to generate and print a
                              ! temperature conversion table. The table
                              ! will show the Celsius equivalents to
                              ! Fahrenheit temperatures ranging from a
                              ! high of 100 degrees to a low of 0
                              ! degrees in 10 degree increments.

                              ! We want to use the full screen for our
                              ! output, so we'll define channel #1 as
                              ! the full screen, and OPEN it.

OPEN #1: SCREEN 0,1, 0,1

                              ! First, we'll print column headers.

PRINT #1, USING "#########   #######": "Fahrenheit", "CELSIUS"

                              ! Next, we'll generate the table.

FOR fahrenheit = 100 TO 0 STEP -10

   LET celsius = (5/9) * (fahrenheit - 32)

                              ! The PRINT USING option allows us to
                              ! control the format of the output.

   PRINT #1, USING "     ###        -##.#": fahrenheit, celsius

NEXT fahrenheit

CLOSE #1                      ! Since we opened the screen,
                              ! we must close it.

                              ! The PAUSE loop holds the display
                              ! until the user presses a key.

DO
   PAUSE 2
LOOP UNTIL KEY INPUT

END
```

Fig. 7.22: *The temperature conversion program with full screen output.*

corrections can be made on the same screen, with a complete history of this individual's data always visible. After the data have been successively entered, a **CLEAR** statement *(Fig. 7.24)* can be used to erase the window and move the cursor back to the upper left corner. Now the next employee's data can be entered.

The programmer is not limited to line-by-line, top-to-bottom input and output. With a **SET CURSOR** statement *(Fig. 7.25)*, the cursor can be moved to any position

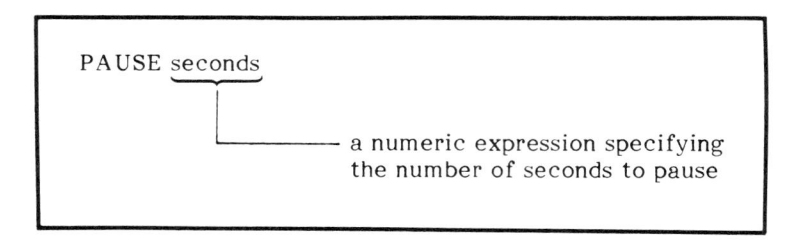

```
┌─────────────────────────────────────────┐
│                                         │
│         PAUSE seconds                   │
│               ‾‾‾‾‾‾‾                   │
│                  └──── a numeric expression specifying │
│                        the number of seconds to pause  │
│                                         │
└─────────────────────────────────────────┘

**Fig. 7.23:** *A PAUSE statement tells the computer to "mark time" for the indicated number of seconds.*

on any line in the window. An **INPUT** or **PRINT** following a **SET CURSOR** statement will begin at whatever position the cursor occupies. The **ASK CURSOR** statement *(Fig. 7.26)* returns the cursor's current line number and character number.

## SUMMARY

This chapter presented several advanced input and output topics. We started with data input, using a guessing game program to introduce the **INPUT** with **PROMPT** statement. We then modified the program, using a **GET KEY** statement to control repetitive play.

Next, we discussed the problem of entering several input values on one line. Instead of coding a single, lengthy statement, two or more **INPUT** statements can essentially be combined by placing a comma after the last variable in all but the final one.

*True BASIC* automatically catches three types of input errors. Enter too few values, and the computer asks for more. Excess data values are ignored. If an illegal value is coded, all the values, starting with the bad one, must be reentered. This can be confusing; options include coding a separate **INPUT** statement for each value and using **LINE INPUT** statements *(see Chapter 10)*.

When **INPUT** statements are used, the data are entered as the program runs. An option is to define several **DATA** statements, and then use **READ** statements to get values from the data pool. **READ** and **DATA** statements are useful for program debugging, for defining data values that change only occasionally, and, by using a **RESTORE** statement, for accessing data values that must be reused.

**Fig. 7.24:** *The **CLEAR** statement erases the current window and moves the cursor to the top left corner.*

    ┌─────────┐
    │  CLEAR  │
    └─────────┘
```

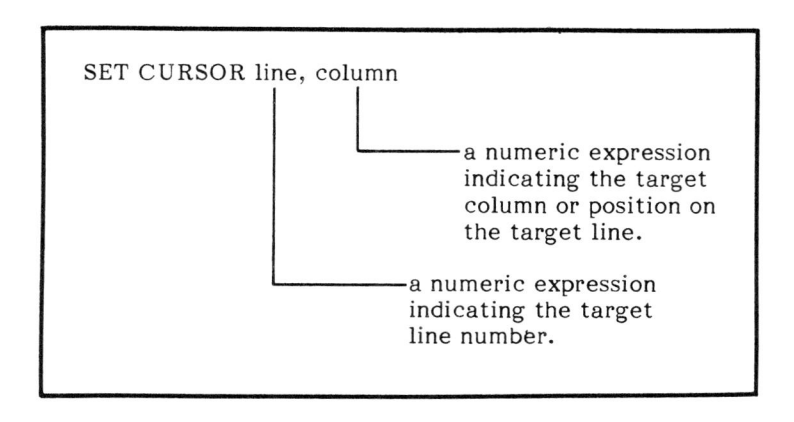

```
SET CURSOR line, column
              │      │
              │      └─── a numeric expression
              │           indicating the target
              │           column or position on
              │           the target line.
              │
              └────────── a numeric expression
                          indicating the target
                          line number.
```

Fig. 7.25: *A SET CURSOR statement moves the cursor to the indicated position on the screen.*

Turning to output, we reviewed the **PRINT** statement, discussing margins, zones, commas, semicolons, and **TAB** functions. Next we introduced **PRINT USING,** and explained how format patterns can be defined to control the appearance of a program's output. A temperature conversion program illustrated several options.

Output is normally displayed in the history window. An option is to send it to the printer. We discussed how to **OPEN** a channel to the printer. Then we introduced the idea of windows, and illustrated how the full screen can be used for input and output.

Fig. 7.26: *An ASK CURSOR statement returns the cursor's current coordinates.*

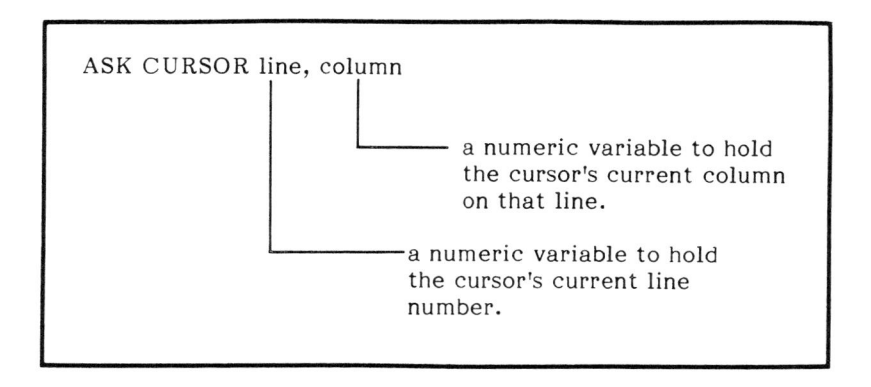

```
ASK CURSOR line, column
              │      │
              │      └─── a numeric variable to hold
              │           the cursor's current column
              │           on that line.
              │
              └────────── a numeric variable to hold
                          the cursor's current line
                          number.
```

REFERENCES

True BASIC Statements

    INPUT PROMPT   Fig. 7.2,   page 193

    GET KEY   Fig. 7.4,   page 195

    READ   Fig. 7.7,   page 199

    DATA   Fig. 7.8,   page 199

    RESTORE   Fig. 7.10, page 201

    PRINT USING   Fig. 7.13, page 205

    OPEN PRINTER   Fig. 7.18, page 209

    CLOSE   Fig. 7.20, page 210

    OPEN SCREEN   Fig. 7.21, page 211

    PAUSE   Fig. 7.23, page 214

    CLEAR   Fig. 7.24, page 214

    SET CURSOR   Fig. 7.25, page 215

    ASK CURSOR   Fig. 7.26, page 215

True BASIC Rules and Syntax

    Format characters   Fig. 7.14, page 205

    Format strings   Fig. 7.17, page 208

    Defining windows   Fig. 7.21, page 212

True BASIC Logical Conditions

    END DATA condition   page 201

    MORE DATA condition   page 201

    KEY INPUT condition   page 211

EXERCISES

1. Suggest input prompts for the following data:

    a. An integer between 1 and 10.

    b. Hours worked and a pay rate for a payroll program.

    c. A dollar amount to be invested.

    d. An interest rate to be input as a percentage; for example, ten percent should be entered as 0.10.

    e. The lengths of the three sides of a triangle, with the longest side entered first.

    f. The elements for computing a grade point average.

    g. A customer's name.

    h. A date in the form: mm/dd/yy.

2. Suggest format strings for the following output data:

    a. A grade point average.

    b. Three 2-digit integers.

    c. A temperature between 0 and 100, followed by the words "degrees Fahrenheit."

    d. The phrase "Average age = " followed by an age between 0 and 80, accurate to a single decimal place.

    e. A check for an amount not to exceed $10,000, with check protect characters (asterisks) replacing leading zeros. Be sure to include appropriate punctuation.

    f. A date in the form mm/dd/yy.

    g. A check stub showing gross pay, federal tax, state tax, local tax, and net pay. Each number has a maximum value of $5,000.00. Replace leading zeros with blanks. There is no need to print a dollar sign for each value.

    h. A partial summary of the results of an examination in the form: "xx students scored A; yy students failed the exam." Note that xx and yy are counters generated by the program.

    i. A name (maximum 15 characters) left justified in its field.

    j. Given that a, b, c, and d are variables, the line: "a plus b minus c equals d."

3. Enter the new version of the number guessing game as we wrote it in this chapter *(Fig. 7.5)*. Compare it to the earlier version we wrote in Chapter 5 *(Fig. 5.9)*. Try both versions. Which one would you rather play?

4. In Chapter 2, Exercise 6, you wrote a program to compute net pay. Revise it, using **INPUT PROMPT** statements.

5. In Chapter 2, Exercise 19, you wrote a program to accept the amount of an investment, the interest rate, and the investment's duration in years. Then you computed its future value, using the formula

$$F = P(1+i)^n$$

Modify the program, adding prompts to the **INPUT** statements and formatting the output.

6. Chapter 3, Exercise 11 asked you to use the Pythagorean theorem

$$a^2 = b^2 + c^2$$

to test for a right triangle. Revise the program, providing explicit prompts for the input data.

7. In Chaper 4, Exercise 2, you were asked to generate a table of Fahrenheit, Celsius, and absolute temperatures. Modify the program to yield formatted output with appropriate column headers. Send your output to the printer. Change the program once again to send your output to a full screen window.

8. In Chapter 4, we developed a program to generate a wind chill table *(Fig. 4.25)*. Modify the program to send formatted output, complete with appropriate column headers, to the printer. Modify the program once again to send the output to a full screen window. Ideally, you should print or display a two dimensional table, with temperatures running down, and wind velocities running across. While not necessary, you might want to use an array *(see Chapter 8)*.

9. In Chapter 4, Exercise 6, you developed a table of the squares and square roots of the integers from 1 to 25. Modify the program to send formatted output, with column headers, to the printer.

10. In Chapter 4, Exercise 7, you wrote a program to generate a distance conversion table. Modify the program to send formatted output, with column headers, to the printer. Modify it again to send its output to a full screen window.

11. In Chapter 4, Exercise 12, you were asked to write a program to compute a grade point average. Modify it to use input prompts and generate formatted output.

12. Chapter 4, Exercise 13 asked you to write a program to generate a loan repayment table. Modify it to use input prompts and produce formatted output with appropriate column headers. Send your output to the printer.

13. Chapter 6, Exercise 1, suggested some modifications to the craps program developed in the chapter. Change it again, using input prompts and formatted output. The nature of the program almost demands full screen output.

14. In Chapter 6, Exercise 2g, you were asked to write a data output subroutine for a payroll program. Modify that subroutine to simulate printing a check and a check stub. Print net pay on the check--include a dollar sign and leading asterisks. Print gross pay, federal tax, state tax, local tax, and net pay on the stub. Perhaps your instructor can provide a sample check as a model. If not, use one of your own. Send your output to the printer.

15. Chapter 6, Exercise 4 described a series of interest computations. The idea was to code each algorithm in its own subroutine, and then use a control module to select the proper algorithm. Modify the program. Start with a full screen. Display a menu, a list of available computations. Use the **GET KEY** statement to accept the user's choice and then call the appropriate subroutine. Display input prompts, the responses, and a clearly labeled and formatted result at the bottom of the page. Pause to let the user read the result; then clear the screen, display the menu, and start over again. One menu option should be to end the program.

16. Write a program to compute the average score on an exam. Define the input data in a series of **DATA** statements; use **READ** statements to access the values *(see Fig. 7.9)*. After computing the average, reread the data and develop a frequency distribution (how many students scored A, how

many scored B, and so on). Use the following rules for assigning individual grades:

Final Grade	Exam Score
A	(average + 15 or more points)
B	(average + 5) to (average + 15)
C	(average - 5) to (average + 5)
D	(average -15) to (average - 5)
F	below (average - 15)

17. Write a program to print, on the printer, a 1-month calendar. Input the day of the week on which the first of the month falls, the number of days in the month, and the month's name. Use format strings for your output. You may want to read Chapter 10 before trying this program.

18. Write a program to update a checking account. Input an old balance. Next, input deposit amounts, one by one, using some sentinel value to mark the end of the deposits. Then enter the checks one by one; again, use a sentinel value to mark the end of data. Print the new balance (old balance, plus the sum of all deposits, minus the sum of all checks). Use input prompts. Clearly format and label the output.

19. Modify Exercise 18 to allow deposits and checks to be entered in any order.

20. Modify exercise 19 to generate a printed checkbook ledger. Print the old balance at the top of the page. For each check, list the amount and subtract it from the balance. For each deposit, list the amount and add it to the balance. Clearly distinguish checks from deposits. Print, on each line, a running balance reflecting the account's status after each transaction. Should the balance drop below zero, print "account overdrawn." Send your output to the printer.

8

Arrays

KEY IDEAS

1. One-dimensional arrays.

    a. Defining an array.

    b. Subscripts.

2. Multidimensional arrays.

3. Using parallel arrays.

4. Matrix statements.

5. Table handling.

6. Passing arrays to a subroutine.

7. Matrix arithmetic.

ONE-DIMENSIONAL ARRAYS

Is there any student in the United States who has never taken a standardized test? With IQ tests, interest tests, achievement tests, and college entrance examinations, probably not. By the time most students graduate from high school, they have taken several.

The scores earned on such tests are a bit unusual. The average IQ is 100, while Scholastic Aptitude Test scores range from a low of 200 to a high of 800. What is a "passing" score? There is none. Standardized tests are not designed to generate grades, but to rank students with respect to others who took the same test. Standardized test scores are intentionally difficult to convert to a traditional grading scale.

The Scholastic Aptitude Test (SAT) is a good example. Individual scores fall between 200 and 800, with the average student scoring 500. As a means for introducing arrays, we'll design and write a program to compute and print examination scores, using the SAT test as a model.

Designing the Program

We'll start by defining the problem *(Fig. 8.1)*. Input data are the individual student raw scores (basically, the number of questions each student answered correctly). An algorithm converts raw scores to test scores. The key to the algorithm is the average raw score. By definition, it represents a test score of 500. Raw scores above the average earn test scores above 500; below average raw scores earn test scores below 500. The rule for computing an individual's test score is

$$\text{test score} = \left[\frac{\text{raw score}}{\text{average raw score}} \right] 500$$

For example, consider the following three students:

Fig. 8.1: *A block level definition of the test scoring problem.*

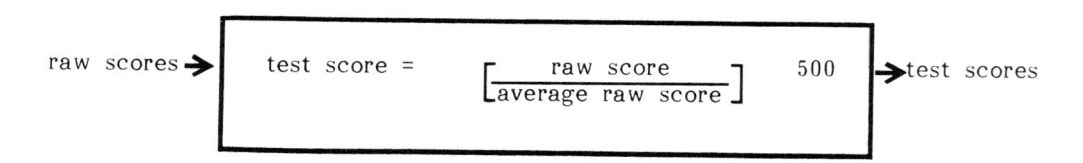

$$\text{raw scores} \rightarrow \boxed{\text{test score} = \left[\frac{\text{raw score}}{\text{average raw score}} \right] 500} \rightarrow \text{test scores}$$

222

Student	Raw score	Average raw score	Test score
Aaron	150	100	750
Baker	100	100	500
Cooper	50	100	250

Use the algorithm to verify the results.

Test scores must lie between 200 and 800. A computed score can lie outside the range. If a score exceeds 800, it is set to 800; if a score drops below 200, it is set to 200.

To compute test scores for a group of students, the data must be used twice. First, we need the average raw score. To find it, each student's raw score must be accumulated and counted. Next, each raw score is divided by the average. Ideally, we should be able to input the raw scores, store them in memory, use them to compute the average, and then use them again to compute the test scores. One solution is to define an array.

What is an Array?

Assume twenty-five students took an SAT-like test. Each student's raw score is needed twice. We could read the scores, use them to compute an average, and then read them again, but it makes more sense to read them once, store them in memory, and then simply use them when needed.

How can we store twenty-five students' scores in memory? We might assign a different variable to each one; for example, **raw01, raw02, raw03, . . ., raw25**. To input the data, we could code

    INPUT raw01, raw02, raw03, . . ., raw25

To find the average raw score, we could

    LET sum = raw01 + raw02 + raw03 + . . . + raw25

and then divide by the number of values. Finally, we could compute and print test scores by coding

    LET test_score = (raw01 / average) * 500

PRINT raw01, test_score

repeating the **LET** and **PRINT** combination for each student.

Imagine keeping track of all those variables. Imagine writing all those instructions. Now, try to picture one hundred raw scores, or one thousand. Defining a separate variable for each value is unacceptable. There must be an easier way to solve this problem.

A variable is simply a name or label assigned to a memory location. Twenty-five variables represent twenty-five names assigned to twenty-five different memory locations. An array defines a set of consecutive memory locations *(Fig. 8.2)*. Memory is addressed by numbering its cells—0, 1, 2, and so on. Because an array is composed of consecutive memory locations, given the address of the first one, we can compute the address of the second, the third, and so on. If we use an array to hold several values, all we need is a name for the first one, and we can compute the locations of the others.

Defining an Array

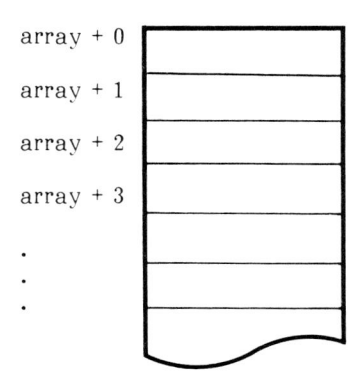

An array is defined in a dimension statement *(Fig. 8.3)*. Following the keyword **DIM**, one or more array names can be listed. Each one must be a valid variable name. String array names must end with a dollar sign.

Following the array's name, enclosed in parentheses, are one or more integers that define the number of elements in the array. For example, the statement

DIM raw_score (25)

defines an array named **raw_score** containing 25 elements, while

Fig. 8.2: *An array defines a series of consecutive memory locations.*

```
DIM array_name (i, j, k, . . .)
                 ⏟
                 └──── dimensions
```

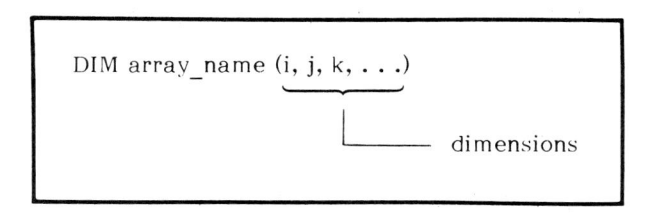

Fig. 8.3: *An array is defined in a dimension (DIM) statement.*

    DIM array (5,2)

defines a two-dimensional array with five rows of two columns each. The statement

    DIM example (2,2,2,2,2)

defines an array of five dimensions with 2*2*2*2*2, or 32 elements. *True BASIC* arrays can have up to 10 dimensions (even more on some machines). We'll return to multidimensional arrays later in the chapter. For now, we'll focus on one-dimensional arrays.

Let's define a relatively small array of five elements so we can visualize it *(Fig. 8.4)*. When *True BASIC* encounters the **DIM** statement, five consecutive memory locations are set aside. The next question is, how do we access those elements?

Fig. 8.4: *This array contains five elements. Individual elements can be accessed by using subscripts.*

Statement	Element	Memory
DIM raw_score (5)	raw_score(1)	
	raw_score(2)	
	raw_score(3)	
	raw_score(4)	
	raw_score(5)	

Subscripts

Note *(Fig. 8.4)* the numbers in parentheses following the array's name under the column header "element." They are subscripts. The array's first element is **raw_score(1)**, or "raw_score-sub-one." The second element is **raw_score(2)**. Just as memory locations are addressed by counting them, so are an array's elements. The count is the subscript.

Using subscripts, an array's individual elements can be accessed just like regular variables. For example, to store an input value in element 1, code

    INPUT raw_score (1)

To add elements 2 and 3, and store the sum in element 4, code

    LET raw_score (4) = raw_score (2) + raw_score (3)

By default, all arrays begin with subscript 1, and end with a subscript equal to the number of items in the array. Our example array *(Fig. 8.4)* starts with **raw_score(1)** and ends with **raw_score(5)**. The programmer can specify the bounds. For example, the statement

    DIM sales_by_year (1986 TO 1995)

defines a ten-element array with subscripts ranging from 1986 to 1995. A subscript must lie within the range defined for the array. Also, the subscript must be an integer. If you specify a non-integer, the subscript is rounded to the nearest integer.

A subscript need not be a constant; any numeric expression will do. Thus we can compute subscript values as the program runs. As we'll see shortly, the fact that subscripts can be computed makes arrays a very flexible tool.

Writing the Program

Let's return to the test scoring problem. The algorithm for computing an individual's score is

$$\text{test score} = \left[\frac{\text{raw score}}{\text{average raw score}} \right] 500$$

We need both the individual raw scores and the average raw score to figure the test scores. To compute the average raw score, we need the individual raw scores. Clearly, the program must begin with the input of the raw scores. Next, the average must be computed. Finally, test scores can be generated. Given this necessary sequence, we can define three major steps: input the data, compute the average, and compute the test scores *(Fig. 8.5)*.

Let's attack the major steps one by one. We'll start with entering the data. The idea is to read all the raw scores and store them in an array. Figure 8.6 outlines the basic logic; Fig. 8.7 shows the equivalent *True BASIC* code. Note that we use a negative raw score as a sentinel value.

Follow the logic. Start with a maximum of five raw scores so we can visualize what happens. The dimension statement defines a five element array. We don't know exactly how many values will be input, so we'll have to count them. Enter the **DO** loop. A student's raw score is input. If the score is positive or zero (we

Fig. 8.5: *The test scoring program can be broken into three major steps.*

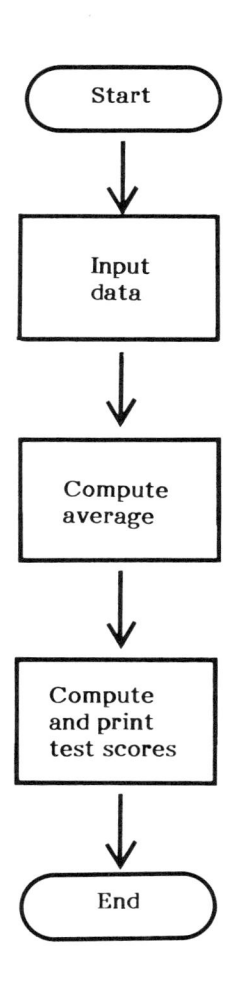

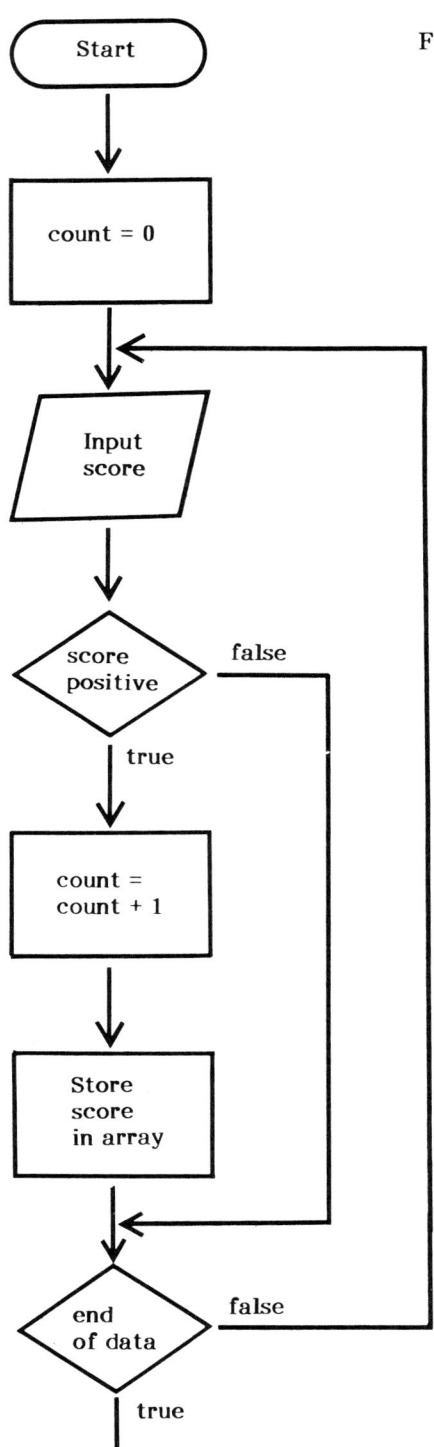

Fig. 8.6: *The first module fills the array with data.*

```
DIM raw_score (5)                   ! The dimension (DIM) statement creates
                                    ! the array.
LET count = 0                       ! The first module fills the array.
                                    ! Since the number of scores to be input
                                    ! is unknown, we must count them.
DO                                  ! Each time through the loop, a single raw
                                    ! score is input. Unless it's negative, it
   INPUT student_score              ! is counted and stored in the array.

   IF student_score >= 0 THEN
      LET count = count + 1
      LET raw_score(count) = student_score
   END IF
                                    ! The loop ends when the user enters the
                                    ! sentinel value, a negative raw score.
LOOP UNTIL student_score < 0
```

Fig. 8.7: *The test scoring program's first module fills the array with data.*

don't want to store the sentinel value), we count the student. The first time through the loop, **count** is 1. Thus, **raw_score(count)** is really **raw_score(1)**. Consequently *(Fig. 8.8)*, the **LET** statement stores the first raw score in memory location **raw_score(1)**.

Following the first pass through the loop, **count** is 1 and **raw_score(1)** is 103. Because **student_score** is positive, the loop repeats. A second raw score is input. Because it's positive, the student is counted. This time, **count** is 2, so **raw_score(count)** is **raw_score(2)**. The third time through, **raw_score(count)** becomes **raw_score(3)**. Eventually, the entire array is filled *(Fig. 8.8)*.

With only five elements, we were able to show the entire array's contents

Fig. 8.8: *After the first module runs, the array's elements are filled with data.*

raw_score (1)	103
raw_score (2)	85
raw_score (3)	98
raw_score (4)	114
raw_score (5)	73

in a brief illustration; that's why we picked such a small number. In a more realistic program, we might need 100, 1000, or even more elements. By changing the number of elements in the **DIM** statement, we could define and fill an array containing any number of elements.

Move on to the second module: computing the average raw score. We've already written programs to compute an average, so the logic should be apparent *(Fig.*

Fig. 8.9: *In the second module, we use the data stored in the array to compute the average raw score.*

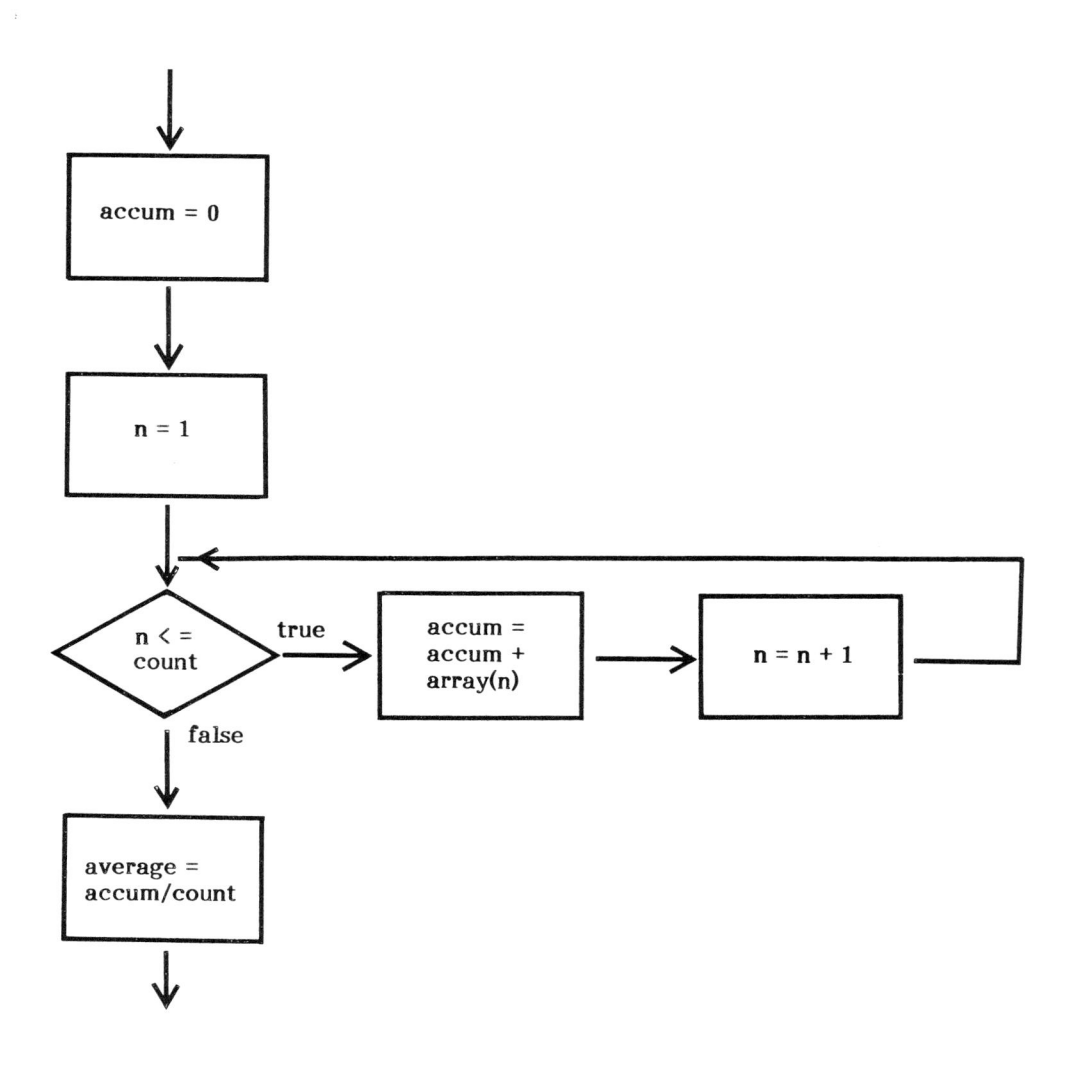

8.9). We know the count; we computed it in the first module. We'll start by initializing an accumulator to zero. Then, we'll accumulate the raw scores stored in the array. After all the values have been accumulated, the average (the sum divided by the count) can be computed.

Let's write the code to compute the average raw score *(Fig. 8.10)* and see how it manipulates the data stored in the array by the first module. Begin by initializing an accumulator to zero. Then, enter the loop. The first time through, **n** is 1. The loop contains the instruction

>   LET accumulator = accumulator + raw_score (n)

Because **n** is 1, the last term refers to location **raw_score(1).** Thus, whatever is stored in the array's first element is added to the accumulator.

The second time through the loop, **n** is 2. Thus, the term **raw_score(n)** is really **raw_score(2).** The second raw score is added to the accumulator. As **n** changes, the subscript changes. As the subscript changes, a different memory location is referenced. When the loop is finished, every value stored in the array is added to the accumulator.

Finally, we move to the third module: computing the test scores. The individual

---

Fig. 8.10: *The test scoring program's second module computes the average raw score, using the data previously stored in the array by the first module.*

```
                                ! The second module accumulates the raw
                                ! scores and computes the average.
LET accumulator = 0
                                ! The count is known from the first module.
FOR n = 1 TO count
    LET accumulator = accumulator + raw_score(n)
NEXT n
                                ! Given the sum of the raw scores and the
                                ! number of scores, we compute the average.
LET average_raw_score = accumulator / count
```

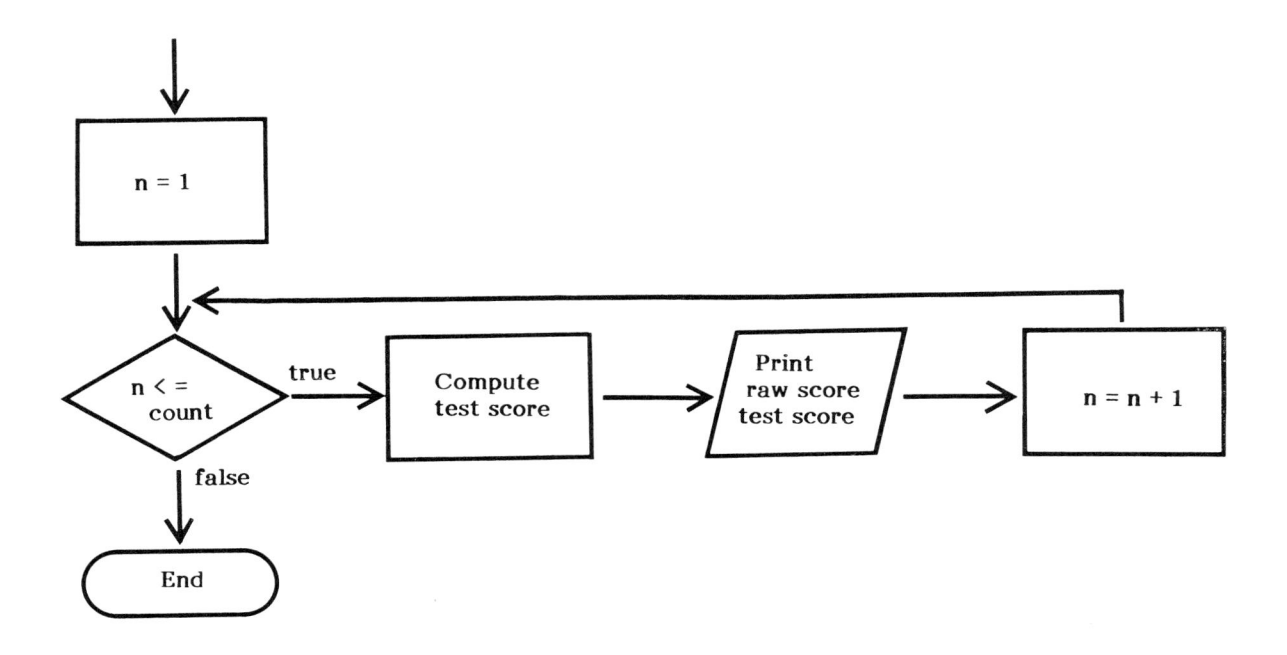

Fig. 8.11: *After the average raw score is computed by the second module, we can compute and print the individual test scores.*

Fig. 8.12: *Given the raw scores stored in the array by the first module, and the average raw score just computed by the second module, this third module computes and prints the individual test scores.*

```
                         ! Finally, given the raw scores and the
                         ! average raw score, the individual test
                         ! scores are computed and output.
FOR n = 1 TO count
   LET test_score = (raw_score(n)/average_raw_score) * 500
   PRINT raw_score(n), test_score
NEXT n

END
```

raw scores are still stored in the array. Variable **average_raw_score** holds the average score. We need another loop to compute the individual test scores *(Fig. 8.11)*. Each time through, one raw score is selected from the array, and its equivalent test score computed. Then, the raw score and the test score are printed. Finally, the control variable is incremented, and the loop repeats. When the loop ends, the program ends. Figure 8.12 shows the instructions for computing test scores. Read the code carefully, and be sure you understand it.

Now that we've planned the modules comprising the examination scoring program, it's time to put the pieces together. We'll increase the array size to a more realistic 100 elements *(Fig. 8.13)*. Otherwise, the instructions stay exactly the same. Read the program carefully. Note how the array values and the count are passed from module to module. You should have little trouble following the logic.

MULTIDIMENSIONAL ARRAYS

We used a one-dimensional array in the test scoring program. It is possible to define arrays of up to 10 dimensions and even more on some computers. For example, the statement

DIM array (5,3)

defines the 5 by 3 array pictured in Fig. 8.14. Each element in a two-dimensional array is identified by two subscripts. Note in the figure that the top left element is **array(1,1)**, while the bottom right element is **array(5,3)**.

As with one-dimensional arrays, the default lower limit on each subscript is 1. The programmer can, however, specify the range for both subscripts. For example, the statement

DIM array_b (1980 TO 1989, -10 TO 10)

defines a two-dimensional, 10 by 21 array whose first subscript can range from 1980 to 1989, and whose second subscript can vary from -10 to 10 (including 0).

A three-dimensional array's elements are accessed by a set of three subscripts. You can visualize a three-dimensional array by picturing a Rubik's cube®. Each small square represents a single array element. To find a given element, you must specify three things: the face, the number of squares from the left, and the number of squares up from the bottom. The elements in a four-dimensional array are identified by a set of four subscripts; the rule is one subscript for each dimension. It's difficult to visualize arrays of four dimensions or more, so we

```
                                    ! This program computes student SAT scores
                                    ! given an array of student raw scores.

                                    ! The dimension (DIM) statement creates
                                    ! the array.
DIM raw_score (5)

                                    ! The first module fills the array.
LET count = 0                       ! Since the number of scores to be input
                                    ! is unknown, we must count them.

DO                                  ! Each time through the loop, a single raw
                                    ! score is input. Unless it's negative, it
   INPUT student_score              ! is counted and stored in the array.

   IF student_score >= 0 THEN
      LET count = count + 1
      LET raw_score(count) = student_score
   END IF

                                    ! The loop ends when the user enters the
                                    ! sentinel value, a negative raw score.
LOOP UNTIL student_score < 0

                                    ! The second module accumulates raw
                                    ! scores and computes the average.
LET accumulator = 0
                                    ! The count comes from the first module.
FOR n = 1 TO count
   LET accumulator = accumulator + raw_score(n)
NEXT n
                                    ! Given the sum of the raw scores and the
                                    ! number of scores, we compute the average.
LET average_raw_score = accumulator / count

                                    ! Finally, given the raw scores and the
                                    ! average raw score, the individual test
                                    ! scores are computed and output.
FOR n = 1 TO count
   LET test_score = (raw_score(n)/average_raw_score) * 500
   PRINT raw_score(n), test_score
NEXT n

END
```

Fig. 8.13: *Now that we've developed the code for each of the modules, we can put the pieces together.*

DIM array (5,2)

array(1,1)	array(1,2)	array(1,3)
array(2,1)	array(2,2)	array(2,3)
array(3,1)	array(3,2)	array(3,3)
array(4,1)	array(4,2)	array(4,3)
array(5,1)	array(5,2)	array(5,3)

Fig. 8.14: *In a two-dimensional array, the first subscript represents the row number and the second subscript identifies the column.*

won't try.

Let's extend the test scoring program to illustrate two-dimensional arrays. It makes sense to link individual student scores with such information as a student identification number or a social security number. That way, if a clerk enters a series of raw scores, and then loses track of the order in which they were entered, we'll still be able to associate test scores with the correct students. Our objective is simply to input the identification numbers with the raw scores, hold them, and then output them with the computed test scores.

We'll do it by defining a two-dimensional array *(Fig. 8.15)*. View it as a table. Each row holds two values: a student's identification number and his or her raw score. There are one hundred rows of two columns each. The first column holds the identification numbers. The second column holds the raw scores. **Element(1,1)** refers to the first student's identification number. **Element(1,2)** holds that same student's raw score.

A new program listing is shown in Fig. 8.16. Start with the dimension statement. Next, move inside the **DO** loop. Note that two values are read and later assigned

Fig. 8.15: *In order to provide for identification of program output, we want to store individual students' identification numbers and raw scores in a two-dimensional array.*

DIM raw_score (100,2)

	Identification number	raw score
1	125739121	103
2	375219538	85
3	212151259	98
4	199814433	114
5	202252298	73
6	.	.
7	.	
8		

1   2

```
                              ! This program computes student SAT scores
                              ! given an array of student identification
                              ! numbers and raw scores.

                              ! The dimension (DIM) statement creates
                              ! the array. In this case, we'll use a
                              ! 2-dimensional array, with identification
                              ! numbers stored in the first column and
                              ! raw scores stored in the second.
DIM raw_score (100,2)
                              ! The first module fills the array.
LET count = 0                 ! Since the number of scores to be input
                              ! is unknown, we must count them.

DO                            ! Each time through the loop, a student's
                              ! identification number and raw score are
                              ! entered. If the raw score is positive,
                              ! the student is counted, and the number
                              ! and score are stored in the array.

   INPUT student_ID, student_score

   IF student_score >= 0 THEN
      LET count = count + 1
      LET raw_score(count,1) = student_ID
      LET raw_score(count,2) = student_score
   END IF

                              ! The loop ends when the user enters the
                              ! sentinel value, a negative raw score.
LOOP UNTIL student_score < 0


                              ! The second module accumulates raw
                              ! scores and computes the average.
LET accumulator = 0
                              ! The count comes from the first module.
FOR n = 1 TO count
   LET accumulator = accumulator + raw_score(n,2)
NEXT n
                              ! Given the sum of the raw scores and the
                              ! number of scores, we compute the average.
LET average_raw_score = accumulator / count
```

Fig. 8.16: *To score both an identification number and a raw score for each student, we can define a two-dimensional array.*

```
                          ! Finally, given the raw scores and the
                          ! average raw score, the individual test
                          ! scores are computed and output.
FOR n = 1 TO count
   LET test_score = (raw_score(n,2)/average_raw_score) * 500
   PRINT raw_score(n,1),raw_score(n,2),test_score
NEXT n

END
```

Fig. 8.16, continued.

to two array elements. Note also that the first subscript is the same for both elements; for example, the fifth student's identification number will be stored in **raw_score(5,1)**, and this same student's raw score will be stored in **raw_score(5,2)**.

Move down to the accumulation step. Note that the second subscript is always 2. We want to accumulate raw scores, not identification numbers. Raw scores are stored in the second column.

Now drop to the final loop. The **LET** statement always references the array's second column. The **PRINT** statement, however, deals with both. What happens when **raw_score(5,1)**, **raw_score(5,2)**, and **test_score** are output? The fifth student's identification number, raw score, and computed test score are displayed.

PARALLEL ARRAYS

Social security numbers are not necessarily the best way to identify people. Although they are unique (there is only one 123-45-6789), most of us would prefer

Fig. 8.17: *It is illegal to mix numeric and string data in the same array. If related string and numeric data values must be stored, define parallel arrays.*

```
DIM name$ (100), raw_score (100,2)
```

Name		Identification number	raw score
Jim Johnston	1	125739121	103
Mary Lopez	2	375219538	85
Tom O'Riely	3	212151259	98
Connie Costa	4	199814433	114
Bilbo Baggins	5	202252298	73
.	6	.	.
.	7		

```
                              ! This program computes student SAT scores
                              ! given student names, identification
                              ! numbers, and raw scores.

                              ! The dimension (DIM) statement creates
                              ! the arrays. In this case, we'll use a
                              ! string array to hold student's names,
                              ! and a 2-dimensional array, with iden-
                              ! tification numbers stored in the first
                              ! column and raw scores in the second.
DIM name$(100), raw_score (100,2)
                              ! The first module fills the array.
LET count = 0                 ! Since the number of scores to be input
                              ! is unknown, we must count them.
DO                            ! Each time through the loop, we read a
                              ! student's name, identification number,
                              ! and raw score. Unless the raw score is
                              ! negative, we'll count the student and
                              ! store the data in the arrays.
   INPUT student_name$, student_ID, student_score

   IF student_score >= 0 THEN
      LET count = count + 1
      LET name$(count) = student_name$
      LET raw_score(count,1) = student_ID
      LET raw_score(count,2) = student_score
   END IF
                              ! The loop ends when the user enters the
                              ! sentinel value, a negative raw score.
LOOP UNTIL student_score < 0


                              ! The second module accumulates raw
                              ! scores and computes the average.
LET accumulator = 0
                              ! The count comes from the first module.
FOR n = 1 TO count
   LET accumulator = accumulator + raw_score(n,2)
NEXT n
                              ! Given the sum of the raw scores and the
                              ! number of scores, we compute the average.
LET average_raw_score = accumulator / count
```

Fig. 8.18: *Numeric and string data cannot be stored in the same array. We can, however, define parallel arrays.*

```
                            ! Finally, given the raw scores and the
                            ! average raw score, the individual test
                            ! scores are computed and output.
FOR n = 1 TO count
   LET test_score = (raw_score(n,2)/average_raw_score) * 500
   PRINT name$(n), raw_score(n,1), raw_score(n,2), test_score
NEXT n

END
```

Fig. 8.18, *continued.*

---

to be known by our names. The raw score is a numeric value. A name is a string value. We can't mix strings and numbers in the same array.

We can, however, use two arrays *(Fig. 8.17).* Figure 8.18 shows a new version of the test scoring program with both a one-dimensional string array to hold the students' names, and a two-dimensional numeric array to hold their identification numbers and raw scores. Note how the two arrays are filled and output together. Whenever a set of related string and numeric data must be stored and manipulated together, consider defining parallel arrays. As long as you keep the subscripts consistent, you'll be able to preserve the relationship between the data elements.

MATRIX STATEMENTS

One way to view an array is as a matrix. In mathematics, single operations can be used to manipulate all the elements in a matrix. While we don't intend to discuss the mathematical details, the idea of using a single operation to input, to output, or to manipulate an entire array is an important one.

For example, consider the **MAT INPUT** statement *(Fig. 8.19).* When a **MAT INPUT** statement is executed, a prompt is displayed on the screen. In response the user is expected to enter, on a single line, all the array's elements, one by one, separated by commas. If they won't fit on one line, end the line with a comma, and continue on the next line. If you enter too many values, the surplus will be

Fig. 8.19: *The MAT INPUT statement allows an entire array's contents to be entered through the keyboard.*

```
MAT INPUT array1, array2, . . .

MAT INPUT PROMPT expression$: array1, array2, . . .
```

ignored. Enter too few, and you'll be asked for more.

Values are assigned to array elements in the order in which they are entered. For one-dimensional arrays, the result should be obvious, but it's less clear for multidimensional arrays. When more than one dimension is involved, the array's subscripts vary in "odometer order." On an automobile's odometer, you can watch the rightmost, tenth-of-a-mile digit change. After a complete cycle of the digits, the mile digit changes. The units position must progress from 0 to 9 before the tens position changes. When data are read by a **MAT INPUT** statement, the array's rightmost subscripts change more rapidly than those to the left. For example, Fig. 8.20 shows the order in which elements are assigned to a 2x2x2 array.

A common problem when reading input data is not knowing exactly how many values to expect. It would be nice if you could enter data until there are no more, and have the computer adjust the array size for you. A special form of **MAT INPUT**, available only for one-dimensional arrays, allows you to do just that. Let's modify the test scoring program to use a **MAT INPUT** statement *(Fig. 8.21)*. Note that the **DIM** statement defines only two elements for **raw_score**. The initial array size is meaningless; the number of elements won't be determined until the data are entered. We have, however, defined a one-dimensional array.

Move down to the **MAT INPUT** statement. Note that the array name is followed by a question mark. In response to a prompt, type values, one by one, separating them with commas. If there are too many to fit on a single line, end the line with a comma and continue typing on the next line. To indicate the end of data, type the last item and press enter. (Note: do not type a comma after the last item.) The array will automatically be redimensioned to hold every item you type.

Unfortunately, we don't know how many values are stored, and we need the count in subsequent modules. A **Ubound** function (see the instruction following **MAT INPUT** in Fig. 8.21) returns the array's upper bound. The **Lbound** function returns the lower bound; the **Size** function returns the number of elements in the array.

In the above example, the array was *implicitly* redimensioned. It is also possible to *explicitly* redimension an array. For example, start with

Fig. 8.20: *A MAT INPUT statement fills a multi-dimensional array in odometer order.*

DIM array (2,2,2)

1	(1,1,1)
2	(1,1,2)
3	(1,2,1)
4	(1,2,2)
5	(2,1,1)
6	(2,1,2)
7	(2,2,1)
8	(2,2,2)

```
                        ! This program computes student SAT scores
                        ! given an array of raw scores.

                        ! The dimension (DIM) statement creates the
                        ! array. In this case, we'll create a dummy
                        ! array of only two elements. The MAT INPUT
                        ! statement will redimension it at run time.
DIM raw_score (2)
                        ! The first module fills the array. In this
                        ! version of the program, we'll use a MAT
                        ! INPUT statement.
MAT INPUT raw_score (?)
                        ! The MAT INPUT statement fills the array,
                        ! storing as many values as we enter. We
                        ! don't know how many that is, so we'll
                        ! use a Ubound function to find out.
LET count = Ubound (raw_score)

                        ! The second module accumulates raw
                        ! scores and computes the average.
LET accumulator = 0
                        ! The count comes from the first module.
FOR n = 1 TO count
   LET accumulator = accumulator + raw_score(n)
NEXT n
                        ! Given the sum of the raw scores and the
                        ! number of scores, we compute the average.
LET average_raw_score = accumulator / count

                        ! Finally, given the raw scores and the
                        ! average raw score, the individual test
                        ! scores are computed and output.
FOR n = 1 TO count
   LET test_score = (raw_score(n)/average_raw_score) * 500
   PRINT raw_score(n), test_score
NEXT n

END
```

Fig. 8.21: *This version of the test scoring program uses a single MAT_INPUT statement to fill the array.*

    DIM array (5,3)

It's a 5x3 array containing fifteen elements. If the statement

    MAT INPUT array (10,5)

is executed, the array is changed to a 10x5 array containing fifty elements. By using variables, such as

    MAT INPUT array (i,j)

the array's dimensions can be determined as the program runs. You can set upper and lower limits at run time, too; for example

    MAT INPUT (2 TO 10, 1983 TO last_year)

The **MAT READ** statement *(Fig. 8.22)* resembles a **MAT INPUT** statement. It has similar redimensioning rules. **MAT PRINT** and **MAT PRINT USING** *(Fig. 8.23)* display all an array's elements. In a **MAT PRINT** statement, if you follow the array's name with a semicolon, the output is printed as if the elements were listed individually and separated with semicolons. Multidimensional arrays are printed in odometer order. The output starts on a new line each time a dimension's upper bound is reached.

One array can be assigned to another in a **MAT** assignment statement. For example,

    MAT a = b

copies every element in array **b** into array **a**. The target array's dimensions are automatically adjusted to hold the array to the right of the equal sign. Both arrays

Fig. 8.22: *The general form of the MAT READ statement.*

    MAT READ array1, array2, . . .

```
MAT PRINT array1, array2, . . .

MAT PRINT USING format$: array1, array2, . . .
```

Fig. 8.23: *The general form of the MAT PRINT statement.*

must have the same number of dimensions. A **MAT** assignment statement can have only one operator.

Be careful of matrix assignment statements. They can have surprising results. Unless you know exactly what you are doing, limit yourself to arrays that have the same upper and lower bounds, and the same number of dimensions.

To assign the same value to every element in an array, code a statement such as

MAT a = 0

This statement assigns the constant 0 to every element in array **a**. For a numeric array, any numeric expression can be coded to the right of the equal sign. For a string array, code a string variable or a string constant.

TABLE MANIPULATION

Arrays are often used as tables. For example, Fig. 8.24 shows a typical state tax withholding table. Imagine that an individual earns exactly $300 in a given week. Read down the table's first two columns; they define a series of tax brackets. This person's gross pay lies between $200 and $500, so the tax is computed using

Fig. 8.24: *A table for determining the amount of state income tax to be withheld from an employee's pay.*

For gross pay between	the tax is	of excess over
0 and 25	0	
25 and 50	0 + 1%	25
50 and 100	0.25 + 2%	50
100 and 200	1.25 + 3%	100
200 and 500	4.25 + 4%	200
500 and up	16.25 + 5%	500

the constants in the fifth row.

Move to the right. The minimum tax for this bracket is $4.25. Additionally, a 4 percent tax is collected on the "excess" income over $200, the bracket's lower limit. The excess income is $100; 4 percent of $100 is $4.00. Add the percentage tax to the bracket's minimum tax, and you get $8.25, the amount to be withheld from this individual's pay.

One way to compute state tax is to use a decision structure. An alternative is to define the tax table as an array *(Fig. 8.25)*, and, using the computed gross pay as a key, to select the appropriate base tax, percentage, and bracket limits in a loop. Use a **MAT INPUT** or **MAT READ** to fill the array. Figure 8.26 shows a state tax subroutine that uses table lookup.

Let's desk check the logic. Start with a $125 gross pay. Refer to the table pictured in Fig. 8.25; keep track of the value of n, and follow the instructions. Compare the subroutine to the one you may have written for Chapter 6, Exercise 2d. While looping through an array may not be as obvious as checking bracket limits in a **SELECT CASE** structure, the loop is much more compact.

ARRAYS AS PARAMETERS

Like simple variables, arrays can be passed to a function or a subroutine. Parameters are physically copied to a function. Because an array represents several memory locations, a great deal of memory space may be copied. Avoid passing arrays to functions. Subroutines are different. Parameters are not physically copied to a subroutine; only their addresses are passed. Thus, there are no space implications associated with passing arrays to subroutines.

An array is different from a regular variable because it represents several

Fig. 8.25: *Define the table as a two-dimensional array.*

```
DIM state_tax_table (6,4)
```

row	lower limit	upper limit	base tax	percent tax
1	0	25	0.00	0.00
2	25	50	0.00	0.01
3	50	100	0.25	0.02
4	100	200	1.25	0.03
5	200	500	4.25	0.04
6	500	max	16.25	0.05

1   2   3   4
column

```
                              ! A subroutine to compute the state tax
                              ! to be withheld from an employee's pay.
                              ! Gross pay and a tax table are passed to
                              ! the subroutine. State tax is returned.

SUB Compute_state_tax (gross_pay, state_tax_table(,), state_tax)

                              ! Using gross pay as an argument, the tax
                              ! table is searched for the proper bracket.
                              ! Then, the base tax, the percentage tax
                              ! and the excess income are set, and the
                              ! search loop ends.
    LET n = 1
                              ! The table's first row holds the various
                              ! brackets' lower limits.

    DO WHILE gross_pay > state_tax_table (n,1)

                              ! The table's second row holds the various
                              ! brackets' upper limits. If gross pay
                              ! lies between the lower and upper limit,
                              ! the employee's bracket has been found.

        IF gross_pay < state_tax_table (n,2) THEN

            LET bracket_base = state_tax_table (n,1)
            LET base_tax = state_tax_table (n,3)
            LET tax_percentage = state_tax_table (n,4)

        END IF

        LET n = n + 1

    LOOP
                              ! When the loop ends, 3 local variables
                              ! hold the values to compute state tax.

    LET state_tax = base_tax + ((gross_pay - bracket_base) * tax_percent)

END SUB
```

Fig. 8.26: *In this subroutine, an array is used as a table.*

memory locations. A multidimensional array is different from a one-dimensional array because it requires more than one subscript. A subroutine is defined in a **SUB** statement. Array names can be included in the parameters list. The actual dimensions need not be repeated because they are defined in a **DIM** statement. However, the number of dimensions must be indicated.

To pass a one-dimensional array, follow the array name with a set of empty

245

parentheses; for example,

    SUB Example_1 (array_1(), parameter2, . . .)

To pass a two-dimensional array, include a single comma between the parentheses; for example,

    SUB Example_2 (array_2(,), parameter2, . . .)

The comma indicates that there are two subscripts. For a three-dimensional array, code (,,); for a four-dimensional array, code (,,,), and so on.

Subroutines are accessed by **CALL** statements. Following the keyword **CALL** is a series of arguments. In the arguments list, just code the array's name; for example,

    CALL Example_1 (array_1, parameter2, . . .)

    CALL Example_2 (array_2, parameter2, . . .)

Do not include parentheses or commas in a **CALL** statement's arguments list.

MATRIX ARITHMETIC

The field of linear algebra defines a number of arithmetic operations that can be performed on two-dimensional arrays. An introduction to linear algebra is beyond the scope of this book. For those who know matrix algebra, however, *True BASIC* offers a host of arithmetic operations, constants, and functions that allow the programmer to

1. Initialize a matrix's elements to 1.

2. Initialize an identity matrix.

3. Initialize a null (string) matrix.

4. Initialize a matrix's elements to 0.

5. Add two matrices.

6. Subtract one matrix from another.

7. Multiply a matrix by a scalar.

8. Multiply two matrices.

9. Invert a matrix.

10. Transpose a matrix.

11. Find a determinant.

12. Compute the dot product of two matrices.

See the *Reference Manual* for details.

SUMMARY

An array is defined in a **DIM** statement. Following the keyword **DIM** is the array's name and one or more integers separated by commas. The integers represent the array's dimensions. *True BASIC* can support up to ten dimensions (more on some machines). By default, for each dimension, the array's lower bound is 1, and its upper bound is the number of elements defined for the dimension. The programmer can override the default, coding a dimension's upper and lower bounds.

Individual array elements are accessed by using subscripts. One subscript is needed for each dimension. Any numeric expression can be used as a subscript. Subscript values must, however, be integer. If an expression's value is not an integer, *True BASIC* rounds it to the nearest integer.

To illustrate one-dimensional arrays, we developed and coded an examination scoring program. Then we modified the program, adding an identification number and using a two-dimensional array. Finally, we added a parallel array to hold string values.

An array can be viewed as a matrix. Certain matrix statements manipulate all an array's elements. For example, a single **MAT INPUT** statement can be used to fill an entire array. We considered a special form of **MAT INPUT** that allowed us to enter an unknown number of input values and store them in a one-dimensional array. The array's size was automatically adjusted to hold the number of values entered. We then modified the examination scoring program to use **MAT INPUT.** We briefly discussed **MAT READ, MAT PRINT, MAT PRINT USING,** and **MAT** assignment statements, explaining both implicit and explicit redimensioning.

Arrays can also be viewed as tables. We designed and wrote a state income tax subroutine to illustrate. Next, we considered passing arrays to a subroutine. The chapter ended with a brief overview of matrix arithmetic.

REFERENCES

True BASIC Statements

DIM	Fig. 8.3, page 225
MAT INPUT	Fig. 8.19, page 239
MAT READ	Fig. 8.22, page 242
MAT PRINT	Fig. 8.23, page 243
Matrix Arithmetic	page 246

EXERCISES

1. Write a program to input a series of three integers, store them in an array, and output them in reverse order.

2. In Chapter 4 *(Fig. 4.25)*, we developed a program to generate a table of wind chill factors. Modify the program. As you compute wind chills for the various combinations of temperatures and wind velocities, store the results in a two-dimensional array. After completing all computations, print the array as a two-dimensional table with wind velocities running across the top and temperatures running down the side.

3. Write a program to generate random numbers ranging between 00 and 99. As you generate the numbers, develop a frequency distribution, counting how many lie between 00 and 09, between 10 and 19, between 20 and 29, and so on. Keep your counts in an array. After generating and categorizing 1000 random numbers, print the results.

4. In the chapter, we developed a test scoring program using SAT scores as a model. In a different test, the average raw score becomes a test score of 18. The minimum possible score is zero; the maximum possible score is 30. Modify the test scoring program *(Fig. 8.13)* to use this new algorithm.

5. Write a program to generate a multiplication table. Define a 10x10 array. Store the 1-times table in the first row, the 2-times table in the second row, and so on. After filling the table, display it, printing one row per line.

6. Write a program to read ten or more values (in random order) into an array. Search the array and find the largest value. Search it again and find the smallest value. Print the largest value, the smallest value, and their difference.

7. An automobile dealership employs ten salespeople. Each year, a competition is held. The employee who sells the most cars is identified. The employee selling the fewest is also identified, and the difference between their sales totals computed. The high salesperson receives a bonus of $25 times this difference. The low salesperson moves back to used car sales. Monthly sales statistics for the past year were:

	J	F	M	A	M	J	J	A	S	O	N	D
1	12	7	7	4	4	0	9	5	0	9	4	6
2	0	9	2	11	0	5	3	9	4	5	5	7
3	5	2	6	6	8	7	8	0	4	12	6	5
4	3	10	15	6	1	9	6	3	4	9	5	3
5	4	7	7	5	7	4	15	2	5	3	1	9
6	9	2	2	5	3	5	12	16	13	0	5	5
7	8	0	6	8	9	3	6	2	3	1	7	5
8	8	0	0	5	4	9	4	2	2	7	8	2
9	8	2	4	2	3	8	3	2	0	6	8	5
10	6	5	7	4	9	8	0	8	6	3	7	6

Identify the high salesperson and the low salesperson, and compute the bonus.

8. Read at least ten values into an array, in random order. Sort the array's values into ascending order (smallest first). Print the sorted array. Next, sort the array into descending order (smallest last), and print the sorted array. Hint: compare the value stored in the first element to each of the other elements and, if appropriate, switch their order. Then compare the second element to each of the others.

9. Two common statistical computations are the mean and the standard deviation. The mean is simply the sum of all the data values divided by the number of values. The standard deviation requires both the individual data points and the mean. One by one, subtract the computed mean from each data point and square the difference. Accumulate the sum of these squares. When you're finished, divide the accumulated sum of the squares by the number of data points minus 1. The standard deviation is the square root of the quotient. Write a program to input a series of data values and compute and print their mean and their standard deviation.

10. A speciality shop stocks ten items. The current stock on hand for each of the ten items is:

Item	Quantity	Item	Quantity
1	14	6	37
2	28	7	18
3	4	8	9
4	95	9	42
5	12	10	11

During the week, the following transactions took place:

Day	Item	Code	Quantity	Day	Item	Code	Quantity
M	2	2	5	W	7	2	8
M	5	2	10	R	3	2	12
M	9	2	23	R	6	2	10
T	2	2	15	R	8	2	20
T	1	2	10	F	1	1	25
T	4	2	15	F	10	2	3
T	5	2	2	F	4	2	32
W	8	1	25	F	6	2	10
W	7	2	8	F	7	1	25
W	3	1	25				

Code 1 means an addition to inventory; code 2 is a deletion from inventory.

Write a program to track inventory. Start by initializing the start-of-week inventory levels as described above. Then, process the transactions one by one, adding the quantity to inventory for a code 1, and subtracting from inventory for a code 2. (Hint: use the item number as a subscript.) After processing all the transactions, print an inventory report showing, for each item, the item number, the start-of-week stock on hand, the sum of all deletions from inventory, the sum of all additions to inventory, and the ending stock on hand.

11. In Chapter 6, Exercise 2c, you were asked to write a subroutine to compute the amount of federal income tax to be withheld from an employee's pay. Modify the subroutine. Define the table in an array, and search the array to find the proper rates.

12. In Chapter 6, Exercise 2d, you were asked to write a subroutine to compute the amount of state income tax to be withheld from an employee's pay. Modify the subroutine to use an array and table lookup.

13. In Chapter 6, Exercise 2e, you were asked to write a subroutine to compute the amount of local tax to be withheld from an employee's pay. Modify the subroutine to use an array and table lookup. Use the city code as a subscript.

14. Write a program to compute and print a running bowling score. Set up an array with one element for each of the ten frames. Generate random numbers to determine how many pins are knocked down by each ball. Update the score after each ball is thrown; print the score at the end of each frame. (If you don't know how to score bowling, don't try this program.)

15. Write a program to simulate a game of bingo. Define a 5x5 matrix, and use random numbers to initialize the array. Column 1 holds numbers between 1 and 15; column 2 holds numbers between 16 and 30, and so on. Once the "card" is initialized, use random numbers to generate the play. As a number is "called," check the card; if the number is present, mark it in some way. A card wins when five numbers in the same row, the same column, or (here's the tough one) the same diagonal are marked.

    After you learn how to play a single bingo card, expand the game to handle two, three, or four. You might let players play against each other, and even simulate a jackpot. Don't forget the principles of modular program design. Also, remember to use subroutines. The ultimate version of this game will display bingo cards graphically *(see Chapter 9)*.

16. Define an array of five elements. Use random numbers to simulate dealing a five card hand, and store it in the array. Print the hand. Assume a standard, 52-card deck.

    Modify the program to evaluate the hand after dealing it. Use the standard rules of poker; in other words, look for a pair, two pair, three of a kind, and so on. In addition to printing the hand, print its value.

    Ultimately, develop a program to allow two or more people to play poker against each other, or one person to play against the machine. This is another potential application for computer graphics *(Chapter 9)*.

17. Write a program to simulate playing a game of tic-tac-toe. Start with a 3x3 array. Allow the player to enter the row and column number of a square. Store a 1 (or an X, if you want to use a string array) in the designated square. Then have the computer pick one of the remaining squares and mark it with a 0 (or an O). Display the array, and allow the player to select another square. Continue until either the player or the computer gets three in a row.

Initially, generate the computer's moves with random numbers. After you have the program working, see if you can improve the computer's strategy. If you haven't already done so, switch to a string array, and use X and O to mark the squares. Consider full screen output, or even graphics to display the changing matrix.

18. A gymnastics event is scored by five judges. Scores range from a low of 0 to a high of 10, and are accurate to one decimal position. To compute a competitor's total score for an event, input the five judges' scores, discard the high and the low score, and average the remaining three. Print the score.

    Expand the program to keep track of the scores earned by each of 25 competitors in each of 5 events. Also maintain, for each competitor, a running total of points earned on all events.

19. Write a program to generate a frequency distribution. Input values are grouped into classes. The class interval is the number of values in each class. The class limits represent the initial values of the upper and lower "open" classes. For example, in the frequency distribution

    90 and above

    80-89

    70-79

    60-69

    below 60

    the class interval is 10 and the class limits are 90 and 60. Your program should input the class interval, the upper (or lower) class limit, and the number of classes. Then, input several values, classify them, and print the completed frequency distribution.

9

Graphics

KEY IDEAS

1. *Some basic concepts.*
2. *Elementary plotting.*
   a. *Points.*
   b. *Lines.*
   c. *Text.*
3. *Color.*
4. *Plotting areas.*
5. *The **BOX** statements.*
   a. *Shapes.*
   b. *Animation.*
6. *Graphic input.*
7. *Pictures.*
8. *Windows.*

SOME BASIC CONCEPTS

It has been said that "a picture is worth 1000 words." That old adage is as true for computers as for any other medium. Graphic output can summarize volumes of data on a single screen. Perhaps even more important, however, particularly for beginners, is that graphics is fun! Write a program to generate a bar chart or a simple animation. When you look at the output for the very first time, try not to smile.

Unfortunately, it's difficult (and a bit frustrating) to produce graphic output in most programming languages. *True BASIC* is an exception. Its graphics features are remarkably clear and easy to use. If you understand the basics of programming, you know enough to generate sophisticated graphic images in *True BASIC*.

You should know a few things about graphics before you begin, however. First, your computer must be equipped with a graphics card. To find out if you have one, run your system's diagnostic program or try one of the sample graphics programs stored on your *True BASIC* disk (**HANOI**, for example). You'll get an error message if you don't have a graphics card.

The standard graphic output device is the display screen. The surface is divided into tiny dots called picture elements or pixels *(Fig. 9.1)*. Points, lines, shapes, and characters are displayed by turning selected pixels on and off. The number of pixels determines the screen's resolution--the greater the number, the sharper the image. A typical medium-resolution screen has 320 x 200 pixels, while a high-resolution screen might display 640 x 200 pixels.

Pixels are turned on and off by an electron beam that scans the screen from left to right and from top to bottom, thirty times a second or more. On a color monitor three beams (usually, red, green, and blue) scan together. Thus a single

Fig. 9.1: *For graphic output, a screen is divided into picture elements or pixels. Images are formed by a scanner that selectively turns selected pixels on and off.*

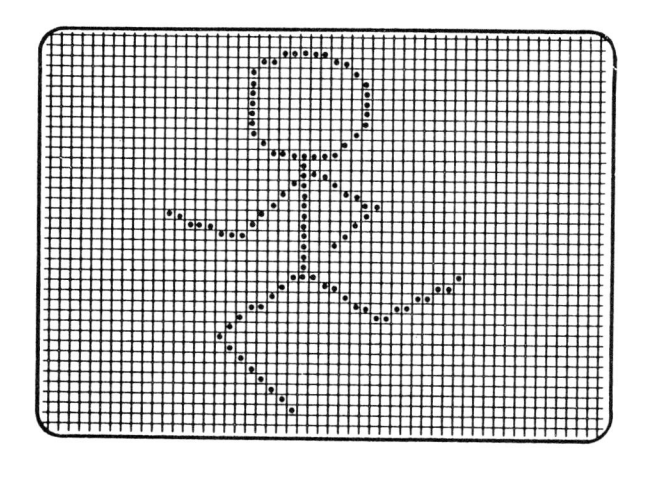

Fig. 9.2: *In True BASIC, individual points are represented by sets of x-y coordinates. By default, both x and y values can range from 0 to 1, and the origin, point 0,0, is at the screen's lower left.*

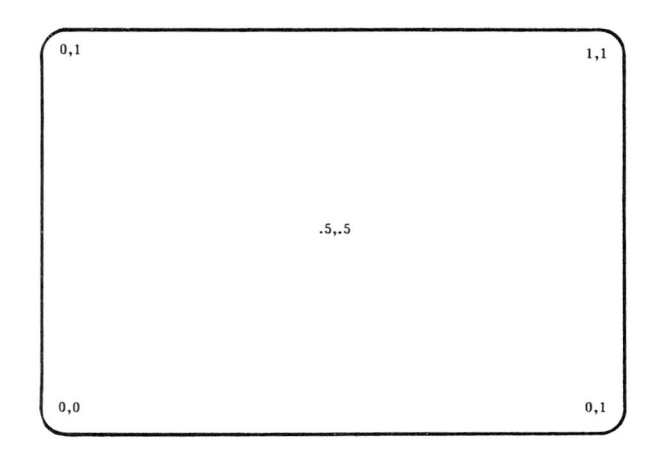

```
0,1                              1,1



              .5,.5



0,0                              0,1
```

pixel can be colored red, green, blue, a combination of those colors, or black (off).

How does the electron beam know which pixels to turn on? Typically, the graphics card contains memory. Each pixel is assigned several bits of this memory. A pixel's first bit might indicate its state—on (1) or off (0). Other bits might indicate colors. The content of this memory determines the control signals sent to the scanner.

Fortunately, you don't have to worry about any of these details. You'll work with standard x-y coordinates, and the necessary translation to pixel addresses will be taken care of for you. That's what makes *True BASIC* graphics so easy to use. You can think in your own terms. You don't have to think like a computer.

Superimpose a set of x-y coordinates on a blank screen *(Fig. 9.2)*. Points on the screen are identified by an x-value (a distance along the horizontal axis) and a y-value (a distance along the vertical axis). By default, the screen's lower left corner is point 0,0, the origin. The top left corner is point 0,1 (x = 0, y = 1). The bottom right is 1,0; the top right is 1,1; 0.5,0.5 marks the center of the screen. As you'll discover later, you can move those axes wherever you please and designate any set of minimum and maximum values for x and y. No matter what scale you might choose, *True BASIC* automatically translates your x-y coordinates to the necessary pixel addresses.

There is one technical detail that *True BASIC* can't handle for you, however. Not all screens are the same shape. Moving from one screen to another, the ratio between the horizontal and vertical measurements can change. Consequently, the distribution of pixels can spread out or compress. A circle drawn on one screen may look like an ellipse on another. Different screens have different aspect ratios, and you'll have to experiment a bit to determine how to draw proper shapes on yours. Later in the chapter, we'll show you how to check your display's aspect ratio.

ELEMENTARY PLOTTING

Points

That's enough background; let's get started. Remember that any point on the screen can be identified by its x and y coordinates. We can illuminate selected points by coding a **PLOT POINTS** statement *(Fig. 9.3)*. For example, assuming the default screen layout, the statement

> **PLOT POINTS: 0.5,0.5**

would turn on a single point in the center of the screen. If only one point is coded, a shorthand form can be used; for example,

> **PLOT 0.5,0.5**

is identical to the statement coded above. If more than one point is listed, sets of x-y coordinates are separated by semicolons, and the shorthand form may not be used.

Figure 9.4 illustrates the **PLOT POINTS** statement. The **Rnd** function returns random numbers between 0 and 1. The program simply generates two random numbers, uses them as x and y coordinates, and plots a point. Then it loops back, generates another set of random numbers, and plots another point. The loop continues until a key (any key) is pressed (see Chapter 7 for an explanation of the **KEY INPUT** condition).

Enter the program and run it. After a few seconds, your screen will resemble a pattern of stars on a clear night. Incidentally, there is a version of this program

Fig. 9.3: *Individual points can be plotted by listing their coordinates in a PLOT POINTS statement.*

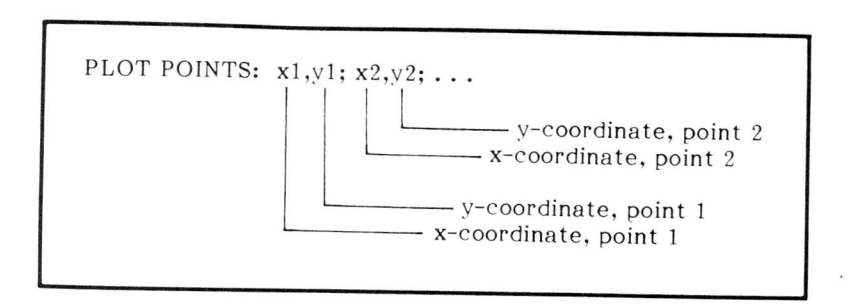

```
PLOT POINTS: x1,y1; x2,y2; ...
                │ │   │ │
                │ │   │ └── y-coordinate, point 2
                │ │   └──── x-coordinate, point 2
                │ └──────── y-coordinate, point 1
                └────────── x-coordinate, point 1
```

```
! Program to illustrate plotting points.
! The output resembles a pattern of stars
! on a clear night. Press any key to end
! the program.
DO
    PLOT Rnd,Rnd
LOOP UNTIL KEY INPUT    ! Here's the loop's terminal condition.
END
```

```
True BASIC here.
Version 1.0
Copyright (c) 1985 by True BASIC, Inc.
Published by Addison-Wesley Publishing Company, Inc.
Ok. old stars
Ok.
```

Fig. 9.4: *This simple program illustrates how points are plotted in True BASIC.*

on your *True BASIC* disk—type **OLD STARS** to get it. The only thing it lacks is the loop's exit condition.

In this example, we used the default ranges. The x-axis ran from 0 to 1. The y-axis ran from 0 to 1. If we executed the statement

PLOT POINTS: 0,2; 2,0; 2,2

nothing would appear on the screen because each point lies outside the range in at least one direction. Later in the chapter, we'll show you how to change the default ranges, but the rule will still hold: points lying outside the range for x, y, or both cannot be displayed.

Fig. 9.5: *To illustrate several plotting features, we'll design and code a frequency distribution program. The first step is problem definition.*

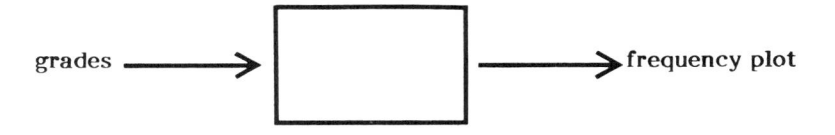

grades ⟶ ☐ ⟶ frequency plot

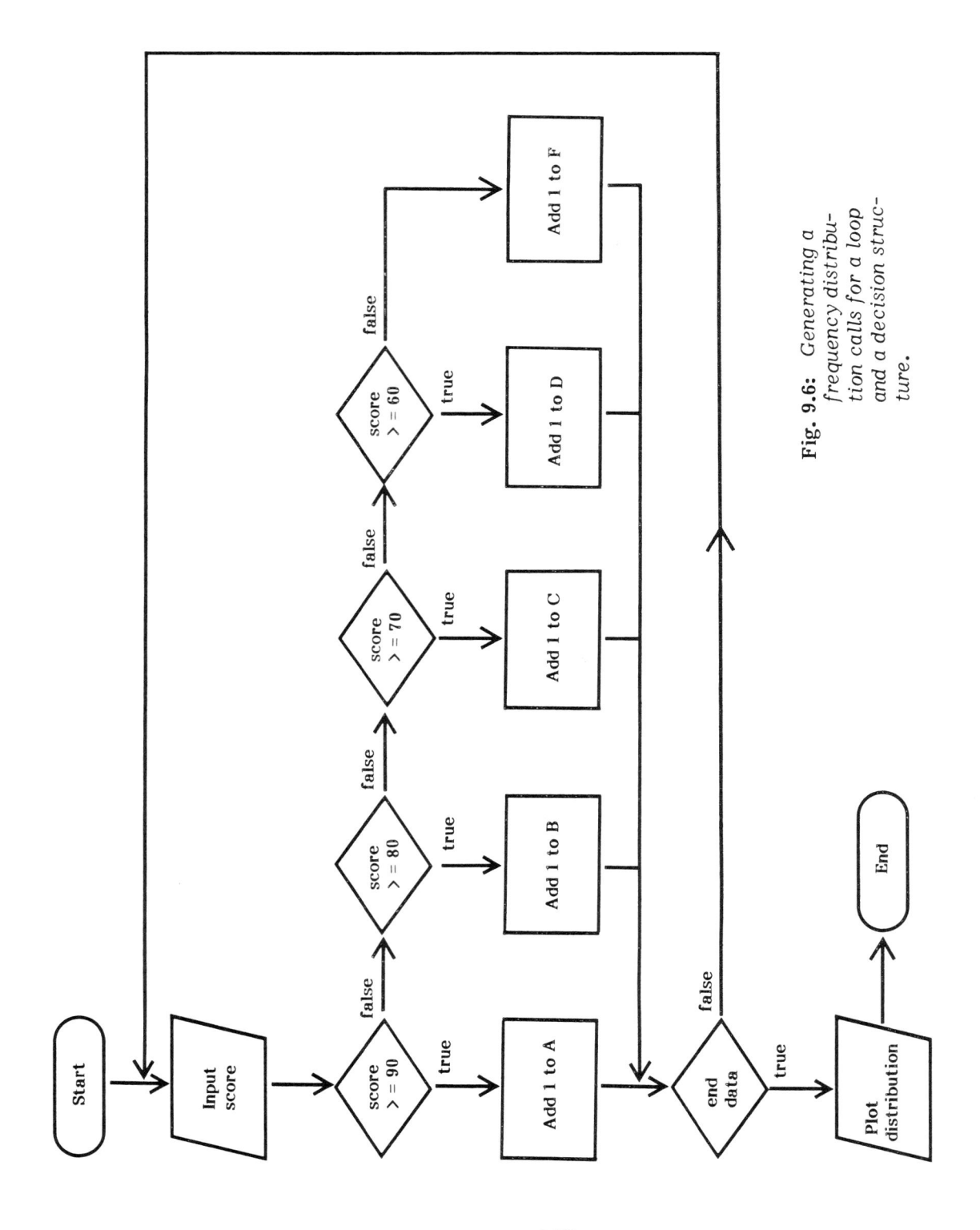

Fig. 9.6: *Generating a frequency distribution calls for a loop and a decision structure.*

Planning a Plot

Plotting points can be useful, but lines, curves, and shapes can convey more meaning. For example, imagine that we want to plot a frequency distribution of student grades. A series of grades will be input in random order *(Fig. 9.5)*. The number of As, Bs, Cs, Ds, and Fs will be counted. Finally, using the counts as data points, the frequency distribution will be displayed. Figure 9.6 shows the program's basic logic.

Generating the grade counts is easy. The key is a loop *(Fig. 9.7)*. An exam score is input. A **SELECT CASE** structure determines and counts the grades, and the loop continues until there are no more exam scores to be entered. There is nothing new in this module. The output, however, *is* different. We want to plot the frequency distribution. Before we write the code to produce that output,

---

Fig. 9.7: *This program module reads a series of exam grades and uses them to develop a frequency distribution. In several subsequent examples, we'll explore several options for plotting this frequency distribution.*

```
                                    ! Program to plot a frequency distribution
                                    ! of student grades. In this first module,
                                    ! student grades are read and grouped into
                                    ! A, B, C, D, and F ranges. The sentinel
                                    ! value is a negative grade.
DO
    INPUT grade

    SELECT CASE grade

        CASE IS < 0                 ! A negative grade is the sentinel value.

        CASE 90 TO 100              ! A grade of 90 or above is an A.
            LET a = a + 1

        CASE 80 TO 89               ! A grade in the 80s is a B.
            LET b = b + 1

        CASE 70 TO 79               ! A grade in the 70s is a C.
            LET c = c + 1

        CASE 60 TO 69               ! A grade in the 60s is a D.
            LET d = d + 1

        CASE ELSE                   ! A grade below 60 is an F.
            LET f = f + 1

    END SELECT

LOOP UNTIL grade < 0
```

we must plan it.

Start with a sheet of scratch paper and some test data. Imagine, for example, that a class has the following grade distribution:

Grade	Number of students
A	5
B	12
C	15
D	9
F	4

The expected output should look something like Fig. 9.8. The possible grades--A, B, C, D, and F--are arrayed along the x-axis. The counts are plotted along the y-axis. For example, to indicate the number of students earning an A, we would move along the x-axis to A (or 1), and then move up to 5--that's point 1,5. B's frequency is point 2,12; C is 3,15, and so on. By connecting the five points, we get a plot of the grade distribution.

Analyze the rough draft of the frequency plot. While our assumed counts will almost certainly change, we can draw some general conclusions. First, how many points will we need along the x-axis? The answer is five--one each for A, B, C, D, and F. It might improve the appearance of our output if we leave some space to the left and to the right of our plot; thus we'll define the limits of the x-axis as 0 and 6.

How many points will we need along the y-axis? That depends on the counts we generate. In our example, the maximum count was 15. If we allowed y-values to range from 0 to 15, we'd have enough room for all the counts. Why couldn't

Fig. 9.8: *Before writing the instructions to generate a plot, take the time to plan your output. Start with a set of test data, and lay out the expected output on a sheet of paper.*

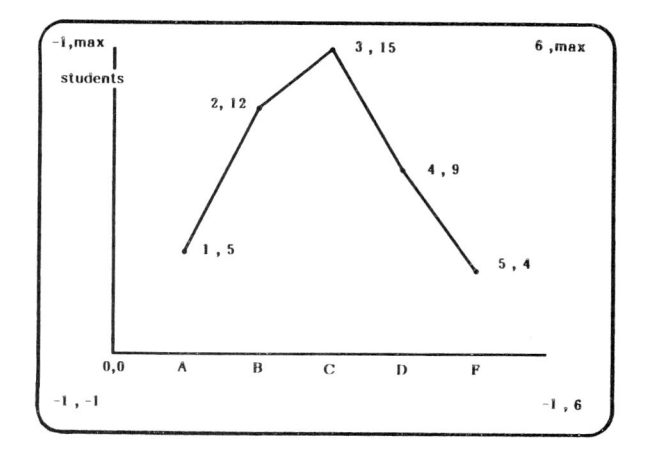

we set the limit at 12? Because point 3,15 (grade C) would lie beyond our limits, and thus could not be plotted. In our example, the lowest possible count for any given grade is zero. The maximum is 15. Thus the range of possible y-values is 0 to 15.

Of course, with other data that maximum could change. How can we find the maximum count? One possibility is to always use the count for a grade of C, but not every exam produces a normal grade distribution. It's better to compare the counts, select the biggest, and use it as the maximum y-value.

In addition to plotting a curve, we want to label it. The letters A, B, C, D, and F are to appear along the x-axis. The word "students" is to appear near the top of the y-axis. We must leave space for these words. Thus, the range for x-values is -1 to 6, and the range for y-values is -1 to the maximum count. Look at Fig. 9.8 again. A screen has been superimposed on the sketch and the x-y coordinates of the four corners labeled.

Plotting Lines

Now that we've planned our output, we're ready to code it. A finished version is shown in Fig. 9.9; let's go through it line by line. As we begin, remember that the program's first module generates the grade counts, so we have values for **a, b, c, d,** and **f**. To set the y-axis's range, we need the biggest count. We'll use an external function to find it. You can see the function near the end of the program; because it's external, it must be declared.

The next step is defining ranges for the x and y axes. The defaults, remember, are 0,1 and 0,1, and they won't do for this application. To override the default ranges, code a **SET WINDOW** statement *(Fig. 9.10)*. In this case, we want x-values to range from -1 to 6, and y-values to range from -1 to the maximum count, so we code

> **SET WINDOW -1,6, -1,ymax**

Given the ranges, we can plot the x and y axes. Lines are drawn by a **PLOT LINES** statement *(Fig. 9.11)*. For example, the statement

> **PLOT LINES: 0,0; 0,ymax**

draws the y-axis. The line's end points are defined as x-y coordinate pairs. The points are separated by semicolons, which tell the system to keep the electron beam on as it scans from point to point. Thus, we get lines. Find the instruction that plots the x-axis *(Fig. 9.9)*. The keyword **LINES** is optional; for example, the statement

```
                                    ! Given the grade frequencies, we define
                                    ! the x and y coordinates for plotting a
                                    ! frequency distrubution. The function
                                    ! Biggest finds the grade earned by the
                                    ! largest number of students; we'll use
                                    ! it to set an upper limit on our y axis.

DECLARE DEF Biggest
LET ymax = Biggest (a,b,c,d,f)

SET WINDOW -1,6,-1,ymax             ! Both x and y start at -1 to allow room
PLOT LINES: 0,-1; 0,ymax            ! to label the graph. Given the window's
PLOT LINES: -1,0;6,0                ! limits, we can plot the x and y axies.

PLOT 1,a;2,b;3,c;4,d;5,f            ! Next, we plot the distribution. Note
                                    ! that the keyword LINES is optional.

PLOT TEXT, AT 1,-1: "A"             ! Finally, we label the graph. It might
PLOT TEXT, AT 2,-1: "B"             ! make sense to move the PLOT TEXT
PLOT TEXT, AT 3,-1: "C"             ! statements to an internal subroutine.
PLOT TEXT, AT 4,-1: "D"
PLOT TEXT, AT 5,-1: "F"
PLOT TEXT, AT -1,(ymax - 1): "Students"

END

                                    ! Function to find the grade earned
                                    ! by the most students.
DEF Biggest (a,b,c,d,f)
   LET work = MAX (a,b)
   LET work = MAX (work,c)
   LET work = MAX (work,d)
   LET Biggest = MAX (work,f)
END DEF
```

Fig. 9.9: *Given the distribution of grades, this module plots a frequency distribution "curve."*

Fig. 9.10: *The maximum and minimum ranges for both x and y are defined in a SET WINDOW statement.*

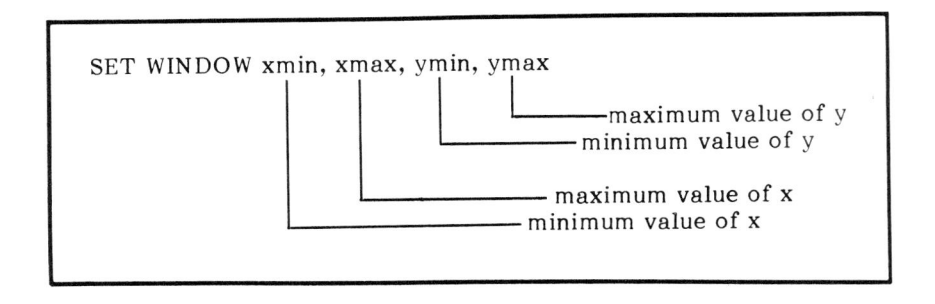

```
SET WINDOW xmin, xmax, ymin, ymax
                            │     │     │     │
                            │     │     │     └── maximum value of y
                            │     │     └────── minimum value of y
                            │     └──────────── maximum value of x
                            └────────────────── minimum value of x
```

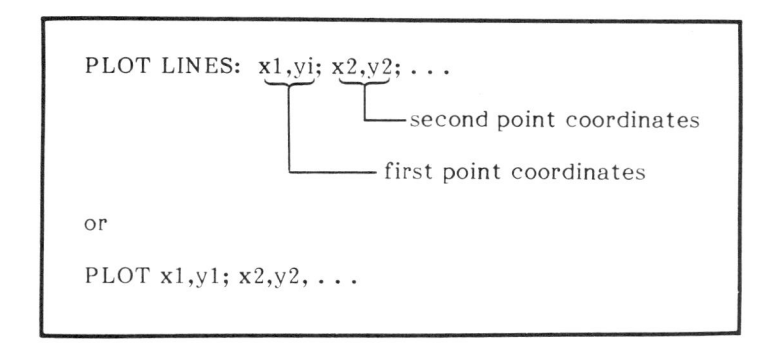

```
PLOT LINES: x1,y1; x2,y2; . . .
                ⏟      ⏟
                │      └─ second point coordinates
                └─ first point coordinates

or

PLOT x1,y1; x2,y2, . . .
```

Fig. 9.11: *The PLOT LINES resembles a PLOT POINTS statement. Note that the x-y coordinate pairs are separated by semicolons. The semicolon tells the system to keep the electron scanner on as it moves from point to point; the result is a line.*

PLOT 0,0; 6,0

is equivalent to the **PLOT LINES** statement in the program.

A single statement can plot several lines. For example,

PLOT 1,a; 2,b; 3,c; 4,d; 5,f

plots point **1,a**, links it to point **2,b**, links that point with **3,c**, and so on. The result is our frequency distribution *(Fig. 9.12)*. Note that the output covers a

Fig. 9.12: *Here's the plotted grade frequency distribution.*

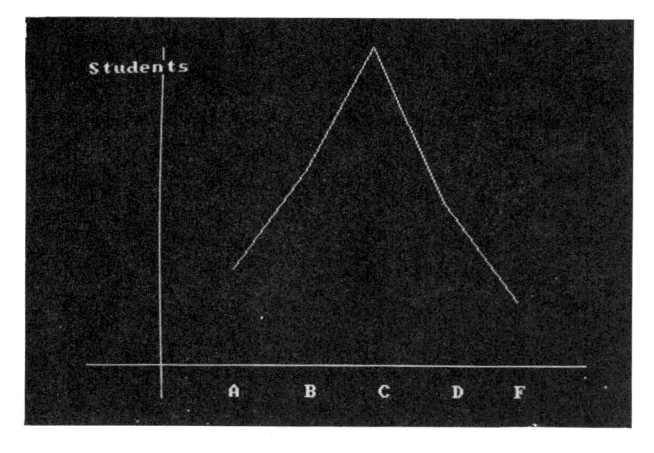

full screen instead of just the history window. When graphics instructions are used, *True BASIC* automatically switches from its two window default to full screen output.

A **PLOT** statement that links several points can easily exceed a single line. When this happens, spread the points over two or more statements and code a semicolon at the end of all but the last one. The semicolon keeps the electron beam on, so you'll get a line linking the last point in the first **PLOT** with the first point in the second one. This same trick can be used when a series of points is generated one by one in a loop. If you end the **PLOT** statement with a semicolon, all the points will be linked. A **PLOT** with no points turns the beam off.

Plotting Text

The output *(Fig. 9.12)* is labeled. We put the labels there with a series of **PLOT TEXT** statements *(Fig. 9.13)*. You can see them in Fig. 9.9; let's select one,

    PLOT TEXT, AT 1,-1: "A"

and study it. Following **PLOT TEXT** is another keyword, **AT**. Next comes a set of x-y coordinates specifying the location of the message's lower-left corner. A colon follows the coordinates. Then comes the string expression to be displayed. Look at the other **PLOT TEXT** statements. Find the output each one generates in Fig. 9.12.

One problem with plotting text is that the physical size of the characters does not change to match the scale of your plot. As you develop labeled plots, you may find it necessary to experiment with several ranges before you find one that looks right with the text in place.

Fig. 9.13: *Captions can be added to a plot by using the PLOT TEXT statement.*

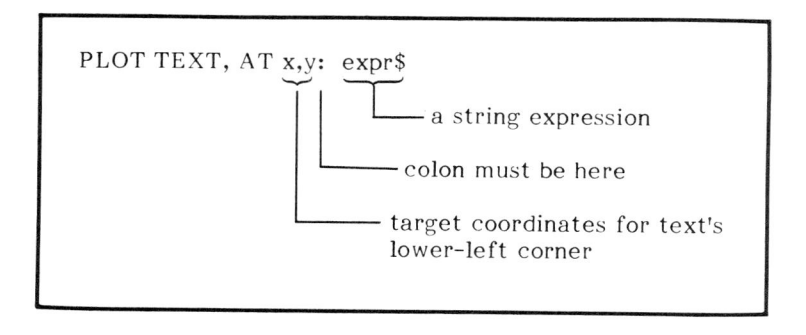

```
PLOT TEXT, AT x,y:  expr$
              |        |
              |        └── a string expression
              |
              └── colon must be here
              
              └── target coordinates for text's
                  lower-left corner
```

```
        red                         cyan
        magneta                     brown
        yellow                      white
        green                       black
        blue                        background
```

"Background" is the current background color. See your *User's Guide* for a detailed description of colors on your computer.

Fig. 9.14: *On most computers, the True BASIC programmer can work with these colors.*

COLOR

Color can add a great deal to your graphic output. In *True BASIC*, you can define one background color and several different foreground colors.

Points, lines, areas, and text are plotted against the background. In *True BASIC*, you have a choice of several colors *(Fig. 9.14)*. Not all computers can display all the colors. Others can display more. On some computers, a color doesn't match its name. Once again, you'll have to experiment. Refer to your *User's Guide* for more detailed information.

The background color is defined by a **SET BACKGROUND COLOR** statement *(Fig. 9.15)*. The color can be specified as a string ("red" or "blue", for example), or as a number. Check your *User's Guide* for your computer's color numbers. For example, to set the background color to blue, code

Fig. 9.15: *The background color is defined in a SET BACKGROUND COLOR statement.*

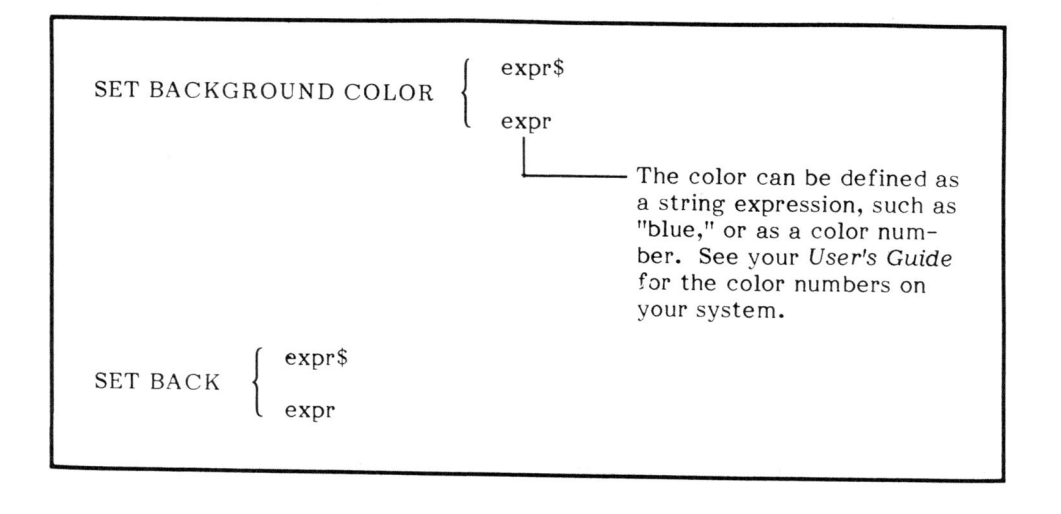

```
                              ⎧ expr$
    SET BACKGROUND COLOR      ⎨
                              ⎩ expr
                                    └──── The color can be defined as
                                          a string expression, such as
                                          "blue," or as a color num-
                                          ber. See your User's Guide
                                          for the color numbers on
                                          your system.


                ⎧ expr$
    SET BACK    ⎨
                ⎩ expr
```

>   **SET BACKGROUND COLOR "blue"**

or

>   **SET BACK "blue"**

Place the **SET BACKGROUND COLOR** statement after the associated **SET WINDOW** statement.

The foreground color is specified in a **SET COLOR** statement *(Fig. 9.16)*. Generally, you have the same choices as before. Once again, some computers support more colors, and others fewer, and a given color won't always match its name. For example, on an IBM PC®, foreground colors are selected from one of two "palettes:" green, red, and yellow, or cyan, magenta, and white. You can refer to colors by name or by number; check your *User's Guide* for details.

Both the foreground and the background colors can be set in a single statement:

>   **SET COLOR "foreground/background"**

We'll illustrate the use of color in the next section.

PLOTTING AREAS

For many applications, points or lines are fine, but shapes are more dramatic. Start with points. To plot lines, you connect them. To plot an area, you define its corners, link them with lines, and then fill the enclosed area with the current

Fig. 9.16: *The current foreground color can be defined in a SET COLOR statement.*

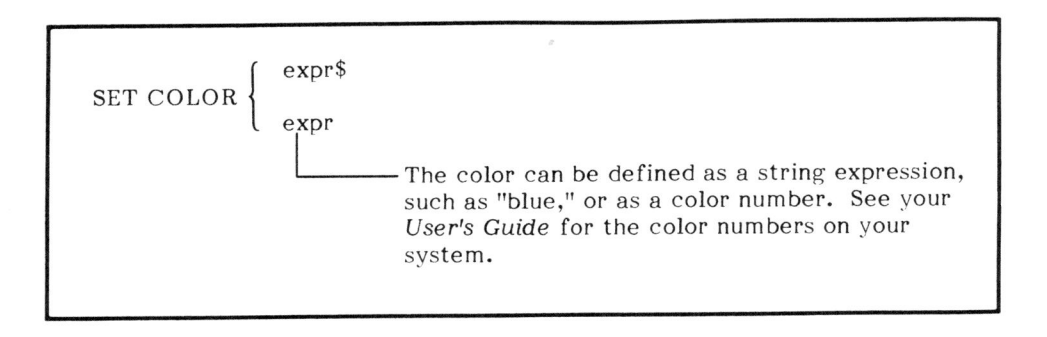

```
SET COLOR  { expr$
           { expr
                └── The color can be defined as a string expression,
                    such as "blue," or as a color number. See your
                    User's Guide for the color numbers on your
                    system.
```

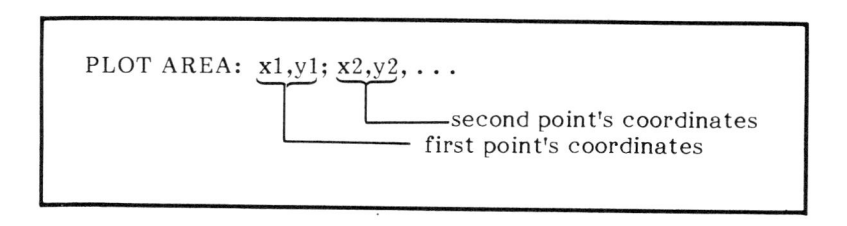

```
┌─────────────────────────────────────────────────┐
│                                                 │
│       PLOT AREA:  x1,y1; x2,y2, . . .           │
│                   └─┬─┘  └─┬─┘                  │
│                     │      └──second point's coordinates │
│                     └─────────first point's coordinates  │
│                                                 │
└─────────────────────────────────────────────────┘
```

Fig. 9.17: *The PLOT AREA statement connects a series of points, draws a line linking the last and the first points, and then fills the enclosed area with the current foreground color.*

foreground color. To define a triangle, you need three points. To define a rectangle, you need four. A pentagon calls for five, and so on. The points are listed in a **PLOT AREA** statement *(Fig. 9.17)*.

In our grade distribution program, we plotted a frequency distribution. Let's change the program to display a bar chart. Again, we'll ignore the first part of the program and concentrate on the graphic output *(Fig. 9.18)*. Read through the logic. Near the top, the background color is set to blue. Next, the foreground color is set to green, and the x and y axes are plotted.

Move along to the logic that plots the bars. Focus on the first bar; the relevant instructions are shaded. The first step is setting the foreground color

    SET COLOR "red"

Next, the statement

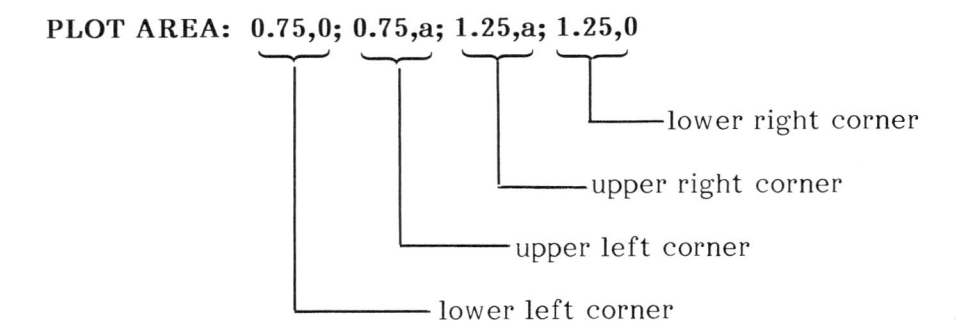

    PLOT AREA: 0.75,0; 0.75,a; 1.25,a; 1.25,0
                    │   │   │   └── lower right corner
                    │   │   └──────── upper right corner
                    │   └────────────── upper left corner
                    └──────────────────── lower left corner

is executed. Look at the x-values: 0.75 and 1.25. Our bar will be 0.5 units wide, and centered on x = 1. Now look at the y-values. The bar will range from 0

```
                                        ! Given the grade frequencies, we define
                                        ! the x and y coordinates for plotting a
                                        ! frequency distrubution. The function
                                        ! Biggest finds the grade earned by the
                                        ! largest number of students; we'll use
                                        ! it to set an upper limit on our y axis.
DECLARE DEF Biggest
LET ymax = Biggest (a,b,c,d,f)

SET WINDOW -1,6,-1,ymax                 ! Both x and y start at -1 to allow room
SET BACK "blue"                         ! for labeling the graph. We'll set the
SET COLOR "green"                       ! background and foreground colors, and
PLOT -1,0; 6,0                          ! then plot the x and y axes.
PLOT 0,-1; 0,ymax
                                        ! Next, we plot the distribution.
SET COLOR "red"
PLOT AREA: 0.75,0; 0.75,a; 1.25,a; 1.25,0
SET COLOR "yellow"
PLOT AREA: 1.75,0; 1.75,b; 2.25,b; 2.25,0
SET COLOR "green"
PLOT AREA: 2.75,0; 2.75,c; 3.25,c; 3.25,0
SET COLOR "red"
PLOT AREA: 3.75,0; 3.75,d; 4.25,d; 4.25,0
SET COLOR "yellow"
PLOT AREA: 4.75,0; 4.75,f; 5.25,f; 5.25,0

SET COLOR "green"
PLOT TEXT, AT 1,-1: "A"                 ! Finally, we label the plot. It might
PLOT TEXT, AT 2,-1: "B"                 ! make sense to move the PLOT TEXT
PLOT TEXT, AT 3,-1: "C"                 ! statements to an internal subroutine.
PLOT TEXT, AT 4,-1: "D"
PLOT TEXT, AT 5,-1: "F"
PLOT TEXT, AT -1,(ymax - 1): "Students"

DATA 93,87,70,62,65,52,73,75,83,85,68,92,72,77,64,78,57,90,88,72,76
DATA 82,81,75,66,79
END

                                        ! Function to find the grade earned
                                        ! by the most students.
DEF Biggest (a,b,c,d,f)
  LET work = MAX (a,b)
  LET work = MAX (work,c)
  LET work = MAX (work,d)
  LET Biggest = MAX (work,f)
END DEF
```

Fig. 9.18: *This module uses the grade distribution developed earlier to plot a bar chart.*

to **a** units high. Variable **a** is our count.

Read the rest of the program *(Fig. 9.18)*; plotting each of the bars follows the same pattern. Note that they are centered on x = 1, 2, 3, 4, and 5 respectively. Note also that each bar's height is determined by one of the counts. The output is shown in Fig. 9.19.

Pie Charts

Bar charts are useful for graphically showing relative proportions. A pie chart, a circle divided into "slices," is an option. The relative size of each slice conveys the same sense of proportion as the relative height of each bar.

The secret to drawing a pie chart is plotting a series of arcs, each one representing a proportionate fraction of a circle. Drawing an arc requires an understanding of trigonometry. This primer assumes a very limited mathematical background, so we won't attempt to develop a pie chart program. For those who know trig, the x-y coordinates of any point on a circle are defined by

$$\text{Cos(angle)*radius, Sin(angle)*radius}$$

THE BOX STATEMENTS

PLOT AREA statements can be used to generate any shape. However, many applications call for only a few basic shapes such as rectangles and circles. If such shapes will do, *True BASIC*'s **BOX** statements offer real advantages. For one thing, they are easy to code. They also display shapes much more quickly than equivalent **PLOT AREA** statements. In fact, the **BOX** statements work so quickly they can be used for animation.

Fig. 9.19: *Compare this bar chart with the simple "curve" illustrated in Fig. 9.12. Note how much more visually appealing it is.*

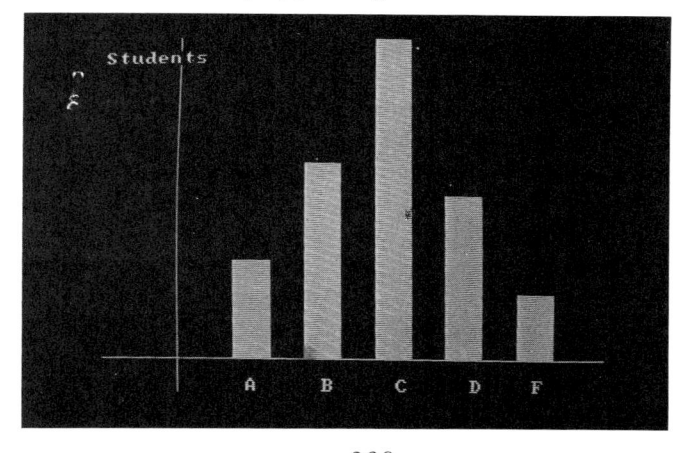

Figure 9.20 summarizes three key **BOX** statements. **BOX LINES** outlines a rectangle having the specified maximum and minimum x and y coordinates. **BOX ELLIPSE** (or **BOX CIRCLE**) draws the ellipse that fits inside the specified box. A **BOX AREA** statement displays a rectangle and fills it with the current foreground color.

Figure 9.21 shows a new version of the frequency distribution program. Compare it to Fig. 9.19. The **PLOT AREA** statements have been replaced by **BOX AREA** statements; nothing else is changed. If you run both versions, however, you'll see an almost amazing difference in plot speed. It's easy to claim that **BOX** statements are fast. Run the two programs, however, and you'll see exactly what fast means.

Testing the Aspect Ratio

Another advantage of the **BOX** statements is their simplicity. As an example, let's write a routine to draw a circle, and then use the output to check our screen's aspect ratio. If the shape looks like a circle, fine. If it looks like an ellipse, then we'll have to make an adjustment.

We'll use the screen's default coordinates. The statement

   BOX CIRCLE 0,1, 0,1

Fig. 9.20: *Rectangles and ellipses can be plotted quickly by using True BASIC's BOX statements.*

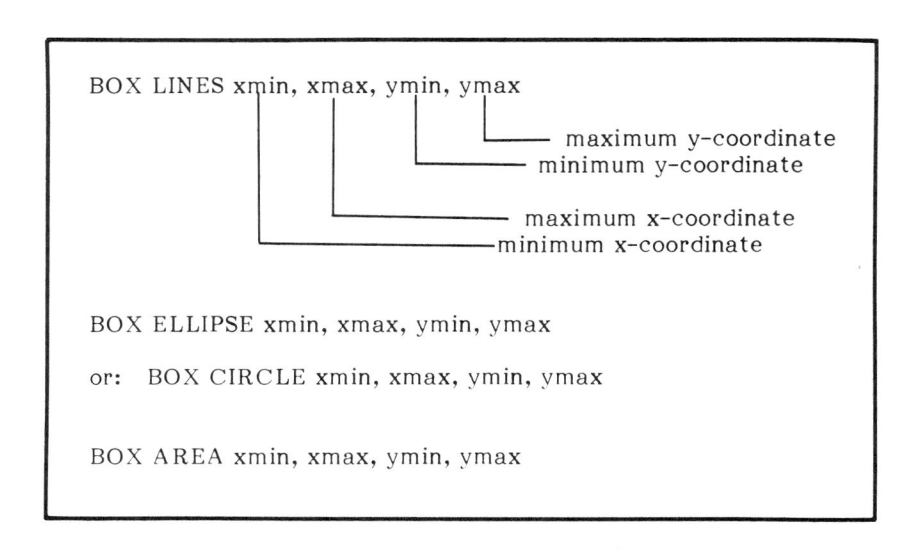

```
BOX LINES xmin, xmax, ymin, ymax
                         │      └── maximum y-coordinate
                         └──────── minimum y-coordinate
              │      └──────────── maximum x-coordinate
              └─────────────────── minimum x-coordinate

BOX ELLIPSE xmin, xmax, ymin, ymax

or:  BOX CIRCLE xmin, xmax, ymin, ymax

BOX AREA xmin, xmax, ymin, ymax
```

```
                                    ! Given the grade frequencies, we define
                                    ! the x and y coordinates for plotting a
                                    ! frequency distrubution. The function
                                    ! Biggest finds the grade earned by the
                                    ! largest number of students; we'll use
                                    ! it to set an upper limit on our y axis.
DECLARE DEF Biggest
LET ymax = Biggest (a,b,c,d,f)

SET WINDOW -1,6,-1,ymax             ! Both x and y start at -1 to allow room
SET BACK "blue"                     ! for labeling the graph. We'll set the
SET COLOR "green"                   ! background and foreground colors, and
PLOT -1,0; 6,0                      ! then plot the x and y axes.
PLOT 0,-1; 0,ymax
                                    ! Next, we plot the distribution.
SET COLOR "red"
BOX AREA 0.75,1.25, 0,a
SET COLOR "yellow"
BOX AREA 1.75,2.25, 0,b
SET COLOR "green"
BOX AREA 2.75,3.25, 0,c
SET COLOR "red"
BOX AREA 3.75,4.25, 0,d
SET COLOR "yellow"
BOX AREA 4.75,5.25, 0,f

SET COLOR "green"
PLOT TEXT, AT 1,-1: "A"             ! Finally, we label the plot. It might
PLOT TEXT, AT 2,-1: "B"             ! make sense to move the PLOT TEXT
PLOT TEXT, AT 3,-1: "C"             ! statements to an internal subroutine.
PLOT TEXT, AT 4,-1: "D"
PLOT TEXT, AT 5,-1: "F"
PLOT TEXT, AT -1,(ymax - 1): "Students"

DATA 93,87,70,62,65,52,73,75,83,85,68,92,72,77,64,78,57,90,88,72,76
DATA 82,81,75,66,79
END

                                    ! Function to find the grade earned
                                    ! by the most students.
DEF Biggest (a,b,c,d,f)
  LET work = MAX (a,b)
  LET work = MAX (work,c)
  LET work = MAX (work,d)
  LET Biggest = MAX (work,f)
END DEF
```

Fig. 9.21: *This routine also plots a bar chart, but it uses BOX statements instead of PLOT AREA statements. Run this version, and compare its plot speed with the version in Fig. 9.18.*

Fig. 9.22: *To determine your screen's aspect ratio, use a BOX CIRCLE statement, study the output, and adjust the coordinates until the output looks like a circle.*

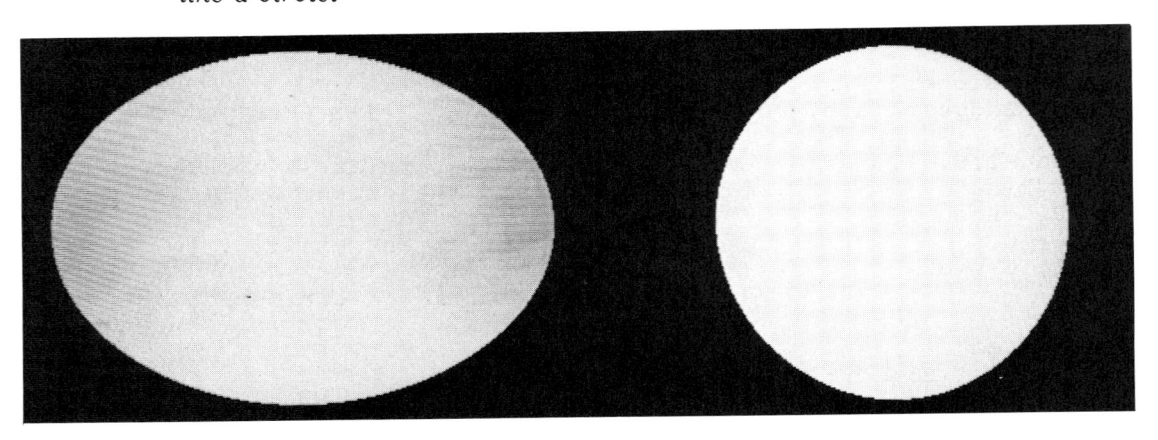

    a. BOX CIRCLE 0,1, 0,1   b. BOX CIRCLE 0.15,0.85, 0,1
       END   END

specifies an ellipse that just fits inside a 1 by 1 rectangle. That "rectangle" should be a square, and the "ellipse" should be a circle. Figure 9.22a shows how this statement's output appears on an IBM color monitor. Clearly, it isn't a circle. What can we do to make it a circle?

Look at the shape. It's too fat. Let's cut the width. This time, we'll code

BOX CIRCLE 0.15,0.85, 0,1

Note that we've moved the minimum and maximum values of x closer to the center of the screen, but we've left the y limits alone. The **BOX** statement now defines a rectangle that is 0.70 units wide (0.85 - 0.15 = 0.70) and 1.00 units high. It shouldn't be a circle, but, as Fig. 9.22b shows, it is. If we want circles to look like circles, at least on an IBM color monitor, we must make them 70 percent as wide as they are high. Conduct a similar experiment to determine how to correct for your own screen's aspect ratio.

The last **BOX CIRCLE** statement appears in Fig. 9.23, along with a new statement: **FLOOD** *(Fig. 9.24)*. When a **FLOOD** statement is executed, the specified point is set to the current foreground color. Then the color begins to spread from that "seed" point, and continues spreading until it hits a line. In our example, the **FLOOD** statement refers to a point in the middle of the circle, so the entire circle is "flooded" with the current foreground color. Specify a point outside the circle, and everything but the circle will be colored.

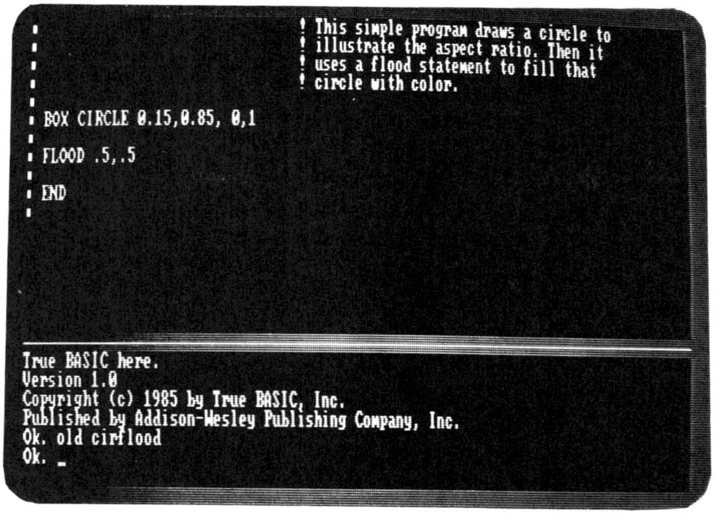

```
! This simple program draws a circle to
! illustrate the aspect ratio. Then it
! uses a flood statement to fill that
! circle with color.

BOX CIRCLE 0.15,0.85, 0,1

FLOOD .5,.5

END


True BASIC here.
Version 1.0
Copyright (c) 1985 by True BASIC, Inc.
Published by Addison-Wesley Publishing Company, Inc.
Ok. old cirflood
Ok. _
```

Fig. 9.23: *On the author's display screen, a shape must be defined 70 percent as wide as it is high if the output is to look like a circle. This simple program also illustrates the FLOOD statement.*

Drawing Multiple Shapes

Another interesting application of the **BOX** statements is drawing multiple shapes to form simple optical illusions. For example, consider Fig. 9.25. Focus on the first **FOR NEXT** loop. It draws a series of boxes, one inside the other; its output is shown in Fig. 9.26. More impressive than seeing the finished output, however, is watching it develop. Enter the first loop and run it. Then try experimenting with the shape of the rectangles.

A **PAUSE** statement *(Fig. 9.27)* follows the first loop. It causes the computer

Fig. 9.24: *The FLOOD statement allows the programmer to fill an area with the current foreground color.*

```
FLOOD x,y
      ⌣
      └── Coordinates of a reference point. This point is set to
          the current foreground color. The color then spreads in
          all directions, and continues spreading until a line is
          encountered.
```

```
                    ! Simple exercise to illustrate BOX LINES
                    ! and BOX CIRCLE.

FOR i = .1 TO 1 STEP .05   ! First we'll draw a series of boxes, one
   BOX LINES 0,i, 0,i      ! inside the other.
NEXT i

PAUSE 5                    ! We'll give you a few seconds to look at
CLEAR                      ! the output. Then we'll clear the screen.

FOR i = .1 TO 1 STEP .1    ! Next, we'll draw a series of successively
   BOX CIRCLE 0,i, 0,i     ! larger circles. The output is almost an
NEXT i                     ! optical illusion. It will stay on until
                           ! you press any key.
END
```

True BASIC here.
Version 1.0
Copyright (c) 1985 by True BASIC, Inc.
Published by Addison-Wesley Publishing Company, Inc.
Ok. old cirflood
Ok. old boxillus
Ok. _

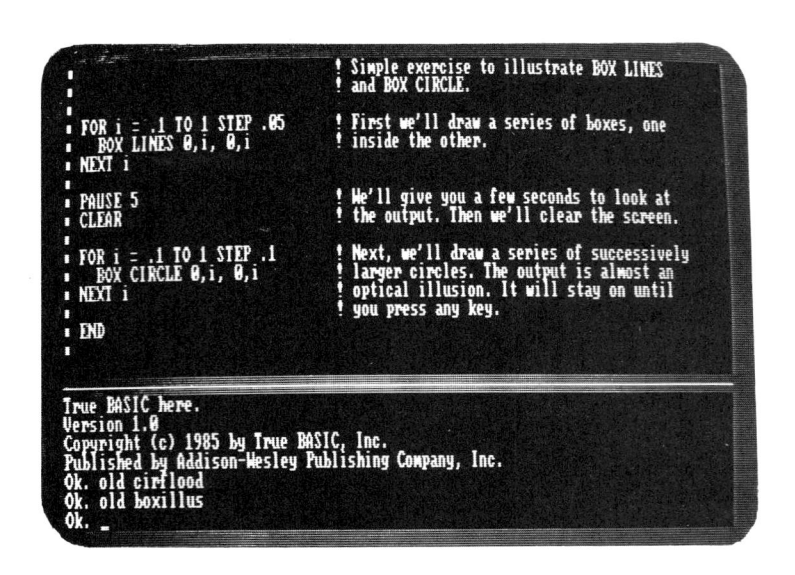

Fig. 9.25: *This program illustrates the BOX statements. Enter it on your computer and run it.*

Fig. 9.26: *Here's the output from the program's first loop.*

```
PAUSE n
      └── time, in seconds
```

Fig. 9.27: *A **PAUSE** statement holds or freezes the screen image so that the user has time to view it.*

```
┌─────────────────────────────────────────────────────────┐
│                                                         │
│   CLEAR                                                 │
│                                                         │
│                    Be careful!  CLEAR erases the screen.│
│                                                         │
└─────────────────────────────────────────────────────────┘
```

Fig. 9.28: *A CLEAR statement erases the screen.*

to wait for a specified number of seconds (in this case, 5) before proceeding. The brief pause gives you time to view the output. Next comes a **CLEAR** statement *(Fig. 9.28)*. As you may have guessed, a **CLEAR** statement erases the screen.

Move on to the second loop *(Fig. 9.25, again)*. It generates a series of successively larger circles; the output is shown in Fig. 9.29. Again, it's more interesting watching the output develop than simply viewing the finished version. Try the program.

Animation

True BASIC's **BOX** statements are fast enough for animation. Start with a **BOX LINES, BOX CIRCLE,** or **BOX AREA** statement, and plot a shape. Use a **BOX KEEP** statement *(Fig. 9.30)* to store the shape in a string variable. Erase it (**BOX CLEAR**), and redraw it at a different spot (**BOX SHOW**). Repeat this sequence and you'll see an illusion of motion.

Let's use a simple example to illustrate. Some of you may remember an early computer game called Pong. A dot moves from one side of the screen toward the other. The player manipulates a "paddle" to intercept the flight of the "ball" and send it back. The game resembles electronic ping pong.

Fig. 9.29: *Here's the output from the second loop in the BOX illustration program (Fig. 9.25).*

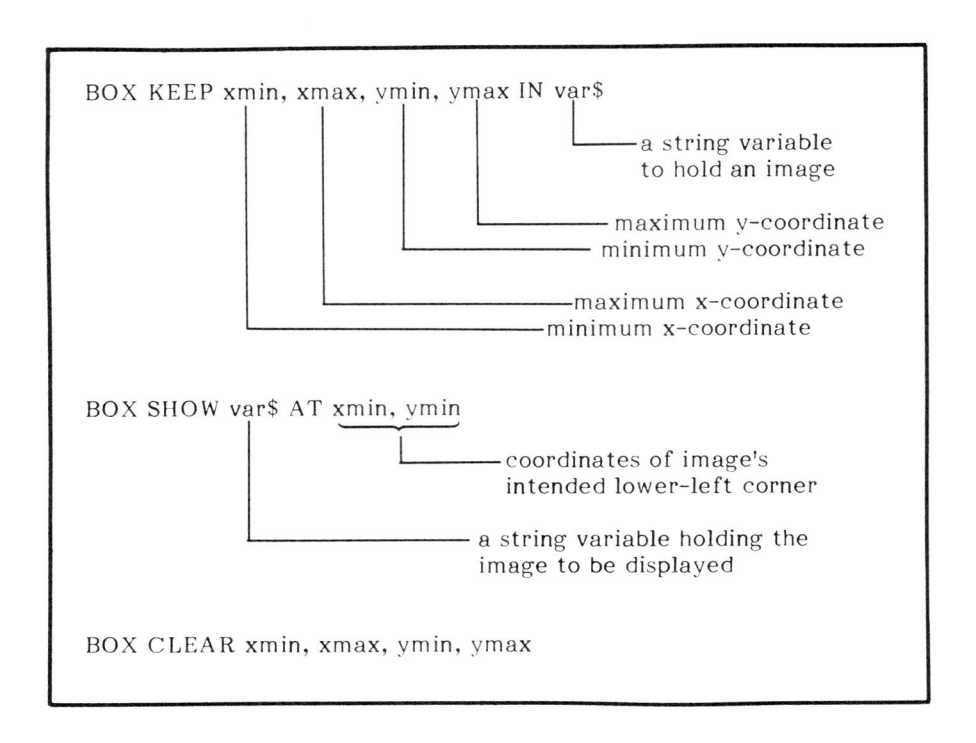

```
BOX KEEP xmin, xmax, ymin, ymax IN var$
                                     └── a string variable
                                          to hold an image
                                 └── maximum y-coordinate
                                 └── minimum y-coordinate
                        └── maximum x-coordinate
                        └── minimum x-coordinate

BOX SHOW var$ AT xmin, ymin
                 └── coordinates of image's
                      intended lower-left corner
         └── a string variable holding the
              image to be displayed

BOX CLEAR xmin, xmax, ymin, ymax
```

Fig. 9.30: *Interesting animation effects can be produced by using the following BOX statements.*

The key is a ball-like shape that rebounds when it hits a wall or a paddle. Figure 9.31 shows a simplified version of this "moving ball" routine. Let's review the program and see how it works.

We begin by defining a window. Note that the origin (point 0,0) is at the screen's center—that's important. Next, using a **BOX CIRCLE** statement, a ball is drawn (it's intentionally quite large) and then filled with the current foreground color (the **FLOOD** statement). The **BOX KEEP** statement stores the shape in a string variable, **ball$**. Note that **BOX KEEP** has the same x-y limits as **BOX CIRCLE**. Now, we're ready to move the ball.

The basic control structure is a **DO UNTIL** loop with a **KEY INPUT** exit condition. Focus on the inner **FOR NEXT** loop. The upper and lower limits and the increment are variables. The increment is 0.5. As we begin, **limit** is 5, so the **FOR NEXT** loop goes from -5 to 5. The "ball" will move from left to right. When the loop ends, the signs of the increment and the limit are flipped. As we return to the top of the **DO** loop, **limit** is -5. Thus, the **FOR NEXT** loop goes from 5 to -5. The "ball" will move from right to left.

Look inside the **FOR NEXT** loop. The **BOX CLEAR** statement erases the original ball. The **BOX SHOW** statement displays a new one; the x-y coordinates

```
                                  ! A simple example of animation. This
                                  ! program simulates a ball bouncing
                                  ! back and forth across the screen.

SET WINDOW -5,5, -5,5             ! First, we'll set the window so that the
                                  ! origin is in the center of the screen.

BOX CIRCLE -5,-4.3, -0.5,0.5      ! Next, we'll draw a circle. The y range
                                  ! is slightly larger than the x range to
                                  ! correct for the aspect ratio.
FLOOD -4.5,0                      ! We'll color the circle.

                                  ! The BOX KEEP statement stores our circle
                                  ! in a string variable called ball$.

BOX KEEP -5,-4.3, -0.5,0.5 IN ball$

LET increment = .5                ! The increment and limit are for a FOR
LET limits = 5                    ! NEXT loop we're about to code.

DO                                ! We continue until a key is pressed.

  FOR i = -limits TO limits STEP increment

                                  ! First, we erase the old ball.

    BOX CLEAR i,i+0.7, -0.5,0.5

                                  ! Then we draw a new one.

    BOX SHOW ball$ AT i + increment, -0.5

  NEXT i                          ! Then we do it again.

  LET increment = -increment      ! These two statements switch the limits
  LET limits = -limits            ! and the increment of the FOR NEXT loop.
                                  ! Next time, the ball will go backward.

LOOP UNTIL KEY INPUT              ! We keep going until a key is pressed.

END
```

Fig. 9.31: *This simple animation program illustrates the basic movement of the traditional computer game called "pong."*

specify the location of the shape's lower left corner. As the loop repeats, that ball is erased and another one appears at yet another position. The result is a convincing animation.

Try the program. Vary the increment to make the ball speed up or slow down. Try clearing less than a full width, and you'll leave a ghost image of the ball's

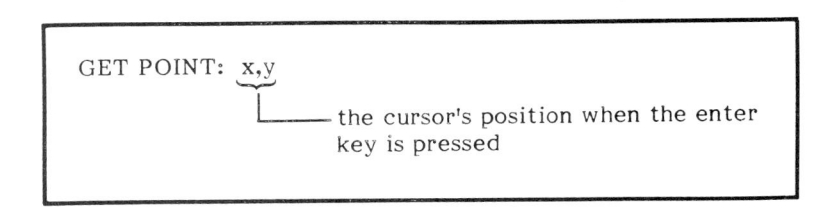

```
GET POINT: x,y
              └─── the cursor's position when the enter
                   key is pressed
```

Fig. 9.32: *A GET POINT statement can be used to input a set of x-y coordinates.*

path. At the end of a loop, the ball hits something. Try modifying the program to make it bounce at a different angle. There is a great deal you can do with this simple animation structure. Check your *Reference Manual* and your *User's Guide* for additional examples.

An extended form of the **BOX SHOW** statement allows the programmer to specify how the saved image is to interact with the existing screen image. Check your *User's Guide* for details.

GRAPHIC INPUT

True BASIC supports two statements that allow points to be input to a computer. When a **GET POINT** statement *(Fig. 9.32)* is executed, the user moves a cursor to the desired spot on the screen and presses enter. The cursor's x-y coordinates are then stored in the statement's variables. Depending on your system, cursor control keys, a mouse, a light pen, or a stylus can be used to position the cursor.

Locate a program called **MONDRIAN** on your *True BASIC* disk. It illustrates the **GET POINT** statement. Run it. A graphic cursor (a set of "cross hairs") will appear on your screen. Move the cursor and press enter; the point will be plotted. Move the cursor to a different spot and press enter again. After the second

Fig. 9.33: *On computers that are equipped with a mouse, a GET MOUSE statement can be used to input a set of x-y coordinates and the current state of the mouse control button.*

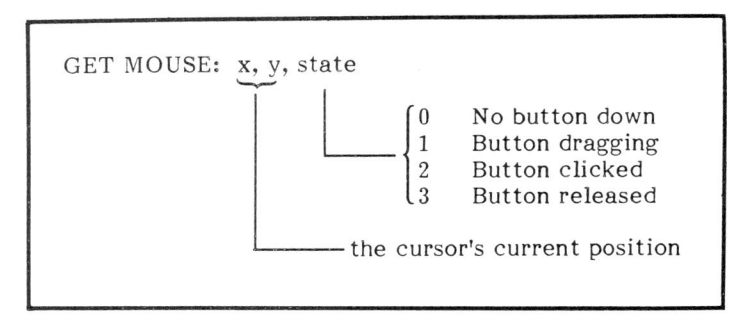

```
GET MOUSE: x, y, state
                 │   └─── ┌ 0   No button down
                          │ 1   Button dragging
                          │ 2   Button clicked
                          └ 3   Button released
                 └─────── the cursor's current position
```

move, a colored rectangle will appear. Keep going. A new rectangle will appear after every second point is entered. The idea is to simulate a Mondrian painting.

The other graphic input statement is **GET MOUSE** *(Fig. 9.33)*. When a **GET MOUSE** statement is executed, three values are input: the cursor's x and y coordinates and the state of the mouse's control button. Obviously, a **GET MOUSE** statement is legal only on a computer equipped with a mouse.

PICTURES

Graphic subroutines, called pictures, are a particularly significant *True BASIC* feature. Like regular subroutines, they can be internal or external, and parameters can be passed to them. What makes this feature so powerful is that transformations can be applied to a picture. Once an image is defined, it can be moved, made larger or smaller, rotated, or twisted with a simple command.

Let's develop a program to illustrate this feature. We'll plot a triangle, place the **PLOT** statement in a picture, and then use the picture to draw a series of triangles. We'll define a right triangle with one corner at the origin. Given its height and its base, we can plot it by coding

PLOT LINES: 0,0; 0,height; base,0; 0,0

Fig. 9.34: *A True BASIC picture is a graphic subroutine. A picture is defined much like a subroutine.*

```
PICTURE Picture_name (var1, var2, ...)
   ___
   ___
      PLOT ...
   ___
   ___
END PICTURE
```

An example:

```
PICTURE Triangle (height, base)
   PLOT 0,0; 0,height; base,0; 0,0
END PICTURE
```

The fourth point is needed to draw a line from the third point back to the origin.

A picture is defined much as a subroutine *(Fig. 9.34)*. It begins with a **PICTURE** statement. Following the keyword is the picture's name (a valid subroutine name), and a list of parameters. Within the picture are one or more statements including at least one **PLOT**. An **END PICTURE** statement ends the graphic subroutine. A picture to plot a right triangle is shown near the bottom of Fig. 9.34.

Pictures are invoked by **DRAW** statements *(Fig. 9.35)*. A simple **DRAW** statement, such as

DRAW Triangle (3,4)

generates a single image, in this case a right triangle with height 3 and base 4. By transforming a picture, we can shift an image's location, make it larger or smaller (in either dimension), rotate it, or tilt it. Figure 9.36 illustrates a **DRAW** statement with rotation. Its output is shown in Fig. 9.37; once again,

Fig. 9.35: *A picture is called or invoked by a DRAW statement. The ability to transform a picture is a particularly powerful feature.*

DRAW Picture_name (var1, var2, . . .) WITH transformation

DRAW Picture_name (parameters) WITH trans1 * trans2* . . .

Built-in transformations:

Shift (a,b)	Move the picture. Coordinate **x** becomes **x + a**; coordinate **y** becomes **y + b**.
Scale (a)	Change the picture's size. Coordinate **x** becomes **x + a**; coordinate **y** becomes **y + a**.
Scale (a,b)	Change the picture's size. Coordinate **x** becomes **x + a**; coordinate **y** becomes **y + b**.
Rotate (a)	Rotate the picture **a** radians (or degrees) counterclockwise about the origin.
Shear (a)	Lean all verticle lines clockwise by **a** radians (or degrees).

```
                              ! This program illustrates PICTUREs.
                              ! A PICTURE is defined to plot a right
                              ! triangle. One corner is at point 0,0.
                              ! The lengths of two sides, a and b, are
                              ! input to the program.
INPUT a,b

SET WINDOW -10,10, -10,10     ! The window is set with its origin at the
                              ! screen's center.

OPTION ANGLE DEGREES          ! We'll use degrees.

                              ! Next, we'll set up a loop to DRAW the
                              ! triangle and then transform it,
                              ! rotating it in 10 degree increments.

FOR angle = 0 TO 360 STEP 10

   DRAW Triangle (a,b) WITH Rotate (angle)

NEXT angle

END

                              ! This picture plots a right triangle
                              ! centered on the origin given values
                              ! for the triangle's height and base.

PICTURE Triangle (height, base)

   PLOT 0,0; 0,height; base,0; 0,0

END PICTURE
```

Fig. 9.36: *In this program, we use a picture to define a triangle, and then draw it repetitively while rotating it around the origin.*

Fig. 9.37: *Here's the output generated by the triangle program.*

OPEN #n: SCREEN 0,0.5, 0.5,1   OPEN #n: SCREEN 0.5,1, 0.5,1

0,1   1,1

0,0   0,1

OPEN #n: SCREEN 0, 0.5, 0,0.5   OPEN #n: SCREEN 0.5,1, 0,0.5

Full screen:

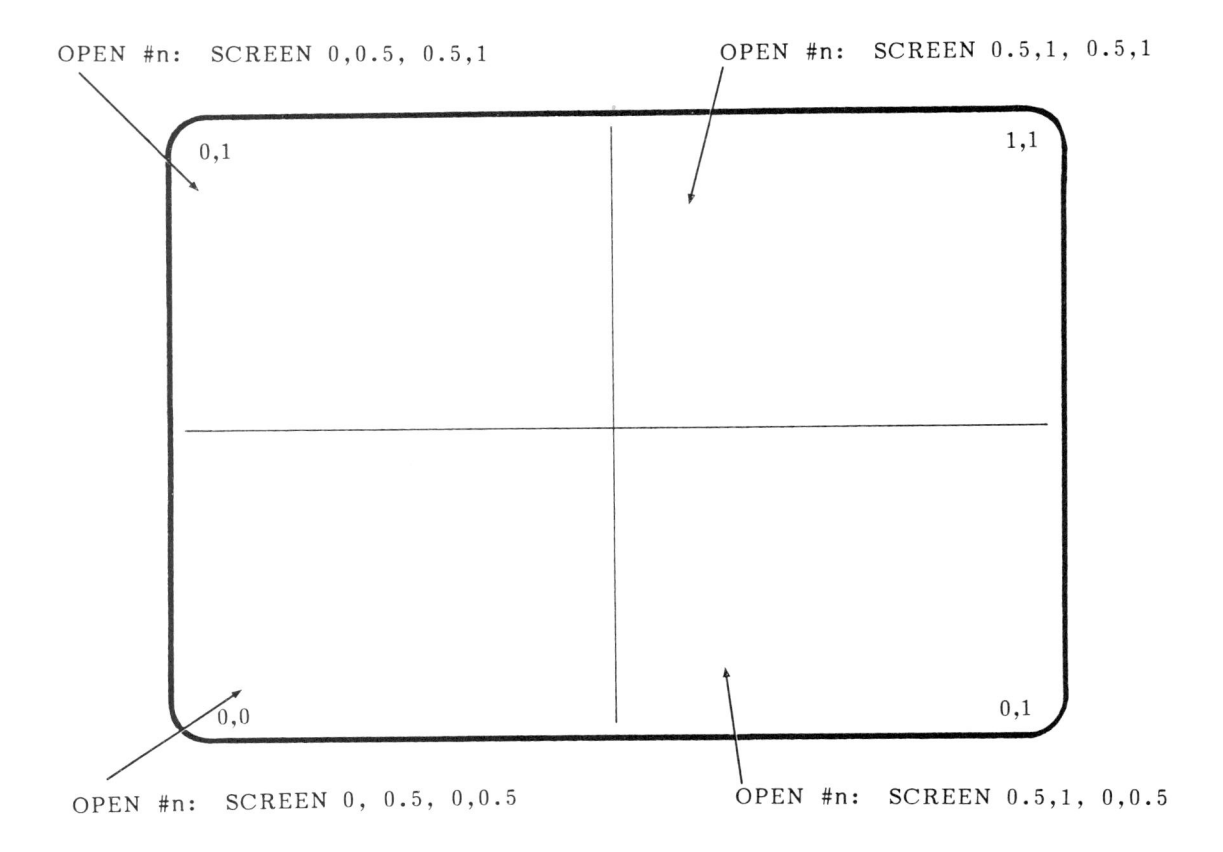

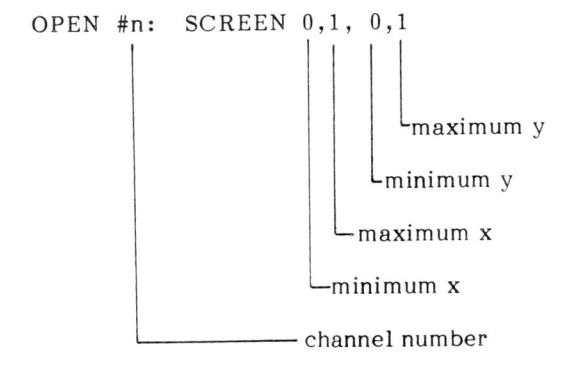

OPEN #n: SCREEN 0,1, 0,1
                         │ │ │ │
                         │ │ │ └─ maximum y
                         │ │ └─ minimum y
                         │ └─ maximum x
                         └─ minimum x
          └─ channel number

Fig. 9.38: *To understand windows, view the screen as an x-y coordinate system. You can OPEN a window simply by specifying its maximum and minimum x and y values.*

```
CLOSE #expr
       └────── a channel or window number
```

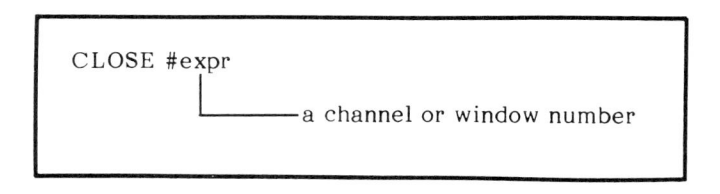

Fig. 9.39: *You should always close your windows when you finish with them.*

watching the display develop is far more interesting than seeing the finished product.

With pictures, you can define a set of standard symbols (flowchart symbols, for example), and then use them to build complex diagrams. Using pictures, you can construct background elements for animations. Take the time to learn this powerful feature. Read your *Reference Manual* and your *User's Guide* for additional details. Incidentally, pictures, like subroutines, can be stored in a library *(see Chapter 12)*.

WINDOWS

All the programs in this chapter used the full screen for their output. It is possible to display output in a window covering only a portion of the screen, and to access several windows concurrently. You define a window by opening it *(Fig. 9.38)*. Start with the screen's default coordinates. Identify the portion of the screen you want to use, assign it a window (or channel) number, list its minimum and maximum x and y values, and open it. The most recently opened window is the current window. **PLOT** statements always work with the current window. When the program ends, close your windows *(Fig. 9.39)*. All windows are closed automatically when the **END** statement is executed.

Several windows can be open concurrently. You can switch between windows by coding a **WINDOW** statement *(Fig. 9.40)*; the number following the keyword **WINDOW** defines the current window. Be careful of overlapping windows, as different systems display them differently.

Fig. 9.40: *The current window can be specified by coding a WINDOW statement.*

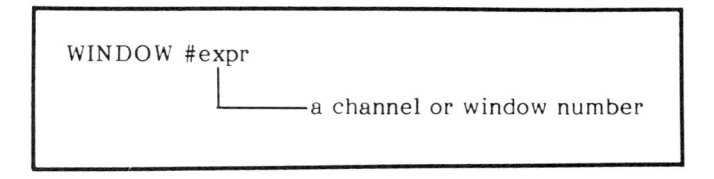

```
WINDOW #expr
        └────── a channel or window number
```

SOME FINAL DETAILS

A **MAT PLOT** statement plots all the points in a two-dimensional array. Read Chapter 8 to gain an understanding of arrays, and then check the **MAT PLOT** statement in the *Reference Manual.*

Several color-related functions are available. **ASK MAX COLOR** returns the maximum number of colors supported on your system. **ASK COLOR** returns the current foreground color; **ASK BACKGROUND COLOR** returns the current background color. Another function, **ASK WINDOW**, returns the coordinates of the current window.

All the plots in this chapter were generated in medium resolution graphics mode. On some systems, it is possible to switch to high resolution mode by coding

SET MODE HIRES

High resolution doubles the number of pixels on the screen, thus yielding sharper images. However, you are limited to a single color on a black background.

If your program contains **BOX** or **PLOT** statements, *True BASIC* automatically switches to graphics mode. You can, however, still use **PRINT** and **INPUT** statements. A **PRINT** statement displays a string of characters in the current window starting at the cursor. An **INPUT** statement accepts values from the current window starting at the cursor. You can't see the cursor in graphics mode. You can, however, control its position by using **SET CURSOR** and **ASK CURSOR** statements—see Chapter 7.

SUMMARY

To take advantage of *True BASIC*'s easy-to-use graphics features, your computer must be equipped with a graphics card. A display screen's surface is divided into a pattern of tiny dots called pixels. Images are formed by an electron beam which scans the surface thirty times a second or more, selectively turning pixels on and off.

Individual points on a screen are identified by a set of x-y coordinates. To illustrate plotting points, we developed a simple program that generated a set of random numbers and used them as coordinates in a **PLOT POINTS** statement. The result looked like a pattern of stars. In this program, we used the default screen coordinates, with both x and y ranging from 0 to 1.

Next, we turned to plotting lines. First, we developed a program to generate a frequency distribution. After coding the main loop, we planned the output, carefully laying out the desired plot. Then we wrote the code using **PLOT LINES** statements. Finally, we added labels with **PLOT TEXT** statements.

Color can add a great deal to graphic output. In *True BASIC*, a **SET BACK-**

GROUND COLOR statement defines the background, and a **SET COLOR** statement defines the foreground color. The specific set of colors available to the programmer varies from computer to computer.

By combining lines and color, it is possible to plot areas. We introduced the **PLOT AREA** statement, and used it to generate a bar chart from the frequency distribution data developed earlier in the chapter. Bar charts show relative size by the height of a bar. An option is plotting a pie chart.

For certain limited shapes, the **BOX** statements offer significant advantages. To illustrate their speed, we modified the frequency distribution program. To illustrate their simplicity, we wrote a two-line program to test a screen's aspect ratio. We introduced the **FLOOD** statement, and then showed how **BOX** statements can quickly draw a series of similar shapes. Finally, a simplified Pong program showed how **BOX** statements can support animation.

Two graphic input statements, **GET POINT** and **GET MOUSE**, were covered briefly.

Pictures (graphic subroutines) are a very significant *True BASIC* feature. The instructions to create a shape can be placed in a picture. Later, when the picture is referenced by a **DRAW** statement, transformations can be applied to move, scale, rotate, and shear the image. To illustrate pictures, we defined an instruction to plot a triangle, placed it in a picture, and then, using the rotate transformation, rotated the triangle on one point around the origin.

The chapter ended with a brief discussion of windows and comments on using **PRINT** and **INPUT** instructions while in graphic mode.

REFERENCES

True BASIC Statements

PLOT POINTS	Fig. 9.3, page 256
PLOT LINES	Fig. 9.11, page 263
PLOT TEXT	Fig. 9.13, page 264
SET BACKGROUND COLOR	Fig. 9.15, page 265
SET COLOR	Fig. 9.16, page 266
PLOT AREA	Fig. 9.17, page 267
BOX LINES	Fig. 9.20, page 270
BOX ELLIPSE (CIRCLE)	Fig. 9.20, page 270

BOX AREA	Fig. 9.20, page 270
FLOOD	Fig. 9.24, page 273
PAUSE	Fig. 9.27, page 274
CLEAR	Fig. 9.28, page 275
BOX KEEP	Fig. 9.30, page 276
BOX SHOW	Fig. 9.30, page 276
BOX CLEAR	Fig. 9.30, page 276
GET POINT	Fig. 9.32, page 278
GET MOUSE	Fig. 9.33, page 278
PICTURE	Fig. 9.34, page 279
DRAW	Fig. 9.35, page 280
OPEN	Fig. 9.38, page 282
CLOSE	Fig. 9.39, page 283
WINDOW	Fig. 9.40, page 283

EXERCISES

1. Read the program **STARS** from your *True BASIC* disk (**OLD STARS**). Add an exit condition to the loop, and run the program. Add a **RANDOMIZE** statement and run it again.

2. Change the **PLOT POINTS** statement in the **STARS** program to a **PLOT LINES** statement, and end the statement with a semicolon. Run the program again. This time, you should see a series of linked straight lines cover the screen.

3. For this exercise, start with the bar chart program developed in the chapter *(Fig. 9.18 or 9.21)*. Rewrite the program so that the bar chart appears

in a window covering the top two thirds of the screen. In the bottom third, **PRINT** information to explain the bar chart, such as the class, the test date, the number of students taking the exam, the instruction, and so on.

4. Use **BOX LINES** instructions to write a program to output a series of "boxes within boxes." Start with a small box in the center of the screen. Then draw a slightly larger box around it, a still larger box around that one, and so on.

5. Use **BOX CIRCLE** or **BOX ELLIPSE** statements to draw a series of concentric circles. Then use **FLOOD** statements to alternately color adjacent circles red and green so that the screen resembles a target.

6. Read the program **MONDRIAN** from your *True BASIC* disk. Run it. Modify the main control loop so that the program asks for fewer points (perhaps ten), and run it again.

7. Start with the picture developed in the chapter *(Fig. 9.36)*. Experiment with several transformations. Use shift to move the triangle around the screen. Use scale to make it larger or smaller. Try increasing and decreasing the degrees of rotation; then specify rotation in radians. Use shear to distort the triangle. Finally, combine two or more transformations; for example, rotate a triangle while changing its size.

8. Start with the Pong program *(Fig. 9.31)*. In addition to changing the ball's x-coordinate within the loop, change the y-coordinate, too. As a result, the ball should move across the screen at an angle. When it hits a side, the top, or the bottom, note the angle at which it strikes and have it rebound 90 degrees from that angle. In other words, if the ball is following a line 30 degrees to horizontal when it strikes a side, it should rebound at 120 degrees to horizontal. You will probably need the trigonometric functions to write this program. When you finish, you should see the ball bounce from screen edge to screen edge, like a cue ball careening from cushion to cushion.

9. Write a program to plot a sine wave. Use a **FOR NEXT** loop to control the value of a variable such as x, and plot points x, sin(x). A semicolon after the x-y coordinate pair will generate a continuous curve linking the points. Add the x and y axes, and label the curve. Run the program several times, varying the loop's increment. Note how changing the increment affects both the plot speed and the curve's sharpness.

10. Start with the bar chart program from the chapter *(Fig. 9.7 and 9.9)*. Change the output to a pie chart, with each "slice" representing the

proportion of one grade. Hint: start with 360 degrees. Convert each grade frequency to a proportion of the total number of grades, and multiply the resulting fractions by 360 to get an equivalent porportion of a complete circle.

11. Use a **BOX CIRCLE** statement to determine your screen's aspect ratio.

12. Use **BOX** statements to simulate a bouncing ball. Start the ball at the screen's top left. Use increments to give it motion both toward the right and down. When the ball hits the bottom of the screen (y = 0), let it rebound, again in increments, to half its original height. When it hits bottom again, let it rebound to half that height, and so on. Run the program several times, varying the forward speed, the downward speed, and the rebound.

13. Use the bar chart routine from this chapter as a model for writing this program. Chapter 8, Exercise 19 outlined a program to compile a general frequency distribution. Start by writing that routine. Write a subroutine to plot a bar given its lower left corner, its height, and its color. One by one, pass the frequencies to the subroutine and plot a frequency distribution.

14. Modify Exercise 13 to output a pie chart.

15. Develop pictures to represent the basic flowcharting symbols: a rectangle, a parallelogram, a diamond, and a terminal symbol (if the arcs present a problem, use short lines to form arrows on each end). Then use **DRAW** statements with transformations to create flowcharts.

16. Try an experiment using windows. By this time, you have probably written several programs. Combine them into one (use **INCLUDE** commands). Divide your screen into four windows, each covering one-quarter of the screen. Plot a bar chart in the upper left. Use **PRINT** statements to generate descriptive comments in the upper right. Plot a sine wave or some other curve in the lower left. Use **PRINT** statements to describe the curve in the lower right window. Use **WINDOW** statements to switch from window to window. For each of your plots, compare the full-screen output to the small window output. Note how *True BASIC* scales the output to fit the window.

17. Develop a routine to simulate a baseball game. Start with a "pitcher" throwing a ball from left to right. Use **Rnd** to vary the speed of the ball. Add a batter--you might represent the bat as a vertical line. Let the "hitter" swing the bat by pressing any key; use the **KEY INPUT** condition to sense if the movement of the bat intercepts the path of the ball, have the ball rebound--it's a hit! If not, it's a strike. Once you get the basic

structure in place, you will certainly think of numerous improvements.

18. Write a program to simulate a game of pool. Place "pockets" in each corner of the screen, and color them a distinctive shade. Place several balls on the "table;" one of them, the cue ball, should be white. Use a **GET POINTS** statement to enter a point. Plot a line between the cue ball's center and that point; the line determines the angle at which the cue ball is struck. Simulate striking the cue ball; it should move along an extension of the line. If it hits another ball, start that ball moving along the same line and stop the cue ball. If a ball strikes a "cushion," it rebounds at 90 degrees from its contact angle. If a ball enters a pocket, it disappears.

    This problem description outlines only the basics. Use your imagination to improve the simulation.

19. Using lines and color, plot a checkerboard pattern on your screen. Superimpose several checkers (colored circles) on the pattern. Use **GET POINT** statements to select a checker, and then to select the square it should be moved to. Using these input points, move the checker. Complete several moves before ending the program.

    Once again, this exercise describes a basic pattern. You might want to develop the pattern to play a full game of checkers. Similar patterns can be used to play several board games.

20. Write a program to play a game of tic-tac-toe. Start by drawing vertical and horizontal lines to form a 3x3 grid pattern. Start with one player against the computer. Use a **GET POINT** statement to allow the player to identify a square, and place an X there. Then have the computer place an O in one of the remaining squares. Continue taking turns until one player, or the computer, marks three squares in a row. An interesting variation is to use colors instead of Xs and Os.

    If you use the right strategy, you'll never lose at tic-tac-toe. Work out the strategy, and program the computer to follow it. Then change the program again to allow the user a choice between playing against the computer or playing against another player.

10

Strings and Sound

KEY IDEAS

1. *String operations.*

2. *String manipulation.*

   a. Concatenation.

   b. Comparing and counting.

   c. Search and replace.

3. *Line input.*

4. *String functions.*

5. *Music.*

6. *Sound.*

STRING OPERATIONS

Strings and numbers are different. A string can hold any combination of letters, digits, punctuation marks, and other symbols, while a number is limited to digits, a sign, and a decimal point. Because numbers are restricted to a handful of symbols, they can be stored inside a computer in a compressed (and highly efficient) shorthand form. Because strings must accommodate any character, they can't be compressed. Strings and numbers are stored in memory in different forms. That's why you can't use a string in an arithmetic operation, and why so many *True BASIC* features distinguish between strings and numbers.

String Constants and Variables

In this chapter, you will learn to manipulate strings. A string constant consists of a series of characters enclosed in a set of quotation marks ("). Any character on your keyboard is legal, but be careful of the quotation mark. Because it could be interpreted as the string's end, you must code two to get one; for example,

> "Code two "" to put one in a string."

String constants can contain as many as 32,000 characters, and even more on some computers. A null or empty string is defined by coding a set of quotation marks with nothing between them ("").

The last character in a string variable or string array name must be a dollar sign ($). Names can be as many as 31 characters long; the dollar sign counts as one of those characters. If a function returns a string value, its name must end with a dollar sign. Subroutine names and numeric function names may not end with a dollar sign.

While arithmetic operations are illegal, other operations *can* be performed on strings. Two or more strings can be concatenated or joined to form a longer string. Characters can be extracted from, modified, or inserted into a string by using substring operations.

The logical operators are legal; strings can be compared to other strings. Inside most microcomputers, characters are stored using the ASCII code *(see Appendix V)*. To understand string comparisons, look at the decimal values associated with the various characters. The bigger the value, the "larger" the character. Thus, capital letters are "greater than" digits, and lower case letters are "greater than" capital letters. Assuming alphabetic data, string comparisons follow normal alphabetic order; for example, the condition

> "A" < "B"

is true, while

"A" > "Z"

is false. Be careful, though; comparing a string to a number generates an error.

STRING MANIPULATION

Word processing is probably the most popular application of string manipulation. To illustrate *True BASIC*'s string handling features, we'll write the instructions to implement some typical word processing features.

Concatenation

First, however, we should explain concatenation *(Fig. 10.1)*. The word means *to join*. The ampersand symbol (&) is the concatenation operator. In our example, two strings are defined and then joined to form one longer string. Look closely

Fig. 10.1: *True BASIC's one string operation, concatenation, is designated by an ampersand (&) symbol. In this example, two short strings are combined to form one longer one.*

```
! This simple program illustrates
! concatenation. Two strings are defined
! and then combined to form a single string.

LET string1$ = "The quick brown fox"
LET string2$ = "jumped over the lazy dog."
LET combo$ = string1$ & " " & string2$

! Finally, the two strings and their combined
! string are printed.

PRINT string1$
PRINT string2$
PRINT combo$

END
```

```
Published by Addison-Wesley Publishing Company, Inc.
Ok. old concat
Ok. run
The quick brown fox
jumped over the lazy dog.
The quick brown fox jumped over the lazy dog.
Ok.
```

at the shaded instruction. Note that a blank is placed between the two strings. Without it, they would run together.

Distinguishing Words

One common word processing feature is counting. Let's start with characters. The function **Len** *(Fig. 10.2)* returns the number of characters in a string; for example,

      Len(combo$)

returns the length of the string **combo$**.

    Counting words is a bit more complex. The first task is distinguishing the words. Start by assuming that adjacent words are separated by blanks. Given this assumption, the number of words can be determined by counting the blanks. Because there is rarely a blank after the last word, we'll have to be sure to count it, too.

    The **Pos** function *(Fig. 10.3)* can be used to search a string for a particular character or group of characters. The function has two forms. In the first, string **a$** is searched for the first occurrence of character pattern **b$**. In the second form, **a$** is searched for **b$**, starting with character position **n**. The function returns the position where pattern **b$** is found. For example, the function reference

      Pos ("abba", "a")

would return 1. What value would

      Pos ("abba","a", 2)

Fig. 10.2: *Given a string, the **Len** function counts the characters and returns the string's length.*

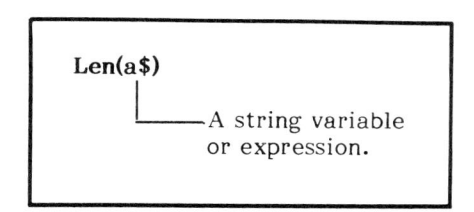

```
Len(a$)
     └──A string variable
        or expression.
```

Fig. 10.3: *The **Pos** function searches a string for occurrences of a specified substring.*

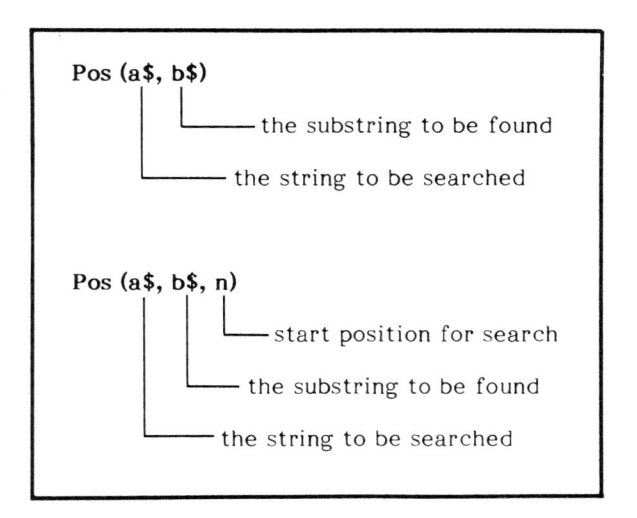

```
Pos (a$, b$)
        │
        └── the substring to be found
    └────── the string to be searched


Pos (a$, b$, n)
           │
           └── start position for search
       └────── the substring to be found
    └───────── the string to be searched
```

return? Start searching at position 2. You've already passed the first **a**. The next **a** you encounter is at position 4. The function would return 4.

If the search pattern is not found, **Pos** returns 0. In the second form, if **n** is less than 1, *True BASIC* uses 1. If **n** exceeds the length of the string, **Pos** returns 0. Note that the search argument can be a single character or a group of characters. If several characters are specified, **Pos** looks for that specific sequence of consecutive characters.

Figure 10.4 shows a program that counts the number of words in a string. We'll start with the same string we used in the concatenation program, print it, and then, using a **Len** function, count the number of characters. The character count will serve as an exit condition for the word-count loop.

Move to the **DO** loop. As you enter it, note that the word count is 0 and the initial search position is 1. Inside the loop, a **Pos** function searches for a blank space. When a blank is found, the word count is incremented, and the loop repeats. This time the search starts just past the position of the last space. The loop repeats until all the string's characters have been checked (**a_space = limit**) or until the **Pos** function returns 0 (no match). When the loop ends, **word_count** holds the number of words in the string.

Search and Replace

Search and replace is another common word processing feature. The basic idea is to search a string for a particular sequence of characters and, assuming the sequence is found, to delete it, move it, or replace it with a different sequence.

Again, let's start with a program *(Fig. 10.5)* and go through it line by line. The first few instructions define a string, print it, and then print directions for the user. Move inside the **DO** loop; that's where the action is. The user is told to type the word or phrase to be changed, followed by the new or corrected ver-

```
                              ! This program starts with a concatenated
                              ! string and, by searching for blanks,
                              ! counts the number of words.

                              ! First, the phrase is formed.

LET string1$ = "The quick brown fox"
LET string2$ = "jumped over the lazy dog."
LET combo$ = string1$ & " " & string2$

                              ! Next, the phrase is printed.
PRINT combo$
                              ! The Len function returns the number of
                              ! characters in the string. We'll find
                              ! the character count, print it, and
                              ! then use it as a search limit.

LET character_count = Len(combo$)
PRINT "The phrase contains "; character_count; " characters."

                              ! The Pos function searches the specified
                              ! string (1st parameter) for a specified
                              ! substring (2nd parameter), starting with
                              ! the position specified in the 3rd para-
                              ! meter. It returns a position number. In
                              ! the DO loop, we search combo$ for blanks.
                              ! Each time we find one, we add 1 to the
                              ! word-counter. The "next" search will
                              ! begin with the "last" blank found.
LET word_count = 0
LET a_space = 1

DO
   LET a_space = Pos(combo$, " ", a_space+1)
   LET word_count = word_count + 1

                              ! The search continues until we reach the
                              ! end of the phrase (a_space = limit) or
                              ! until Pos returns 0 (no match).

LOOP UNTIL (a_space = limit) OR (a_space = 0)

                              ! Finally, the number of words in the
                              ! phrase is printed.

PRINT "The phrase contains "; word_count; " words."
END
```

Fig. 10.4: *This program uses a **Pos** function to count the words in a string.*

```
                            ! In this program, we'll set up a phrase,
                            ! print it, and then allow the user to
                            ! change selected words.

LET string1$ = "The quick brown fox"
LET string2$ = "jumped over the lazy dog."
LET combo$ = string1$ & " " & string2$

PRINT "The string is:"
PRINT
PRINT combo$
PRINT
PRINT "Would you like to change it? If so, type the word or phrase to"
PRINT "be changed, and then, in response to a second prompt, type the"
PRINT "corrected word or phrase. When you've finished, simply type ZZ"
PRINT "in response to the first prompt."
PRINT

                            ! In this loop, we ask the user to enter
                            ! the "old" version of the phrase to be
                            ! changed. If the user enters ZZ, the
                            ! loop ends.
DO
    INPUT PROMPT "Enter phrase to be changed: ": old_phrase$

                            ! Note exit condition.

    IF old_phrase$ = "ZZ" THEN EXIT DO

                            ! Assuming the user enters a valid string,
                            ! we ask for the replacement string.

    INPUT PROMPT "Enter corrected phrase: ": new_phrase$

                            ! Next, we search the string for the
                            ! phrase to be changed.

    LET phrase_position = Pos(combo$,old_phrase$)

                            ! If the phrase isn't found, Pos returns
                            ! 0. If this happens, the user is asked
                            ! to try again.

    IF phrase_position = 0 THEN
        PRINT old_phrase$; " not found. Try again."
        PRINT
```

Fig. 10.5: *In this program, we use the* **Pos** *function to search a string for a particular series of characters, and then use substring operations to change the original string. The program listing is continued on the next page.*

```
        ELSE                            ! If the old phrase is found, we replace
                                        ! it with the new phrase. First, we need
                                        ! the old phrase's length.

          LET phrase_length = Len(old_phrase$)

                                        ! Given the length, we can compute the
                                        ! ending position and replace it.

          LET end_position = phrase_position + phrase_length - 1
          LET combo$[phrase_position: end_position] = new_phrase$

                                        ! Finally, we print the new string
                                        ! and loop back for another change.

          PRINT "The string now reads:"; combo$
          PRINT
        END IF
    LOOP
    END
```

Fig. 10.5, *continued.*

Fig. 10.6: *A substring is a portion of a string. Substrings are specified by their starting and ending positions.*

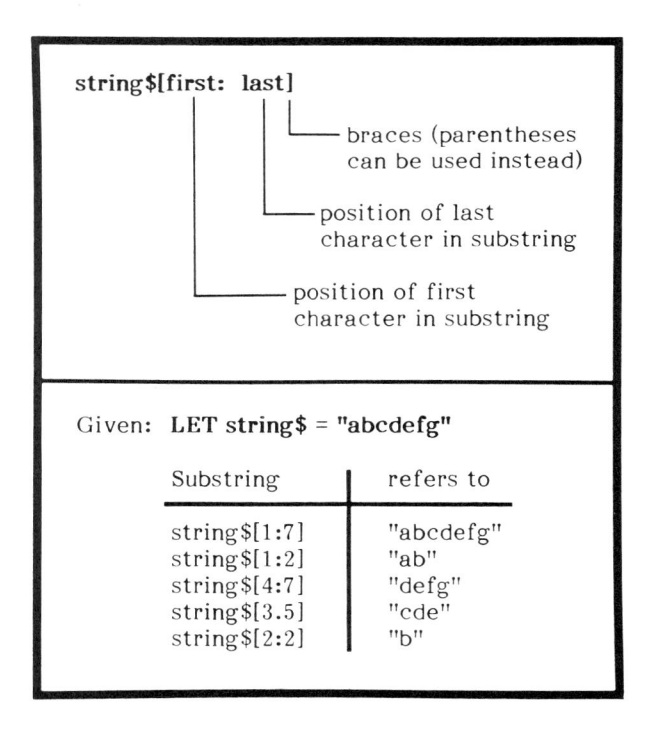

```
string$[first: last]
               │    └── braces (parentheses
               │         can be used instead)
               └──── position of last
                     character in substring
        └──────────── position of first
                     character in substring
```

Given: **LET string$ = "abcdefg"**

Substring	refers to
string$[1:7]	"abcdefg"
string$[1:2]	"ab"
string$[4:7]	"defg"
string$[3:5]	"cde"
string$[2:2]	"b"

sion. Then the program searches the string for the old character pattern.

That search has two possible outcomes—either the substring is there, or it isn't. If the **Pos** function can't find the search pattern, it returns 0; otherwise, it returns a positive value. Thus, the program checks **phrase_position**. If it's 0, a message is printed inviting the user to try again. If **Pos** returns a positive value, the pattern has been found. After the phrase's end position is computed, we're ready to replace it.

Look at the instruction that replaces the old pattern:

LET combo$ [phrase_position: end_position] = new_phrase$

The term to the left of the equal sign is a substring *(Fig. 10.6)*. It defines a portion of **combo$**. Following the string's name, enclosed in brackets and separated by a colon, are the substring's first and last character positions. The assignment statement says to replace a portion of **combo$** with **new_phrase$**. The old substring is erased and the new substring inserted in its place. Note that the substring and the new phrase need not be the same length; the string's length is increased or decreased as necessary to accommodate the change.

Figure 10.7 shows an example of the output generated by the search and replace program. Compare it with the program listing *(Fig. 10.5)*, and try to trace

Fig. 10.7: *Here's an example of the output generated by the search and replace program.*

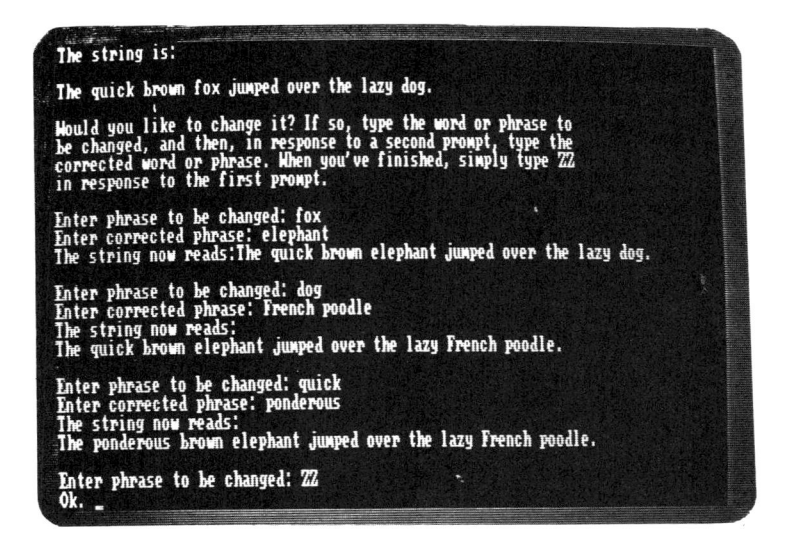

```
The string is:
The quick brown fox jumped over the lazy dog.

Would you like to change it? If so, type the word or phrase to
be changed, and then, in response to a second prompt, type the
corrected word or phrase. When you've finished, simply type ZZ
in response to the first prompt.

Enter phrase to be changed: fox
Enter corrected phrase: elephant
The string now reads:The quick brown elephant jumped over the lazy dog.

Enter phrase to be changed: dog
Enter corrected phrase: French poodle
The string now reads:
The quick brown elephant jumped over the lazy French poodle.

Enter phrase to be changed: quick
Enter corrected phrase: ponderous
The string now reads:
The ponderous brown elephant jumped over the lazy French poodle.

Enter phrase to be changed: ZZ
Ok.
```

the source of each output line.

Several options could be added to this program. For example, we might give the user a choice of changing only the first occurrence of a particular substring, or changing all occurrences. Moving or copying a substring is another possibility. In our example, a substring could be deleted by replacing it with a null string. A clearer delete function would be useful.

Incidentally, we used brackets to code the substring reference. If you prefer, you can use parentheses instead. We'll continue to use the square brackets because they help to distinguish a substring reference from a subroutine, function, or array reference.

LINE INPUT STATEMENTS

One program developed in Chapter 6 computed payroll. Because it was so lengthy, we started with a skeleton mainline and added modules one by one. The program's first module read and verified input data. One concern in planning the data entry module was providing clear, easy to understand error messages so that a nontechnical clerk could use the program with a minimum of training.

There is, however, one type of input error we couldn't control. Try typing a number containing an invalid character; for example, type $5.75 in response to a request for **pay_rate**. The dollar sign is illegal. *True BASIC* traps such errors and displays a cryptic message such as

>   String given instead of number.
>   Please retry from bad item.

It is unreasonable to expect a nonprogrammer to understand such messages. Programs written for nontechnical people must anticipate everything that can possibly go wrong, and display clear, explicit directions to help the user.

Please understand that there is nothing wrong with *True BASIC*'s "cryptic" error messages. They are intended for programmers. As you test a program, if you get one of those standard, built-in messages, you should be able to look at your code, spot the error, and correct it. You would be annoyed if a two or three line explanation followed each typing error; you don't need that kind of support. However, most people are not programmers, and they do.

When data are input, they enter main memory as separate characters--after all, that's what you type. The characters are stored in a string and, after you press enter, parceled out to variables. Remember that strings and numbers are stored differently inside a computer. If a string is assigned to a string variable, no change is necessary. If, however, some or all of that input string is assigned to a numeric variable, the data must be converted to numeric form. *True BASIC* takes care of this data conversion; you don't have to worry about it. However,

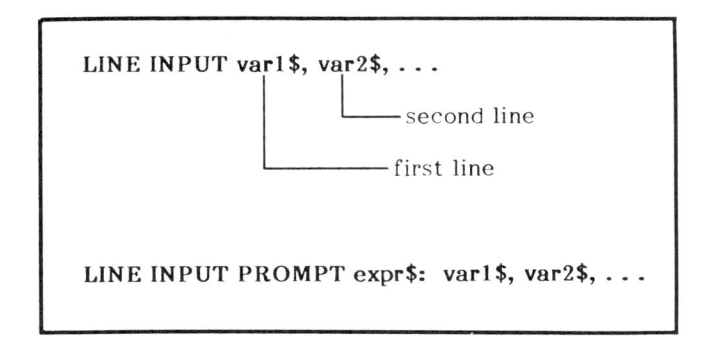

```
LINE INPUT var1$, var2$, . . .
                    |        |
                    |        └── second line
                    └── first line


LINE INPUT PROMPT expr$: var1$, var2$, . . .
```

Fig. 10.8: *The **LINE INPUT** statement assigns a complete input line to a single string variable.*

it is during data conversion that errors are trapped and those "cryptic" messages generated. If you want to generate your own customized input data error messages, you must control data conversion yourself.

Fortunately, this isn't difficult. The key is a **LINE INPUT** instruction *(Fig. 10.8)*. When **LINE INPUT** is executed, all the characters typed on a single line are stored, without change, in a single string variable. Using substring operations, the program then extracts portions of the input line and assigns them to variables. If a substring is assigned to a string variable, no data conversion takes place. If a substring is assigned to a numeric variable, however, it must be converted to numeric form. At this point, an illegal character will generate an error, but the program can trap it and print its own error message.

Parsing

Let's look at a program to input an employee's name, hours worked, and pay rate *(Fig.10.9)*. Start with the **LINE INPUT** statement. The user, probably a clerk, has been told to enter the three values separated by commas, but the **LINE INPUT** statement simply accepts everything from the first character until the enter key is pressed, and stores it in **payroll_data$**. Now, our job is to extract the three fields from that string.

The process of separating the string into meaningful substrings is called parsing *(Fig. 10.10)*. Remember that commas separate the data elements. Assume that the first element, the employee's name, starts in position 1. If we can find the first comma, we'll bracket the name. The **Pos** function in the instruction

        LET comma = Pos(payroll_data$, ",")

returns the position of the string's first comma. The next instruction

```
                              ! This program shows how a LINE INPUT
                              ! statement can be used to enter several
                              ! values. Substrings are used to separate
                              ! the individual values and assign them to
                              ! variables. We'll enter an employee's
                              ! name, hours worked, and pay rate.
PRINT "Enter employee name, hours worked, and pay rate. Use commas to"
PRINT "separate values."
PRINT
LINE INPUT payroll_data$
                              ! Given a line of input data, we'll search
                              ! for the first comma. Everything from the
                              ! start of the line to the comma is assign-
                              ! ed to variable employee_name$.
LET comma = Pos(payroll_data$, ",")
LET employee_name$ = payroll_data$[1:comma-1]
                              ! Starting just past the first comma,
                              ! we search for the second comma.
LET comma2 = Pos(payroll_data$, ",", comma+1)
                              ! All characters lying between the two
                              ! commas are assigned to hours_worked.
                              ! Because payroll_data$ is a string, we
                              ! need the Val function to convert its
                              ! substring to a number.
LET hours_worked = Val(payroll_data$[comma+1:comma2-1])
                              ! Everything from the second comma to the
                              ! string's end is assigned to variable
                              ! pay_rate.
LET pay_rate = Val(payroll_data$[comma2+1:Maxnum])
                              ! To verify our program, we'll print the
                              ! original string and the three variables.
PRINT
PRINT "From the input string: "; payroll_data$
PRINT
PRINT "We extracted: ",employee_name$, hours_worked, pay_rate
END
```

Fig. 10.9: *A **LINE INPUT** statement allows the programmer to bypass True BASIC's normal input error messages, substituting custom error messages instead. Consider **LINE INPUT**s whenever nontechnical people will use your program.*

Bilbo Baggins, 40.0, 8.50

The marker's position is returned by the function Pos (payroll_data$, ",")

payroll_data$[1: comma-1]

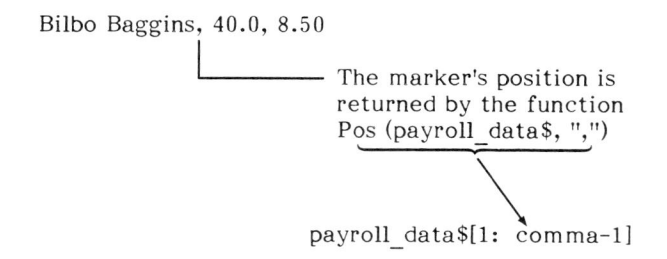

Fig. 10.10: *The process of separating a string into meaningful substrings is called parsing. First, the string is searched for a marker (in our example, a comma). Once the marker's position is determined, a substring operation is used to extract a portion of the string.*

    LET employee_name$ = payroll_data$ [1:comma-1]

assigns the substring to **employee_name$**.

The second value, hours worked, should lie between the first and the second commas. We have the first comma's position. Given it as a starting point, we search for the second comma, coding

    Pos(payroll_data$, ",", comma+1)

Once the second comma's position is known, everything between the two commas is assigned to **hours_worked**.

There is one problem with this assignment operation, however. The data in **payroll_data$** is in string form, and **hours_worked** is a numeric variable. We have to change the data type. The **Val** function converts a string to a number. Its counterpart, **Str$**, converts a number to a string. The instruction

    LET hours_worked = Val (payroll_data$ [comma1+1:comma2-1])

extracts the characters between the two commas, converts them to numeric form, and stores the number in **hours_worked**.

The last value is **pay_rate**. Its characters lie between the second comma and the string's end; in other words, **pay_rate** is the substring

    payroll_data$ [comma2+1:Maxnum]

Maxnum returns the largest number supported on the computer. In a substring reference, if the second value exceeds the string's length, the string's length is substituted. Thus, all the characters between the second comma and the string's end are included in this substring. Using a **Val** function to change the data type, the substring is assigned to **pay_rate**. The program ends with a series of **PRINT** statements that display the extracted data.

That seems like a great deal of effort to do something as apparently simple as reading three data values, and it is. However, trapping errors and generating meaningful error messages is not done for the programmer's benefit. Instead, the objective is to insulate the user from the technical details. If you're writing programs for yourself, don't bother with **LINE INPUT**. If you're writing for someone else, put in the extra time.

Do real programmers actually go to all this trouble? Yes, they do. Good professionals anticipate everything that can possibly go wrong and design logic to handle it. Never should a user be left thinking: "What do I do now?" When it comes to designing a smooth user interface, taking shortcuts is bad programming.

Picture a regular **INPUT** statement with numeric variables. When that statement is executed, data flow into the computer as characters. *True BASIC* then converts the data from string to numeric form. If an error makes that conversion impossible, *True BASIC* generates the error message. Since the designers of the language couldn't possibly anticipate the particular needs of all users, they coded general-purpose error messages. With **LINE INPUT** statements, the programmer codes **Val** or **Str$** functions to control data conversion. Thus, the program can trap errors and generate customized error messages.

How can a program trap errors? One way is anticipating them. For example, what if a clerk types the wrong number of values. The program assumes three values. What if the user types only two? Or more than three? The program won't work. Because values are separated by commas, three values call for two commas. Thus, a first step might be simply counting commas and asking the user to try again if the count is wrong.

Still, when the time comes to convert a substring to a number, errors can occur. For example, numbers can contain illegal characters. If **Val** is passed a string containing illegal characters, *True BASIC* generates one of those "cryptic" error messages we've been trying so hard to avoid. Don't let *True BASIC* respond to the error. Instead, use a **WHEN ERROR IN** structure; see Module D for details. The basic idea is to let the error happen, sense it, and generate explicit error messages to tell the user exactly what is wrong and how to correct it.

STRING FUNCTIONS

True BASIC supports a number of string functions. We've already covered **Len**, **Pos**, **Val**, and **Str$**. Some others are concerned with translating different character codes. For example, most microcomputers use the ASCII code to store characters in main memory. The **Ord** function takes a character and returns its ASCII code number. The **Chr$** function accepts a number and returns the equivalent character.

Because different computers store numbers differently, transferring data between machines can be a problem. An IEEE code helps to solve this problem by establishing a machine-independent standard for numeric data. In this code, numbers are represented as 8-byte strings. The **Num$** function accepts a number and converts it to IEEE 8-byte format. The **Num** function takes an IEEE code and converts it to a number. In a *True BASIC* record file *(see Chapter 11)*, numbers are stored in IEEE form, making these files transportable between various manufacturers' computers.

Other functions are used to format strings. For example, **Rtrim** removes a string's leading blanks, **Ltrim** removes trailing blanks, and **Trim** removes both leading and trailing blanks. The **Using** function can format a series of numeric or string values; see Chapter 7 (**PRINT USING**) for details. The **Repeat** function allows a programmer to replicate a string as many times as desired.

True BASIC statements can be typed using any combination of upper case and lower case letters. Two functions allow a programmer to afford the same flexibility to a program's users. **Lcase** converts all the letters in the referenced string to lower case. **Ucase** converts all the letters to upper case. No matter what the user types, if one of these functions is used, the program will always deal with the same case.

Finally, we consider the date and time functions. **Date** returns the current date in numeric form. A two-digit year is followed by a three-digit day; for example, January 1, 1986 would be 86001, while December 31, 1986 would be 86365. **Time** returns the computer's current clock time measured in seconds past midnight. For example, 1:00 a.m. would be 3600, or 3600 seconds.

Date$** returns the current date as a string with the form "yyyymmdd". For example, January 1, 1986 would be "19860101", while December 31, 1986 would be "19861231". **Time$ returns the current time in string form. Time is measured on a standard 24-hour clock, with midnight as time zero. The general format is "hh:mm:ss". At precisely 1:00 a.m., the **Time$** function will return "01:00:00".

On many computers, the user is expected to set the date and the time as part of the "boot" or startup procedure. If you fail to do so, the system will probably assume a startup time of 12 midnight, and may assume almost any date. If you plan to use date and time functions, set the date and the time accurately.

MAKING NOISE

Two instructions, **PLAY** and **SOUND**, allow the programmer to generate audio output (read that "noise"). Both are driven by character strings.

PLAY *(Fig. 10.11)* allows the programmer to define notes, octaves, note lengths, rests, tempo, and other musical parameters, and instruct the computer to play music. The various music commands are summarized in Fig. 10.12. Figure 10.13 shows a program that plays perhaps the most famous tune in computer history,

```
       PLAY music$
             |
             └──── a string of notes and other
                   musical commands
```

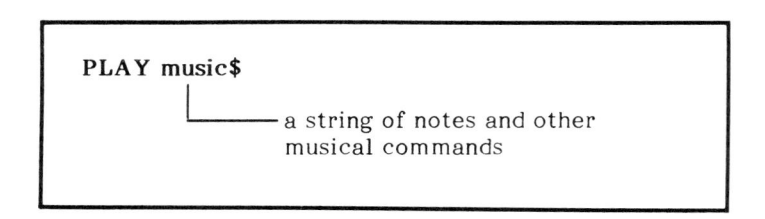

Fig. 10.11: *A **PLAY** statement can be used to generate music.*

"A Bicycle Built for Two." (That's the tune HAL sang in *2001*.) Enter it into your computer and run it. Check your *Reference Manual* and *User's Guide* for additional examples. A program that incorporates **PLAY** instructions, **SMOKY**, can be found on your *True BASIC* disk.

The **SOUND** statement *(Fig. 10.14)* generates a variety of sounds or noises. Use it to simulate a ringing telephone, a police siren, or a "Bronx cheer." As you probably know, sound is produced when sound waves move through a medium (such as air) and enter your ear. The wave frequency (usually measured in hertz, or thousands of vibrations per second) determines the sound's pitch; bass is a relatively low frequency, while treble is higher. Another parameter is the sound's

Fig. 10.12: *A summary of True BASIC's musical commands. See the Reference Manual for additional details.*

Command	Meaning
A to G	A note.
# or +	Sharp (follows a note).
-	Flat (follows a note).
O n	Set octive Middle C is the first note in octive 5.
>	Move up one octive
<	Move down one octive.
L n	Set length of subsequent notes. L1 is a whole note, L2 is a half note, and so on.
R n	Rest for length n.
P n	Same as R n.
"	Play as dotted note (follows note).
T n	Set tempo. T120 plays 120 quarter notes per minute.
MF	Play subsequent music in foreground.
MB	Play subsequent music in background; in other words, execute other instructions as music plays.
MN	Play "normally."
ML	Play "legato," or drawn out.
MS	Play "staccato," or briskly.
blank	*True BASIC* ignores blanks. Include them for legibility.

```
! In the movie 2001, HAL sang this song. Run
! this program, and your computer will do a
! poor imitation.

! First line: Daisy, Daisy, give me your
!             answer do.

LET first_line$ = "T220 MS o4 L2 ge c(g L6ab)c (a4)c6 (g2R4"

! Second line: I'm half crazy all for the
! love of you.

LET second_line$ = "L2 )dg ec L6(ab)c d4e d2"
PLAY first_line$
PLAY second_line$

END
```

True BASIC here.
Version 1.0
Copyright (c) 1985 by True BASIC, Inc.
Published by Addison-Wesley Publishing Company, Inc.
Ok. old daisy
Ok. _

Fig. 10.13: *This program shows the strings that define the notes for the old tune, "A Bicycle Built for Two."*

time or duration.

The best way to understand **SOUND** is to experiment. Figure 10.15 shows a simple program that inputs a frequency and a duration (in seconds), generates a sound, and then loops back for another set of input data. Try a number of different frequencies and durations. If you stumble across a sound you like, make a note and use it in a future program. Also, try two programs on your *True BASIC* disk: **SIREN** and **PHONE**.

When a **PLAY** statement is executed, *True BASIC* waits for the music to end before moving on to the next instruction. It is, however, possible to specify that the music play in the background. When a **SOUND** statement is executed,

Fig. 10.14: *The SOUND statement can be used to generate a variety of sounds.*

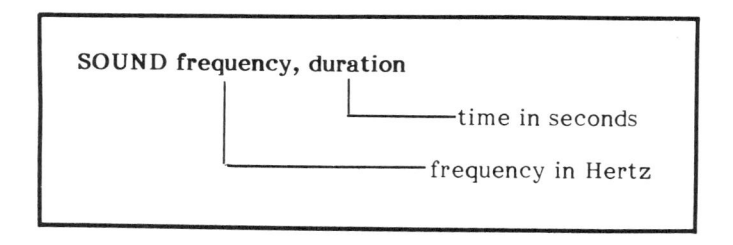

```
SOUND frequency, duration
       │          │
       │          └──── time in seconds
       │
       └──────────────── frequency in Hertz
```

```
!                            ! This program allows a user to experiment
! DO                         ! with various sounds.
!
!     INPUT frequency, duration   ! First, a sound's frequency and duration
!                                 ! are entered.
!     SOUND frequency, duration   ! Then, a sound with that frequency and
!                                 ! duration is played.
!
! LOOP UNTIL frequency = 0        ! The program continues until a frequency
!                                 ! of zero is entered.
! END
!
Published by Addison-Wesley Publishing Company, Inc.
Ok. old daisy
Ok. old sound
Ok. run
? 750,1.5
? 0,0
Ok. _
```

Fig. 10:15: *Use this simple program to experiment with sound output.*

the necessary signals are sent to the speaker, and the computer continues to execute other instructions as the sound is heard. If a subsequent **SOUND** statement is encountered, *True BASIC* waits for the first sound to end before starting the second one.

SUMMARY

The chapter began with a brief explanation of the difference between string and numeric data. Next we discussed string constants and variables, and introduced the string operations: concatenation and substrings. The logical operators can be used with strings; however, it is illegal to compare a string and a number. The outcome of a string comparison is determined by the ASCII code sequence.

The concatenation operator, an ampersand (&), can be used to join two strings. We then turned to a series of examples based on common word processing features, beginning with a **Len** function to count characters. Assuming that the words in a phrase were separated by blank spaces, we used a **Pos** function to search a string for blanks, counted them, and used the count as a word count. Next, we turned to a search and replace operation. Again, the key was a **Pos** function. We searched a string for a particular character pattern and, once we found it, used substring operations to replace the old substring with a new one.

In Chapter 6, we developed a program to compute payroll. One module screened the input data. We introduced the **LINE INPUT** statement as an extension to that module, using it to bypass *True BASIC*'s rather cryptic standard error messages. The **LINE INPUT** statement reads a complete line of data into a single string variable. The next step is parsing the string, searching for markers (such as commas), extracting data items, and assigning them to variables. Because assigning a substring to a numeric variable involves a conversion in data type, we had to use a **Val** function. The **Str$** function converts a number to a string.

Several string functions are supported by *True BASIC*. **Ord** and **Chr$** convert between characters and their ASCII code equivalents. **Num** and **Num$** convert between IEEE 8-byte codes and numbers. Other functions format strings. Functions are also available to return the current date and time.

Finally, we turned to making noise. The **PLAY** instruction transmits a string of music commands to the computer's speaker. The **SOUND** instruction accepts a frequency and a duration and generates a sound. Examples of both were shown.

REFERENCES

True BASIC Statements

    LINE INPUT — Fig. 10.8, page 301

    WHEN ERROR IN — Module D

    PLAY — Fig. 10.11, page 306

    SOUND — Fig. 10.14, page 307

True BASIC Functions

    Len — Fig. 10.2, page 294

    Pos — Fig. 10.3, page 295

    Val — page 303

    Str$ — page 303

    Other string functions — page 304, 305

Rules for:

    concatenation — page 293

    substrings — Fig. 10.6, page 298

music commands   Fig. 10.12, page 306

EXERCISES

1. A palindrome is a word or phrase that reads the same backward as forward. For example, otto is a palindrome, but tom (mot, backward) is not. Write a program to input a word or phrase, reverse its letters, print the backward version, and determine if the phrase is a palindrome.

2. Check your *True BASIC* disk for a program named **HAIKU**. It's an interesting example of concatenation. Try it.

3. Write a program to generate "apartment ads." The secret is to start with a regular sentence and remove all the vowels; for example, "4 rooms river view" becomes "4 rms rvr vw" (which you might recognize as the title of a play). The objective is to convey meaning in as few letters as possible because newspapers charge essentially by the letter.

4. Write a program to input a phrase and translate it into "pig Latin." The rule is simple. Take the first letter from each word, move it to the end of the word, and add the letter a. For example, "see you later" translates to "eesa ouya aterla."

5. Start with the search and replace module we developed in the chapter *(Fig. 10.5)*. Add a delete option. Give the user a choice of replacing only the first reference or all references. Don't start with a string constant; instead input the string to be operated upon.

6. Chapter 6, Exercise 2b, asked you to write a subroutine to verify input data to a payroll program. Modify the subroutine to use a **LINE INPUT** statement. Use substring functions to extract data values from the string and assign them to the appropriate variables. Trap all errors and display meaningful error messages. Ideally, no matter what garbage you might enter, your program should catch it and print a message that gives an unsophisticated user reasonable instructions for recovering. Avoid asking for all values to be reentered; if at all possible, error messages should relate to a single data element.

7. "Mad Libs" is a popular word game. One player starts with a printed paragraph or two containing numerous blank spaces. Without seeing the "story," the other players are asked to suggest adjectives, nouns, verbs, adverbs,

etc. The reader inserts the suggested words into the story, and then reads the often hilarious result.

Write a program to play "Mad Libs." Start by making up a story. Remove selected words. (If you prefer, purchase a "Mad Libs" book at your local book store.) Enter the story as a long string, a series of one or more **DATA** statements *(see Chapter 7)*, a file *(see Chapter 11)*, or a library member *(see Chapter 12)*. After accessing the "story," your program should ask for various words (by part of speech), insert them into the story, and display the result.

8. A common security operation is computing a check digit. For example, imagine that a social security number is used for identification. We might sum the odd digits (positions 1, 3, 5, 7, 9), separately sum the even digits, divide the odd sum by the even sum, and then use the remainder as a tenth check digit. Write one program to generate check digits. Given a nine-digit social security number, it should compute the check digit, concatenate it to the original number, and output a ten-digit identification number. Write a separate program (think of it as a program module) to read a ten-digit identification number, compute the check digit, compare the computed check digit to the tenth digit entered, and either accept or reject the identification number. Note that all input and output values should be strings.

9. Enter the "Bicycle Built for Two" program *(Fig. 10.13)*, and run it. Try **SMOKY** on your *True BASIC* disk, too.

10. If you can read music, take your favorite piece and transcribe the first several bars into *True BASIC* music commands. Then play it on your computer. Start your own library of tunes. Music can add a great deal to a program.

11. Enter the sound generating program *(Fig. 10.15)* and run it. Experiment with various frequencies and durations. Modify the program to generate more sophisticated sounds; use **SIREN** and **PHONE** from your *True BASIC* disk as models. Other examples can be found in the *User's Guide* and the *Reference Manual*. As you discover interesting sounds, add them to your own sound library.

12. Type a series of sentences or phrases. Count the words. Then compute the average word size.

13. Type several sentences into a program. Compute the average number of words per sentence.

14. Type a series of sentences or phrases into a program. Search the string

or strings and replace each word starting with the letter s with asterisks. (Don't change the word's length; just replace it.) Then print the "censored" version.

15. Input a person's name in any form. Sometimes, type the first name, a blank, and the last name. For other names, type the last name, a comma, and the first name. Your program should always output "last-name, first-name".

16. Read a series of names into an array *(see Chapter 8)*. Sort the names into alphabetic order. When strings are sorted, they are placed in ASCII sequence.

17. Write a program to generate address labels. Input a name, a street address, a city, a state, and a zip code. Output a simulated envelope with your name and address at the upper left, and the input name and address down a few lines and just to the right of center. All addresses should be spread over three lines.

18. Input a phrase to a program. Develop a frequency distribution of the letters; in other words, count the As, the Bs, and so on. Print each letter's frequency.

19. Start with Exercise 18. Use the letter frequencies to generate a code. Equate the most frequently occurring letter with a Z, the second most frequently occurring letter with a Y, and so on. Input a second phrase, and, using the code, encode and print it. If any letter did not appear in the original, "key" phrase, don't change it in the encoded phrase.

20. Refer to Exercises 18 and 19. Start by entering the key phrase (the one from Exercise 18). Use it to generate a frequency table. Then read in the encoded phrase and decode it.

11

Files

KEY IDEAS

1. *What is a file?*

2. *Text files.*

   a. *Creating a text file.*

   b. *Accessing a text file.*

3. *Record files.*

   a. *Records.*

   b. *Creating a record file.*

   c. *Accessing a record file sequentially.*

   d. *Accessing a record file directly.*

4. *Byte files.*

WHAT IS A FILE?

A file is a collection of related data. For example, your school probably maintains a file of student grade data, and somewhere in that file is information about you. Your name and grade point average are data elements or fields. Taken together, the data elements related to your grade history represent your student record. The file holds one record for each student.

Note that the file need not be stored on a computer. Your record might be kept in a manila folder, and folders for each student stored in a filing cabinet. However, a modern computer is the most efficient information storage and retrieval tool ever developed. Thus, data structures and files take on a particular importance when we study computers.

Main Memory

A file is a collection of data. A computer manipulates data stored in its main memory, but there are some limitations to main memory. For one thing, it's expensive. Partly because of the cost, and partly because of a computer's design, the amount of available main memory is limited. A grade history for each student in your school, or payroll data for a few thousand employees in a medium-sized firm can easily exceed main memory capacity.

Another problem is volatility. Simply put, main memory loses its contents when the power is cut. Imagine if all your school's student grade histories were stored in a computer's main memory. Every time the computer was turned off, all the data would have to be reentered. In fact, every time a thunderstorm interrupted power for even a brief fraction of a second, all those data would be lost. Reentering data through the keyboard is unacceptably slow, expensive, and error-prone. If main memory were the only available computer storage medium, we'd still be keeping all our data in filing cabinets.

Secondary Storage

Fortunately, there is an alternative--secondary storage. Many types of secondary storage media are available, including magnetic tape, bubble memory, and video disk, but the most popular is magnetic disk. A disk is a flat, circular platter coated with a magnetic material. Data are stored on concentric circles called tracks *(Fig. 11.1)*. The tracks are subdivided into sectors, with each sector holding a fixed amount of data (128 characters is common). Data flow between the disk surface and the computer a sector at a time.

Data are recorded on disk using the same patterns of binary digits used inside a computer. Thus, a disk can store a precise image of main memory's contents. Anything you can represent in main memory, you can store on disk.

Disk has other advantages, too. It's much less expensive than main memory. For about $100, you can buy a set of chips to increase your computer's main memory by roughly 64,000 characters, but a floppy disk with a capacity of 360,000 characters

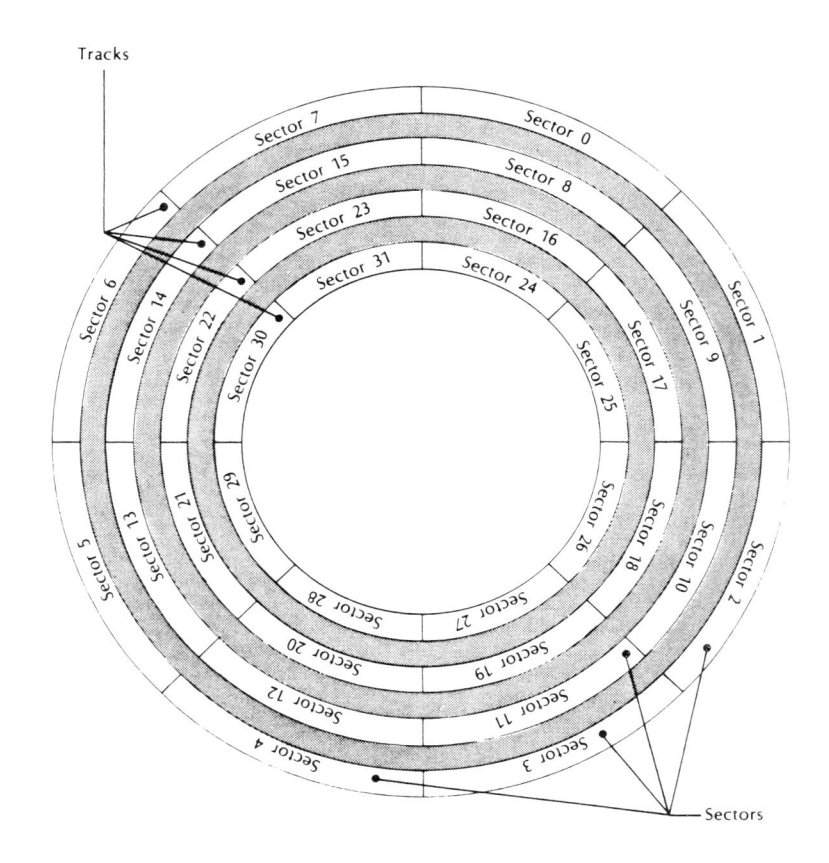

Fig. 11.1: *A disk is a flat, disk-shaped surface coated with a magnetic material. Data are stored around the disk surface on a series of concentric circles called tracks. The tracks are subdivided to form sectors. Data move between the computer and the disk's surface a sector at a time.*

costs $5.00 or less. Disk is also nonvolatile; its data do not disappear when the power is cut. Thus, a disk can be removed from the computer, filed away somewhere, and its data accessed again later. Disk is used for long-term data storage.

Although accessing a disk is much slower than accessing data in main memory, it is much faster than typing the data through the keyboard. Disk is also much more accurate than human data entry. People make typing mistakes. With rare exceptions, data are transferred between a disk and main memory without error.

Please note, however, that a computer's processor cannot manipulate data on disk. Before data stored on disk can be processed, they must be transferred into main memory. In a file's life cycle,

Fig. 11.2: *A disk file's "life cycle."*

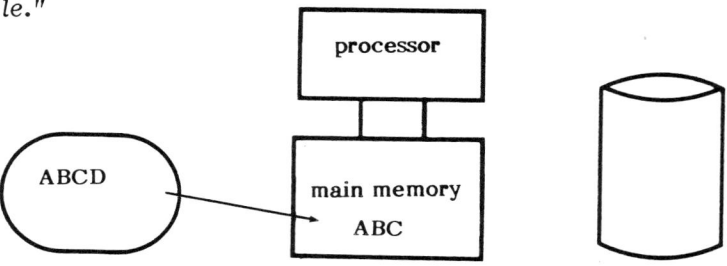

a. *The data are entered through the keyboard and stored in the computer's main memory.*

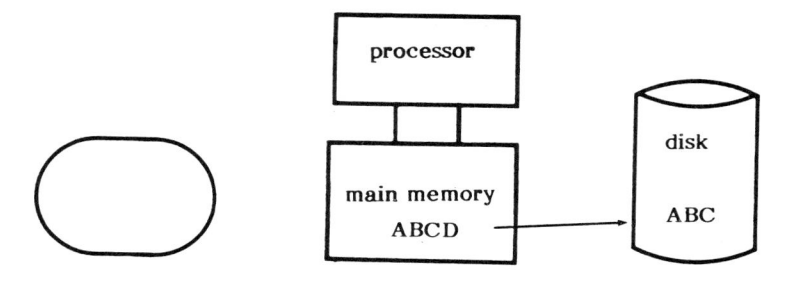

b. *From main memory, the data are copied to the disk's surface.*

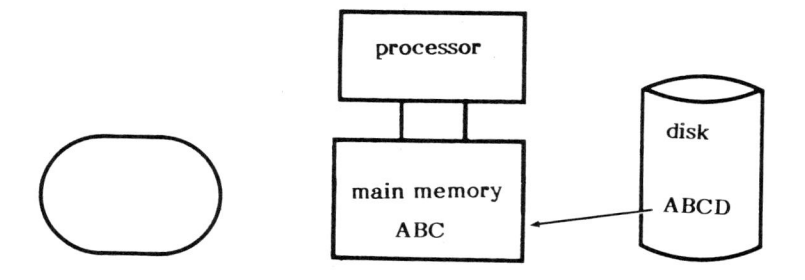

c. *Once the data are stored on disk, they can be read back into main memory and processed as often as necessary.*

1. the original "raw" data are entered by a human being and stored in the computer's main memory *(Fig. 11.2a)*,

2. the file is created by copying the data from main memory to disk *(Fig. 11.2b)*,

3. subsequently, as often as necessary, the data are read from disk back into main memory, and processed *(Fig. 11.2c)*.

Note that the data must be entered only once. After they are stored on disk, the computer can access the data without further human intervention, and, assuming no one physically destroys the disk, the data can be used again and again, literally forever.

True BASIC Files

True BASIC supports three different types of files: text, record, and byte. We'll discuss each one in detail. First, however, because they are common to all files, we'll introduce the **OPEN** and **CLOSE** statements.

A path linking a peripheral device to a computer is called a data channel. Before a device can be accessed by a program, a channel must be established. Channels are defined in an **OPEN** statement *(Fig. 11.3)*. Following the keyword **OPEN** is a channel number. By default, channel #0 refers to the keyboard and the screen. It's always open. For other files, you can use any positive integer as a channel number.

A colon follows the channel number. After the colon comes a keyword. **SCREEN** specifies a display screen window *(see Chapter 9)*. **PRINTER** implies that the output is to go to the printer *(see Chapter 7)*. If the word following the colon is **NAME**, the **OPEN** statement refers to a file on disk.

Several different files can be stored on the same disk. Each file is assigned a name.* The names of all the files on a given disk are collected in the disk's index. A file's name follows the keyword **NAME** in the **OPEN** statement. When the **OPEN** is executed, the computer establishes a channel between main memory and the disk drive, reads the index into main memory, and finds the file. Once the file is located, its data can be accessed.

Several options can be specified in an **OPEN** statement. Consider **ACCESS** first. **OUTPUT** means the file is to be opened for output (write only). **INPUT** means read only. **OUTIN** means you can read and/or write the data. If you don't specify **ACCESS**, **OUTIN** is assumed.

The second option is **CREATE**. **NEW** means that the file doesn't exist, so a new one must be created. **OLD** means that the file already exists. **NEWOLD** gives the programmer the choice of using an old file (if it exists), or creating a new one. The default is **OLD**.

The file's **ORGANIZATION** can be **TEXT**, **RECORD**, or **BYTE**. If the file is old, an entry has already been recorded on the disk's index. If you don't specify **ORGANIZATION** for an old file, the organization recorded on the index will be used. If you do specify an organization, it must match the index. New files are

---

*The rules for naming files vary considerably from computer to computer; check your User's Guide. In this primer, we'll use file names that are valid on most systems.

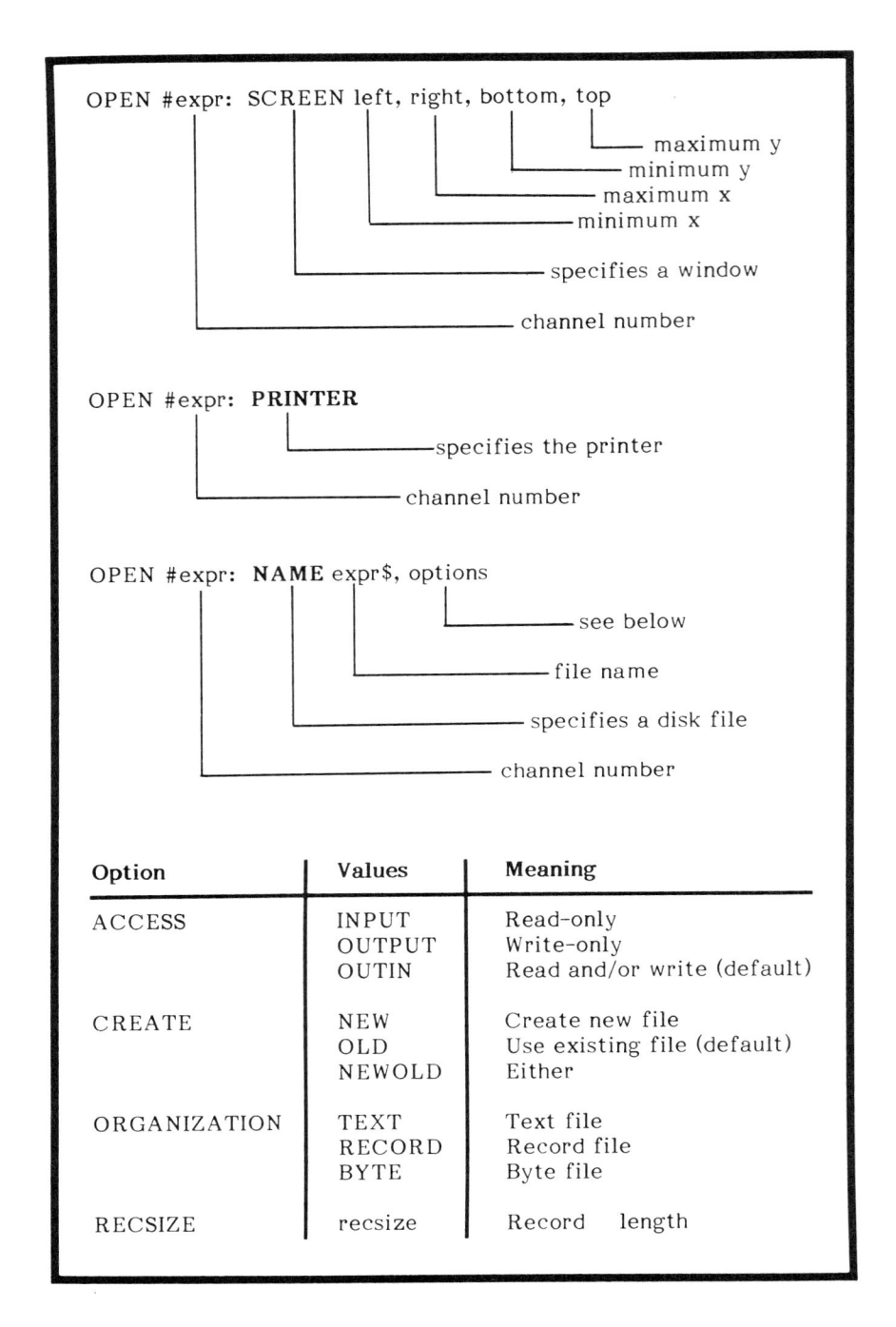

```
OPEN #expr: SCREEN left, right, bottom, top
       │            │     │      │     │
       │            │     │      │     └── maximum y
       │            │     │      └────── minimum y
       │            │     └──────────── maximum x
       │            └──────────────── minimum x
       │    └──────────────────── specifies a window
       └────────────────────── channel number

OPEN #expr: PRINTER
       │        └────── specifies the printer
       └────────────── channel number

OPEN #expr: NAME expr$, options
       │      │    │       └────── see below
       │      │    └──────────── file name
       │      └──────────────── specifies a disk file
       └────────────────────── channel number
```

Option	Values	Meaning
ACCESS	INPUT	Read-only
	OUTPUT	Write-only
	OUTIN	Read and/or write (default)
CREATE	NEW	Create new file
	OLD	Use existing file (default)
	NEWOLD	Either
ORGANIZATION	TEXT	Text file
	RECORD	Record file
	BYTE	Byte file
RECSIZE	recsize	Record length

Fig. 11.3: *An OPEN statement establishes a link, called a channel, between the computer's main processor and an external device.*

different. Because they are new, no index entry exists. If you don't specify an organization, *True BASIC* assumes one. If the first reference to the file is an **INPUT** or **PRINT** statement, the file must be **TEXT**. Record files call for **READ** and **WRITE** statements. A byte file is accessed by **READ**s and **WRITE**s, but there is a special option, **BYTE**, on the **READ** statement. The first input or output statement encountered determines the organization.

Finally, the record size can be specified as an **OPEN** statement option. The record size is meaningful only for record and byte files.

When you've finished accessing a file, **CLOSE** it *(Fig. 11.4)*. Closing a file helps to protect your data. All files are automatically closed when the program ends. Don't take a chance, though. If, for whatever reason, your computer should lose power while a file is still open, you can lose data. To be safe, close your files when you finish with them.

TEXT FILES

The easiest type of file to visualize is a text file. When a **PRINT** statement is executed, a line of data is displayed on the screen. When the output device is a disk file, a similar line is stored on disk. When an **INPUT** statement is executed, a line of data is input from the keyboard. When the source is a text file, a similar line is input from disk. Text file data are stored and retrieved in display form--the same format used for the screen.

Creating a Text File

Perhaps the best way to visualize text files is through an example. We'll start by creating a text file. We want to type a series of data values and output them to disk. While we don't need a formal problem definition or a flowchart for such a simple program, we should take the time to define our data. We'll create an inventory file. For each of ten different parts, we'll input a part number, the part's stock-on-hand, and a description. Then, we'll output the data to a text file. When we finish, our file might contain

Fig. 11:4: *When you finish using a file, close it.*

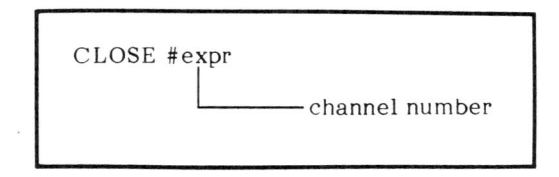

```
CLOSE #expr
       └──── channel number
```

Part number	Stock-on-hand	Description
1	12	baseball
2	17	football
3	42	tennis ball

and so on.

The file creation program *(Fig. 11.5)* begins with an **OPEN** statement. We'll call the file **INVENTRY**. Future references to the file will use that name. It's a **NEW** file (we're about to create it), to be opened for **OUTPUT** only. Finally, it's a **TEXT** file. The **OPEN** statement establishes a link to the disk device and creates an entry on the disk's index under the name **INVENTRY**. Once the **OPEN** is executed, our program can reference the file using channel #1.

Fig. 11.5: *A program to create a text inventory file.*

```
                        ! This program creates an inventory file
                        ! on disk. The file will be accessed by a
                        ! subsequent program. We begin by opening
                        ! the file and assigning it to channel 1.
OPEN #1: NAME "inventry", ACCESS OUTPUT, CREATE NEW, ORGANIZATION TEXT

                        ! For each of ten different parts we store
                        ! a part number, a stock on hand, and a
                        ! description. The part numbers will be
                        ! generated by the program. The user will
                        ! input values for the part's stock on
                        ! hand and description.
FOR part_number = 1 TO 10
    PRINT "enter the stock on hand and a description"
    PRINT "for part number "; part_number;

    INPUT stock_on_hand, description$

    PRINT #1: part_number
    PRINT #1: stock_on_hand
    PRINT #1: description$

NEXT part_number

CLOSE #1
PRINT "Inventory file created."

END
```

Move inside the program's main **FOR NEXT** loop. The loop starts by printing some directions for the user. Then, a particular part's stock-on-hand and description are entered; note that the loop generates and assigns part numbers. Finally, the three values--part number, stock-on-hand, and description--are output to disk, and the next number is generated. When the loop ends, the file is closed, and the message "Inventory file created." is printed on the screen.

Note that each data element is sent to disk through a separate **PRINT** statement. Why couldn't we just code

> **PRINT #1:** part_number, stock_on_hand, description$

We could have; **PRINT** statements listing several variables are legal. However, we would have created problems for ourselves when we tried to retrieve the data. We'll explain why after we've accessed the file.

Accessing a Text File

Now that we've created a text file, let's access it. To illustrate that a file can be passed from program to program, we'll write a separate program to read it and display an inventory list on the screen. Once again, because the program is so simple, we don't need a flowchart. Start with the **OPEN** statement *(Fig. 11.6)*. The organization is still **TEXT**, but the access mode is now **INPUT** (read only), and the create option specifies **OLD** (the file already exists). Consequently, **OPEN** will establish a channel to the disk, find the file named **INVENTRY**, and make it available to the program.

Check the **DO** statement next. The program's main control is a **WHILE** loop with exit condition **MORE #1**. The **MORE #n** condition is true if there are more data on the file. A similar condition, **END #n** is true if there are *no* more data on the file.

Inside the loop, the three **INPUT** statements get values for **part_number, stock_on_hand,** and **description$** from the file. Then the three values are printed to the screen. When the loop ends, a complete inventory list is displayed in the history window.

Why did we input one variable at a time? Earlier, we compared text file data to a series of screen lines. That wasn't just an analogy. That's exactly how the data are recorded. Start with the screen. By default, its right margin is set at 80 characters. Five zones, each 16 characters wide, are used to display data. When data are printed, the first value is displayed in zone 1, the second value in zone 2, and so on. Semicolons, **Tab** functions, and **Using** options override those defaults, and the programmer can set the margin or the zone width with **SET** statements. See Chapters 2 and 7 for details.

Text files follow the same rules. For example, the statement

```
                         | This program lists the inventory file
                         | created by a previously run program.
                         | We begin by opening the file and
                         | assigning it to channel 1.
OPEN #1: NAME "inventry", ACCESS INPUT, CREATE OLD, ORGANIZATION TEXT

                         | First, column headers are printed.

PRINT "Part number", "Stock-on-hand", "Description"

                         | Each time through this loop, the program
                         | reads a part number, a stock on hand,
                         | and a description from the file. Then it
                         | prints these data items. The loop ends
                         | when there are no more data to be read.
DO WHILE MORE #1

    INPUT #1: part_number
    INPUT #1: stock_on_hand
    INPUT #1:description$


    PRINT part_number, stock_on_hand, description$

LOOP

CLOSE #1

END
```

Fig. 11.6: *This program accesses the text file created by the program in Fig. 11.5, and uses the data to generate an inventory list.*

PRINT #1: part_number, stock_on_hand, description$

would generate the following line

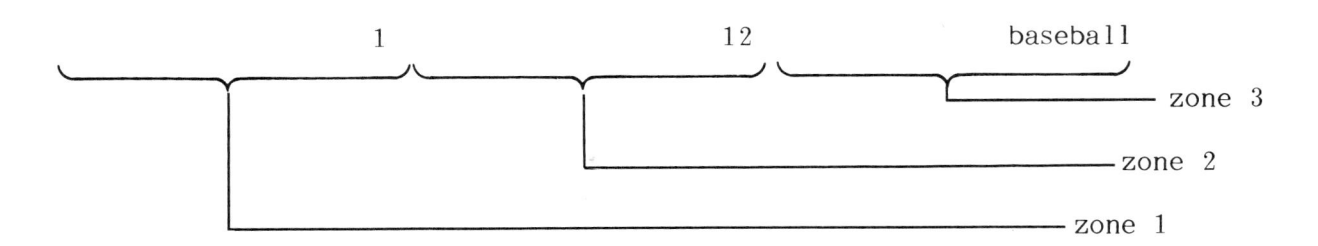

```
                      1                12            baseball
                                                     ───────── zone 3
                                       ─────────────────────── zone 2
                      ───────────────────────────────────────── zone 1
```

322

This 48-character line would then be stored on disk.

An **INPUT** statement expects to find data values separated by commas. If you code

> INPUT #1: part_number, stock_on_hand, description$

you'll get an error message: "String given insead of number." Why? Look at the line. Do you see any commas separating the three values? No. Thus, since there is at least one nonnumeric character in the line, *True BASIC* treats the whole thing as a string and tries to assign it to **part_number.** That's illegal. Hence, the error message.

How can you get around this problem? The easiest way is to code one **PRINT** or one **INPUT** for each variable. Each **PRINT** starts a new output line. With one value per line, the **INPUT** statement doesn't need commas to separate the data elements, because there aren't any values to separate.

An option is inserting your own commas or semicolons between values. For example, the statement

> PRINT #1: part_number; ","; stock_on_hand; ","; description$

outputs a line containing

> 1 , 12 ,baseball

Later, the instruction

> INPUT #1: part_number, stock_on_hand, description$

uses the commas to separate the three data elements. Another option is to use **LINE INPUT** statements to read data from a text file, and then rely on your own substring functions to extract the data values *(see Chapter 10 for details)*.

Features and Options

An **OPEN** statement can be used to create a file, but what if you want to get rid of one? The **ERASE** statement *(Fig. 11.7)* erases a file's contents. However, the file still exists; you can use it to store new data. The **UNSAVE** instruction

Fig. 11.7: *Code an ERASE statement to delete the data stored in a file. After ERASE is executed, the file still exists, and new data can be stored in it.*

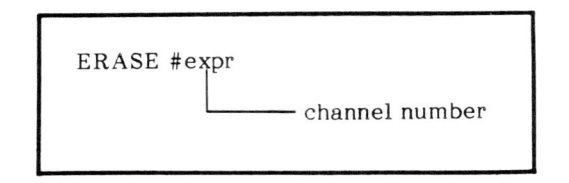

```
ERASE #expr
       └──── channel number
```

(Fig. 11.8) removes a file from the disk's index. Subsequently, since there is no reference to the file, future **OPEN**s will be unable to find it. Thus, following an **UNSAVE**, the file ceases to exist. (Note: **ERASE** and **UNSAVE** can be coded as instructions or as commands.)

A pointer controls access to a text file. When the file is opened, the pointer is set at the first storage position. An **INPUT** instruction will get the contents of this first position; a **PRINT** statement's data will be stored there. After the first **INPUT** or **PRINT**, the pointer moves to the second storage location, and so on. Consequently, the data in a text file are input or output in sequential order, from first to last.

The programmer does have some control over the pointer. By coding a **SET POINTER** statement *(Fig. 11.9)*, the pointer can be moved to the file's beginning or to its end. Set the pointer to the file's end to add more data to an old file. Set it to the beginning to reuse the data.

By default, a **PRINT** statement generates 80-character output lines divided into five 16-character zones. Code **SET MARGIN** or **SET ZONEWIDTH** statements to change those defaults *(Fig. 11.9, again)*. You can also code semicolons or use **Tab** functions to separate values. A **PRINT USING** statement *(see Chapter 7)* formats the output data. While not normally desirable, recording formatted data on disk can prove valuable. For example, in applications that print checks, a common operating procedure is generating the formatted output in one program, writing the lines to a text file, and then printing the checks in a different program. That way, security procedures can control the actual check-writing process.

Use **MAT PRINT** and **MAT INPUT** statements to store and retrieve complete arrays *(see Chapter 8)*. Array elements are output and input in odometer order, with the rightmost subscript changing most rapidly. One element is stored on each line; in other words, the statements access data as though each array element

Fig. 11.8: *To delete a file completely, code an UNSAVE instruction. Following UNSAVE, the file will no longer exist, and further reference to it will generate an error.*

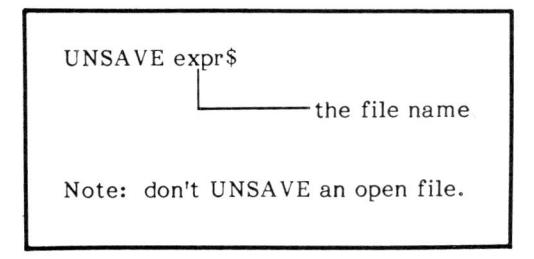

```
UNSAVE expr$
       └──── the file name

Note: don't UNSAVE an open file.
```

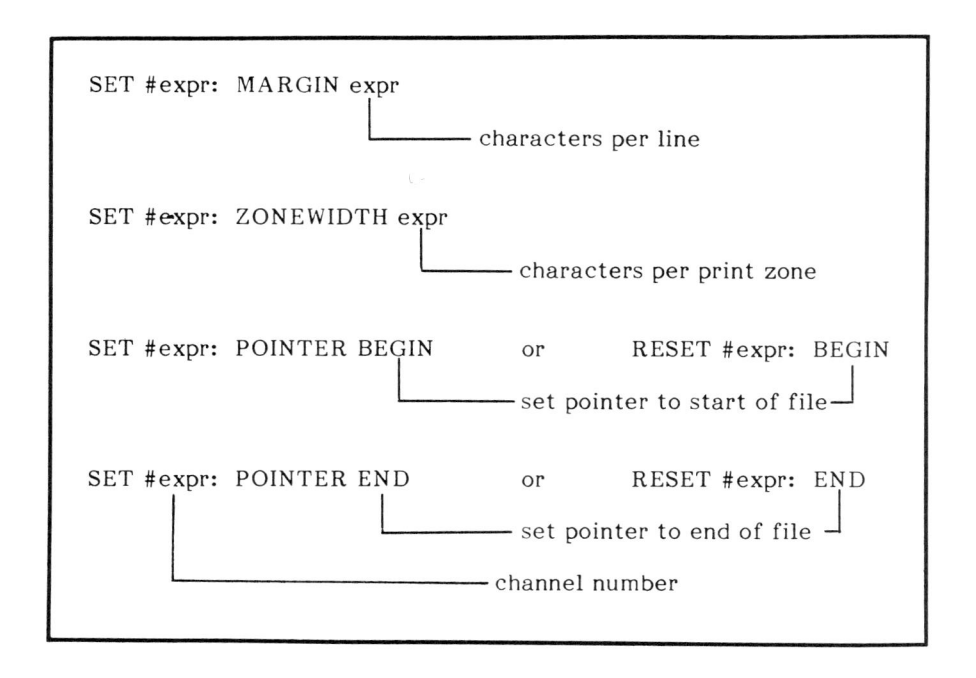

```
SET #expr: MARGIN expr
                  └──────── characters per line

SET #expr: ZONEWIDTH expr
                     └──────── characters per print zone

SET #expr: POINTER BEGIN        or      RESET #expr: BEGIN
                   └──────── set pointer to start of file ──┘

SET #expr: POINTER END          or      RESET #expr: END
           │       └──────── set pointer to end of file ──┘
           └──────────────── channel number
```

Fig. 11.9: *Several SET statement options help the programmer to access text files.*

is output or input by a separate **PRINT** or **INPUT** statement.

Finally, with any file, bad data on input causes a fatal error. If you type $5.75 in response to a request for **pay_rate**, *True BASIC* will identify the dollar sign as an illegal character and ask you to try again. If the dollar sign is stored on disk, the system can't very well ask the disk to correct the data. Thus, the program is terminated.

RECORD FILES

Record files are different. Instead of lines, they store data in a series of storage locations called records. The programmer can directly control the record length. Strings are represented as ASCII characters *(see Appendix V)*. Numbers are stored in IEEE 8-byte format. These formats are common to most microcomputers; thus record files are transportable between *True BASIC* programs written on different types of computers. Data on a record file are accessed by **READ** and **WRITE** statements.

Records

Each record on a record file holds a single number or a single string. Each record is numbered: the first one on the file is 1, the second is 2, and so on. By default, when the file is opened, a pointer is set at the first record. Following each **READ** or **WRITE**, the pointer is advanced one record; thus, like text files, record files are accessed sequentially.

You do have another option with record files, however. In addition to setting the pointer at the file's beginning or end, you can also set it to the next record, move it back to access the same record again, or with a **SET RECORD** statement, set it to any record on the file *(Fig. 11.10)*. Thus, you can access a record file sequentially or directly.

Fig. 11.10: *Several SET statement options can be used when accessing record files.*

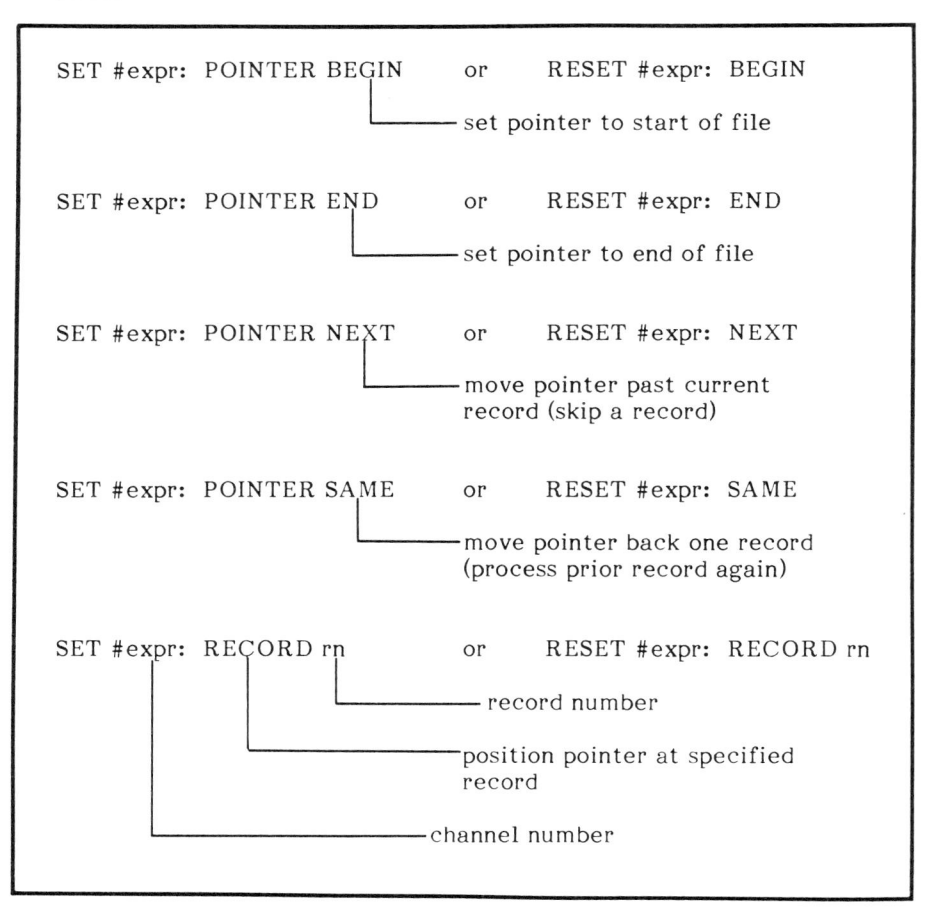

```
SET #expr: POINTER BEGIN      or     RESET #expr: BEGIN
                   └──── set pointer to start of file

SET #expr: POINTER END        or     RESET #expr: END
                   └──── set pointer to end of file

SET #expr: POINTER NEXT       or     RESET #expr: NEXT
                   └──── move pointer past current
                         record (skip a record)

SET #expr: POINTER SAME       or     RESET #expr: SAME
                   └──── move pointer back one record
                         (process prior record again)

SET #expr: RECORD rn          or     RESET #expr: RECORD rn
                        └──── record number
                   └──── position pointer at specified
                         record
           └──── channel number
```

The record size is fixed; in other words, all records on a file must contain the same number of bytes or characters. Before adding the first record, you must set the record size. You can use a **RECSIZE** option on the **OPEN** statement, or you can code a **SET RECSIZE** statement *(Fig. 11.10, again)*. Once the record size is set, it can't be changed. If a program accesses an existing record file, the **SET RECSIZE** statement is illegal.

Storing one data item per record is fine for passing an array or a few values from one program to another, but it's unacceptable for long-term data storage. Rarely are individual data elements truly independent. For example, a grade history file might hold a thousand or more student records, each containing a name, an address, a series of course identifications and grades, and such summary data as the student's total credit hours earned and grade point average. On a record file, each "record" must be the same length. Assume that the student's address is the longest single data element. If we need twenty characters to store it, we need twenty to store every data element. But numbers require only eight characters. Store an eight-character number in a twenty-character record, and you waste twelve characters per record. Store a one-character grade, and you waste nineteen.

In languages such as COBOL and Pascal, a programmer can define data structures containing several related data elements. By packing and unpacking the data, you can do much the same thing in *True BASIC*. The secret is to concatenate the related data elements to form a single string (see Chapter 10 for an explanation of string operations). On input, substring functions are used to extract individual data elements from the string. As we'll see later in the chapter, there are significant advantages to be gained from packing and unpacking records.

Creating a Record File

Let's recreate the text inventory file as a record file. As before, the program will simply read some data and write them to disk, so we won't need a flowchart. However, before we begin writing the code, we should lay out a data structure.

In this case, each part stored on the file requires three data elements: part number, stock-on-hand, and description. Our objective is to combine these three data elements in a single record. On a record file, numbers are stored in IEEE 8-byte format; thus we need eight bytes for each number. A string is stored as a series of ASCII-coded characters. We'll use twenty characters for the description field. Thus, each record in our file should look like Fig. 11.11, with three related data items packed into a single 36-character string.

Figure 11.12 shows a program to create a record file. Let's go through it line by line. Start with the **OPEN** statement. Read the options. Convince yourself that it creates a new record file named **RECINV**. Following **OPEN** is the instruction that sets the record size to 36 characters.

Move inside the **FOR NEXT** loop. User instructions are printed, and then values for stock-on-hand and the part description are input. A subroutine, **Pack_data**, packs the generated part number, along with the two input fields, into a single

Data element	Length	Positions
part number	8	1-8
stock-on-hand	8	9-16
description	20	17-36

Fig. 11.11: *A key step in planning a record file is laying out data structure. Here's how the inventory data elements will be grouped to form a record.*

Fig. 11.12: *As this program shows, the process of creating a record file is similar to creating a text file.*

```
                        ! This program creates an inventory file
                        ! using the record file format. Each
                        ! record holds a part number, a stock on
                        ! hand, and a part description. The part
                        ! number will serve as a relative record
                        ! number. Subsequent programs will access
                        ! the inventory file either directly or
                        ! sequentially. We begin by opening the
                        ! file and assigning it to channel 1.
OPEN #1: NAME "recinv", ACCESS OUTPUT, CREATE NEW, ORGANIZATION RECORD
SET #1: RECSIZE 36
                        ! For each of ten different parts we
                        ! store a part number, a stock on hand,
                        ! and a description. The part numbers will
                        ! be generated by the program. The user
                        ! will input values for the part's stock
                        ! on hand and description.
FOR part_number = 1 TO 10
    PRINT "enter the stock on hand and a description"
    PRINT "for part number "; part_number;

    INPUT stock_on_hand, description$

                        ! Next, we'll call a subroutine that will
                        ! pack the three data items into a record.

    CALL Pack_data (record$, part_number, stock_on_hand, description$)

    WRITE #1: record$

NEXT part_number

CLOSE #1
PRINT "Inventory file created."

END
```

```
                              ! This subroutine accepts 2 numbers and a
                              ! string and packs them into a record.
SUB Pack_data (record$, first_number, second_number, string$)

                              ! First, we pad the string to 20 charac-
                              ! ters by concatenating 20 blanks to its
                              ! end (making it at least 20 characters
                              ! long), and then taking a substring of
                              ! the first 20 characters of the result.

   LET string$ = (string$ & Repeat$(" ",20))[1:20]

                              ! Now we can build the record.

   LET record$ = Num$(first_number) & Num$(second_number) & string$
END SUB
```

Fig. 11.12, *Continued.*

36-character string, **record$**. Then **record$** is written to disk, and the loop repeats. A total of ten records are output.

For those who have already read about string manipulation *(see Chapter 10)*, the subroutine **Pack_data** is quite interesting. The first instruction makes sure the description contains exactly twenty characters. Look to the right of the equal sign. First, twenty blanks are concatenated to the string's end. Then, a substring consisting of the first twenty characters replaces the original string. An option is to check the initial description's length, subtract that value from 20, and use the difference as the **Repeat$** function's second parameter.

The subroutine's second statement creates the 36-character record. Numbers, remember, are stored in IEEE 8-byte format. The **Num$** function accepts a *True BASIC* number and converts it to IEEE form. The ampersand character (&) is a concatenation operator; the statement simply joins the two numbers and the 20-character description, and assigns the resulting string to **record$**.

Accessing a Record File Sequentially

There is very little difference between accessing a record file sequentially and accessing a text file sequentially. When the file is opened, a pointer is set at record number 1. Thus, the first **READ** or **WRITE** refers to record number 1. Following any input or output operation, the pointer is incremented by one record. Thus, by default, records are read in the order they were written.

Let's write a program to generate an inventory list from the record file we just created. Start *(Fig. 11.13)* with the **OPEN**. We intend to input data from an existing record file named **RECINV**. Note that there is no **SET RECSIZE** state-

```
                              ! This program lists the inventory file
                              ! created by a previous program. The
                              ! file is a record file. The OPEN assigns
                              ! it to channel 1.
OPEN #1: NAME "recinv", ACCESS INPUT, CREATE OLD, ORGANIZATION RECORD

                              ! First, column headers are printed.
PRINT "Part number", "Stock-on-hand", "Description"

                              ! Each time through the loop, a record
                              ! is read. Then a subroutine is called.
                              ! The subroutine unpacks the record into
                              ! a part-number, a stock_on_hand, and a
                              ! description. Then it prints the data.
                              ! The loop ends when there are no more
                              ! data to be read.
DO WHILE MORE #1

    READ #1: record$
    CALL Unpack (record$, part_number, stock_on_hand, description$)

    PRINT part_number, stock_on_hand, description$

LOOP

CLOSE #1

END

                              ! This subroutine accepts a 36 character
                              ! string and unpacks it into two numbers
                              ! and a 20 character string.
SUB Unpack (record$, first_number, second_number, string$)

    LET first_number = Num(record$[1:8])
    LET second_number = Num(record$[9:16])
    LET string$ = record$[17:36]

END SUB
```

Fig. 11.13: *This program reads the record file sequentially, producing an inventory list.*

ment. Because the file exists, the record size has already been set, and we don't have to code it again. (In fact, if we do, we'll get a compilation error.)

Move inside the **DO** loop. **MORE #1** is our exit condition. The first statement reads a record from the file. Next, a subroutine unpacks the 36-character string into three separate variables. Finally, the part number, the stock-on-hand, and the description are printed to the screen, and the loop repeats.

If you understand string operations, look at the subroutine that unpacks the data. The **Num** function accepts an IEEE 8-character code and converts it to a *True BASIC* number. We stored the part number in position 1 through 8 of the record string. The first statement in the subroutine passes a substring consisting of the record's first eight characters to a **Num** function and stores the result in **first_number**. Compare the **CALL** statement's arguments with the **SUB** statement's parameters, and you'll see that **first_number** is really **part_number**. The next two statements extract **stock_on_hand** and **description$**.

Direct Access

If all we had was sequential access, there wouldn't be much point to using record files. They are more efficient than text files, and are transportable between different manufacturer's computers, but those considerations are of importance to professional programmers, not beginners.

Direct or random access *is* useful to beginners, however. With sequential files, data are read and written in strict sequence, and accessing a particular record depends on its relative position in the file. With direct access, individual records can be stored or retrieved without regard for their position in the file. For example, using direct access, if you want inventory information for part number 7, you can read record number 7 without first reading 1 through 6.

Remember that individual records on a record file are numbered; the first one is record 1, the second is record 2, and so on. Those record numbers are the secret to direct access. Using a **SET RECORD** statement *(see Fig. 11.10)*, the programmer can position the file's pointer at any record and read or write it next.

For example, consider the program in Fig. 11.14. Start with the **OPEN** statement; it references the inventory file created earlier. Move inside the **DO** loop. The first instruction accepts a single part number. After checking to make sure it's positive (a negative part number is the loop's exit condition), the file's pointer is set to **part_number**. Next, the record indicated by the pointer is read. Finally, a subroutine unpacks the record into individual data elements, and the values are printed.

An error is generated if the pointer refers to a record that doesn't exist on the file. It would have been wise to check the input part number to be sure that it lay between 1 and the number of records on the file. Because we wanted to keep the program simple, we skipped the data verification step. When you write direct access routines, don't.

How did we know which record held the data we wanted? In our case, when we created the file, we used the record number as a part number, but that's not always possible. For example, picture a grade file. Imagine that social security numbers are used to identify students. The only way we could use a student's social security number as a record number is if we stored 999,999,999 records,

```
                              ! This program accesses the inventory file
                              ! directly, printing the inventory levels
                              ! of selected part numbers. The OPEN
                              ! assigns the file to channel 1.
OPEN #1: NAME "recinv", ACCESS INPUT, CREATE OLD, ORGANIZATION RECORD

                              ! Each time through this loop, the program
                              ! asks the user to enter a part number. It
                              ! then retrieves and displays data for
                              ! that part number. The loop ends when the
                              ! user enters a negative part number.
DO
    INPUT PROMPT "Enter part number ": part_number
    IF part_number > 0 THEN
                              ! Given a valid part number, the pointer
                              ! is set to that relative record number.
        SET #1: RECORD part_number
                              ! Next, the record is read and unpacked.
        READ #1: record$
        CALL Unpack (record$, part_number, stock_on_hand, description$)

                              ! And the data are printed.
        PRINT
        PRINT "Part number ";part_number; description$
        PRINT "stock on hand = "; stock_on_hand
        PRINT

    END IF

LOOP UNTIL part_number <= 0

CLOSE #1

END
```

Fig. 11.14: *In this program, individual records are accessed directly.*

one for each possible social security number. How many students attend your school? The file would contain mostly empty records, and that's not efficient.

Fortunately, there are alternatives. One is to create an index. For example, we might start with an array containing, for each student, a social security number and the number of that student's record. Given the array, a user could ask for a student's data by entering a social security number. Given the identification

```
                              ! This subroutine accepts a 36 character
                              ! string and unpacks it into two numbers
                              ! and a 20 character string.
SUB Unpack (record$, first_number, second_number, string$)

    LET first_number = Num(record$[1:8])
    LET second_number = Num(record$[9:16])
    LET string$ = record$[17:36]

END SUB
```

Fig. 11.14, *Continued.*

number, the program would search the array, find the student's social security number, find the associated record number, and use it to read the data. For added efficiency, sort the index into identification number sequence. Another option is to create an array (or parallel arrays) holding the students' names and associated record numbers. Then we could find a student's data by entering his or her name. See Chapter 8 for an explanation of arrays.

A third option is to use an algorithm to generate a record number. Start by creating a file of empty (blank) records. To add data to the file, read a record's identification key, pass it through an algorithm, and compute a record number. Later, to retrieve the data, input the identification key, pass it to the same algorithm, and generate the record number.

Using an algorithm to compute a record number is called randomizing. Several different types of algorithms can be used. For example, you might divide the identification number by the number of records in the file and use the remainder as a record number. Or you might extract the key's three or four low order digits and use them as a record number. Selecting a randomizing algorithm demands considerable skill and experience. Spend some time studying direct access techniques before you try to create your own. For a beginner, the search-key-equals-record-number or the index approach are probably better choices.

You can do a great deal with the data stored on a file once you get it. Of course, you can use it in computations. A common application is updating the file; for example, changing the stock-on-hand of a particular part number to reflect additions to and deletions from inventory. To update a file, use **ACCESS OUTIN** on your **OPEN** statement. Set the pointer to the record you want, and read it. Modify the data as necessary. Then reset the pointer to the same record number and write the record back to disk.

Other Record File Features

Use **MAT READ** and **MAT WRITE** statements to move complete arrays between main memory and the disk surface. Both work as though individual array elements were manipulated, in odometer order, by a series of independent statements. Additionally, the **ERASE** and **UNSAVE** instructions work just as they did with text files. Finally, again as with text files, input data errors are fatal.

BYTE FILES

Byte files allow the programmer to access the "raw data." For example, using byte files, data created by your favorite word processor or spreadsheet program can be manipulated by a *True BASIC* program, and data created by a *True BASIC* program can be passed to another software package. No structure is imposed on a byte file; the programmer is completely responsible for interpreting data. **READ** and **WRITE** statements are used to access byte files. You must set the record size, either with a **SET RECSIZE** statement or a **BYTE** option on the **READ** statement, before reading data.

Byte files are an advanced topic requiring an in-depth understanding of the data formats generated by various software packages. A brief explanation would be meaningless to those who don't know much about computer internals, and useless to those who do, so we won't try. See the *Reference Manual* for details.

FINAL COMMENTS

True BASIC's **ASK** instruction can be used to discover details about a file. Several options are summarized in Fig. 11.15.

A channel number can be passed as a parameter to a subroutine (but not to a function). The channel number must be specified as a number (for example, #1) in both the **CALL** statement's arguments list and the subroutine's parameters list. For example, refer to channel #999 in the **SUB** statement. When parameters are passed, the **CALL** statement's argument replaces the subroutine's dummy channel number.

Local channels can be defined within a subroutine or a function. A local channel is closed automatically when the subroutine or function ends. The number assigned to a local channel is local, too; for example, channel #1 in the main program differs from channel #1 in a subroutine. Local channels are useful for applications such as filling a table from a file.

SUMMARY

The chapter began with a brief definition of the term file. We then explored the basic data hierarchy: data element, record, and file. Main memory is expensive, limited, and volatile; thus it is a poor choice for storing large amounts of data or for long-term data storage. Secondary storage, often disk, is a better choice because it is inexpensive and nonvolatile. The process of storing data on disk

Statement	Option	Returns
ASK #expr:	ACCESS var$	INPUT, OUTPUT, or OUTIN.
	FILESIZE var	File size in bytes or records.
	MARGIN var	Current margin or line width.
	Name var$	The file name, or a null string for a window.
	ORGANIZATION var$	TEXT, RECORD, BYTE, or WINDOW.
	POINTER var$	BEGIN, MIDDLE, or END. The position of the file's pointer.
	RECORD var	The file's current pointer position.
	RECSIZE var	The file's record size.
	ZONEWIDTH var	Characters per print zone.

Fig. 11.15: *Several ASK statement options can be used to gain information about a file.*

was briefly explained.

True BASIC supports three types of files: **TEXT, RECORD,** and **BYTE**. External devices are linked to a computer by a channel. The **OPEN** statement was introduced, and the **ACCESS, CREATE,** and **ORGANIZATION** options explained. After accessing a file, you should close it.

Next, the chapter turned to creating a text file. The **OPEN** instruction was explained, and a program to read data and output them to the file developed. Data are output to a text file by a **PRINT** statement. In a second program, we read the text file data sequentially and produced an inventory list. An **INPUT** statement is used to read a text file. Data are recorded on the file as screen line images. The **ERASE** and **UNSAVE** instructions were briefly discussed. A **SET POINTER** statement can be used to position the file's pointer at the file's beginning or end.

Creating a record file is similar to creating a text file. Instead of screen line images, however, a record file stores data in a series of memory locations called records. One number or one string is stored in each record. By packing several data elements into a single long string, it is possible to create a simple data structure. On input, individual data elements are unpacked from the record string into individual variables.

We used another program to illustrate creating a record file. A **SET RECSIZE** statement followed the **OPEN**. After accepting the data to be recorded from the screen, we used a subroutine to pack them, and then used a **WRITE** statement to send the resulting string to the file. In a subsequent program, the data were read sequentially by a **READ** instruction, and then unpacked in another subroutine. Taking advantage of the **SET RECORD** statement, we then wrote a third program to access the file's data directly. Several direct access techniques were briefly explained.

Byte files allow the programmer to get at the raw data, accessing, for example, data generated by a spreadsheet or a word processor. Because accessing raw data requires advanced knowledge of computer internals, we did not cover this topic in depth.

The chapter ended with a brief summary of **ASK** statement options and the rules for passing a channel number to a subroutine. Local channels are supported by *True BASIC*.

REFERENCES

True BASIC Statements

OPEN	Fig. 11.3, page 318
CLOSE	Fig. 11.4, page 319
ERASE	Fig. 11.7, page 324
UNSAVE	Fig. 11.8, page 324
SET (text files)	Fig. 11.9, page 325
SET (record files)	Fig. 11.10, page 326
ASK	Fig. 11.15, page 335

True BASIC Logical Conditions

MORE #n	page 321
END #n	page 321

EXERCISES

1. Enter the text file creation program developed in the chapter *(Fig. 11.5)*, and run it. Then enter the file access program *(Fig. 11.6)*, and run it. Pay particular attention to the disk drive. You'll hear it start and stop as the program runs. Check the code, and see if you can figure out why.

2. Enter and run the record file creation program developed in the chapter *(Fig. 11.12)*. Then enter and run the sequential file access program *(Fig. 11.13)*.

3. Assuming that you have already created the record inventory file, enter and run the program that accesses it directly *(Fig. 11.14)*. Modify the program to update the inventory file. Accept as input a part number, a transaction type (add to inventory, delete from inventory), and a quantity. For an add transaction, add the quantity to the old stock-on-hand for the referenced part number, and rewrite the record. For a deletion from inventory, subtract and then rewrite.

4. Add to Exercise 3 an option to allow the user to request a complete current inventory listing.

5. Write a program to maintain a running checkbook register. Start with an initial deposit. Accept transactions consisting of a code (C for check, D for deposit), a date, the name of the payee, and the check or deposit amount. Read the prior transaction to get the amount left in the checking account. Output a new transaction at the end of the file containing this transaction's date, payee, and amount, and the new account balance. Assign a number to each transaction; use the old transaction number plus 1. The program should allow you to sign off the computer, come back at a later time, and process subsequent transactions.

6. Write a program or group of programs to create and maintain your own, personal name and address file. Enter a name, mailing address, and telephone number for each of several friends. Design the program so that information on new friends can be added to the file. Include an option to print the file upon request.

7. Modify Exercise 6. Use a record file, and pack the data for a given friend into a single record. Then create an index of names and record numbers. When you want a friend's address or telephone number, you should be able to simply type his or her name. In response, the program will search the index, find the individual's record number, read the record, and display the data.

8. Set up a file to keep track of your *True BASIC* programs. It should include, for each program, the program's name, a description of the program's function, the date it was written, and the number of the disk on which it is stored. Include an option to print the list on request.

9. Write a program to create and maintain an inventory of your own records and tapes. Include the artist, the title, the date you purchased the recording, and the purchase price. Include options to add new recordings, delete old ones, and correct any errors you might detect. Ideally, you should be able to access your library by artist or by title. After writing the basic program or programs, see if you can add these two indexes.

10. In a payroll application, such information as an employee's pay rate, number of dependents, and filing status is stored on a personnel file. Instead of manually entering these relatively constant data each time payroll is run, they are read from disk. Write a program or programs to create and maintain a personnel file. For each employee, store social security number, name, pay rate, number of dependents, and filing status. Be sure to verify the input data; see Fig. 6.18 for ranges on the various data items.

11. In Chapter 6, Exercise 2b, you were asked to write a data input subroutine. Modify the subroutine to get pay rate, dependents, and filing status from the file created in Exercise 10 above.

12. In Chapter 6, Exercise 2c, you were asked to write a subroutine to compute federal income tax from a tax table. Modify the program so that another subroutine reads the tax table from a file. Do the same thing for Chapter 6, Exercises 2d and 2e. Both call for table lookup. Create subroutines to fill all the tables. Of course, you will have to write programs to create the table files.

13. Another requirement of most payroll applications is keeping track of each employee's year-to-date earnings. For example, at the beginning of the year, year-to-date gross pay is set to zero. Each pay period, the current gross pay is added to the year-to-date figure which, at any given pay period, contains the accumulated sum of all the gross pay earned since the beginning of the year. Modify the payroll program once again. To the personnel file created in Exercise 10 above, add fields to hold year-to-date gross pay, federal tax, state tax, local tax, social security tax, and net pay. After computing the current value of each variable, add it to the appropriate year-to-date accumulator. At the end of the program, rewrite the employee's personnel record.

14. If you did Exercise 13, write a new program to read the personnel file and generate an end-of-year earnings statement for each employee. If you've

held even a part-time job, you have probably received a similar statement, called a W-2 form, from your employer. If you have one, use it as a model.

15. Modify the payroll system yet again. Instead of sending the simulated checks directly to the printer, format the data, pack them into a single string, and write them to a record file. Dump the simulated checks to the printer in a subsequent program. See Chapter 7 for a description of data formatting.

16. Write a program to keep track of performance statistics for your favorite athletic team. Include each player's number and name, and, depending on the sport, relevant statistics. Keep the data on a file. After each game, add the new data to the file and compute and print summary statistics.

17. Imagine that you are an instructor. Write a program to create and maintain a grade book. Record each student's name and identification number. Then record the various grade factors—exam grades, homework grades, project grades, and so on. Include the necessary algorithms to convert grade factors to a final grade. If possible, use the grade factors for this course. Otherwise, select a course in which the instructor clearly defined the grading criteria, and use them.

18. Write a program to play a trivia game. Store a series of questions and answers in a file. Define separate files for each of several categories. Roll dice *(see Chapter 6 for a dice function)* to select a category. Then use a random number to select a question from the appropriate file. Keep score according to the rules of your favorite trivia game.

    For an interesting extension to this game, incorporate computer graphics *(see Chapter 9)*. Plot a game board and playing pieces. Use a **GET POINT** statement to move a piece. You might even get fancy and display the playing board in one window, roll the dice in a second, and ask questions in a third.

19. Insurance companies strongly recommend that policy holders maintain an inventory of their belongings. Use the computer to set up one for your own house or apartment.

20. Set up an engagement calendar for yourself. In addition to the date and the day of the week, you should leave room to record appointments, social events, birthdays, examinations, due dates, and other important activities for each day. Your program should start by executing a **Date** function and displaying today's, yesterday's, and tomorrow's reminders. The user should be able to request information on any day in the year, add new entries, delete old ones, and correct entries. This program is tricky. Think about it before starting to write it. Try defining a one month calendar before

tackling a full year. Eventually, modify the program so that it tracks the current month, a year into the future, and six months into the past. You might also consider using graphics and/or windows to make the display look better.

12

Libraries, Chaining, and Recursion

KEY IDEAS

1. *Libraries.*
    a. *Creating a library.*
    b. *Accessing a library.*
    c. *Maintaining a library.*
    d. *Existing libraries.*
2. *Chaining.*
3. *Recursion.*

LIBRARIES

In computer terms, a library is an indexed collection of programs, subroutines, functions, or data files. Usually, the members of a particular library are related in some way; for example, an organization might maintain a library of production programs, and another library of computational subroutines.

True BASIC supports a powerful library feature that allows a programmer to define and access groups of subroutines, functions, and/or pictures. Several libraries can be found on your *True BASIC* disk. An option is creating your own. For example, you might develop libraries of game playing routines, statistical functions, graphics routines, shapes, sounds, or tunes. Once stored in a library, your subroutines, functions, or pictures can be inserted into any program. Why reinvent the wheel? Build a module once, put it in a library, and use it over and over again.

Creating a Library

Using existing libraries can save a great deal of time and effort, but the general purpose routines they often contain may not exactly match your needs. If that's the case, build a custom library. For example, imagine that we plan to develop programs to play a variety of card games. Certain tasks, such as dealing cards and organizing a hand, are common to most games. Thus, we'll define subroutines to perform those tasks, and use them in all the programs.

A *True BASIC* library consists of an **EXTERNAL** statement *(Fig. 12.1)* followed by any number of modules. You can mix functions, subroutines, and pictures in the same library. The routines can be stored in source or compiled form. When a library is accessed, its members are added to a program after the **END** statement; in other words, they are external. If the library contains functions, don't forget to declare them in the main program.

Figure 12.2 shows a library of card-playing subroutines. Start at the top and read the description of its contents. It contains routines to pick a suit, pick a card, deal a card, deal a hand, and organize a hand into sequence. Read through the subroutines. In particular, look at **Deal_a_card** and **Deal_a_hand**. Note that they call other library members. Once defined, a library's members can be used as building blocks.

Creating a library is similar to creating a program. Start with a **NEW** command. Type an **EXTERNAL** statement. Then code the necessary comments, **SUB, DEF, PICTURE,** and **END** statements, and executable instructions. After entering the members, assign the library a name and **SAVE** it.

Accessing the Library

Accessing a library is easy. To illustrate, we'll write a program to deal and display several cards. First, we'll call **Deal_a_card**. Then, we'll print the card, loop back, and deal and display another one.

Fig. 12.1: *A library begins with an **EXTERNAL** statement. Complete subroutines, functions, and/or pictures follow the **EXTERNAL** statement.*

```
EXTERNAL
SUB  subroutine1 (...)
   ___
   ___
   ___
END SUB
DEF function1 (...)
   ___
   ___
   ___
END DEF
PICTURE picture1 (...)
   ___
   ___
   ___
END PICTURE
   .
   .
   .
```

Fig. 12.2: *This library contains a series of subroutines that deal and arrange playing cards. Continued on next page.*

```
EXTERNAL
REM ****************************************************************
REM * This library contains a series of subroutines that generate   *
REM * playing card values. Subroutines include:                     *
REM *     1. Pick_a_suit (a$). Assigns a suit -- hearts, diamonds,  *
REM *        clubs, or spades -- to a card.                         *
REM *     2. Pick_a_card (a$, b). Assigns a value -- A, K, Q, J, etc.*
REM *        -- to a card. Returns a string value and a numeric value*
REM *        in the range 2 (duce) through 14 (Ace).                *
REM *     3. Deal_a_card (a$, b). Returns the value of a single card*
REM *        both as a string (value, suit) and as a numeric value. *
REM *     4. Deal_a_hand (a$(), b(), n). Returns arrays containing n*
REM *        card values. Array a$ holds the string values of the   *
REM *        cards. Array b holds numeric values (2-14).            *
REM *     5. Organize_hand (a$(), b(), n). Sorts n "cards" into     *
REM *        numeric order. Array a$ holds the cards' string values.*
REM *        Array b holds their numeric values. Sorting is done on *
REM *        array b. Values are returned ace high.                 *
REM ****************************************************************
```

```
SUB Pick_a_suit (a$)            ! Subroutine to select a suit: "Hearts",
                                 ! "Diamonds", "Clubs", or "Spades".
  LET n = Int(Rnd * 4 + 1)       ! Select random integer between 1 and 4.
  SELECT CASE n
    CASE 1
      LET a$ = "Hearts"
    CASE 2
      LET a$ = "Diamonds"
    CASE 3
      LET a$ = "Clubs"
    CASE 4
      LET a$ = "Spades"
  END SELECT
END SUB

                                 ! Subroutine to select a card. Returns
                                 ! "A", "K", "Q", "J", or a string
                                 ! numeric value (2-10). Also returns a
SUB Pick_a_card (a$, b)          ! number between 2 and 14.

  LET b = Int(Rnd *13 +1) + 1    ! Select random number between 2 and 14.
  SELECT CASE b
    CASE 14
      LET a$ = "A"
    CASE 13
      LET a$ = "K"
    CASE 12
      LET a$ = "Q"
    CASE 11
      LET a$ = "J"
    CASE ELSE
      LET a$ = Str$(b)
  END SELECT
END SUB
```

Fig. 12.2, *Continued.*

Each library accessed by a program must be listed in a **LIBRARY** statement *(Fig. 12.3)*. The file names following the keyword must match the names under which the libraries are stored.* Code them as string constants enclosed in quotation marks. The subroutines, functions, and pictures contained in each specified library are gathered to form a pool of external modules.

Individual library members can contain **LIBRARY** statements of their own. If they do, the lower-level libraries are added to the pool. Be careful, though.

*The rules for defining file names vary with the computer; check your User's Guide for details. The string constants you specify are passed, without change, to your system's control program.

```
                              ! Subroutine to deal a single card. The card
                              ! value is returned both as a string and as
                              ! a number.
SUB Deal_a_card (a$,b)
  CALL Pick_a_card (card$, b)
  CALL Pick_a_suit (suit$)
  LET a$ = card$ & " of " & suit$
END SUB
                              ! Subroutine to deal a hand of n cards. The
                              ! card values are returned as strings (array
                              ! a$), and as numbers (array b).
SUB Deal_a_hand (a$(), b(), n)
  FOR i = 1 TO n
    CALL Deal_a_card (a$(i), b(i))
  NEXT i
END SUB
                              ! Subroutine to sort a hand of n cards
                              ! into numeric order. Array a$ holds cards'
                              ! string values. Array b holds cards'
                              ! numeric values. Sort is on array b. Arrays
                              ! returned ace high.
SUB Organize_hand (a$(), b(), n)
  FOR i = 1 TO (n-1)
    FOR j = (i+1) TO n
      IF b(i) < b(j) THEN
        LET temp = b(i)
        LET temp2$ = a$(i)
        LET b(i) = b(j)
        LET a$(i) = a$(j)
        LET b(j) = temp
        LET a$(j) = temp2$
      END IF
    NEXT j
  NEXT i
END SUB
```

Fig. 12.2, *Continued.*

Fig. 12.3: *To access a library, include a **LIBRARY** statement in the main program.*

```
LIBRARY "filename1" , "filename2" , ...
                 └─────One or more file names.
```

Each member of the pool must have a unique name.

Figure 12.4 shows the program. Read through it carefully. The **LIBRARY** statement comes first. When you run the program, the library is read from disk. Because we stored it in source form, its statements must be compiled. If compilation errors are detected in any library module (whether it's called or not), you'll get an error message.

Assuming the program compiles, it will begin running. The first step inside the loop calls a subroutine. Then the card value returned by the subroutine is printed, and the loop repeats. Run the program. When you do, you might see some unusual results. For example, it is possible to get the same card twice. Card suits and card values are generated by a random number function, and random numbers can repeat. To avoid this problem, define another subroutine to keep track of the cards already dealt. Probably the best way to track cards is to maintain an array. To "shuffle" the deck, initialize the array. Arrays are discussed in Chapter 8.

An array can also be used to hold a hand of cards. After dealing a hand, write the logic to implement the rules of a particular card game. Another possibility is adding graphics. Write a picture to draw a card. Then, using transformations, plot card images in different positions and add the card values.

Fig. 12.4: *All libraries accessed by a program must be listed in a **LIBRARY** statement. This program accesses the card subroutine library of Fig. 12.2.*

```
                        ! This program accesses the card playing
                        ! library and simulates dealing five cards.

 LIBRARY "cardsubs"     ! Several subroutines in the "cardsubs"
                        ! library are accessed.
 RANDOMIZE

 FOR n = 1 TO 5         ! Five cards will be dealt and their
                        ! values printed.

    CALL Deal_a_card (card$, value)

    PRINT card$, value

 NEXT n

 END

Ok, run
Q of Spades      12
9 of Spades       9
10 of Diamonds   10
Q of Diamonds    12
A of Spades      14
Ok.
```

Subroutine name	Function
frame	Frames a window.
axes	Draws a set of x-y axes.
ticks(x,y)	Draws a set of x-y axes with "ticks" or marks x (x-axis) and y (y-axis) units apart.
polygon (x1,x2,y1,y2,n)	Draws an n-sided polygon inside the box defined by the x and y values.
bars(data() ,n)	Draws a bar chart of the data in array data.
arc(x,y,r,a1,a2)	Draws an arc with center x,y and radius r, between angles a1 and a2.
fplot(a,b)	Plots a function (which you define) from a to b.

Fig. 12.5: *The following subroutines can be found in a library named* **GRAPHLIB** *on your True BASIC disk. To see the subroutines, type* **OLD GRAPHLIB**.

Maintaining a Library

Libraries are not static. As you begin developing an application using a library's modules, you will probably think of new ones to add. You'll also want to correct, modify, and delete members. Fortunately, maintaining a library is easy.

To change an existing library, start by reading it into memory (an **OLD** command). Then make your changes, adding, deleting, and modifying code. When you finish, copy the new version back to disk (**REPLACE**).

Using Existing Libraries

Several libraries can be found on your *True BASIC* disk. **GAMESLIB** contains subroutines to roll a set of dice and to flip a coin. The graphic subroutines stored on **GRAPHLIB** are summarized in Fig. 12.5. A particularly time-consuming programming task is preparing menus to guide a user through a program's functions. The subroutines in **MENULIB** *(Fig. 12.6)* can help.

Four libraries contain computational functions stored in compiled form *(Fig. 12.7)*. Included are hyperbolic functions, trigonometric functions in radians, trigonometric functions in degrees, and mathematical functions. The file names are shown in IBM PC® form; see your *User's Guide* if you have a different computer. The function names are valid on any computer.

The functions stored in a library are added to a main program after the **END** statement—they are external. Thus they must be declared in the main program.

Subroutine name	Function
menu_set (. . .)	Create a menu
menu_show (. . .)	Display a menu.
menu_ask (. . .)	Get user response.
menu (. . .)	Display menu and get response.
menu_all (. . .)	Create, display, and get response.

Fig. 12.6: *The following subroutines can be found in a library named **MENULIB** on your True BASIC disk. To see the subroutines, type **OLD MENULIB**. Because these subroutines have so many parameters, we won't list them all here.*

In addition to the libraries themselves, a set of associated **DECLARE** statements can be found on your *True BASIC* disk. The second column in Fig. 12.7 lists the name of each library's **DECLARE**. To add it to your program, type the **LIBRARY** statement first, and then issue an **INCLUDE** command. For example, if you're using an IBM PC and you want to access the mathematical functions, type

    LIBRARY "FNMLIB.TRC"

as the first statement in your program, and press enter. Then drop back to the history window and type

    INCLUDE FNM

The statement

    DECLARE DEF logbase, erf, normal, factrl, . . .

will appear immediately after the **LIBRARY** statement. Note *(Fig. 12.7, again)* that the names assigned to the **DECLARE** statements match the first characters in the associated library name.

    Because *True BASIC* uses standard linkage conventions, most existing subroutines, even those written in other languages, can be added to a *True BASIC* program. Linking modules written in different languages requires a knowledge

Library	Include	Function	Returns
FNHLIB.TRC	FNH	Sinh (a) Cosh (a) Tanh (a) Coth (a) Sech (a) Csch (a) Asinh (a) Acosh (a) Atanh (a) Acoth (a) Asech (a) Acsch (a)	Hyperbolic sine of a. Hyperbolic cosine of a. Hyperbolic tangent of a. Hyperbolic cotangent of a. Hyperbolic secant of a. Hyperbolic cosecant of a. Hyperbolic arcsine of a. Hyperbolic arccosine of a. Hyperbolic arctangent of a. Hyperbolic arccotangen of a. Hyperbolic arcsecant of a. Hyperbolic arccosecant of a.
FNTLIB.TRC	FNT	Cot (a) Sec (a) Csc (a) Asine (a) Acos (a) Acot (a) Asec (a) Acsc (a)	Cotangent of a. Secant of a. Cosecant of a. Arcsine of a. Arccosine of a. Arccotangent of a. Arcsecant of a. Arccosecant of a.
FNTDLIB.TRC	FNTD	Cot (a) Sec (a) Csc (a) Asine (a) Acos (a) Acot (a) Asec (a) Acsc (a)	Cotangent of a. Secant of a. Cosecant of a. Arcsine of a. Arccosine of a. Arccotangent of a. Arcsecant of a. Arccosecant of a.
FNMLIB.TRC	FNM	Logbase (x,b) Erf (x) Normal (a,b) Norm1 (x) Factrl (n) Binom(n,j,p) Binompr (n,j,p) Poisson (m,j)	Log of x to the base b. Error function: Erf (x) = 2*Norm1 (Sqr(2) * x) Area under the normal curve from a to b. Area under the normal curve from 0 to x. n factorial. Binomial coefficient. Binomial distribution. Poisson Distribution.

Fig. 12.7: *Your True BASIC disk also holds a number of computational functions. The functions are added after the main program's **END** statement (they are external). Thus they must be declared. Each "include" file listed below contains a **DECLARE** statement listing all the functions in the associated file.*

of data formats, an advanced topic we won't cover. However, you should know that the ability to access a vast pool of existing scientific, statistical, and graphic subroutines is a powerful feature.

CHAINING

It's sometimes necessary to create a series of related programs and run them in sequence. Some applications are so large they won't fit in main memory. Instead of buying a bigger computer, break the logic into smaller programs, and load and execute them one by one. Other programs contain routines that are needed only occasionally. A good technique is writing a separate program to house the rarely needed logic, and loading it when necessary.

Checkpoints represent yet another reason to spread logic over two or more related programs. When an application processes a great deal of data, or performs time-consuming computations, it makes sense to stop occasionally, write the data to a disk file, and then resume processing in a new program. That interruption is called a checkpoint. Without checkpoints, if a power failure or other problem causes the computer to "go down," all the work is lost. With them, processing can resume with the most recent checkpoint, so only a portion of the work is lost.

Security controls are often implemented by shifting sensitive logic to a separate program. For example, a payroll program might be designed to output formatted check data to a file. A separate program then asks for proper authorization and ensures that the correct check forms are loaded on the printer before printing the checks.

Most computer centers maintain utility programs to perform such common functions as sorting a file, or generating a backup copy of a file. Whenever one of these standard functions is called for, it makes sense simply to use the utility. For example, an inventory application might call for screening transactions, sorting the transactions, and updating the inventory file. Thus, three programs must run in sequence.

Finally, there is the problem of related systems. In a business environment, few applications stand alone. For example, the total value of the checks printed by a payroll program is an important expenditure that must be entered on the firm's ledger. The ledger is updated by another program. Thus, output generated by payroll may be input to general ledger. Rather than risk a clerical error, it makes sense to link the two programs, and update the ledger immediately.

Programs are linked by **CHAIN** statements *(Fig. 12.8)*. The basic form of a **CHAIN** statement contains only the keyword and a program name. When it is executed, the current program stops, its memory space is freed, and the named program is read from disk and given control. An alternate form allows an argument to be passed to the new program. The string **arg$** can contain a single value, or, with packing *(see Chapters 10 and 11)*, several values.

Note that when a **CHAIN** statement is executed, the program that was in memory is gone. You can't return to it. However, *True BASIC* does support a return

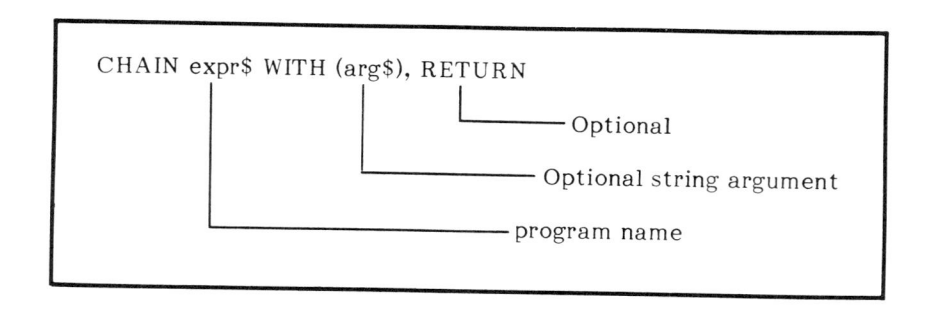

```
CHAIN expr$ WITH (arg$), RETURN
                                │
                                └── Optional
                         │
                         └── Optional string argument
      │
      └── program name
```

Fig. 12.8: *A CHAIN statement is used to transfer control from one program to another. Options include a string argument and RETURN.*

option. If **RETURN** is coded, the **CHAIN** statement becomes, in effect, a **CALL** statement. The original program remains in memory. The chained program is read into memory and given control. When it ends, control goes back to the instruction immediately following **CHAIN**. This option is particularly valuable when a utility program's functions are needed as part of another program.

Although a single string can be passed from one program to another, passing parameters is not as important as it is with subroutines. More often, the first program generates an output file that is read by the second one. In effect, the intermediate file serves to pass data between the programs.

Any program invoked by a **CHAIN** statement must begin with a **PROGRAM** statement *(Fig. 12.9)*. The name following the keyword must be a valid variable name. (It's ignored, but it must be there.) Use the program's name. The string variable in the alternate form holds the string passed by the **CHAIN** statement.

Chaining programs is an advanced topic; thus, no example will be presented.

Fig. 12.9: *A program that is invoked by a CHAIN statement must begin with a PROGRAM statement.*

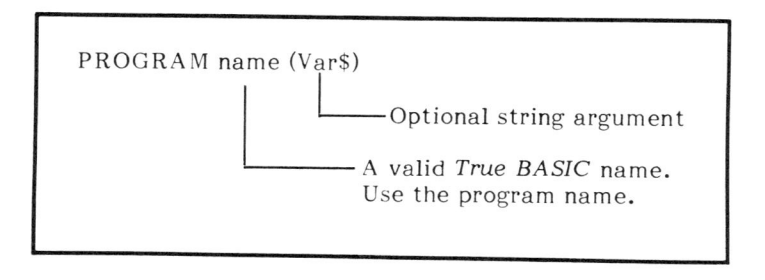

```
PROGRAM name (Var$)
              │
              └── Optional string argument
     │
     └── A valid True BASIC name.
         Use the program name.
```

RECURSION

True BASIC supports recursion. A recursive module is defined in terms of itself (for example, a subroutine, function, or picture that calls itself). Recursion can yield simple, elegant solutions to certain complex problems.

Let's use an example to illustrate. A number's factorial is the product of all integers less than it; for example, 5! is 5*4*3*2*1, and 4! is 4*3*2*1. Note that we can write 5! as 5*4!. More generally, we can define the factorial of any number as

$$n! = n * (n-1)!$$

A mathematician would say that n! is defined inductively.

Figure 12.10 shows a function that computes a factorial recursively. Focus on the second **LET** statement

LET Factorial = n * Factorial (n-1)

Fig. 12.10: *This program features a recursive factorial function.*

```
                              ! Program to illustrate recursion.
DECLARE DEF Factorial
INPUT n
PRINT n, Factorial(n)
END

                              ! Subroutine to compute a factorial recursively.
DEF Factorial (n)
   IF n <= 1 THEN             ! 0! and 1! both equal 1.
      LET Factorial = 1
   ELSE
      LET Factorial = n * Factorial (n-1)
   END IF
END DEF

Q of Diamonds    12
A of Spades      14
Ok. old recfact
Ok. run
? 13
  13          6227020800
Ok.
```

Relate it to the inductive definition of n! developed above. Do you see that **Factorial** calls or invokes itself? That makes it recursive.

Because **Factorial** uses no local variables, it could be an internal function. That's dangerous, however. If you plan to code recursive functions, subroutines, or pictures, define them externally. With external modules, local variables are reset and local **DATA** statements restored each time the module is invoked.

If you are mathematically inclined, consider recursion for any function that is defined inductively. With a little thought, recursive calls can replace many iterative loops. If you continue your computer science studies, you may eventually encounter a course in compiler design, where recursion is a particularly important tool.

Incidentally, you may wonder why recursion is grouped with libraries and chaining. Frankly, it belongs with subroutines and functions; we should have covered it in Chapter 6. However, Part I was aimed at the true beginning, and recursion is an advanced topic. It doesn't fit with the other chapters in Part II, either, but because they are longer than Chapter 12, recursion appears here.

SUMMARY

A *True BASIC* library is a collection of subroutines, functions, and/or pictures. Libraries are created just like programs. Each library must begin with an **EXTERNAL** statement, and may contain any combination of functions, subroutines, and pictures. We used a library of card-playing subroutines as an illustration.

A program that accesses a library must contain a **LIBRARY** statement. One or more file names, coded as string constants, follow the keyword **LIBRARY**. When the program is run, the modules in the referenced library are read into memory and grouped after the **END** statement, making them external; thus functions must be declared in the main program. To illustrate accessing a library, we wrote a program to simulate dealing several cards by taking advantage of the subroutines created earlier.

To maintain a library, read the old version into memory (an **OLD** command), modify it, and write it back to disk (**REPLACE**). Our coverage of libraries ended with a brief overview of several existing *True BASIC* libraries.

Next we turned to the **CHAIN** statement. There are several reasons for executing two or more programs in sequence. A **CHAIN** statement transfers control to a new program. We briefly considered the program name, an optional string argument, and the **RETURN** option.

The chapter ended with a discussion of recursion. A recursive routine is one that calls itself; we wrote a factorial function to illustrate.

REFERENCES

True BASIC Statements

EXTERNAL	Fig. 12.1, page 343
LIBRARY	Fig. 12.3, page 345
CHAIN	Fig. 12.8, page 351
PROGRAM	Fig. 12.9, page 351

EXERCISES

1. Develop your own library of sounds *(see Chapter 10)*.

2. Develop your own library of musical tunes *(see Chapter 10)*.

3. Develop a library of functions, subroutines, or pictures to support tasks common to your major or your profession.

4. Enter the card-playing library *(Fig. 12.2)* and store it on your computer.

5. Using the library created in Exercise 4, write a program to play a game of high-low, or "acey-ducy."

6. Using the library created in Exercise 4, write a program to play a game of blackjack, or 21.

7. Using the library created in Exercise 4, write a program to play solitaire.

8. Using the library created in Exercise 4, write a program to play a game of gin against the computer.

9. If you're really ambitious, use the library created in Exercise 4 and write a program to simulate a game of bridge.

10. Write a **PICTURE** to display a card image on the screen. Add it to the card-playing library *(Exercise 4)*. Then write a program to deal a hand of cards and graphically display them.

11. Create a library of flowchart shapes. Then write a program to display them and draw a flowchart.

12. Expand Exercise 11. Include, in a secondary window, a set of sample flowchart shapes (icons). Use a **GET POINT** statement to allow a user to select a symbol by "pointing to it." Then, draw the shape in the "next" block of the primary window.

13. Create a library of word processing functions such as word count, search and replace, compress, and so on. Then use them to write a small word processing program.

14. Develop a library of subroutines to pack and unpack numbers and strings into or from a record.

15. Chapter 11, Exercise 15 asked you to output formatted check data to a record file, and then print them in a subsequent program. Chain to that program.

16. Fibonacci numbers are defined by the relationship

$$F_{n+1} = F_n + F_{n-1} \text{ if } n > 0$$

where the first two numbers are 1, 1. Design a recursive function that accepts a positive integer n and returns the nth Fibonacci number.

17. Check the program **HANOI** on your *True BASIC* disk. It's an interesting example of recursion.

PART III

Tools and Techniques

A. *True BASIC and the IBM PC*

B. *The True BASIC Editor*

C. *Flowcharting*

D. *Error Handling and Debugging*

E. *True BASIC and Traditional Basic*

Learning to program involves more than just learning a language. Although the focus of this primer is True BASIC, a programmer must know how to plan, enter, and debug a program, and these skills are language independent. Part III presents a series of brief tutorials and reference materials on specific tools and techniques related to True BASIC and to programming in general. We will refer to these modules throughout the text.

Module A

True BASIC and the IBM PC

In this module, we will explore how True BASIC is implemented on an IBM PC® or compatible computer. We'll consider key hardware features, discuss the process of preparing a True BASIC disk, explain how files are saved and retrieved through PC/DOS®, and outline IBM's display modes and available colors. Our objective is to cover True BASIC features unique to the IBM PC®. Refer to your User's Guide for more detailed information.

THE IBM PC

Figure A.1 shows the components of a typical IBM Personal Computer system. The heart of the system is the cabinet located near the center of the picture. Inside it are the processor, main memory, and interface boards for the various input and output devices. The standard input device is a keyboard; the standard output device is a display unit. To the right is an optional printer.

In the front of the cabinet are two diskette drives. Conventionally, the one on the left is the A-drive, or system drive, and the one on the right is the B-drive. When the computer is turned on, the hardware is designed to look for its first program in the A-drive. If your system has only one drive, that's your A-drive. Many computer systems are equipped with a hard disk which can be designated A, B, C, or D. Special instructions may be needed; see your *User's Guide* for details.

Some IBM PCs are equipped with a monochrome screen. Such systems can display characters, but not graphics. To generate graphic output, your monitor must be linked to the system through a graphics card, a set of electronic circuits that plugs into a slot inside the cabinet. If you don't have one and you try to run a graphics program, you'll get an error message. A graphics card can be added to most IBM PCs; check with the people who sold you your computer.

Before you start to work with an IBM PC, it's important that you learn the keyboard *(Fig. A.2)*. Although similar to a standard typewriter keyboard, there are differences. Ignore the numeric keypad for a moment, and start near the upper right. The left-pointing arrow in the top row is a backspace key. Press it, and the most recently typed character is erased. Move down to the "bent" left-pointing arrow. That's the enter key. Directly below it is a key marked *PrtSc/**. Press it and you type an asterisk. Just to its left is a shift key. It shifts the character keys from lower to upper case. If you press the shift key and the *PrtSc* key simultaneously, whatever is currently displayed on your screen

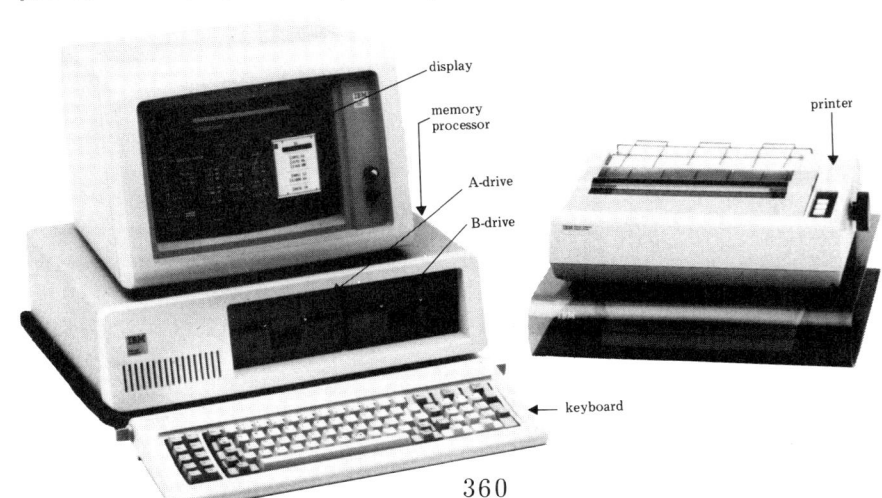

Fig. A.1: *A typical IBM Personal Computer system.*

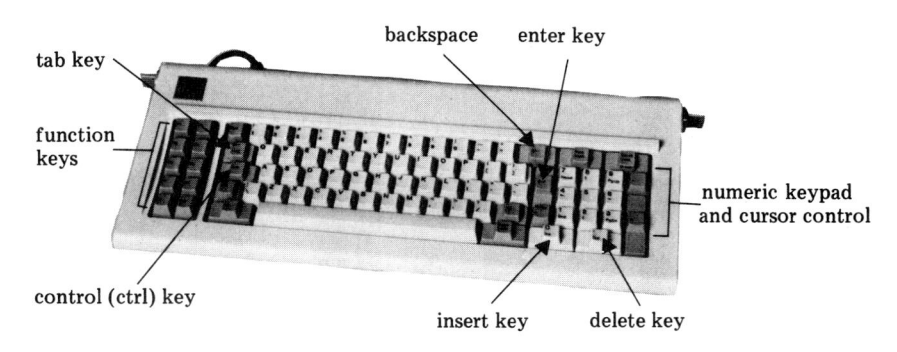

Fig. A.2: *Before starting to work with an IBM PC, take the time to familiarize yourself with the keyboard.*

is copied to the printer. Pressing *Shift-PrtSc* is a good way to get a quick listing of a limited amount of material.

Directly below the shift key is the *Caps Lock* key. Normally, pressing *A* yields a lower-case a, while pressing *Shift-A* yields a capital A. However, if you press *Caps Lock* first, the *A* key will generate a capital A, while *Shift-A* will generate a lower-case letter. Nonalphabetic keys are not affected; for example, the numeric keys in the top row will still generate digits, and not punctuation marks. The *Caps Lock* key works like a switch. Press it once, and all the alphabetic keys generate capital letters. Press it again, and they generate lower-case letters.

Move across the space bar to the left of the keyboard. The *Alt* (or alternate) key is used in combination with selected keys to change their meaning; it's rarely used in *True BASIC*. Directly above it is another shift key. Then comes the *Ctrl* (or control) key. Like the *Alt* key, it is used in combination with other keys; read Module B, "The *True BASIC* Editor," for several examples. Above the *Ctrl* key is the tab key. Press it, and *True BASIC*'s editor advances the cursor to the start of the next word. Press shift and tab together, and the cursor is moved back to the start of the last word. Directly above the tab key is the *Esc* (escape) key. In many applications, *Esc* is used to interrupt a running program.

To the left of the main keyboard are ten function keys labeled *F1* through *F10*. In *True BASIC*, the function keys are used in place of certain commands; for example, to run a program, you can type **RUN** or simply press *F9*. Figure A.3 shows the meanings assigned to an IBM PC's function keys.

To the right of the keyboard is a numeric keypad. Normally, these keys control the cursor. Focus on the keys numbered 1 through 9. Arrows are printed on 2, 4, 6, and 8; they move the cursor down, left, right, and up, respectively. Key 1 (*End*) moves the cursor to the end of a program; key 7 (*Home*) moves it to the beginning. Key 3 moves down a page (*PgDn*), while key 9 moves up a page (*PgUp*). At the bottom of the numeric keypad are the insert (*Ins*) and delete (*Del*) keys. *Del* deletes a single character. Like *Caps Lock*, *Ins* works like a switch. Normally,

Function Key	Meaning
F1	Move cursor to editing window.
F2	Move cursor to history window.
F3	FIND
F4	MARK
F5	COPY
F6	MOVE
F7	RESTORE
F8	Unassigned
F9	RUN
F10	HELP

Fig. A.3: *True BASIC assigns the following meanings to an IBM PC's function keys.*

True BASIC functions in insert mode, with new characters added in front of existing characters. Press *Ins*, and *True BASIC* switches to overstrike mode, with new characters replacing old ones. Press *Ins* again, and you're back in insert mode.

At the top of the keypad is the *Num Lock* key. It's another switch. Press it, and the numeric keypad no longer controls the cursor. Instead, it becomes a numeric keypad, generating numbers, a decimal point, and computational signs. Press it again, and the keypad reverts to cursor control. Incidentally, pressing a shift key and one of the numeric keypad keys generates a digit.

At the keyboard's upper left is a key marked *Scroll Lock* and *Break*. *Scroll Lock* is inactive; it's really a *Break* key. If you press *Crtl-Break*, the current program stops running. Use *Ctrl-Break* to terminate an out-of-control program.

PREPARING YOUR *TRUE BASIC* DISK

The standard *True BASIC* package contains a *Reference Manual*, a *User's Guide*, a function key template, and a disk which holds your master copy of the compiler. Don't risk that disk. Always work with a copy. That way, if anything happens to your work disk, you can prepare a new one. Lose the original, however, and you've lost *True BASIC*.

Fortunately, making a copy is easy. Two steps are involved. First, the *True BASIC* master disk is copied, without change, to a work disk. Next, key operating system routines are added to the copy. The computer can't execute programs unless certain key operating system routines are in main memory. Normally, in a process known as booting, these key routines are read into memory when the computer is turned on. Adding these operating system routines to the *True BASIC* work disk makes it self-booting.

Why aren't the operating system routines included on your *True BASIC* disk? Why must you copy them? Basically because the operating system, PC/DOS, belongs to IBM Corporation, and distributing portions of it is a violation of federal copyright laws. Thus, you must purchase PC/DOS and add key routines to the *True BASIC* work disk.

Copying *True BASIC*

The first step in copying *True BASIC* is loading the operation system (PC/DOS, release 2.0 or higher). Slide the operating system disk into drive A, and turn on the computer. You'll experience a slight delay as the computer checks its circuits. Then a message will appear asking you to enter the date *(Fig. A.4)*. Respond with the current date. Next you'll be asked to enter the time. Following a brief copyright statement, an *A>* prompt will appear (see the last line in Fig. A.4); the system is waiting for you to issue a command.

Must you enter the date and the time? No. The system generates a default date and time; if you simply press enter in response to each request, the defaults are accepted. However, whenever a file is stored on disk, the operating system records the date and time, and you may someday find this information valuable. Also, *True BASIC* contains functions to get the current date and time from the system, and they won't return valid results unless you set the date and time cor-

Fig. A.4: *The first step in creating a True BASIC work disk is loading the operating system, PC/DOS, release 2.0 or higher.*

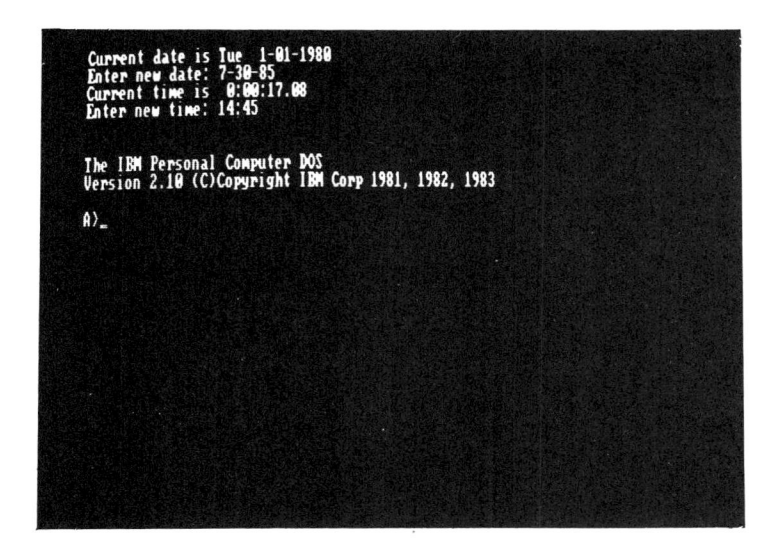

```
Current date is Tue  1-01-1980
Enter new date: 7-30-85
Current time is  0:00:17.08
Enter new time: 14:45

The IBM Personal Computer DOS
Version 2.10 (C)Copyright IBM Corp 1981, 1982, 1983

A>_
```

rectly. It's a good idea to enter the current date and at least estimate the current time.

The next step is copying the *True BASIC* master disk to a work disk. Type the command

>   *A>*diskcopy a: b:

It says to copy the disk in drive A to the disk in drive B; use any combination of upper and lower case letters. As soon as you press enter, a message will appear on your screen *(Fig. A.5)*. The *True BASIC* master disk is your source disk; insert it in drive A. Then, insert a blank disk in drive B and press any key. The copy process will begin. When the copy is made, you'll be asked if you want to make another. Type N, for no.

What if you make a mistake and insert the *True BASIC* disk in drive B? Will you destroy its contents? No. Look at the *True BASIC* master disk, and compare it to a work disk. The work disk should contain a notch near the upper right. Cover that notch with a piece of tape, and the disk is write-protected; in other words, you can't write to it. Remove the tape, and you *can* write to the disk, destroying its old contents. The *True BASIC* disk has no notch. It is *always*

Fig. A.5: *Use a* **diskcopy** *function to copy the True BASIC master disk to a work disk.*

```
Enter new date: 7-30-85
Current time is 0:00:17.08
Enter new time: 14:45

The IBM Personal Computer DOS
Version 2.10 (C)Copyright IBM Corp 1981, 1982, 1983

A)diskcopy a: b:

Insert source diskette in drive A:

Insert target diskette in drive B:

Strike any key when ready

Copying 9 sectors per track, 2 side(s)

Copy complete

Copy another (Y/N)?n
Insert COMMAND.COM disk in drive A
and strike any key when ready

A)_
```

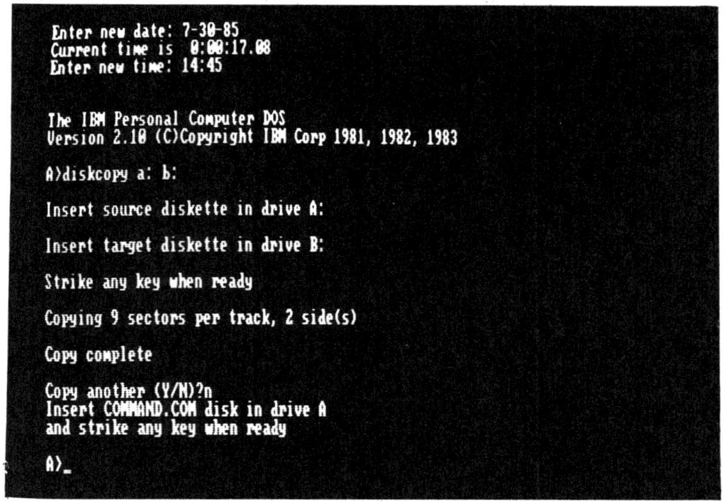

write-protected. You can't write to it. If you insert the *True BASIC* disk in the wrong drive, you'll get an error message, and you'll have to start over, but you can't destroy the disk's contents.

What if you have only one disk drive? You'll have to switch disks several times. After typing the **diskcopy** command, load the *True BASIC* master disk first. A portion of the disk's contents will be read into main memory. Then you'll be asked to insert the target disk; simply remove *True BASIC* and insert your work disk. The source, *True BASIC*, will be called drive A; the target, your work disk, will be called drive B. Just follow the instructions, switching disks when a message tells you to. If you make a mistake the worst that can happen is that you'll have to start over—*True BASIC* is write-protected.

When you've finished copying *True BASIC*, you'll be asked if you want to make another copy. Respond by typing N. A system prompt will appear on the next line; once again, the system is waiting for you to issue a command. Remove your *True BASIC* disk and put it in a safe place; you won't need it again until you decide to make another copy. Remove your work disk and label it.

Adding the Operating System

Now you're ready to add key operating system modules. If you have two drives, insert the operating system into drive A, and the *True BASIC* work disk you just created into drive B. Then type

    *A>***b:install**

This command tells the system to run a program named **install**. The **b:** indicates that the program is found on the disk in drive B (your *True BASIC* work copy). A series of messages will describe the system's progress *(Fig. A.6)*. When the operation is finished, your work copy of *True BASIC* is ready to use. Put your operating system disk away; you won't need it anymore.

What if you have only one drive? Start with the drive empty. Then type the same install command (**b:install**). A message will tell you to insert a diskette for drive B. Insert your *True BASIC* work disk, and press any key. Then, follow the instructions and swap disks. When the system references drive A, it wants the operating system. When it references drive B, it wants the *True BASIC* work disk. Keep swapping disks until you get two *A>* prompts in succession. When that happens, put your operating system disk away.

Loading *True BASIC*

Just to be sure you've prepared your *True BASIC* work disk correctly, insert it into drive A. Then, simultaneously hold down three keys: *Ctrl*, *Alt*, and *Del* (you'll need both hands to do it). Whatever is displayed on your screen should

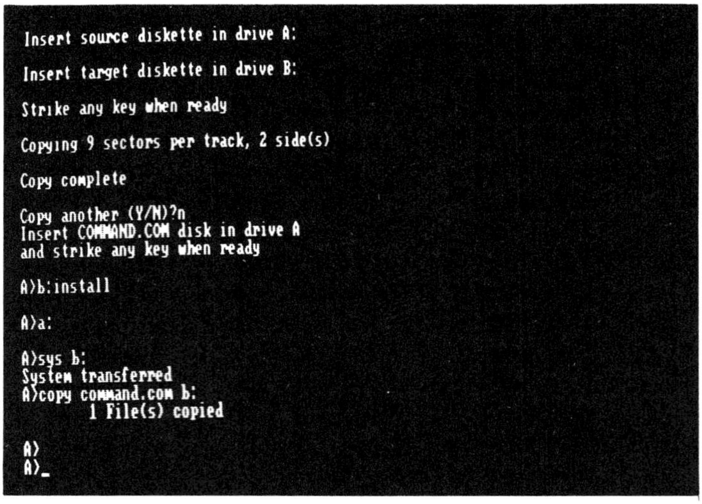

Fig. A.6: *Once you've created a work copy of True BASIC, use the **install** routine to add key operating system modules. When you are finished, your True BASIC work disk is ready to use.*

disappear. A few seconds later, you'll be asked to enter the date and the time. Next, you'll get a system prompt. Respond by typing

    *A>***HELLO**

using any combination of upper and lower case characters *(Fig. A.7)*. A few seconds later, the standard *True BASIC* screen should appear *(Fig. A.8)*. At this point, you can begin using *True BASIC*. When you finish, type **BYE**, and the operating system's prompt (*A>*) will reappear.

SAVING AND RETRIEVING FILES

True BASIC does not directly store or retrieve files. Instead, the language relies on the operating system to perform these functions. Thus the rules for accessing a file are defined not by *True BASIC* but by PC/DOS. File references in *True BASIC* commands or instructions are simply passed to the operating system, without change.

    Fortunately, accessing files under PC/DOS is relatively easy. Each file is assigned a name. A valid file name consists of from 1 to 8 letters, digits, and/or

Fig. A.7: *To test your work disk, insert it into drive A and press Ctrl-Alt-Del. After typing the date and the time, respond to the operating system's A> prompt by typing HELLO.*

Fig. A.8: *Shortly after you issue a HELLO command, True BASIC's standard windows should appear on your screen.*

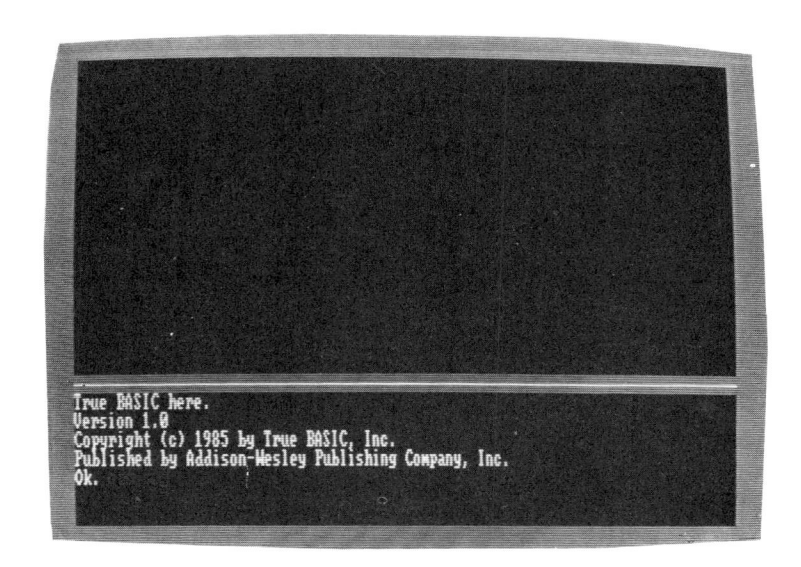

the following special characters: $ # & @ ! % ( ) - { } ' _ '. Lower-case letters are translated to upper case. A three-character extension can be used to distinguish files of different types. If you omit the extension, *True BASIC* assigns **.TRU** to source files and **.TRC** to compiled programs. Thus, the source version of **PGMA** is stored under the name **PGMA.TRU**, while a compiled version of the same program is **PGMA.TRC**.

By default, your A-drive is always active. Thus, if you code

    SAVE program1

PROGRAM1.TRU is saved on the disk in your A drive. Unless you specify otherwise, **SAVE, UNSAVE, REPLACE, INCLUDE,** and **FILES** refer to drive A.

What if you want your programs stored on a separate work disk? After starting *True BASIC*, remove the *True BASIC* disk from drive A and insert a work disk. Future commands will refer to files on the work disk. Be careful, though. Your *True BASIC* disk holds numerous standard libraries and the **HELP** feature. A better idea is keeping the *True BASIC* disk on line and inserting your work disk only when needed.

If you have two drives, use them. Insert your *True BASIC* disk in drive A, and a work disk in drive B. If you want a program or a file from the disk in drive B, precede its name with a **b:** prefix; for example, type

    b:program1

to get **program1** from drive B. Note that the program's name is still **program1**. The **b:** prefix identifies the drive, not the program. If the disk containing **program1** were loaded in drive A, you could get it by coding

    program1

To display a list of the files and programs stored on the disk in your A-drive, type

    FILES

To see the names of the files and programs stored on the disk in your B-drive, code

FILES b:

Once again, the **b:** refers to drive B.

Any file name that is legal under PC/DOS is legal under *True BASIC*. The specified file name is passed directly to the operating system, without change. You can even use directory names, a powerful PC/DOS feature that we won't get into here.

A file name valid on an IBM PC may not be valid on a different computer, but file names that start with a letter and consist of no more than eight letters and digits are legal on most systems. We'll use such restricted file names throughout this primer.

SCREEN MODES AND COLORS

If your computer is equipped with an IBM monochrome display, *True BASIC* operates in **MONO** mode. 256 different characters can be displayed, 80 to a line, but graphics and color are not supported. If your display is linked to the system via a color graphics card, a variety of modes is available. Conventionally, mode **"80"** is used when graphics are not needed. Under mode **"80"**, you get 256 different characters displayed 80 to a line. If your monitor is a standard television set, use mode **"40"** to generate legible characters--you'll get only 40 per line, but they'll be larger. You can set foreground and background colors in mode **"80"** or mode **"40"**.

If you're working in any of the text modes, you can have your IBM PC output blinking characters. Simply add a third option to the **SET COLOR** statement:

    SET COLOR "foreground/background/BLINK"

Most plotting is done in **GRAPHICS** mode. The resolution is 320 x 200 pixels. **PLOT TEXT** statements can display 128 different characters, 40 per line. A full complement of foreground and background colors can be used. In **HIRES** (high resolution) mode, the resolution is increased to 640 x 200 pixels, and 80 characters are displayed per line. The character set is, however, still limited to 128 characters, and only one foreground color can be defined against a black background. High resolution generates sharper graphics, but plotting speed is slower, and the appearance of some shapes can be affected.

You can set the mode by coding

    SET MODE expr$

Color Number	Color Name	Meaning
0	"black"	black
1	"blue"	blue
2	"green"	green
3	"cyan"	cyan (cyano--dark blue)
4	"red"	red
5	"magenta"	magenta
6	"brown"	brown (or yellow)
7	"white"	white
8		gray
9		bright blue
10		bright green
11		bright cyan
12		bright red
13		bright magenta
14	"yellow"	yellow (or brown)
15		bright white

Fig. A.9: *Unless **MONO** mode is used, the True BASIC programmer can choose from the following foreground and background colors on an IBM PC.*

If you aren't sure what mode you're in, code

ASK MODE expr$

Normally, it makes sense to accept *True BASIC*'s default modes.

Unless you are in **MONO** mode, you can use color, selecting foreground and background colors from the list shown in Fig. A.9. Use **SET COLOR** to set the foreground color and **SET BACK** to select a background color. Note that colors can be specified by name or by number. In **GRAPHICS** mode, you can use more than one foreground color concurrently. On an IBM PC, however, you are restricted to one of two "palettes" *(Fig. A.10)*. If you start with colors from one palette, and then switch to a color in the other, every foreground color on the screen will change.

Fig. A.10: *On an IBM PC, a True BASIC programmer can choose one of two color "palettes" for the foreground.*

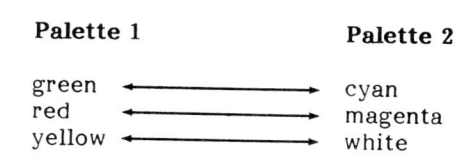

Palette 1		Palette 2
green	⟷	cyan
red	⟷	magenta
yellow	⟷	white

Module

B

The True BASIC Editor

True BASIC's editor greatly simplifies writing a program. This module introduces the editor, presenting a brief tutorial that guides you through entering, correcting, and running a simple program. Don't just read it. Instead, sit down with your personal computer and follow the steps. After the tutorial, several more advanced editing features are overviewed.

Before you begin, take time to review your keyboard. The IBM PC's keyboard is described in Module A. If you have a different type of computer, check your User's Guide or your system's reference manual. The tutorial assumes that your keyboard has function keys. If your system uses a mouse, point-and-select operations will probably replace the function keys. Again, check your User's Guide for details.

CREATING A PROGRAM

Sign on *True BASIC*. Once the standard editing and history windows appear, type a **NEW** command *(Fig. B.1)*, such as

NEW PAY

where **PAY** is the program's name. Press enter. The cursor should move to the top left corner of the editing window. Now you're ready to write instructions.

Before you do, however, experiment a bit with moving between the windows. Find your computer's function keys. Press key *F2*. The cursor should shift to the history window. Now press *F1*. The cursor should move back to the editing window. Move the cursor a few times to get used to the function keys.

Several instructions are listed in Fig. B.2. Make sure the cursor is in the editing window, and enter them. They contain intentional errors. Don't correct the errors; enter the statements as they appear. If you make an unintentional typing error, backspace to erase the character, and retype it. When you complete a statement, press the enter key. When you finish, your screen should look like Fig. B.3. Note the markers at the beginning of each line. They're called line tags, and we'll refer

Fig. B.1: *The first step in writing a program is typing a **NEW** command.*

```
          INPUT hours worked, pay_rate
          LET gross_pay = hours_worked * pay_rate
          LET federal_tax = gross_pay % 0.10
          state_tax = gross_pay * 0.025
          LET local_tax = gorss_pay * 0.015
          LET deductions = federal_tax + state_tax + local _tax
          LET net_pay = gross_pay - deductions
          PRINT net_pay
          END
```

Fig. B.2: *As you begin this tutorial, type the following True BASIC instructions. Four of the statements contain intentional errors. Don't correct them yet. Correcting the errors is part of the tutorial.*

to them throughout the chapter.

Correcting Errors

The editor allows you to correct errors anywhere in the editing window. The key is moving the cursor. Locate your computer's cursor control keys; for example, on an IBM PC they lie near the right edge of the keyboard. Press the key with

Fig. B.3: *After the statements are entered, the screen should look like this.*

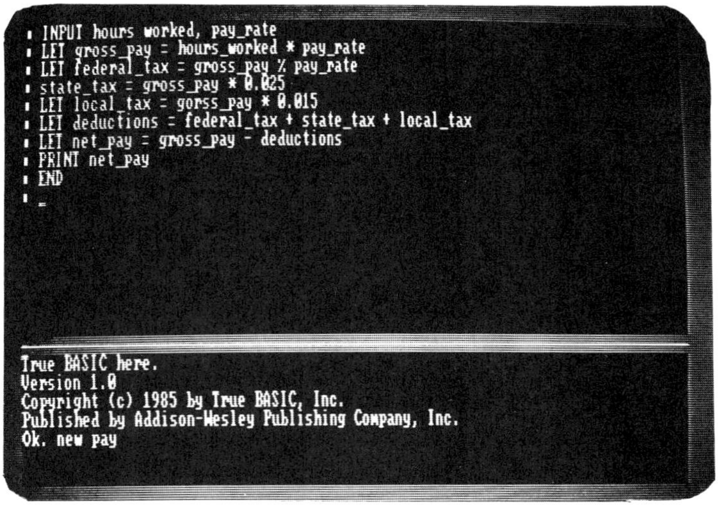

the downward pointing arrow. Watch the cursor move down. Other arrows point to the right, up, and to the left; each moves the cursor in the indicated direction. Experiment. Move the cursor around the screen. When you're finished, be sure it sits under the first character in the first line (the letter I).

On many computers, a character, usually a number, is printed near the top of each cursor control key. Find the *Num Lock* key and press it. Now try moving the cursor. Each time you press a control key, you'll see a digit displayed. Why? *Num Lock* is a shift key. Press it, and the top characters are activated. Press it again, and the keys revert to controlling the cursor. Return the cursor to the upper left corner. Use the delete (*Del*) key to erase any characters you may have added. The screen should look like Fig. B.3 again.

The first of several intentional errors in this program can be found on the very first line. We typed variable name **hours worked**. The blank is illegal; it should be **hours_worked**. Let's correct it. Move the cursor to the blank space between **hours** and **worked**. Press the delete key. The space should disappear. Now hold down the shift key and press the underscore key. An underscore character should appear between the two words *(Fig. B.4)*. By default, *True BASIC* operates in insert mode, adding characters in front of the cursor's current position.

It is also possible to type characters in overstrike mode. For example, move the cursor to the fifth line,

Fig. B.4: *To add an underscore between hours and worked, move the cursor to the blank, delete it, and type an underscore.*

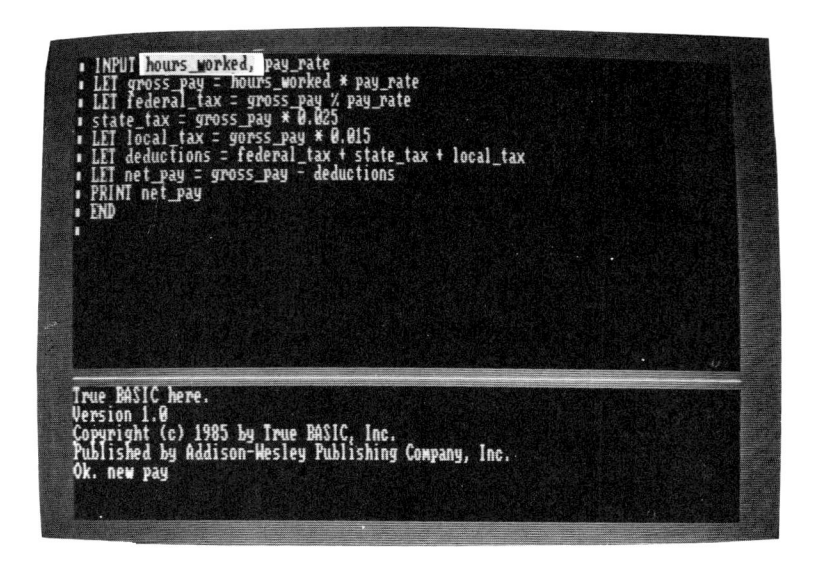

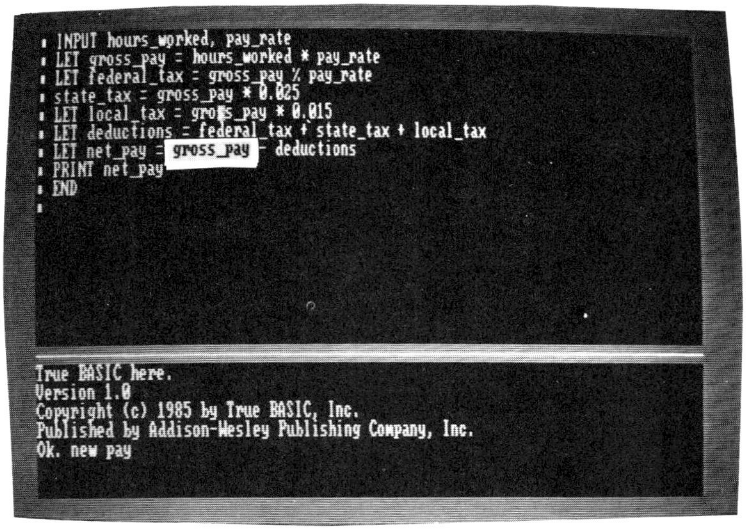

Fig. B.5: *To change "gorss" to "gross", press the insert key and overstrike the "or".*

    LET local_tax = gorss_pay * 0.025

The variable following the equal sign should read **gross_pay.** Move the cursor under the **o.** Then press the insert key. The cursor's appearance should change. Now type **ro.** The letters you type should replace the old letters. When you finish, the screen should resemble Fig. B.5. Press the insert key again to return the cursor to its original form. You're back in insert mode.

Adding and Deleting Lines

Now that we've corrected a few errors, let's add some comments to the program. Move the cursor to the first line's tag, and press enter. A blank line should appear above the **INPUT** statement. Try using a control key to move the cursor to the right. It won't move. Cursor movement is limited to characters already typed. Now try the space bar. A blank space is a character; thus you'll see the cursor move to the right. Count 30 blank spaces and leave the cursor near the middle of the first line. Then type

                        ! Program to compute an individual's

and press enter. The cursor should move to a new blank line under the first comment line.

Press the tab key. The cursor will move directly under the first line's exclamation point. Type the second comment line:

> ! net or take-home pay. First, hours

and press enter again. The cursor will move to the start of a new blank line.

Let's delete this blank line. Move the cursor to the third line's tag and press delete. The line will disappear. If the cursor rests on a line tag, the delete key erases the line. Otherwise, it erases a single character.

The cursor should now rest on the **INPUT** statement. Press the tab key. The cursor moves ahead one word. Press it again, and again; watch how the tab key advances the cursor word by word. Position the cursor under the second line's exclamation point, and start the third comment line *(see Fig. B.6)*. Then add a fourth comment. Leave a blank line between the last comment and the first **LET** statement.

Try one more experiment. Move the cursor to the first **LET** statement's line tag, and press delete. The line will disappear. Don't move the cursor. Instead,

Fig. B.6: *After comments are added, your screen should look like this.*

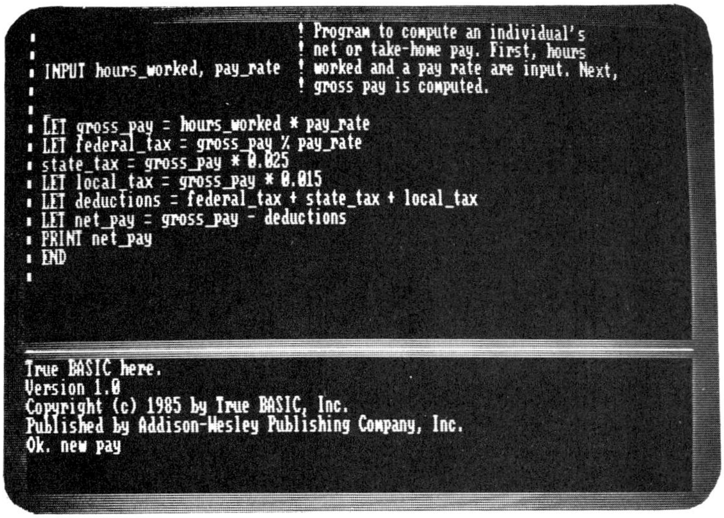

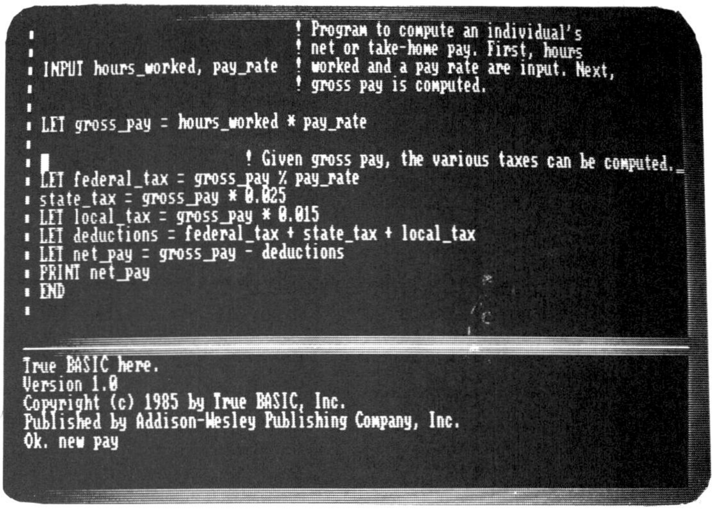

Fig. B.7: *When a line's width exceeds the screen width, True BASIC displays a marker and the eighty characters closest to the cursor.*

find function key *F7*, and press it. The **LET** statement reappears. *F7* is a restore key; it restores the most recent deletion, or erases the most recent addition.

Long Lines

Move the cursor to the second **LET** statement's line tag (**LET federal_tax . . .**). Press enter twice; two new blank lines will appear above the statement. Start the cursor on the second blank line, and type thirty spaces. Then add

> ! Given gross pay the various taxes can be computed.

all on one line. Note what happens. The line's length exceeds the screen's width--the box to the line's left *(Fig. B.7)* tells you that. Note also that the exclamation point is not aligned with the others. The comment is shifted to the left. Why?

When a line exceeds the screen's width, *True BASIC* displays a marker and the eighty characters closest to the cursor. However, the entire line, including the thirty blanks, is still in the computer; nothing has been lost. *True BASIC* can store up to 32,767 (32K) characters on each line. Still, to avoid confusion, it's a good idea to stay within your display unit's line width. Move the cursor to the blank separating "taxes" and "can." Hold down the delete key and watch the remaining characters disappear. Then press enter, press the tab key, and type the balance of the comment on a new line. Your program should look like Fig. B.8.

RUNNING THE PROGRAM

Not all errors can be spotted as a program is typed. Some aren't apparent until it is run. Now that we have a program in memory, let's run it. Use function key *F2* to return to the history window. Once there, type **RUN** or press function key *F9* to run the program.

We buried some intentional errors in this program, so it won't run. Instead, a message is displayed in the history window *(Fig. B.9)*. At the same time, the cursor is shifted automatically to the editing window where it marks the bad instruction. The error message, "Doesn't belong here.", is rather cryptic; you'll find a more detailed explanation in Appendix B of your *Reference Manual*. However, looking up the error message is not usually necessary. Read the statement. Something's wrong. In fact, the cursor marks the incorrect character or word. Clearly, the percent sign doesn't belong in a numeric expression. Delete it, and type the asterisk you really want. Then press *F2* to return to the history window.

Fig. B.8: *Although each program line can hold in excess of 32,000 characters, it's better to limit lines to the screen's width. Here, the comment describing tax computations is spread over two lines.*

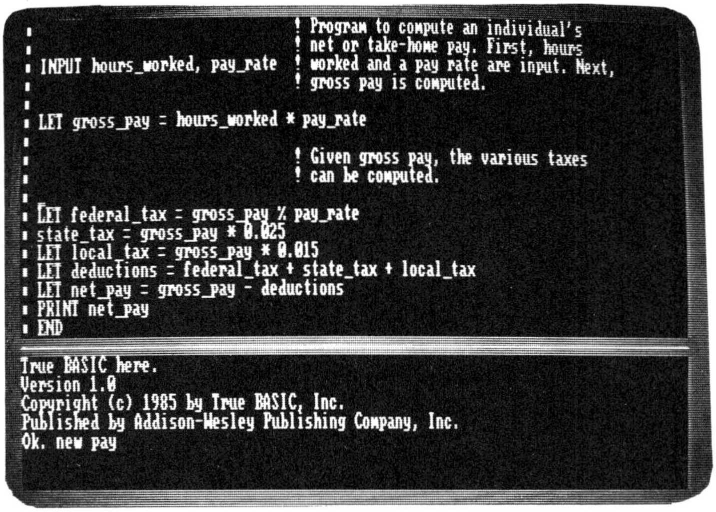

```
! 
!                           ! Program to compute an individual's
!                           ! net or take-home pay. First, hours
! INPUT hours_worked, pay_rate ! worked and a pay rate are input. Next,
!                           ! gross pay is computed.
!
! LET gross_pay = hours_worked * pay_rate
!
!                           ! Given gross pay, the various taxes
!                           ! can be computed.
!
! LET federal_tax = gross_pay ▮ pay_rate
! state_tax = gross_pay * 0.025
! LET local_tax = gross_pay * 0.015
! LET deductions = federal_tax + state_tax + local_tax
! LET net_pay = gross_pay - deductions
! PRINT net_pay
! END

True BASIC here.
Version 1.0
Copyright (c) 1985 by True BASIC, Inc.
Published by Addison-Wesley Publishing Company, Inc.
Ok. new pay
Ok. run
Doesn't belong here.
```

Fig. B.9: *Because the program still contains errors, it won't run. Instead, following a **RUN** command, an error message is generated. The cursor marks the bad statement.*

Almost immediately, another error message appears *(Fig. B.10)*. True BASIC has found something else wrong with your code. Once again, the cursor marks the bad statement. This time, the message says: "Illegal statement." Look at the instruction. We forgot the keyword **LET**. Add it, and press *F2*.

This time, the standard prompt *"Ok."* should appear in the history window. If it doesn't, you may have made additional typing errors. Correct them. When finally the standard prompt appears, press *F9* or type **RUN**. You should see a question mark *(Fig. B.11)*. Respond by typing values for hours worked and an hourly pay rate. Press enter, and the computed gross pay is displayed. If the displayed value is zero, check the spelling of your variable names. Inconsistent spelling is a common beginner's error.

SAVING THE PROGRAM

Now that the program runs, let's save it. We already assigned it a name (the **NEW** statement). Thus, typing

    SAVE

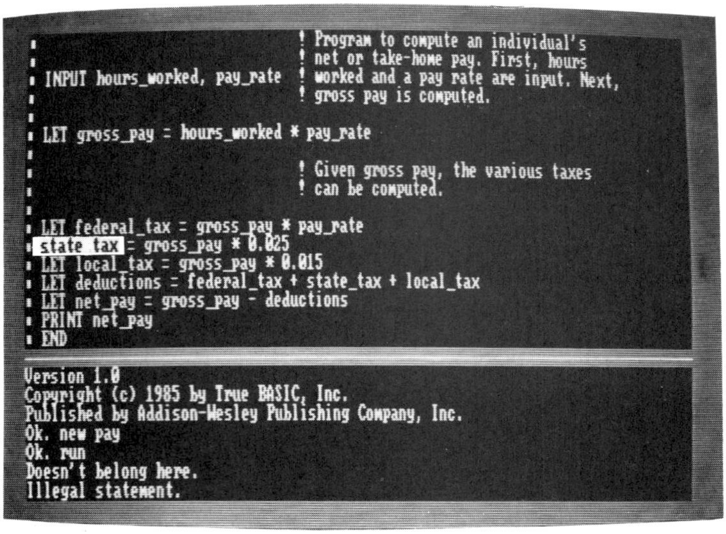

Fig. B. 10: *After pressing function key F2, a second error message appears. Note that the percent sign in the federal tax* **LET** *statement has already been changed to an* asterisk.

Fig. B.11: *Now that the errors have been corrected, the program will run.*

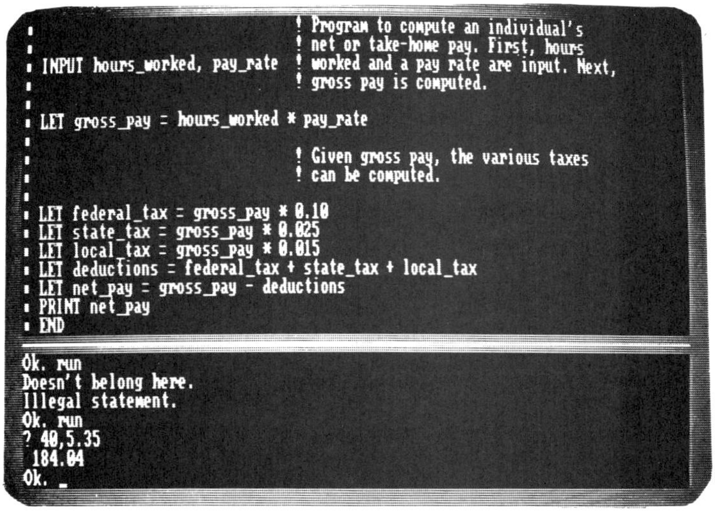

380

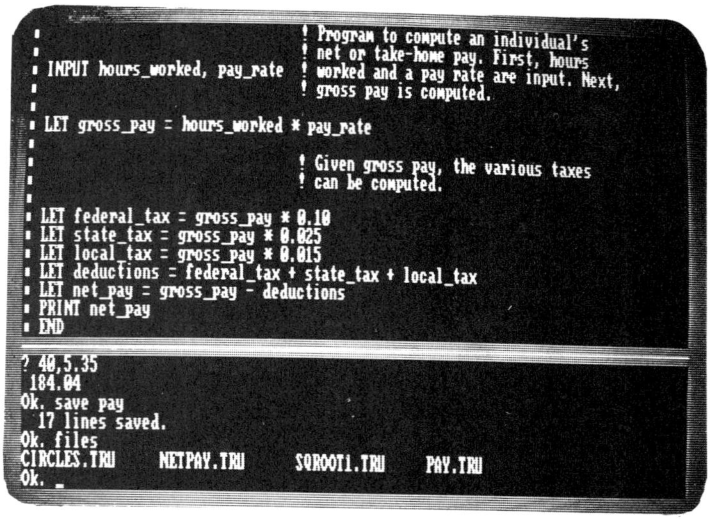

Fig. B.12: *To copy the program to disk, type a **SAVE** command. In this slide, a subsequent **FILES** command verifies that the program **PAY** is indeed stored on disk.*

copies the program to disk and stores it under the name **PAY**. If we had not assigned a file name, we could have typed

    SAVE PAY

to achieve the same result. To verify that the program is on disk, type **FILES**. A list of the files stored on your disk will appear in the history window. Figure B.12 shows the **SAVE** command and a subsequent **FILES** command. Note that **PAY** appears in the list.

    A copy of the program is now stored on disk. You can turn your computer off, walk away, come back later, and access **PAY** again. Try it. If you don't want to turn the machine off, just type **BYE**, and then type **HELLO** again. Or, type **NEW**, and pretend you're going to start a new program. In any case, the program we've called **PAY** disappears from the editing window. How do you get it back? Simple. Just type

    OLD PAY

and the copy from disk is read back into main memory and displayed on your screen. Once it's in memory, you can run it or modify it.

CHANGING THE PROGRAM

Now that the program is back in memory, let's change it. For example, given the logic of this program, federal, state, and local taxes can be computed in any order. Let's move the **LET** statements that compute state and local taxes above the one that computes federal tax.

We'll start by marking the two lines to be moved. To mark a line, move the cursor to its line tag, and press function key *F4*. As an exercise, mark the **LET** statement that computes state tax. Then, move the cursor down to the **PRINT** statement's line tag, and mark it. You'll see that the entire block of five statements is marked. Move the cursor back to the first statement in the block, position it on the line tag, and press *F4* again. The mark disappears. To mark a line or a block of lines, press *F4*. To unmark them, press *F4* again.

The cursor should be sitting on the line tag of the **LET** statement that computes state tax; if it isn't, move it there. Mark the statement. Drop down one line and mark the one that computes local tax. Your screen should look like Fig. B.13.

Next, we'll copy those two lines. Move the cursor to the target line; in this

Fig. B.13: *The first step in making global changes is often marking a block of code.*

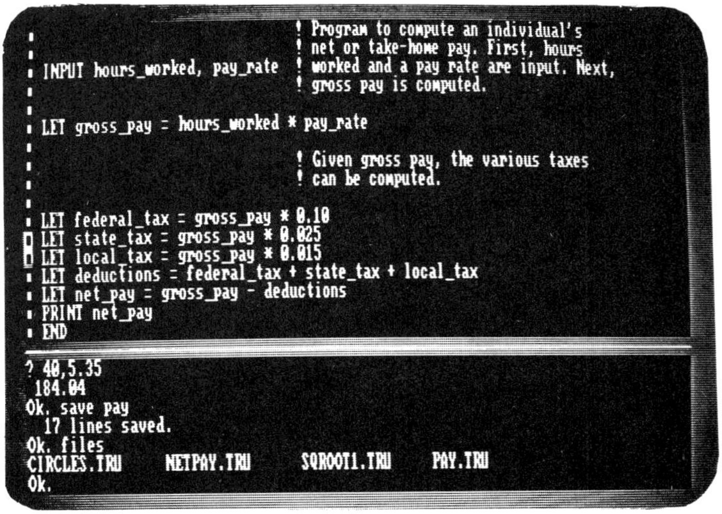

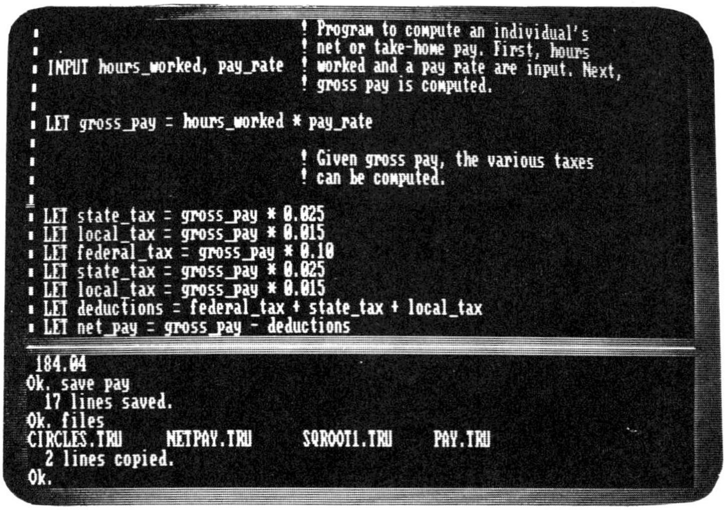

Fig. B.14: *The **COPY** command duplicates a marked block.*

case, move it to the line preceding the **LET** statement that computes federal tax. Press function key *F5*, the copy key. Almost immediately, you'll see another copy of the two marked lines appear below the target line *(Fig. B.14)*. Note that the old state and local tax statements are still there.

Delete the two new lines. Move the cursor to the first one, press delete, and then press delete again. Or, mark the first line, mark the second one, move the cursor back to the first line, and press delete. Now mark the original state and local **LET** statements; your screen should look like Fig. B.13 again. Position the cursor on the line tag of the blank line just above **LET federal_tax = . . .**, and press *F6*, the move key. This time, a new set of **LET** statements will appear above the one that computes **federal_tax**, and the two marked statements will disappear *(Fig. B.15)*. Function key *F5* copies code; *F6* moves code.

REPLACING THE PROGRAM

We've modifed the program in main memory, but we haven't changed the version stored on disk. It still contains the original instructions. If we read it into memory again, the computations of state and local tax would come after federal tax. If we want the new version to be "official," we have to replace the old version on disk.

```
! Program to compute an individual's
! net or take-home pay. First, hours
! INPUT hours_worked, pay_rate    ! worked and a pay rate are input. Next,
!                                 ! gross pay is computed.
!
! LET gross_pay = hours_worked * pay_rate
!
!                                 ! Given gross pay, the various taxes
!                                 ! can be computed.
!
! LET state_tax = gross_pay * 0.025
! LET local_tax = gross_pay * 0.015
! LET federal_tax = gross_pay * 0.10
! LET deductions = federal_tax + state_tax + local_tax
! LET net_pay = gross_pay - deductions
! PRINT net_pay
! END

Ok. save pay
  17 lines saved.
Ok. files
CIRCLES.TRU    NETPAY.TRU    SQROOT1.TRU    PAY.TRU
  2 lines copied.
  2 lines moved.
Ok.
```

Fig. B.15: *A **MOVE** command shifts a marked block from one place to another. Note that the moved lines no longer appear in their old location.*

Try typing

SAVE PAY

You'll get an error message. When a program is copied to disk, the old version is destroyed. When you type **SAVE**, *True BASIC* assumes that you are saving the program for the very first time. If you accidentally forgot about an old program named **PAY**, you'd destroy it. Instead, you get an error message.

To replace a previously saved program, use a different command:

REPLACE

Usually, no file name or program name is necessary, because you provided the name in an earlier **OLD** command, but you can code a file name if you want to. Replace the payroll program.

How can you discard a file or program you no longer need? Just type an **UNSAVE** command. Try an experiment. Save the program in memory under a garbage name such as **XYZ**; for example, type

>   **SAVE XYZ**

Next, type **FILES**. You should see both **PAY** and **XYZ** in the list of files. Then, type

>   **UNSAVE XYZ**

followed by **FILES**. The garbage file **XYZ** will be gone.

ADVANCED EDITING

This ends our tutorial. In addition to the basic functions described above, *True BASIC*'s editor supports a number of advanced features. Some of these features are summarized below. Check your *Reference Manual* and *User's Guide* for details.

Function Keys

If your computer is equipped with function keys, complex operations can often be reduced to a single keystroke. The meanings of individual function keys can vary from computer to computer. Figure B.16 summarizes the function keys on an IBM PC®.

Fig. B.16: *On computers equipped with function keys, True BASIC normally makes the following assignments.*

Function Key	Meaning
F1	Move cursor to editing window.
F2	Move cursor to history window.
F3	FIND
F4	MARK
F5	COPY
F6	MOVE
F7	RESTORE
F8	Unassigned
F9	RUN
F10	HELP

Help

Function key *F10* is *True BASIC*'s help key. Press it once, or type **HELP**, and an overview of the help feature appears on your screen. Press any key to get back to where you were. You can get more help on a number of specific topics. Type

> **HELP TOPICS**

for a list of topics. Then type **HELP** followed by a topic name to view detailed information. Because the explanations are stored on disk and not in main memory, your *True BASIC* disk must be loaded before you type **HELP**.

Special Keys

On most computers, the standard left, right, up, and down keys move the cursor one character or one line at a time. Often, it is useful to move to the next word, the beginning or end of the current line, or the beginning or end of the program.

Fig. B.17: *In addition to the function keys, the following special keys or key combinations are available on an IBM PC.*

Cursor control	Left	left one character
	Right	right one character
	Up	up one line
	Down	down one line
	Home	beginning of program
	End	end of program
	PgUp	back up one screen
	PgDn	move to next screen
	Tab	start of next word or number
	Shift-Tab	start of prior word or number
	Ctrl-left	beginning of current line
	Ctrl-right	end of current line
Editing	Backspace	delete previous character
	Del	delete current character
	Ctrl-Home	delete previous word
	Ctrl-PgUp	delete current word
	Esc	delete from cursor to start line
	Ctrl-END	delete from cursor to end of line
	Del	on a line tag, delete line

We did use the tab key to move the cursor a word at a time, but *True BASIC* supports other special keys and key combinations, too. Figure B.17 summarizes the special keys on an IBM PC®; if you have a different computer, check your *User's Guide*. In addition to moving the cursor, other keys perform editing functions.

Global Changes

To this point, we have focused on changing individual characters or words. Often, it is useful to make more global changes. *True BASIC* has a number of commands that support such global changes.

Many global commands refer to a block of code. A block is simply a set of lines. One way to define a block is to mark the lines; you did this in the tutorial when you copied and then moved some statements. A subroutine, function, or picture is, by definition, a block. Finally, a block can be defined as a set of statement numbers.

True BASIC statements don't have numbers, though. How can you refer to statement numbers? Once a program is written, a useful technique is to number the statements, use the numbers to edit the code, and then unnumber the statements. To add statement numbers, type the command

DO NUM

To remove them, code

DO UNNUM

Normally, global commands *(see Fig. B.18 for a summary)* refer to the entire program. To limit them to a single block, type an **EDIT** command.

Most computers equipped with function keys have one assigned to a find function (on an IBM PC®, it's *F3*). When the find key is pressed, the keyword find is displayed, and the user is asked to enter a target or search field. Then, a search starts at the cursor. When the first occurrence of the specified word or number is located, searching stops and the cursor is positioned on the target. At this point, you can modify the code. Pressing the find key again continues the search for the "next" occurrence. Normally, only complete words or numbers can be located. To find a partial word (for example, to find the "Ex" in "Exercise"), enclose the search pattern in quotation marks. On computers not equipped with function keys, a **LOCATE** command performs the same function.

A **CHANGE** command searches a program for all occurrences of a specified word or number, and replaces them with a different pattern. Once again, specify complete words or numbers; if you must change a portion of a word, enclose it

Command	Meaning
CHANGE a,b	Searches program for occurrences of string or number **a**, and replaces each one with string or number **b**.
COMPILE	Converts the source code currently in main memory to compiled form.
COPY a,b	Copies block **a** to position **b**.
DELETE a	Deletes block **a**.
DO program	Runs a preprocessor or formatting program against your current source program. For example, **DO NUM** adds statement numbers to a program, **DO RENUM** renumbers the statements after changes have been made, **DO UNNUM** removes the statement numbers, and **DO FORMAT** formats a program.
EDIT a	Limits the scope of global commands to block **a**.
KEEP a	Deletes everything but block **a**.
LIST a	Prints block **a** to the printer. If no block is specified, prints the entire program.
LOCATE a	Displays all lines containing word or phrase **a**.
MARK a	Marks block **a**.
MOVE a,b	Moves block **a** to position **b**.
SPLIT n	Draws line separating history and editing windows **n** lines from the top.
TO a	Moves cursor to position **a**.
TRY a,b	Searches program for occurrences of word or number **a**. When it finds one, it replaces **a** with **b** only if the user approves.

Fig. B.18: *The following commands support global editing of a program or other document. Check your Reference Manual and User's Guide for details.*

in quotation marks. Normally, *True BASIC* does not distinguish between upper case and lower case letters. When you enclose a phrase in quotation marks, upper and lower case letters are different, however. **TRY** is similar to **CHANGE** except that it asks for verification before changing a word or number. Thus, you can modify a program selectively, changing some occurrences of the search pattern while leaving others alone.

The **TO** command moves the cursor to the start of a specified block. In the tutorial, we used function keys to mark, copy, and move blocks of code; **MARK**, **COPY**, and **MOVE** perform equivalent functions. A **DELETE** command allows the user to erase a complete block, while **KEEP** deletes everything but a specified block. Check your *Reference Manual* and *User's Guide* for details.

The Program Listing

Throughout this primer we have stressed indenting code to make logical blocks easy to spot. The command

DO FORMAT

automatically formats a program for you. (The process is sometimes called "pretty printing.") Try it. Also, you can use the symbols (>) and (<) to indent or to shift to the left a marked block.

At some point, you will probably need a printed listing of your program. To get one, type

LIST

If you follow the keyword with a block identifier, only the specified block is printed; otherwise, the entire program is listed.

The Screen

Most screens display characters of one color on a darker background. If you have a color display, you may be able to control the background and foreground colors in both the history and editing windows. Try it. With the cursor in the history window, hold down the control key (*Ctrl*) and press *b* (for background). The history window should change color. Press *Ctrl-b* again to get a different background color. Pressing *Ctrl-f* changes the foreground color (the color of the characters). Shift the cursor to the editing window, and set its colors. Pressing *Ctrl-e* (for edge) outlines the two windows. Try working with a red history window, a blue editing window, and a green edge. Then, select contrasting foreground colors that generate characters you find easy to read. A simple thing like adding color can help reduce the eye strain so often associated with video displays.

By default, most screens display 25 lines. The line separating the history and editing windows is drawn at line 18, yielding a 17-line editing window and a 7-line history window. On many computers, you can change that by coding a **SPLIT** command. For example,

    SPLIT 10

redraws the division at line 10, yielding a 9-line editing window and a 15-line history window. Try it. The specified line number must be positive, and at least one line must be left in the history window (otherwise, you won't be able to issue future commands).

Compiling a Program

Normally, *True BASIC* programs are stored in memory or on disk in source statement form. As a result, each time the program is run, it must be compiled, and that takes time. You can save the time by storing the program in compiled form.

To compile a program, write it in the usual way, remove any errors, and save the source code on disk. Then type

    COMPILE

The source program will disappear from your display; you won't be able to view it again. Now you can **RUN** it or **SAVE** it. (Use different file names for the source and compiled versions of the program). You'll find that the compiled version begins executing much more quickly.

Time isn't the only reason for compiling a program, however. Normally, a compiled version occupies less memory space than the source version. Also, compiled programs are private—their statements can't be displayed. If you or your company use or market programs you don't want others duplicating, consider compiling the code.

Many computer systems assign a special file name suffix to compiled programs. Check your *User's Guide* or your system reference manual for details.

Module C

Flowcharting

A flowchart is a graphical representation of a program, a subroutine, or a function. Used as planning aids, flowcharts allow a programmer to visualize logic before writing the code. They are language independent; in other words, they can be used to plan logic that will eventually be coded in assembler, BASIC, COBOL, or any other language. Flowcharts are also valuable as documentation.

PROGRAM LOGIC FLOWCHARTS

In this primer, we'll use five basic flowcharting symbols *(Fig. C.1)*. Terminal symbols mark both the beginning and the end of a program, function, or subroutine. A rectangle represents a process that changes or manipulates data. Input and output operations are identified by a parallelogram. A decision point is represented by a diamond. A fifth symbol, a small circle called an on-page connector, is sometimes used to "continue" lengthy flowcharts.

A flowchart's symbols are linked by flowlines. By convention, logic flows from the top down, and from left to right; arrowheads must be added if the direction of flow deviates from this standard pattern. Since arrowheads make a flowchart easier to read, we will always use them.

Program logic can be expressed as combinations of three basic patterns: sequence, decision, and repetition. Sequential logic *(Fig. C.2)* is executed

Fig. C.1: The flowcharting symbols used in this primer.

Symbol	Name	Description
⬭	Terminal point	Marks the beginning or end of a program function, or subroutine.
▭	Process	Indicates any operation that changes or manipulates data.
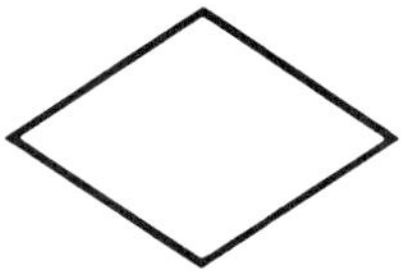 ◇	Decision	Indicates a logical test to be performed by the program.
 ▱	Input or Output	Indicates any input or output operation.
 ○	On-page connector	Indicates that the flowchart is to be continued.

Fig. C.2: *Sequential logic is executed in sequence.*

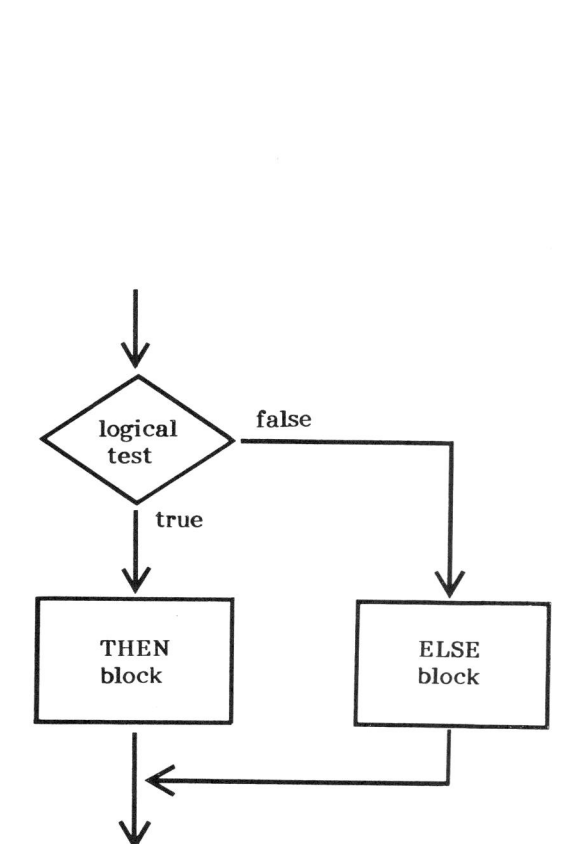

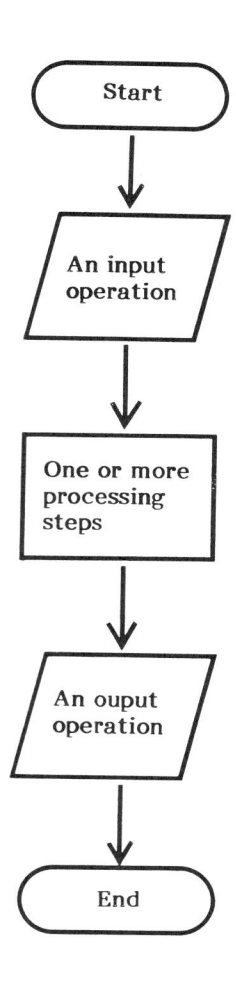

Fig. C.3: *A decision structure begins with a logical test. If the test is true, the THEN block is executed. If the test is false, the ELSE block is executed.*

Fig. C.4: *One decision structure's THEN block can hold another decision structure.*

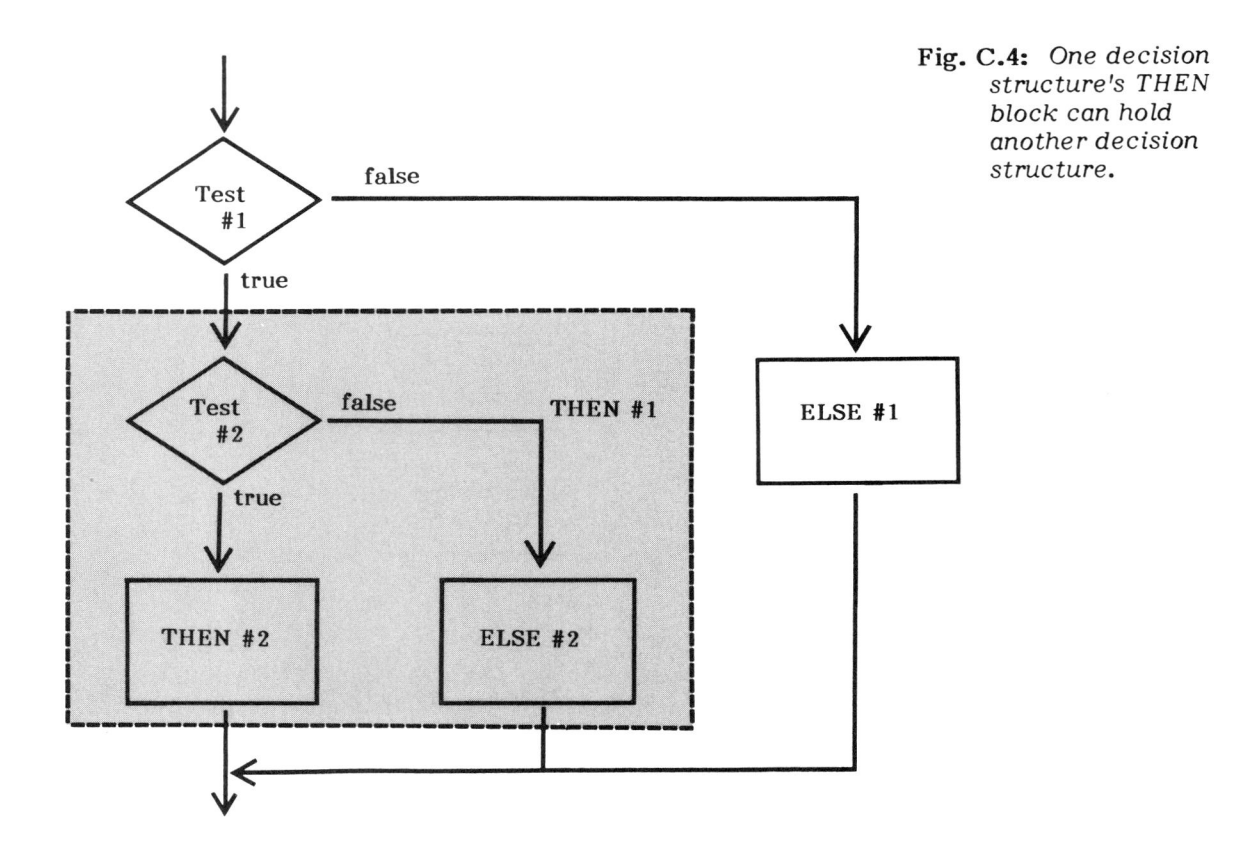

sequentially, one block after another. Each symbol represents one or more actual instructions.

A decision structure *(Fig. C.3)* begins with a condition (the diamond symbol). If the condition is true, the THEN block's logic is executed and the ELSE block is skipped. If the condition is false the ELSE block is executed and the THEN block is skipped.

A decision structure can contain both a THEN block and an ELSE block. Each block can represent one or more actual instructions. On a high-level flowchart, a block might represent a subroutine or a function. A THEN block can even hold another decision block *(Fig. C.4)*: a nested IF. Decision logic can be nested on the ELSE branch too *(Fig. C.5)*, and nesting can occur on both paths.

Two basic patterns are used to show repetitive logic. In a DO WHILE structure *(Fig. C.6)*, a test is performed at the top of the loop. If the condition tested is true, the loop's logic is executed and control is returned to the top for another test. If the condition is false, the loop is skipped and control is transferred to the block following the loop's end. In a DO UNTIL structure *(Fig. C.7)*, a test is performed at the end of the loop. If the condition is false, the loop's logic is repeated; if the condition is true, the loop ends.

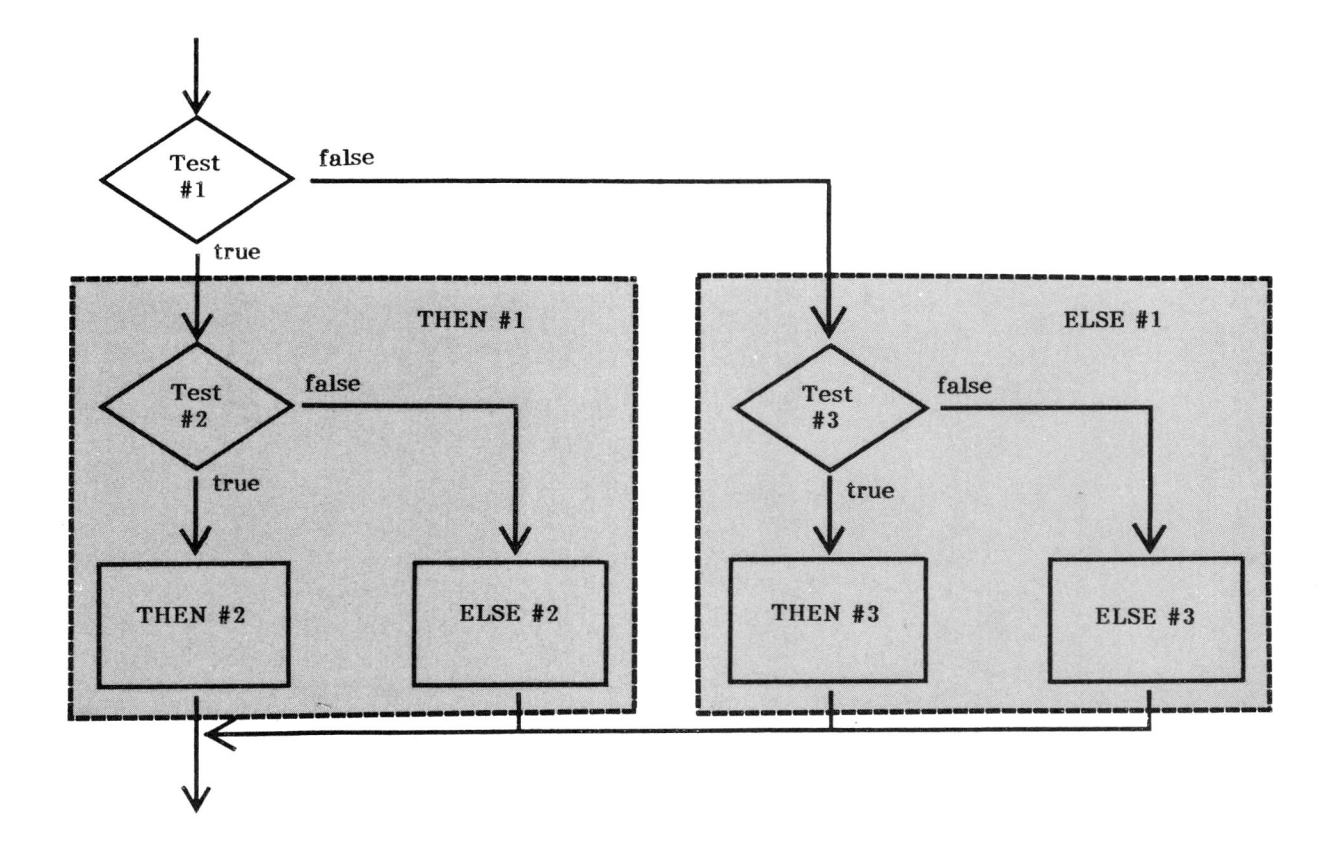

Fig. C.5: *Decision structures can be nested on both the THEN and ELSE blocks.*

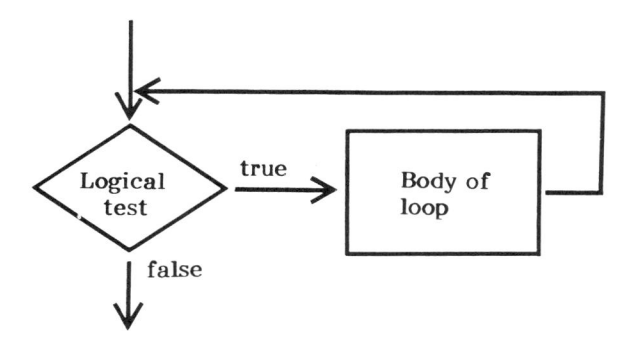

Fig. C.6: *In a DO WHILE loop, a logical test is performed at the top of the loop. As long as the test is true, the loop repeats.*

Fig. C.7: *In a **DO UNTIL** loop, a logical test is performed at the end of the loop. If the condition is true, the loop ends; if the condition is false, the loop repeats.*

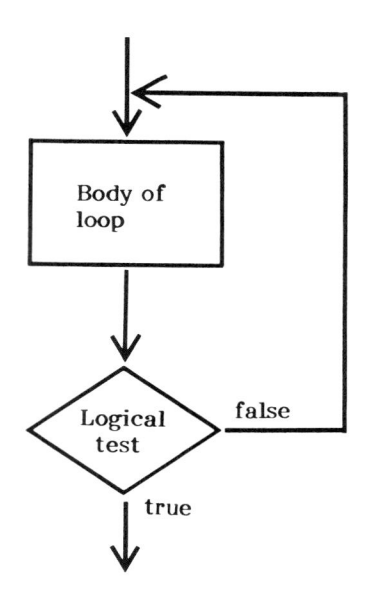

A program is ultimately composed of combinations of these three basic structures. It doesn't take a very large flowchart to fill a page, and that's where the connector symbol proves useful. Look at Fig. C.8. The flowchart starts at the top left and flows down the page. At the bottom left is a connector symbol. It means that the flowchart is to be continued. Look toward the top right, and find another connector symbol. When you find it, continue reading the flowchart from the top, down.

A properly prepared flowchart illustrates logical flow at a glance. However, lengthy flowcharts are often difficult to follow. A single flowchart tracing the detailed logic of a large program is usually a waste of time and effort.

In this primer, our flowcharts will be limited to a single page. Instead of attempting to flowchart a complete, complex program, we will separately flowchart each of the its independent logical units (mainline, subroutines, functions). If a one-page flowchart can't be drawn, the module it represents may be trying to accomplish too much. If that's the case, it should be decomposed into lower-level modules.

Examples of flowcharts are found throughout the primer.

REFERENCES

1. Bohl, Marilyn (1978). *Tools for Structured Design.* Chicago: Science Research Associates, Inc.

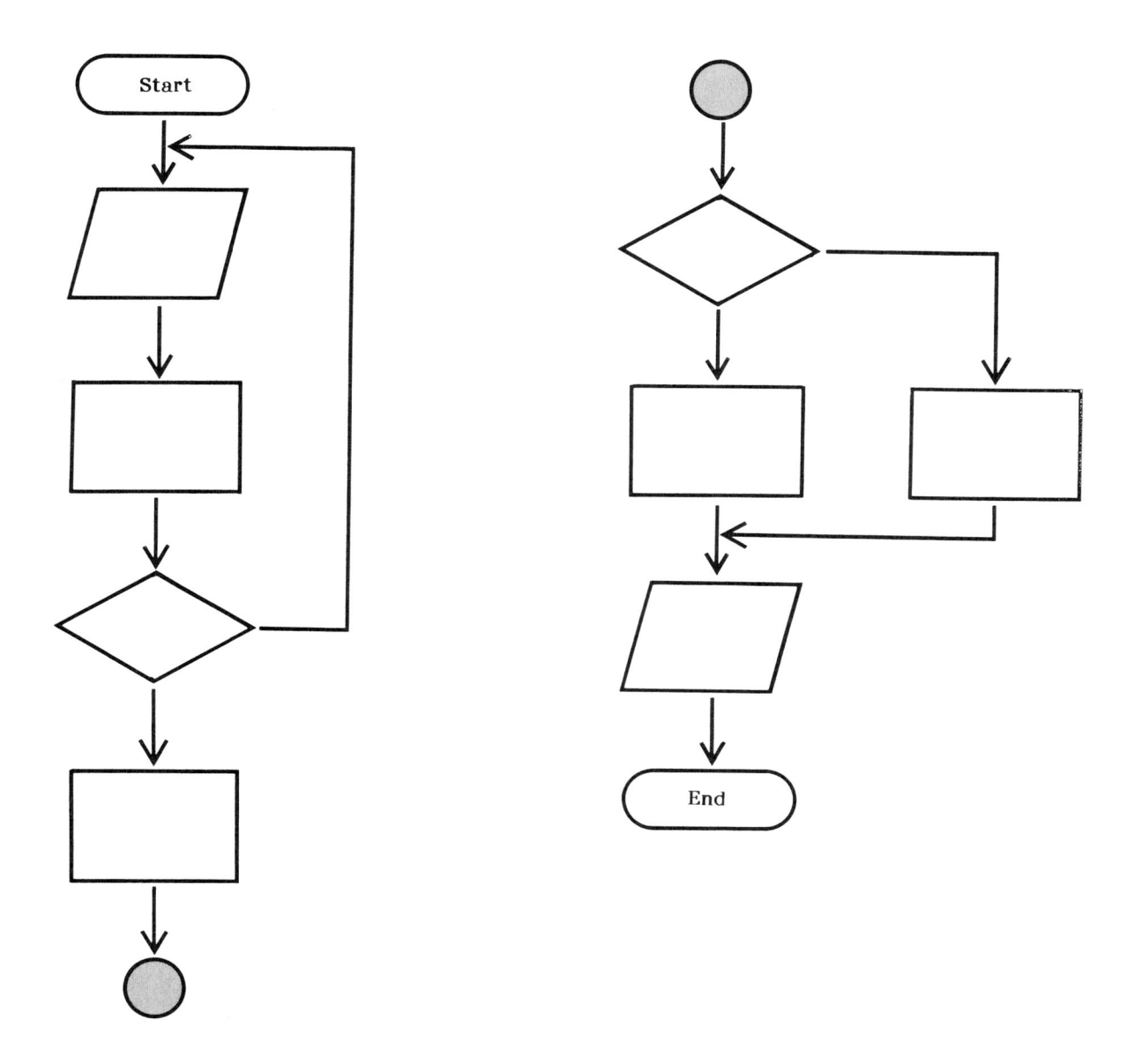

Fig. C.8: *Connector symbols are used to continue a lengthy flowchart.*

Module

D

Error Handling and Debugging

The focus of this module is locating and correcting programming errors. Syntax errors must be fixed before a program can run; fortunately, they are generally easy to find. Run-time errors occur when your instructions tell the computer to do something it can't do; they can be difficult to locate. Most tricky are the logical errors that must be isolated when an apparently valid program generates incorrect output. This module describes the various error types and suggests strategies for dealing with them.

COMMAND ERRORS

Let's start with the easiest type of error to correct, an invalid command. When you type an incorrect command, *True BASIC* responds by displaying "What?" and inviting you to use the **HELP** feature. The message is quite clear: *True BASIC* didn't understand you. The solution is usually obvious. Read what you just typed; you probably misspelled the command. Simply retype it. If you aren't sure what to do, check the command in Appendix III or in your *Reference Manual*, or type **HELP**.

SYNTAX ERRORS

Syntax errors are caused by incorrectly coded instructions that cannot be translated by *True BASIC*. As the program is compiled, a message identifying the error is displayed in the history window, and the cursor is positioned on the bad instruction. At this point, you can correct the error. When you finish, return to the history window. Almost immediately, a message describing the next error appears. Continue correcting errors until you reach the end of the program. Then run it again.

How do you identify and correct a syntax error? Assuming that you understand the program, the error messages are usually quite clear. Read the erroneous statement. In most cases, you'll know what is wrong. If you're still not sure, look up the detailed description of the error message in Appendix B of the *Reference Manual*. Then, look up the instruction and make sure you're coding it correctly.

Occasionally, syntax errors can be misleading. For example, try pressing & instead of * to signify multiplication (the keys are side by side). Clearly, the problem is a bad operator. When you run the program, however, the error message "Wrong type." is displayed, and a *variable* is flagged. Why? The ampersand is a valid string operator. *True BASIC* keys on the operators first, and then checks the variables. The compiler accepts the concatenation operation as legal, and tells you that numbers can't be concatenated.

Another interesting problem occurs when you're working with arrays and you forget to code a dimension statement. Every statement that references a subscripted array element will be flagged, even though there may be nothing wrong with them. The real program is the missing **DIM**; since it isn't there, *True BASIC* can't mark it wrong.

Sometimes, correcting one error corrects several others. For example, if you misspell **DEF**, the function definition will be flagged as an error. If you correct it and then continue compiling, every reference to that function will still be flagged, even though you corrected the real error. That's annoying.

You may need several compilation cycles to remove all the syntax errors from a lengthy program. Occasionally, one will stump you. A common problem is seeing what you *thought* you typed, instead of what's really there. Try retyping the instruction. Even better, ask someone else to look at it. It's amazing how often

400

you can overlook the most obvious error in your own work. Other people won't. Don't forget this primer or your *Reference Manual,* either; a quick review of the instruction's format can clear up a great deal of confusion.

RUN-TIME ERRORS

Run time errors occur when your instructions tell the computer to do something it can't do. The result is usually an error message followed by program termination. Such errors can be difficult to find.

What exactly causes run-time errors? Many things. For example, division by zero is illegal on virtually all computers. Perhaps the division by zero results from bad input data. Maybe a variable name is misspelled. A different spelling means a new variable, and *True BASIC* initializes all new variables to zero. Sometimes, a logical error can generate a division by zero in a program that normally runs correctly. That's what makes run-time errors tricky. The cause is not always obvious.

Run-time errors can arise on input or output operations. For example, typing a string in response to a request for a number will cause an error. If the input device is the keyboard, you'll get a chance to correct it. However, if the same error occurs on file input, the result is program termination. Your program will also fail if you attempt to access a device that doesn't exist or hasn't been opened. You might, for example, open channel #1, but attempt to read data from channel #2. Or, you might open channel #1 and assign it to the printer, but then forget to turn on the printer. In either case, the device you referenced is not available. The system can't recover from such errors, so the program is terminated.

Errors can also occur as the program runs. Often, the cause is an out-of-control loop. Maybe you're modifying the control variable inside the loop. Maybe you should be, but you aren't. As a result you can generate an out-of-range subscript, run out of memory, or read past the end of data. Even more mystifying is the endless loop that runs on and on without generating output or an error message. You'll code one someday; everyone does. After a few seconds, you'll sense that nothing is happening. When you reach that point, press *Ctrl-Break*. The program will terminate, leaving the cursor on the instruction that was about to be executed. Unless you were overly impatient, that instruction will lie in a loop. Check the loop carefully. You probably missed its exit condition.

Search Strategies

Run-time errors are sometimes called bugs, and they must be located and removed. The key to debugging a program is knowing what the program is supposed to do. That's important. If you don't understand the code, you can't debug it. Assuming that you understand the program's logic, the error message is often enough to tell you what is wrong. If it isn't, trace the logic.

Start with an idea (positive, negative, zero, nonzero, large, small) of the value each variable in the failed instruction should hold. Then look at the values they actually hold. Working in the history window, you can type *True BASIC* instructions as though they were commands. For example, type **PRINT** followed by a list of variables. When you press enter, the latest value of each listed variable is displayed just under the **PRINT** command. Look for an unreasonable value. When you find one, you've probably found the error.

For example, imagine a zero divide occurs on the instruction

    LET x = (y/a) + (z/b)

Either **a** or **b** (or both) must be zero. Return to the history window and type

    PRINT a,b

Values for these two variables will be displayed. Find the zero, and you've identified the problem.

That doesn't mean you've solved it, however. Why is the value zero? To find out, trace the variable. Start with a **LOCATE** command, and generate a list of all the statements that reference the variable. Work backward from the bad statement. Focus on other statements that change the variable's value. If there are none, you forgot to initialize it. **PRINT** the variables in those other statements, and look for an unreasonable value. Variables don't take on values by accident; everything that happens on a computer happens because an instruction told the machine to take a particular action.

Errors that occur in loops or decision structures can be particularly difficult to find. Try printing all variables in all affected statements, especially loop control variables and variables that control a decision structure. If you have a sense of what the data should be, an unreasonable value will literally jump out at you.

Try desk checking the logic. Write the affected instructions on a sheet of scratch paper, or list them on the printer. Go through a cycle or two by hand, generating data values. Then turn back to the computer, print data values one by one, and see how they compare with your values. Focus on the differences; they'll tell you what is wrong.

Once you've found an error, correct it and run the program again. Maybe the program will work this time. Maybe you'll just move on to the next error. In either case, assuming you understand the logic, you'll have a sense of making progress. Eventually, you'll isolate and correct the real error.

What if you don't understand the logic, however? You may find yourself guessing, trying things, or, worse yet, copying someone else's code. Don't. That's not the way to learn to program. If it's necessary, go back to the beginning and start over. If you don't understand what you're doing, you aren't programming. You're just writing instructions, and that's a frustrating waste of time.

Trapping Run-time Errors

It's one thing to encounter run-time errors as you debug a program *you* have written. It's quite different when such bugs occur after a program has been "successfully" debugged and released to nontechnical users. People don't like programs that fail. Unfortunately, certain types of run-time errors can't be avoided because they are caused by bad input data. Such errors can, however, be trapped.

The first step is verifying the user's input *(see Chapters 7 and 10)*, perhaps by using **LINE INPUT** statements and checking to be sure that each value lies within an acceptable range. The input data are the only values the programmer cannot directly control. It makes sense to screen them carefully.

Eventually, however, it will be necessary to assign a portion of the input string to a numeric variable, or to use a value in a computation. To trap errors that might occur on such operations, use *True BASIC*'s error handler structure *(Fig. D.1)*. Between **WHEN ERROR IN** and **USE**, code the instruction or instructions that could generate an error. Between **USE** and **END WHEN**, code your own error handler routine. If no error occurs in the protected block, the error handler logic is skipped. Should an error occur, your error handler logic is given control. Instead of generating a cryptic error message and terminating the program, your error handler might display a clear error message and give the user a chance to try

Fig. D.1: *To trap errors in selected True BASIC statements, surround them with a WHEN ERROR in structure. If an error occurs in the affected block, the error handler logic gets control. If no error occurs, the error handler block is ignored.*

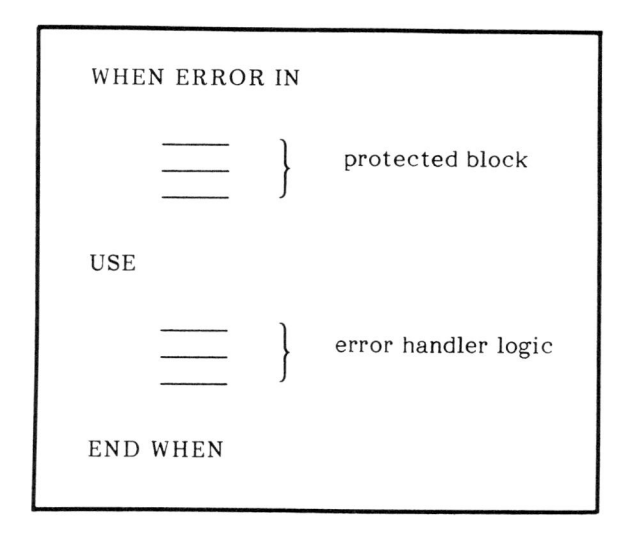

```
WHEN ERROR IN

    ___
    ___  } protected block
    ___

USE

    ___
    ___  } error handler logic
    ___

END WHEN
```

again.

For example, consider the simple program shown in Fig. D.2. The main control loop starts with the entry of a numerator and a denominator. The subsequent division is protected. If the user should enter a negative denominator, the error handler gets control, prints a message, and gives the user a chance to try again.

LOGICAL ERRORS

By far the most difficult type of error to correct is a logical error. By the time you encounter logical errors, your program has been successfully compiled and run, and, rather than terminating abnormally, has generated output. The problem is that the output is wrong. Even more frustrating is a program that has run successfully many times, but suddenly abnormally terminates. The problem might be an unusual combination of data, or bad input data. Then again, it might result from an error in an untested portion of your program. Such bugs can be very difficult to find.

The real key to finding and correcting logical errors is anticipating them. "Murphy's law" states that if anything can go wrong, it will. Expect problems, because they will occur. As you're writing a program, you'll be tempted to take shortcuts to "simplify" or streamline the code. Don't. You might save some coding

Fig. D.2: *This program illustrates the WHEN ERROR IN structure.*

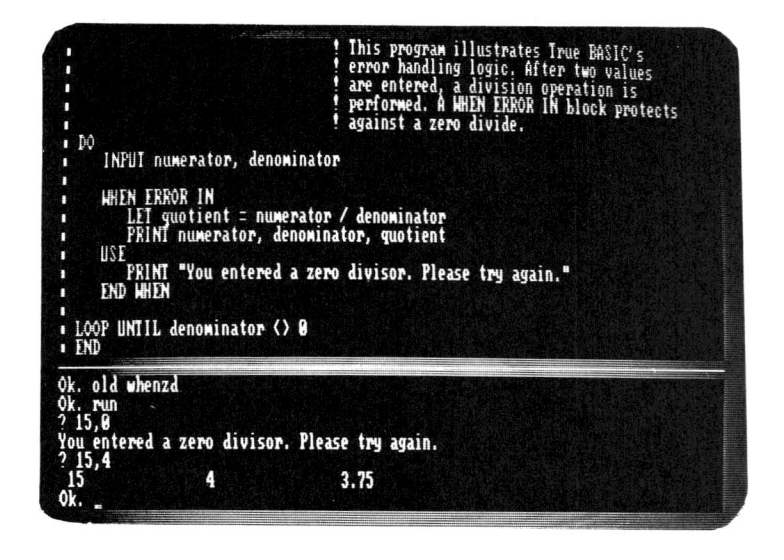

```
! This program illustrates True BASIC's
! error handling logic. After two values
! are entered, a division operation is
! performed. A WHEN ERROR IN block protects
! against a zero divide.
DO
    INPUT numerator, denominator

    WHEN ERROR IN
        LET quotient = numerator / denominator
        PRINT numerator, denominator, quotient
    USE
        PRINT "You entered a zero divisor. Please try again."
    END WHEN

LOOP UNTIL denominator <> 0
END
```

```
Ok. old whenzd
Ok. run
? 15,0
You entered a zero divisor. Please try again.
? 15,4
 15             4              3.75
Ok.
```

time, but you'll pay the price during program debug.

Some techniques you should use while writing code are obvious. Start with clear, descriptive variable names. Sure **r** is easier to type than **radius**, but it's much tougher to find in a complex program. Modularize your code. Remember the three basic logical structures—sequence, decision, and repetition. Write your program as a series of logical blocks. Use subroutines and functions to perform complex logical functions. Remember the rules:

1. A program's logic flows from the top, down.

2. Individual logical blocks should be restricted to a single printed page or a single screen.

Finally, use comments to explain the function of each logical block. A well written program resembles a collection of little programs, each one logically complete. If you follow these simple rules, you'll find debugging much easier.

Once you finish writing a program, test it thoroughly. Almost before you begin writing the code, start developing test data. Don't just include normal input data, however; add extreme values, both high and low. As you write the code, make sure your test data force each module or each logical block to be executed at least once. For example, for each decision structure, include values that force the logic through both the **THEN** and **ELSE** branches. As you code new logical blocks, add to your test data. Take the time to work out each set of test data's expected output. The objective is to catch errors. Before you can spot an error, you must know what the answer should be.

The idea is simple. When you begin testing your program, your test data should exercise every module, and thus force existing errors to occur. If *you* force the errors, you'll be able to find them. If, for example, your third set of test data was designed to flush out errors in a particular subroutine, and an error occurs, you'll know exactly where to look. Let a user generate the error, however, and you won't even know where to start. Don't take shortcuts during coding, documentation, or testing. They can come back to haunt you.

Of course, in spite of your best efforts, it is almost inevitable that some errors will slip through. How can you find them? While we can offer some suggestions, there are no absolute rules. In many cases, you'll simply have to dig into the code. If you've used meaningful variable names, modularized, and commented, your task will be much easier.

The first step is desk checking the logic. For example, if the value of a particular variable is wrong, start with the module that outputs it. Then work back through the other modules that change its value. Use find or **LOCATE** to get a list of all the modules that use the variable *(see Module B)*. Compare the list with the modules you know should access that variable. Look for misspelled variable names. It's surprising how often simply inverting two letters can cause problems.

What if desk checking doesn't reveal the error? What next? A good approach is allowing the computer to trace the logical flow. Start with the list of modules or statements that reference the bad variable. Go through the logic by hand and compute the variable's value following each instruction that changes it. Then stick a **PRINT** statement after each potentially bad instruction. Include in the output list both a string to identify a position in the program (a line number, perhaps) and the variable's current value. Then run the program.

In addition to the regular output, you'll get a series of "trace" messages. Follow them. Compare the sequence of messages to the sequence you expected. If the order is different, then the program isn't following the expected path. Start with the spot where the actual order deviates from your expected order, and figure out what happened. Often, that exercise will reveal the error. Also look at the output values generated by your trace messages, and compare them to the values you expected. Find the first instruction where expectation and reality vary, and you've probably located the error.

An option is including a series of **BREAK** commands *(Fig. D.3)*. Start by marking the statement you want to check. Then return to the history window and type **BREAK**. A breakpoint will be inserted into your program; the affected line will be marked in some way.

When your program runs, *True BASIC* will stop execution just before the marked instruction. At this point, you can return to the history window and issue instructions as though they were commands. For example, you can **PRINT** the values of selected variables, or code **LET** statements to check a computation or to modify a value. When you've finished analyzing a particular breakpoint, just type **CONTINUE,** and your program picks up where it left off. If you changed a value, that new value stays with the program. In this way, you can check to see if a planned change really fixes the problem. You can include as many breakpoints as you want. To remove a breakpoint, simply re-mark the affected statement and type another **BREAK** command.

Fig. D.3: *To insert a breakpoint into a program, mark the statement on which you want to break execution, drop to the history window, and type a BREAK command. Alternately, you can reference a block; the break will be placed on the first statement in the block. When you've finished checking a breakpoint, type CONTINUE, and the program will pick up where it left off. To remove a breakpoint, re-break the affected statement.*

```
            BREAK
    or:                      CONTINUE
            BREAK block
```

Module E

True BASIC and Traditional Basic

True BASIC is a new language. It represents a significant improvement over the old BASIC dialects. Unfortunately, however, it is incompatible with most other BASICs; simply put, programs written in another BASIC will require substantial modification to run under True BASIC. This module explores the reasons for this incompatibility and suggests techniques for converting existing BASIC programs to True BASIC.

A BRIEF HISTORY OF BASIC

BASIC was developed in 1964 by two Dartmouth College professors, John Kemeny and Thomas Kurtz. A key part of the Dartmouth time-sharing system, it was among the first significant interactive programming languages. Aimed at beginners, it was an easy-to-use, hardware-independent, general-purpose language that could be applied to a variety of programming problems. Quickly accepted as a standard, it wasn't long before most major computer suppliers offered a version of Dartmouth BASIC.

In 1975, the company that was to become Microsoft developed a BASIC interpreter for the Altair® microcomputer system. Derived from Digital Equipment Corporation's version of Dartmouth BASIC, it established BASIC as the language of choice for small computers. As the microcomputer revolution accelerated, BASIC remained in the forefront. Today, it is the world's most popular programming language, available on virtually all microcomputer systems.

Unfortunately, the language evolved haphazardly. Early microcomputers contained very little main memory, and changes were needed to get around that limitation. New versions of BASIC were developed with their own unique improvements and special features, many of which were added to enhance performance on a particular machine. In fact, there *was* no single language called BASIC. Instead, as we entered the 1980s, we had a group of dialects based loosely on 1964-vintage Dartmouth BASIC, many of which contained features that violated BASIC's original design principles.

True BASIC

Meanwhle, Kemeny and Kurtz continued developing their language. The principles of structured programming, widely accepted in the 1970s, were incorporated into Dartmouth BASIC. New decision structures, repetitive structures, and subroutines were added; the **GOTO** statement was deemphasized. Technology changed, with video displays and graphic devices replacing the printing terminals of 1964. The language accommodated the new devices. With display monitors came full-screen editing. Thus the need for statement numbers disappeared. As it evolved, however, Dartmouth BASIC remained true to its original design principles: easy-to-use, hardware-independent, and general-purpose.

Recently, an American National Standards Institute (ANSI) committee chaired by Thomas Kurtz released the draft of a proposed ANS standard BASIC. Rejecting any existing version, the committee envisioned a drastic update of the language. Many features were derived from the new Dartmouth BASIC. Other proposed ANSI standards were incorporated into Dartmouth BASIC.

In 1984, Kemeny and Kurtz announced *True BASIC*, the first implementation of the proposed ANSI standard. Rooted in original BASIC and derived from the latest Dartmouth version, it represents a major breakthrough in microcomputer programming. Like its ancestor, it promises to set a new standard.

COMPATIBILITY

Consider the criteria used in developing *True BASIC*. Begin with BASIC's original design principles. Kemeny and Kurtz wanted to teach beginners how to program, so the language had to be easy to use. They didn't want their students worrying about the details of a particular hardware system, so they made BASIC hardware-independent. Finally, they wanted a general-purpose language powerful enough to solve a variety of programming problems. These same principles guided *True BASIC*'s designers.

Next, consider the advances in computer science since 1964. The sense of what makes a program good has changed dramatically. In the 1960's, the emphasis was on machine efficiency. Today, clear, easy-to-maintain code is the objective. A good computer program is constructed from sequence, decision, and repetitive building blocks grouped to form independent, single-function modules. A modern programming language must generate well-structured, modular programs.

Technology is another factor. Clear, easy-to-use graphics are essential to a modern language. The ability to access a variety of different input and output devices is equally important. New peripherals are announced almost continuously. A modern language must be flexible enough to accommodate them.

Finally, there is the question of compatibility. A program written on one computer should run, with little or no change, on a different computer. The various BASIC dialects are not compatible with each other, but ANS BASIC represents a realistic new standard. Eventually, every computer manufacturer will support ANS BASIC. *True BASIC* follows that proposed standard.

True BASIC meets all these criteria. Note, however, that compatibility with existing BASIC dialects was not listed. *True BASIC* is *not* compatible with other BASICs. Consequently, most existing programs must be substantially revised before they can run under *True BASIC*.

This primer is aimed at beginners. Our focus has been learning to write programs correctly. Few beginners worry about converting existing, nonstructured BASIC programs to *True BASIC*. Thus we will offer only a few general comments on compatibility code conversion; check your *Reference Manual* for additional details.

PROGRAM STRUCTURE

The statements in a traditional BASIC program are numbered; *True BASIC* statements are not. In the past, statement numbers were needed for several reasons. A program's logical flow was governed by **GOTO** and conditional **GOTO** statements that transfered control to a specific instruction. Also, in 1964, most terminals printed output a line at a time. Line editors were used, with a programmer modifying a line by referencing its number.

True BASIC relies on current technology. Program logic flows through **IF...THEN...ELSE, DO WHILE, DO UNTIL, FOR...NEXT,** and **SELECT CASE**

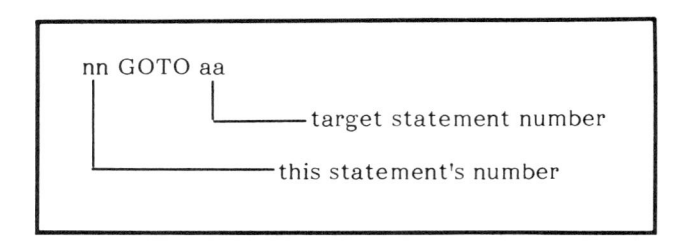

```
nn GOTO aa
   │       └── target statement number
   └── this statement's number
```

Fig. E.1: *If all a program's statements are numbered, True BASIC supports the old **GOTO** statement.*

structures. The standard output device is a display unit; thus, full-screen editing can be used. Because moving the cursor is easier than referencing a line number, there is simply no need for line numbers.

Statement numbers *are* legal in *True BASIC*, however. If one statement is numbered, all must be numbered. You can type the numbers as you type the statements. To add line numbers to a completed program, drop to the history window and type **DO NUM**. Each statement will be assigned a number starting with 100 or 1000 (depending on the program's length) in increments of 10. On a lengthy program, it sometimes makes sense to assign statement numbers, perform necessary global editing functions, and then remove the numbers using a **DO UNNUM** command. If substantial changes are made, renumber the statements (**DO RENUM**).

If the lines are numbered, certain old control structures can be used. A **GOTO** statement *(Fig. E.1)* unconditionally transfers control to the referenced statement. A simple **IF** *(Fig. E.2)* is a conditional transfer, sending control to the specified statement only if the tested condition is true. An **IF** statement can be used to control a loop *(Fig. E.3)*; consider recoding such loops as **DO** structures. The simple **IF** can also be used to perform logical tests *(Fig. E.4)*. True BASIC's **IF...THEN...ELSE** structure usually results in much clearer logic, however.

Traditional BASIC supports a restricted form of subroutine call: **GOSUB** and

Fig. E.2: *Logical tests can be performed using a simple **IF** statement.*

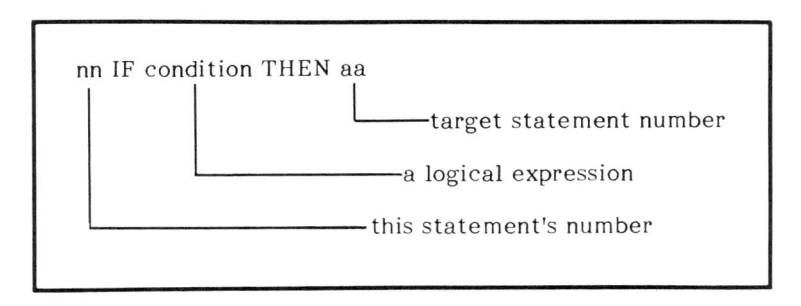

```
nn IF condition THEN aa
   │     │           └── target statement number
   │     └── a logical expression
   └── this statement's number
```

Traditional BASIC	True BASIC

200 LET s = 0
210 INPUT x
220 LET s = s + x
230 IF s < 100 THEN 210
240 -----
250 -----
	LET s = 0
	DO
	   INPUT x
	   LET s = s + x
	LOOP UNTIL s >= 100
	----- 	

Fig. E.3: *A simple IF can be used to control a loop, but a* **DO WHILE** *or* **DO UNTIL** *structure is much more clear.*

RETURN *(Fig. E.5).* When a **GOSUB** statement is executed, control is transferred to the specified instruction. Later, when the **RETURN** is executed, control returns to the statement immediately following **GOSUB**. In effect, **GOSUB** is equivalent to an internal subroutine **CALL** with no parameters, and **RETURN** is equivalent to an **END SUB** statement. Replace **GOSUB**s with **CALL**s and define standard *True BASIC* subroutines.

Many versions of BASIC support **ON-GOTO** and **ON-GOSUB** statements *(Fig. E.6).* If the index is equal to 1, control is transferred to the first statement number; if the index is 2, control goes to the second statement number, and so on. Replace these statements with a **SELECT CASE** structure.

True BASIC does support the old control structures. **GOTO, IF, GOSUB, RETURN, ON-GOTO,** and **ON-GOSUB** will work as long as all statements are numbered. They are not recommended (in fact, we intentionally avoided them in this primer). Because they are supported, some existing BASIC programs will run under *True BASIC* with little or no change. In fact, any program that conforms to the old ANS minimal BASIC standard should run under *True BASIC*.

Fig. E.4: *A simple IF can also be used to code complex decision logic. However, an IF...THEN...ELSE block is usually much clearer.*

Traditional BASIC	True BASIC

200 INPUT x
210 IF x >= 0 THEN 240
220 PRINT "error"
230 GOTO 260
240 LET s = Sqr (x)
250 PRINT x, s
260 -----
270 -----
	INPUT x
	IF x >= 0 THEN
	   LET s = Sqr (x)
	   PRINT x, s
	ELSE
	   PRINT "error"
	END IF
	----- 	

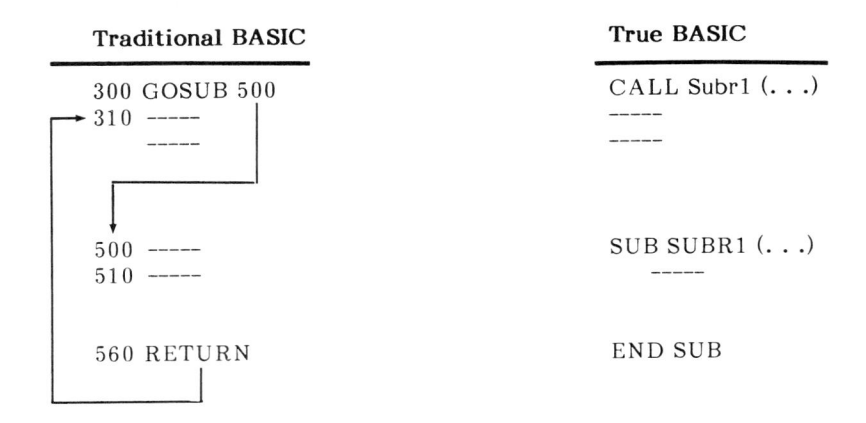

```
      Traditional BASIC                          True BASIC

      300 GOSUB 500                              CALL Subr1 (. . .)
      310 -----                                  -----
          -----                                  -----


      500 -----                                  SUB SUBR1 (. . .)
      510 -----                                  -----


      560 RETURN                                 END SUB
```

Fig. E.5: *Traditional BASIC's **GOSUB** and **RETURN** statements support a limited form of subroutine call. Replace them with real subroutines.*

CONVERTING TO *TRUE BASIC*

Few programs conform to the old minimal BASIC standard, however. Most take advantage of one or more features of their BASIC dialect. Such programs must be modified before they can run under *True BASIC*. Specific conversion rules vary with the version of BASIC. We can, however, offer a few general guidelines.

Many BASIC dialects allow the programmer to take shortcuts. For example, the keyword **LET** is often optional, and the **END** statement can often be omitted. **LET** must be coded in *True BASIC*, and an **END** statement is needed to separate internal and external program units.

Fig. E.6: *Replace **ON-GOTO** and **ON-GOSUB** statements with a **SELECT CASE** structure.*

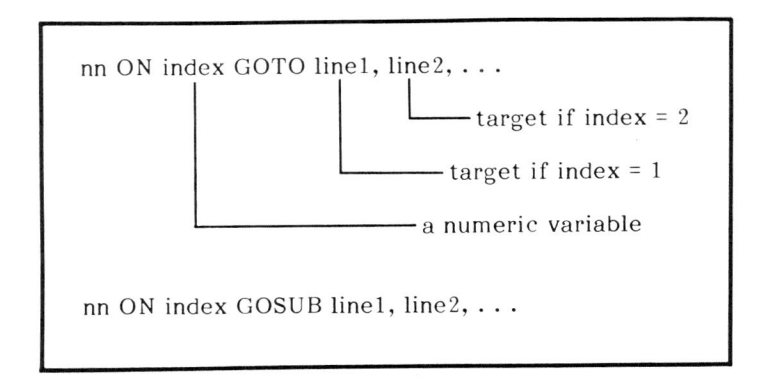

```
   nn ON index GOTO line1, line2, . . .
                               └── target if index = 2
                         └── target if index = 1
          └── a numeric variable

   nn ON index GOSUB line1, line2, . . .
```

Another popular shortcut is coding several statements on a single line. That's illegal in *True BASIC*, where the rule is one statement per line. Also, the *True BASIC* programmer must leave at least one space between variable names, operators, and constants, coding

LET a = b

instead of

LETa=b

In some BASIC's, multiple assignment statements such as

LET a = b = c = 0

are legal. The *True BASIC* equivalent is

LET a, b, c = 0

Many BASICs allow the programmer to specify the form of a numeric variable, using a special character to indicate integer or double precision. *True BASIC* automatically selects the most efficient data type. Remove special characters from variable names. Another feature of many BASICs is defining string length through a declare statement or a set of parameters. *True BASIC* strings are variable in length; they expand or contract as necessary. Remove any instructions or parameters that define string length.

Many BASICs convert numbers to integers by truncating, for example, changing 2.9 to 2. *True BASIC* rounds, so 2.9 becomes 3. If program logic depends on generating integer values, an old program can produce surprising results when converted to *True BASIC*. Consider using a **Truncate** or **Round** function to control conversion to integer.

True BASIC does *not* support logical (**AND, OR, NOT**) operations. Remove them from your program and replace them with conditional expressions.

In many BASIC dialects, generating graphic output means working with pixels. Often, the best solution is to rewrite such graphic routines, but rewriting a routine is not always an option. To use the old graphics logic under *True BASIC*, define your x-y coordinates to match the pixel coordinates.

When it comes to accessing disk, telecommunication devices, or other peripherals, the various BASIC dialects tend to be quite hardware specific. Expect to recode any logic that refers to any device other than the keyboard or the video display.

True BASIC accesses peripheral devices through channels. The channel approach is compatible with the hardware architecture of many small computer systems; thus, one peripheral device calls for much the same logic as any other. Telecommunication is, however, an exception. Several incompatible protocols are in common use, and no clear leader has emerged. Consequently, *True BASIC* does not presently support telecommunication. The experienced programmer who wants to work in a telecommunication environment can write an assembler language subroutine to access the network.

Many versions of BASIC allow the programmer directly to manipulate the contents of main memory with **PEEK** and **POKE** instructions, and *True BASIC* is no exception. Additionally, *True BASIC* supports assembler language subroutines. Given access to assembler language, a programmer can utilize the computer's complete instruction set. It's a very powerful feature, but an advanced one; see the *Reference Manual* for details.

Appendix

I. *True BASIC* Instructions

II. *True BASIC* Built-in Functions

III. *True BASIC* Commands

IV. Errors and Error Codes

V. The ASCII Character Set

VI. Answers to Selected Exercises

I. *TRUE BASIC* INSTRUCTIONS

This appendix lists, in alphabetical order, text references to *True BASIC* syntax rules, statements, and logical conditions.

Syntax Rules

Rule	Figure	Page
arithmetic operators	2.6	26
concatenation		293
expressions		26-29
format characters	7.14	205
format strings	7.17	208
logical expressions	3.7	57
locical operators	3.8	58
music commands	10.12	306
numeric constants	2.3	23
priority of operators	2.10	29
SELECT CASE tests	3.19	75
string constants	2.4	24
substrings	10.6	298
variable names	2.5	25
windows	7.21	212

Statements

Statement	Figure	Page
ASK, files	11.15	335
ASK CURSOR	7.26	215
BOX AREA	9.20	270
BOX CIRCLE	9.20	270
BOX CLEAR	9.30	276
BOX ELLIPSE	9.20	270
BOX KEEP	9.30	276
BOX LINES	9.20	270
BOX SHOW	9.30	276
CALL	5.25	144
CHAIN	12.8	351
CLEAR	7.24	214
	9.28	275
CLOSE	7.20	210
	9.39	283
	11.4	319

Comments		35
DATA	7.8	199
DECLARE	5.18	135
DEF	5.8	125
DIM	8.3	225
DO	4.13	99
DO UNTIL	4.15	101
DO WHILE	4.17	102
DRAW	9.35	280
ELSEIF	3.22	70
END	2.17	37
END DEF	5.8	125
END PICTURE		279
END SUB	5.22	141
END WHEN	D.1	403
ERASE	11.7	324
EXIT DO		99
EXIT FOR		93
EXTERNAL	12.1	343
FLOOD	9.24	273
FOR. . .NEXT	4.6	91
GET KEY	7.4	195
GET MOUSE	9.33	278
GET POINT	9.32	278
GOSUB	E.5	411
GOTO	E.1	410
IF, simple	E.2	410
IF. . .THEN	3.5	56
	3.6	56
IF. . .THEN. . .ELSE	3.15	64
INPUT	2.14	36
INPUT with PROMPT	7.2	193
LET	2.11	29
LIBRARY	12.3	345
LINE INPUT	10.8	301
MAT INPUT	8.19	239
MAT PRINT	8.23	243
MAT READ	8.22	242
ON-GOSUB		411
ON-GOTO	E.6	412
OPEN	9.38	282
	11.3	318
OPEN PRINTER	7.18	209
OPEN SCREEN	7.21	211

PAUSE	7.23	214
	9.27	274
	9.34	279
PICTURE	10.11	306
PLAY	9.27	267
PLOT AREA	9.11	263
PLOT LINES	9.3	256
PLOT POINTS	9.13	264
PLOT TEXT	2.15	36
PRINT	7.13	205
PRINT USING	12.9	351
PROGRAM	5.11	127
RANDOMIZE	7.7	199
READ	7.10	201
RESTORE	3.28	75
SELECT CASE	9.15	265
SET BACKGROUND COLOR	9.16	266
SET COLOR	7.25	215
SET CURSOR	11.10	326
SET, record files	11.9	325
SET, text files	10.14	307
SOUND	5.22	141
SUB	11.8	324
UNSAVE	D.1	403
WHEN ERROR IN	9.40	283
WINDOW		

Logical Conditions

Condition

	Page
END DATA	201
END #n	321
KEY INPUT	211
MORE DATA	201
MORE #n	321

I I. *TRUE BASIC* FUNCTIONS

This appendix summarizes material taken from the *Reference Manual*.

A. Mathematical Functions

Function	Description
Abs(x)	Returns the absolute value of **x**.
Divide (x,y,q,r)	This subroutine must be called. Divides **x** by **y**, and returns their quotient **q** and their remainder **r**.
Eps(x)	Returns the smallest number that can be added to or subtracted from **x** so that the result differs from **x**. **Eps(0)** returns the smallest value *True BASIC* can handle on your computer.
Exp(x)	Returns e^x. The inverse of the **Log** function.
Int(x)	Returns the greatest integer less than or equal to **x**.
Log(x)	Returns the natural (base e) logarithm of **x**.
Log2(x)	Returns the base 2 logarithm of **x**.
Log10(x)	Returns the base 10 logarithm of **x**.
Max(x,y)	Returns the larger value, **x** or **y**.
Maxnum	Returns the largest positive integer your computer can handle.
Min(x,y)	Returns the smaller value, **x** or **y**.
Mod(x,y)	Returns "**x** modulo **y**." Roughly the remainder of **x** divided by **y**, where **y** may not be zero.
Remainder(x,y)	Returns the remainder of **x** divided by **y**, where **y** may not be zero.

Rnd	Returns a "pseudo-random" number between 0 and 1.
Round(x)	Returns **x** rounded to an integer.
Round(x,n)	Returns **x** rounded to **n** decimal places.
Sgn(x)	Returns 1 if **x** is positive, 0 if **x** is zero, or –1 if **x** is negative.
Sqr(x)	Returns the square root of **x**.
Truncate(x,n)	Returns **x** truncated to **n** decimal places.

B. **Trigonometric Functions**

   Note: By default, *True BASIC* measures angles in radians. You may override this default by coding an **OPTION ANGLE DEGREES** statement early in the program before any trigonometric functions are used.

Function	Description
Angle(x,y)	Returns the counterclockwise angle between the positive x-axis and the point **(x,y)**.
Atn(x)	Returns the arctangent of **x**.
Cos(x)	Returns the cosine of angle **x**.
Deg(x)	Returns **x** radians converted to degrees.
PI	The constant π (3.1415926...).
Rad(x)	Returns **x** degrees converted to radians.
Sin(x)	Returns the sine of angle **x**.
Tan(x)	Returns the tangent of angle **x**.

C. String Functions

Note: String functions ending in a dollar sign ($) return a string value. Functions not ending in a dollar sign return a number.

Function	Description
Chr$(n)	Takes a number, **n,** and returns a single-character string corresponding to that number from the ASCII character set *(see Appendix V)*.
LEN(a$)	Returns the number of characters in the string, **a$**.
Lcase$(a$)	Returns the string, **a$**, with each capital letter changed to lower case.
Ltrim$(a$)	Returns the string, **a$**, with leading spaces trimmed off.
Num$(n)	Takes a number, **n**, and converts it to a standard 8-character string representation.
Ord(a$)	Takes a 1-character string, **a$**, and returns the ASCII code for that character. This function is the inverse of **Chr$(n)**.
Pos(a$,b$)	Looks for the first occurrence of **b$** within **a$**, and returns the character location of the first match. If no match is found, returns 0.
Pos(a$,b$,n)	Looks for occurrences of **b$** within **a$** at or after character **n**. If no match is found, returns 0.
Repeat$(a$,n)	Returns the string, **a$**, repeated **n** times.
Rtrim$(a$)	Returns the string, **a$**, with trailing spaces trimmed off.
Str$(n)	Returns the number, **n**, converted to a string.

	Trim$(a$)	Returns the string, **a$**, with both leading and trailing spaces trimmed off.
	Ucase$(a$)	Returns the string, **a$**, with all lower case letters changed to upper case.
	Using$(format$, expr1,expr2,...)	Returns a string containing all the expressions as formatted by the format string.
	Val(a$)	Returns the string, **a$**, converted to a number. The string must represent a proper number.

D. Date and Time Functions

Function	Description
Date	Returns the current date as a number with format YYDDD, where January 1 is day 001, January 2 is day 002, and so on.
Time	Returns the current time measured in seconds since midnight.
Date$	Returns the current date as a string with the format "yyyymmdd."
Time$	Returns the current time as a string with the format "hh:mm:ss". Hours are measured on a 24-hour clock with midnight as 00.

E. Logical Functions

Function	Description
KEY INPUT	True if any key has been pressed since the last input was read from the keyboard.
END DATA	True if there are no more **DATA** items available for subsequent **READ** statements.
MORE DATA	True if there are more **DATA** items available for subsequent **READ** statements.

	END #expression	True if the pointer to file **#expression** is at the end of the file.
	MORE #expression	True if the pointer to file **#expression** is at the beginning or in the middle of the file.

F. **Array Functions**

Function	Description
Con	Sets every element of the array to which it is assigned to 1.
Con(x,y,...)	Sets every element in an **x** by **y** by ... array to 1.
Det	Returns the determinant of the last array inverted by the **Inv** function. If no array has been inverted, returns 0.
Det(x)	Returns the determinant of the square matrix **x**. If **x** is singular, returns 0.
Dot(x,y)	Returns the dot product of the two vectors **x** and **y**.
Idn	Initializes the array to which it is assigned to an identity matrix.
Idn(x)	Initializes an **x** by **x** identity matrix.
Idn(x,y)	The long way of writing **Idn(x)**; **x** and **y** must be equal.
Inv(x)	Returns the inverse of the square matrix **x**. Use **Det** to check on the validity of the results returned by **Inv**.
Lbound(a)	Returns the lower bound of the 1-dimensional array **a**.
Lbound(a,n)	Returns the lower bound of the **n**th dimension of array **a**.

Nul$	Initializes to the null string each element in the array to which it is assigned.
Size(a)	Returns the current number of elements in array **a**.
Size(a,n)	Returns the current number of elements in the **n**th dimension of array **a**.
Trn(x)	Returns the transpose of matrix **x**.
Ubound(a)	Returns the upper bound of the 1-dimensional array **a**.
Ubound(a,n)	Returns the upper bound of the **n**th dimension of array **a**.
Zer	Sets to zero each element of the array to which it is assigned.
Zer(x,y,...)	Initializes each element in an **x** by **y** by ... array to zero.

III. *TRUE BASIC* COMMANDS

This appendix summarizes material from the *Reference Manual*. Several of the command descriptions refer to a *block*. A block is a set of lines previously marked or otherwise identified as a range of statement numbers, or as a function, subroutine, or picture name.

General form	Description
BREAK block	Inserts a breakpoint at the first marked line, or at the first line in the specified block. Useful for program debugging. To remove a breakpoint, "**BREAK**" the line again.
BYE	Marks the end of a *True BASIC* session, and returns control to the operating system.
CHANGE a,b	Changes all occurrences of word or number **a** to word or number **b**.
COMPILE	Replaces the current source program with the equivalent compiler object code. After compiling the program, you may **SAVE** and/or **RUN** it.
COPY block,target	Copies a block of lines from one part of a program to another. The target can be a line number, or a function, subroutine, or picture name. Note that **COPY** does not erase the source block.
DELETE block	Deletes the designated block.
DO program	Runs a preprocessor or formatting program against your current source program. For example, **DO FORMAT** runs a formatting program that indents your code and capitalizes keywords. You can write your own preprocessors; see the *Reference Manual*, Appendix G.
DO NUM	Adds line numbers to a program. When editing a program, it is sometimes useful to add line numbers, use them to define blocks, and then remove them from the finished program (see **DO UNNUM**).
DO UNNUM	Removes line numbers from a program.

EDIT block	Restricts editing to the named block.
FILES	Displays a list of all *True BASIC* files on your disk. See *True BASIC User's Guide* or your system reference manual for any extensions your computer might support.
HELP	Displays on-screen explanations of various *True BASIC* subjects. Type **HELP TOPICS** for a list of specific subjects. Then type **HELP** followed by the topic's name. On many computers, function key F10 is a **HELP** key.
INCLUDE filename	Inserts a saved file into your current program. Useful for adding subroutines or functions to a program. When the functions or subroutines are stored in a library, use a **LIBRARY** statement instead.
KEEP block	Deletes all but the designated block from your current program.
KEY	Allows you to redefine selected keys on your keyboard. See the *Reference Manual* for details.
LIST block	Generates a listing of the designated block on your printer. If no block is indicated, lists the entire program on the printer.
LOCATE a	Finds and displays all lines containing the indicated word or number.
MARK block	Designates a block of lines for future editing operations.
MOVE block,target	Moves the designated block to the target location (a line number, or a function, subroutine, or picture name). Unlike **COPY**, **MOVE** erases the source block.
NEW filename	Clears the editing window and moves the cursor to the editing window's first line so that you can start a new program.
OLD filename	Retrieves a previously saved program from disk.

REPLACE filename   Overwrites or replaces an existing file or program on disk.

RUN   Executes the current program. Following a **RUN** command, the program in main memory is compiled and errors are identified. If no errors are detected, the program is executed.

SAVE filename   Copies the program currently in main memory to disk.

SPLIT n   Controls the location of the dividing line between the history and the editing windows, where **n** is a line number from the top of the screen. Not available on all versions of *True BASIC*.

TO block   Moves the cursor to the start of the designated block in your current program.

TRY a,b   Similar to **CHANGE**. Searches current program for occurrences of word or number **a**. When an occurrence is found, the user is asked if he or she wishes to change **a** to **b** by responding yes, no, or quit. Responding quit terminates the operation.

UNSAVE filename   Deletes an unwanted file from disk.

IV. ERRORS AND ERROR CODES

Most *True BASIC* error messages are self-explanatory. Listing them here or repeating the reference manual descriptions would be a waste of space. If you encounter an unclear error message, check the *Reference Manual. (Appendix B)*.

Three types of errors are possible:

1. *Command errors.* You typed an invalid command. If you type a command that *True BASIC* simply can't figure out, the response is: "What? (Please type HELP.)" This message usually means you've misspelled the command. More explicit command messages usually mean you've incorrectly specified the parameters that follow the command itself.

2. *Compilation errors.* These errors can only occur following a **RUN** or **COMPILE** command. Once the program itself begins executing, compilation errors can no longer occur.

3. *Run-time errors.* These errors occur after your program has been compiled and begins executing. Run-time error messages are assigned numbers. You can trap these errors *(see Module D)* and use the **Extype** and **EXtype$** functions to obtain the numeric code and the error message. A list of runtime errors and error codes is shown below.

Extype	Extext$
1000	Overflow.
1051	String too long.
2001	Subscript out of bounds.
3001	Division by zero.
3002	Negative number to non-integral power.
3003	Zero to negative power.
3004	LOG of number <=0.
3005	SQR of negative number.
3006	MOD and REMAINDER can't have 0 as 2nd argument.
3008	Can't use ANGLE(0,0).
3009	Can't invert singular matrix.
4001	VAL string isn't a proper number.
4003	Improper ORD string.
4004	SIZE index out of range.
4005	TAB column not between 1 and margin.
4006	Margin less than zonewidth.

4007	ZONEWIDTH out of range.
4008	LBOUND out of range.
4009	UBOUND out of range.
4010	REPEAT$ count < 0.
4020	Improper NUM string.
4501	Error in PLAY string.
5000	Out of memory.
6001	Mismatched array sizes.
6002	DET needs a square matrix.
6003	INV needs a square matrix.
6004	IDN must make a square matrix.
7001	Channel number must be 1 to 1000.
7002	Can't use #0 here.
7003	Channel is already open.
7004	Channel isn't open.
7101	Unknown OPEN option
7102	Too many channels open.
7103	File's record size doesn't match OPEN RECSIZE.
7104	Wrong type of file.
7202	Must be record or byte file for SET RECORD.
7250	Can't SET RECSIZE on non-empty record file.
7251	Must be byte file or empty for SET RECSIZE.
7252	File pointer out of bounds.
7301	Can't erase file not opened as OUTIN.
7302	Can't output to INPUT file.
7303	Can't input from OUTPUT file.
7350	Can't PRINT to middle of text file.
7351	Must be byte file for READ BYTES.
8001	Reading past end of data.
8002	Too few input items.
8003	Too many input items.
8011	Reading past end of file.
8101	String given instead of number.
8103	Data item isn't a number.
8104	Data item isn't a string.
8105	Badly formed input line.
8201	Badly formed USING string.
8202	No USING item for output.
8301	Output item bigger than RECSIZE.
8302	Input item bigger than RECSIZE.
8304	Must SET RECSIZE before WRITE.
8501	Must be text file.
8502	Must be record or byte file.
8601	Cursor set out of bounds.
8700	No GET MOUSE on this computer.

9001	File is read or write protected.
9002	Trouble using disk or printer.
9003	No such file.
9004	File already exists.
9005	Diskette removed, or wrong diskette.
9006	Disk full.
9666	Program stopped.
10001	ON index out of range, no ELSE given.
10002	RETURN without GOSUB.
10004	No CASE selected, but no CASE ELSE.
10005	*
11000	Can't do graphics on this computer.
11001	Window minimum = maximum.
11002	Screen minimum > = maximum.
11003	Screen bounds must be 0 to 1.
11004	Can't SET WINDOW in picture.
11005	Channel isn't a window.
11008	No such color.

True BASIC always supplies the Extype 10005 for any error that halts a **CHAIN** statement. The error message, however, describes the particular error that occurred. Thus, even a compile-time error like "illegal statement" could be coupled with Extype 10005, and trapped by an error handler in a program that **CHAIN**ed and **RETURN**ed.

V. THE ASCII CHARACTER SET

This table lists the ASCII characters supported on all *True BASIC* computers. A total of 128 different patterns are listed. (000 - 127). Many computers support additional characters with codes 128 - 255. To see if your computer does, consult your *User's Guide* or your computer's reference manual.

Decimal	Name*	Hex	Decimal	Name*	Hex
000	nul	00	026	sub	1A
001	soh	01	027	esc	1B
002	stx	02	028	fs	1C
003	etx	03	029	gs	1D
004	eot	04	030	rs	1E
005	enq	05	031	us	1F
006	ack	06	032	sp	20
007	bel	07	033	!	21
008	bs	08	034	"	22
009	ht	09	035	#	23
010	lf	0A	036	$	24
011	vt	0B	037	%	25
012	ff	0C	038	&	26
013	cr	0D	039	'	27
014	so	0E	040	(	28
015	si	0F	041	)	29
016	dle	10	042	*	2A
017	dc1	11	043	+	2B
018	dc2	12	044	,	2C
019	dc3	13	045	—	2D
020	dc4	14	046	.	2E
021	nak	15	047	/	2F
022	syn	16	048	0	30
023	etb	17	049	1	31
024	can	18	050	2	32
025	em	19	051	3	33

*These names can be used as arguments to the Ord function.

+The first 33 characters are control signals and other special characters.

Decimal	Name*	Hex	Decimal	Name*	Hex
052	4	34	090	Z	5A
053	5	35	091	[	5B
054	6	36	092	\	5C
055	7	37	093	]	5D
056	8	38	094	^	5E
057	9	39	095	_ UND+	5F
058	:	3A	096	` GRA	60
059	;	3B	097	a LCA	61
060	<	3C	098	b LCB	62
061	=	3D	099	c LCC	63
062	>	3E	100	d LCD	64
063	?	3F	101	e LCE	65
064	@	40	102	f LCF	66
065	A	41	103	g LCG	67
066	B	42	104	h LCH	68
067	C	43	105	i LCI	69
068	D	44	106	j LCJ	6A
069	E	45	107	k LCK	6B
070	F	46	108	l LCL	6C
071	G	47	109	m LCM	6D
072	H	48	110	n LCN	6E
073	I	49	111	o LCO	6F
074	J	4A	112	p LCP	70
075	K	4B	113	q LCQ	71
076	L	4C	114	r LCR	72
077	M	4D	115	s LCS	73
078	N	4E	116	t LCT	74
079	O	4F	117	u LCU	75
080	P	50	118	v LCV	76
081	Q	51	119	w LCW	77
082	R	52	120	x LCX	78
083	S	53	121	y LCY	79
084	T	54	122	z LCZ	7A
085	U	55	123	{ LBR	7B
086	V	56	124	| VLN	7C
087	W	57	125	} RBR	7D
088	X	58	126	~ TIL	7E
089	Y	59	127	del	7F

*These names can be used as arguments to the Ord function.

+These names are designed for use with computers that do not distinguish between upper- and lowercase letters.

VI. ANSWERS TO SELECTED EXERCISES

CHAPTER 1

The exercises in chapter 1 are self-explanatory.

CHAPTER 2

1. (a.) legal   (b.) legal   (c.) comma
   (d.) legal   (e.) legal   (f.) dollar sign
   (g.) dashes   (h.) two decimal points   (i.) legal
   (j.) legal   (k.) blank   (l.) legal

2. (a.) legal number   (b.) first character   (c.) legal number
   (d.) legal number   (e.) legal string   (f.) first character
   (g.) dash   (h.) legal number   (i.) legal number
   (j.) legal number   (k.) ampersand   (l.) legal number

3. (a.) side^2
   (b.) length * width
   (c.) 0.5 * base * height
   (d.) 3.1416 * height * radius^2
   (e.) hits / times_at_bat
   (f.) ((x + y)^3) - ((x + y)^2) + 18
   (g.) (a^3) + ((a^2) * b) - ((a * (b^2)) + (b^3)
   (h.) (a + b + c) / 2
   (i.) ((a + b + c) / (x + y + z))^2
   (j.) ((-b) + (b^2 - (4 * a * c))) / (2 * a)
   (k.) ((a * b)^2)^2
   (l.) grade_points / credits_earned

4, 5, 6. Self-explanatory.

Listed below are suggested solutions to the odd-numbered programming exercises.

```
! Chapter 2, Exercise 7
! Area of a square.

INPUT side
LET area = side * side
PRINT side, area
END
```

```
! Chapter 2, Exercise 9
! Area of a triangle.

INPUT base, height
LET area = 0.5 * base * height
PRINT base, height, area
END
```

```
! Chapter 2, Exercise 11
! Batting average.

INPUT hits, times_at_bat
LET batting_average = hits / times_at_bat
PRINT hits, times_at_bat, batting_average
END



! Chapter 2, Exercise 13
! Points scored.

INPUT field_goals, fouls_made
LET points = fouls_made + (field_goals * 2)
PRINT fouls_made, field_goals, points
END



! Chapter 2, Exercise 15
! Evaluate polynomial.

INPUT x
LET y = (2 * x^3) + (3 * x^2) - (4 * x) + 3
PRINT x, y
END



! Chapter 2, Exercise 17
! Distance light travels in x years.

INPUT years

! miles/second * seconds/minute * minutes/hour *
! hours/day * days/year * years

LET distance = 186000 * 60 * 60 * 24 * 365 * years
PRINT years, distance
END



! Chapter 2, Exercise 19
! Compound interest.

INPUT investment, rate, years
LET future_value = investment * ((1 + rate) ^ years)
PRINT investment, rate, years, future_value
END
```

CHAPTER 3

1. (a.) radius > 0
   (b.) pay_rate < 15.50
   (c.) grade_points >= 90
   (d.) grade_point_average >= 3.5
   (e.) a^2 = (b^2 + c^2)
   (f.) account_balance < 0
   (g.) account_balance >= 50
   (h.) (hours_worked >= 20) AND (hours_worked <= 75)
   (i.) ((x + y) >= 0) AND ((x+y) <= 25)
   (j.) (class = 3) AND (sex = 2) AND (major = 317)

2, 3, 4, 5, 6. Self-explanatory

Listed below are suggested solutions to the odd-numbered programming exercises. Note that Exercise 18 is shown rather than Exercise 19.

```
! Chapter 3, Exercise 7
! Select smallest value.

INPUT x, y, z
LET smallest = x
IF y < smallest THEN LET smallest = y
IF z < smallest THEN LET smallest = z
PRINT smallest
END


! Chapter 3, Exercise 9
! Compute postage due.

INPUT ounces
IF ounces <= 12 THEN
   LET postage = 0.22 + 0.17 * (ounces - 1)
   PRINT ounces, postage
ELSE
   PRINT "Over 12 ounces. Use alternate rate."
END IF
END


! Chapter 3, Exercise 11
! Pythagorean theorem.

INPUT a, b, c
IF a^2 = (b^2 + c^2) THEN
   PRINT "Right triangle"
ELSE
   PRINT "Not a right triangle"
END IF
END
```

```
! Chapter 3, Exercise 13
! Roots of a quadratic equation.

INPUT a, b, c
LET descrim = b^2 - (4 * a * c)
IF descrim > 0 THEN
   LET root1 = ((-b) + descrim) / (2 * a)
   LET root2 = ((-b) - descrim) / (2 * a)
   PRINT root1, root2
ELSEIF descrim = 0 THEN
   LET root1 = (-b) / (2 * a)
   PRINT root1
ELSE
   PRINT "No real roots."
END IF
END



! Chapter 3, Exercise 15
! Impact.

! Compute time to intersection.
LET time_car_a = 2 / 35
LET time_car_b = 3 / 55

! Assume 0.1 seconds to clear.

IF (time_car_a - time_car_b) < 0.1 THEN
   PRINT "Impact!"
ELSE
   PRINT "No impact"
END IF
END



! Chapter 3, Exercise 17
! Grade conversion.

INPUT grade_points
SELECT CASE grade_points
   CASE 90 TO 100
      LET grade$ = "A"
   CASE 80 TO 89
      LET grade$ = "B"
   CASE 70 TO 79
      LET grade$ = "C"
   CASE 60 TO 69
      LET grade$ = "D"
   CASE IS < 60
      LET grade$ = "F"
   CASE ELSE
      LET grade$ = "error"
END SELECT
PRINT grade_points, grade$
END
```

```
! Chapter 3, Exercise 18
! Federal tax.

INPUT gross_pay
SELECT CASE gross_pay
    CASE 0 TO 27
        LET federal_tax = 0.00
    CASE 27.01 TO 84
        LET federal_tax = 0.12 * (gross_pay - 27)
    CASE 84.01 TO 185
        LET federal_tax = 6.84 + 0.15 * (gross_pay - 84)
    CASE 185.01 TO 292
        LET federal_tax = 21.99 + 0.19 * (gross_pay - 185)
    CASE 292.01 TO 440
        LET federal_tax = 42.32 + 0.25 * (gross_pay - 292)
    CASE 440.01 TO 556
        LET federal_tax = 79.32 + 0.30 * (gross_pay - 440)
    CASE 556.01 TO 663
        LET federal_tax = 114.12 + 0.34 * (gross_pay - 556)
    CASE IS > 663
        LET federal_tax = 150.50 + 0.37 * (gross_pay - 663)
    CASE ELSE
        PRINT "error"
END SELECT
PRINT gross_pay, federal_tax
END
```

CHAPTER 4

```
! Chapter 4, Exercise 1
! Sum odd digits.

LET sum = 0
FOR n = 1 TO 100 STEP 2
    LET sum = sum + n
NEXT n
PRINT sum
END
```

```
! Chapter 4, Exercise 3.
! Average with negative grade.

LET count = 0
LET sum = 0
                                  ! In a DO loop, individual values are input,
                                  ! counted, and accumulated. A negative value
DO                                ! indicates the end of data.
    INPUT x
    IF x = 999 THEN               ! A negative number means no more data. We
        LET sum = sum + x         ! do not want to count and accumulate this
        LET count = count + 1     ! sentinel value.
    END IF
LOOP UNTIL x = 999                ! Here is the loop's exit condition.
```

```
LET average = sum / count        ! After exiting the loop, the average is
PRINT sum, count, average        ! computed and printed.
END



! Chapter 4, Exercise 5.
! Wind chill modified.

                                 ! The control variable for the outer loop
                                 ! is wind velocity.

FOR wind_velocity = 10 TO 50 STEP 10

                                 ! The control variable for the inner loop
                                 ! is temperature. Because the formula
                                 ! for computing a wind chill factor is
                                 ! complex, we'll break it into steps.

    FOR temperature = -30 TO 30 STEP 10

        LET term1 = 0.288 * (wind_velocity ^ 0.5)
        LET term2 = 0.019 * wind_velocity
        LET term3 = 91.4 - temperature
        LET wind_chill = 91.4 - ((term1 + 0.450 - term2) * term3)
        PRINT temperature, wind_velocity, wind_chill

    NEXT temperature

    PRINT                        ! Print a blank line to separate
                                 ! wind velocities.
NEXT wind_velocity

END



! Chapter 4, Exercise 7.
! Distance table.
FOR miles = 1 TO 25
   LET feet = 5280 * miles
   LET yards = 1760 * miles
   LET kilometers = 1.609344 * miles
   PRINT miles, feet, yards, kilometers
NEXT miles
END



! Chapter 4, Exercise 9.
! Compute factorial.
INPUT n
LET factorial = 1
FOR i = 1 TO n
   LET factorial = factorial * i
NEXT i
PRINT n, factorial
END
```

```
! Chapter 4, Exercise 11.
! Quartiles.
LET first = 0
LET second = 0
LET third = 0
LET fourth = 0
DO
   INPUT n
   SELECT CASE n
      CASE IS < 0
      CASE IS <= 25
         LET first = first + 1
      CASE IS <= 50
         LET second = second + 1
      CASE IS <= 75
         LET third = third + 1
      CASE IS <= 100
         LET fourth = fourth + 1
      CASE ELSE
   END SELECT
LOOP UNTIL n < 0
PRINT first, second, third, fourth
END

! Chapter 4, Exercise 13.
! Loan repayment.
INPUT loan, rate, payment
LET beginning = loan
LET ending = loan
DO WHILE ending > 0
   LET interest = beginning * (rate/12)
   LET principle = payment - interest
   LET ending = beginning - principle
   IF ending < 0 THEN
      LET payment = beginning + interest
      LET principle = beginning
      LET ending = 0
   END IF
   PRINT beginning, payment, interest, principle, ending
   LET beginning = ending
LOOP
END


! Chapter 4, Exercise 15.
! Estimate square root.
INPUT value
LET old = value/2
DO
   LET new = 0.5 * ((old + value) / old)
   LET test = (old - new) / old
   IF test < 0 THEN LET test = -test
   LET old = new
   PRINT new
LOOP UNTIL test < 0.001
PRINT value, new
END
```

```
! Chapter 4, Exercise 17.
! Making change.
LET count = 0
FOR half = 0 TO 2
   FOR quarter = 0 TO 4
      FOR dime = 0 TO 10
         FOR nickel = 0 TO 20
            FOR cent = 0 TO 100 STEP 5
               LET sum = (half*50)+(quarter*25)+(dime*10)+(nickel*5)+cent
               IF sum = 100 THEN LET count = count + 1
            NEXT cent
         NEXT nickel
      NEXT dime
   NEXT quarter
NEXT half
PRINT count
END


! Chapter 4, Exercise 19.
! Tax table.
LET tax_amount = 0.01
FOR sale = 0.01 TO 1.00 STEP 0.01
   LET tax = sale * 0.055
   IF tax > tax_amount THEN LET tax_amount = tax_amount + 0.01
   PRINT sale, tax_amount
NEXT sale
END


! Chapter 4, Exercise 21.
! Discomfort index.
FOR temperature = 70 TO 110 STEP 5
   FOR humidity = 0.60 TO 1.00 STEP 0.05
      LET discomfort1 = (0.55 - 0.55 * humidity)
      LET discomfort2 = (temperature - 58)
      LET discomfort = temperature - (discomfort1 * discomfort2)
      PRINT temperature, humidity, discomfort
   NEXT humidity
NEXT temperature
END
```

CHAPTER 5

```
! Chapter 5, Exercise 1.
! Max and min.
PRINT Maxnum, Eps(0)
END
```

```
! Chapter 5, Exercise 3.
! Square roots.
FOR n = 1 TO 25
   LET square_root = Sqr(n)
   LET root = n ^ 0.5
   PRINT n, square_root, root
NEXT n
END


! Chapter 5, Exercise 5.
! Trig table.
OPTION ANGLE DEGREES
FOR angle = 10 TO 360 STEP 10
   PRINT Sin(angle), Cos(angle)
NEXT angle
END

! Chapter 5, Exercise 7.
! Dice.
RANDOMIZE
FOR count = 1 TO 10
   LET die = Int(Rnd*6 + 1)
   PRINT die
NEXT count
END



! Chapter 5, Exercise 9.
! Combinations and permutations.

DECLARE DEF Factorial
INPUT students, group_size

LET nfactorial = Factorial(students)
LET rfactorial = Factorial(group_size)
LET difference = Factorial(students - group_size)

LET combinations = nfactorial / (rfactorial * difference)

LET permutations = nfactorial / difference

PRINT students, group_size, combinations, permutations

END
```

```
! Chapter 5, Exercise 11.
! Electric bills.
INPUT code, kilowatt
SELECT CASE code
  CASE 1
     CALL General_rate (kilowatt, bill)
  CASE 2
     CALL Total_electric (kilowatt, bill)
  CASE 3
     CALL Industrial (kilowatt, bill)
  CASE ELSE
     PRINT "Error. No such code."
END SELECT
PRINT code, kilowatt, bill
END


! Chapter 5, Exercise 13.
! Grade point average.
LET credits = 0
LET grade_points = 0
DO
  INPUT hours, grade
  IF hours > 0 THEN
    LET credits = credits + hours
    LET grade_points = grade_points + hours * grade
  END IF
LOOP UNTIL hours < 0
CALL Compute_gpa (credits, grade_points, average)
PRINT credits, grade_points, average
END

SUB Compute_gpa (credits, grade_points, average)
   LET average = grade_points / credits
END SUB

! Chapter 5, Exercise 15
! Estimate roots.
INPUT value
LET old = value / 2
DO
   LET new = 0.5 * (old + (value/old))
   LET error = (old - new) / old
   IF error < 0 THEN LET error = -error
   LET old = new
LOOP UNTIL error < 0.001
PRINT value, new
END
```

No solutions are suggested for Chapters 6 through 12.

Index

ACCESS option, 317,333
Accessing b: drive, 368
Accumulation, 88,231
Algorithm, 14,20,26,38,54,
    65,73,87,103-105,107,152,
    160-162,222,333
Animation, 275-278,283
ANS OR ANSI, 7,408
ANS BASIC, 7,8,408,409
Area, plotting, 266-278
Argument, 246
Arithmetic operator, 26
Array as parameter, 244-246
Array, general, 324
Array, multidimensional,
    233-239
Array name, 224
Array, one-dimensional,
    222-233
ASCII code, 195,292,304,325,
    327
ASK BACKGROUND COLOR
    statement, 284
ASK COLOR statement, 284
ASK CURSOR statement, 214,
    284
ASK MAX COLOR statement,
    284
ASK MODE statement, 370
ASK statement, files, 334
ASK WINDOW statement, 284
ASK ZONEWIDTH statement, 202
Aspect ratio, 255,270,272
Assembler language, 414

Background color, 265,
    266,369,370,389
Bar chart, 267
BASIC, history, 408
Bug, 401,403
Binary, 7
Black box, 119,127,130,
    141,161,162,181
Blinking character, 369
Block diagram, 20,38,54
Block of code, 387,389
Boot procedure, 305,362
BOX AREA statement,
    270,275
BOX CIRCLE statement,
    270,272,275,276
BOX CLEAR statement,
    275,276
BOX ELLIPSE statement,
    see BOX CIRCLE
BOX KEEP statement,
    275,276
BOX LINES statement,
    270,275
BOX SHOW statement,
    275,276,278
BOX statements, 269-278
BREAK command, 406
Building blocks, 44,110,
    152
Built-in function, 119-125
BYE, 13,366,381
Byte file, 334
BYTE option, 317,319,334
b: drive (IBM PC), 368

443

Calculator, 5,6
CALL statement, 141,142,145, 246,334,411
CASE ELSE, 73
Case structure, 73-77
  (see also SELECT CASE)
Checkpoint, 350
CHAIN statement, 350,351
Chaining, 350,351
CHANGE command, 387,389
Channel, 209,211,283,317, 320,321,334
Channel as parameter, 334
Chr$ function, 305
CLEAR statement, 213,275
CLOSE statement, 209,211,283, 319
Cohesion, 181
Color, 265,266,370,389
Command, 9,10
Command error, 400
Commands, *True BASIC*, 425-427
Comment, 35,158
Compatibility, 8,409
Compilation, 10,390
COMPILE command, 390
Compiler, 7
Computational functions, 347
Computer, 4-7
Computer system, 4,5
Concatenation, 292,293,294,327, 329
Condition, 52,53,56,86
Constant, 22,32,33
CONTINUE command, 406
Control structure, 156,158, 162,163,179
Coordinates, 255,256
COPY command, 389
Copy function, 382,383
Count loop, 87-95
Counting characters, 295
Counting words, 295,296
CREATE option, 317

Current window, 283
Cursor, 41,42,372,374
Cursor control keys, 361, 362,373,386,387

Dartmouth BASIC, 7,8
Data, 4,14
Data conversion, 300,301, 303,304
Data element, 314,327
Data pool, 200
Data processing, 4,6
DATA statement, 199-201
Data structure, 327,328
Data verification, 172-179
Date function, 305
Date$ function, 305
Debug, 181,200,399-406
Decision, 44,52,53,54, 77,110,394
DECLARE statement, 134,145,348
DEF statement, 124,125, 134,136
Default, 317,319
Default coordinates, 257, 270,283
DELETE command, 389
Desk checking, 59,244, 402,405
DIM (dimension) statement, 224,225,230,233, 240,245
Direct access, 326,331-333
Directory, 369
Disk or diskette, 4,8,42, 314-317,319
Diskcopy routine, 364,365
Display, 4,254
Division by zero, 401,402
DO FORMAT, 389
DO loop, 95-106
DO loop, simple, 97-99
DO NUM, 387,410
DO RENEM, 410

DO UNNUM, 387,410
DO UNTIL loop, 86,99-101,
  106,140,394
DO WHILE loop, 86,91,
  101-107,394
Documentation, 158,160
DRAW statement, 180
Edge of screen, 389
EDIT command, 387
Editing window, 9,41,42,
  372,373,378,389
Editor, 42,371-390
ELSE, 62,68
ELSEIF, 69-73
END DATA condition, 201
END DEF, 125
END IF, 56,59,63
END PICTURE, 280
END SELECT, 73,74
END statement, 37,126,136
END SUB, 141
END WHEN, 403
END #n condition, 321
Endless loop, 86,401
Equal sign, 31
ERASE statement, 323,324,
  334
Error correction, 373-275,
  399-406
Error handler routine, 403
Error, input, 300,301,304
Error message, 300,301,304,
  378,379,400,401,403
Error trapping, 403,404
Errors, 198-200,300,301,304,
  325,331,399-406
EXIT DO statement, 99,140
EXIT FOR statement, 93,99
Exit condition, 86,87,93,97,
  101,110
Explicit redimensioning, 240,242
Expression, 26-29
External function, 126-136,172
EXTERNAL statement, 342
External subroutine, 136,137,172
  178,181

File, 314-334,366-369
File name, 317,320,344,
  366,368,369
File name extension, 368
File update, 333
FILES command, 9,42,
  368,381
Find function, 387,405
Floating-point, 22
FLOOD statement, 272,276
Flow of logic, 31-33,39
Flowchart, 21,22,39,40,
  52,54,62,67,70,71,73,
  391-397
FOR...NEXT loop, 89-95,
  107
Foregound color, 265-267,
  272,284,369,370,389
Format characters (using
  function), 204-208
Frequency distribution,
  259-260
Full screen I/O, 209-214,
  264,283
Function, 118-136,152,
  156,244
Function key, 42,361,371,
  377,378,382,383,385,387
Function name, 122,124
FUNCTION statement, 136
Functional decomposition,
  179-182

GAMESLIB library, 347
GET KEY statement, 194,
  195
GET MOUSE statement, 279
GET POINT statement,
  278-279
Global data, 129,130,136,
  162,172,178
Global editing, 387,389
GOSUB statement, 410,411
GOTO statement, 408-410
Graphic cursor, 278

445

Graphic input, 278,279
Graphics, 11,254-284,360
Graphics card, 254,255,360, 369
GRAPHICS mode, 369-370
GRAPHLIB library, 347

Hard disk, 360
HELLO command, 9,43,366,381
HELP feature, 368,386,400
Hierarchy chart, 162
High resolution, 254,284,369
HIRES option, 369
History window, 9,36,42,209, 378,389

IBM PC, 8,359-370,373
IEEE code, 305,325,327,329,331
IF, simple, 410
IF statement, 55-58,59
IF...THEN, 54-56,58
IF...THEN...ELSE, 52,53, 62-65,410
Implicit redimensioning, 340
INCLUDE command, 125,127, 348
Identation, 59,60,64
Independence, 127-131, 136, 172, 178,181
Index, disk, 317,320
Index, file, 332,333
Information, 4,14
Input, 4,20,193-201
Input errors, 198,199
INPUT option, 319,321,323,324
INPUT statement, 35,36,39,193, 195,196,211,319,321,323,324
INPUT statement, graphics mode, 284
INPUT with PROMPT statement, 193
Insert mode, 374,375
INSTALL routine, 365
Instruction, 4,14

Instruction as command, 402,406
Int function, 124
Interface board, 360
Internal function, 122-125, 128,129
Internal subroutine, 136, 137,172,178,181

KEEP command, 389
Key input, 194,195
KEY INPUT condition, 211,256
Keyboard, 4,360-362,371

Lbound function, 240
Lcase function, 305
Len function, 294,295,304
Lengthy input lists, 195-198
LET statement, 29-31, 38,40
Library, 125,283,342-350
Library access, 342-346
Library creation, 342-346
Library, existing, 347-350
Library maintenance, 347
LIBRARY statement, 344, 346,348
Line, 34
Line number, 387,409,410
LINE INPUT statement, 199,300-304,323,403
Line tag, 372,376
Lines, plotting, 261-264
LIST command, 389
Listing, program, 389
Local channel, 334
Local data, 130,136,178,181, 201
LOCATE command, 387, 402,405
Logical error, 404-406
Logical expression, 56-59
Logical operator, 56,58,292
Long line, 377

Loop, 86-110
Ltrim function, 305

Macintosh, 8
Machine language, 7,8
Main memory, 5,7,30,314,360
Mainline, 158
Margin, 202
MARK command, 389
Marking lines, 382,383,387
MAT (matrix) statements, 239-244
MAT assignment statement, 242,243
MAT INPUT statement, 239,240, 242,244,324
MAT PLOT statement, 284
MAT PRINT statement, 242,324
MAT PRINT USING statement, 242
MAT READ statement, 242,244,333
MAT WRITE statement, 333
Matrix arithmetic, 246,247
Matrix manipulation, 239-243, 246,247
Maxnum function, 303,340
Medium resolution, 254,284
Memory, 5
MENULIB library, 347
Message characters (Using function), 204,205
Minimal BASIC, 411,412
MODE "40", 369
MODE "80", 369
Modular programming, 145,146, 152,156-160
Module, 163,179
Monitor, 254
MONO mode, 369,370
Monochrome screen, 360,369
MORE DATA condition, 201
MORE #n condition, 321,330
Mouse, 279,371
MOVE command, 389
Move function, 383
Music commands, 305,306

NAME option, 317
Nested IF, 68-73,394
Nested loops, 106-110
NEW command, 41,42, 372
NEW option, 317,320
NEWOLD, 317
Nonvolatile memory, 315
Null string, 292,300
Num function, 305
Numeric constant, 22,23
Numeric function, 121
Numeric variable, 301, 303
Numeric versus string, 292,300
Num function, 331
Num$ function, 305,331

Odometer order, 240,242
OLD command,10,11,43, 381
OLD option, 317,321
ON-GOSUB statement, 411,412
ON-GOTO statement, 411,412
OPEN statement, 209,311, 282,283,317-319,320,321, 327,329,331,333
Operating system, 362,373, 365,366,369
Operator, 26
Ord function, 304
ORGANIZATION option, 317
Origin, graphics, 255,276
OUTIN option, 317,333
Output, 4,20,202-214
OUTPUT option, 317,320
Overstrike mode, 374,375

Pack, 327-329
Palette, color, 266,370

Parallel arrays, 237,239
Parameter, 119-121,127,130,136, 141,142,181,244-246,280
Parameter, array, 244-246
Parameter, channel, 334
Parentheses, 28,29
Parsing, 301-304
Passing parameters, 120,130,142, 145
PAUSE statement, 211,214,273, 275
PC/DOS, 363,366,369
PEEK statement, 414
PICTURE statement, 280
Pictures, 279-283
Pie chart, 269
Pixel, 254,255,369
Planning, program, 160-162
PLAY statement, 305-307
PLOT AREA statement, 267-269
PLOT LINES statement, 261-264, 279
PLOT POINTS statement, 256, 257
PLOT TEXT statement, 264, 369
Plotting areas, 266-278
Plotting lines, 261-264
Plotting points, 256,257
Plotting text, 264
Pointer, 200,324,326,329,331, 333
Points, plotting, 256,257
POKE statement, 414
POS function, 294,295,299,301, 303,304
Precision, 22
Preparing *True BASIC* disk, 362-366
Pretty printing, 389
PRINT, graphics mode, 284
PRINT statement, 36,193,202-209, 319,321,323,324
PRINT USING statement, 204-208, 324

Print zone, 36,37,202,203
PRINTER option (OPEN), 209,317
Printer output, 208,209
Priority of operators, 27-29
Problem definition, 20,38, 54,60
Processor, 5,360
Program, 7,14
Program development process, 14,20-22
Program listing, 389
Program name, 41
Program planning, 20-22
PROGRAM statement, 351
Prompt, 9,13,36,193,194, 379
Pseudo-random number, 125

Quotation mark (string constant), 292

Random number, 122,124, 125
RANDOMIZE statement, 125
Randomizing, 333
READ statement, 199-201, 326,329,334
Record, 314,325-327,329, 331
Record file, 305,325-334
Record file, creation, 325-328
Record file, direct access, 331-333
Record file, sequential access, 329-331
Record length (or record size), 319,325
RECORD option, 317
RECSIZE option, 327
Recursion, 122,352,353

Redimensioning, explicit, 240, 242
Redimensioning, implicit, 240
Relational operator, 56,57
REM statement, 35,158
Repeat$ function, 305,329
Repetition or repetitive logic, 44,86-110
REPLACE command, 368,384
Resolution, screen, 254,369
RESTORE statement, 201
RETURN option (CHAIN), 351
RETURN statement, 411
Rnd function, 122,124,125,256
Rtrim function, 305
RUN command, 10,11,42,378
Run-time error, 401-404

SAVE command, 42,368,379, 381,384
Scientific notation, 22
Screen, 254,389,390
SCREEN option (OPEN), 211,317
Search and replace, 295-300
Searching a string, 295,299
Secondary storage, 4,314-317
Sector, 314
Security, 324,350
SELECT CASE, 73-77
Semicolon, (PLOT), 264
Semicolon (PRINT), 193,203, 208,324
Sentinel value, 97,101,140, 201
Sequence, 32,33,43,44,52, 77,110,392,394
Sequential access, 324,326, 329-331
SET BACK statement, 265, 266,370
SET BACKGROUND COLOR statement, 265,266
SET COLOR statement, 265,267, 369,370
SET CURSOR statement, 213,214,284

SET MARGIN statement, 203,324
SET MODE statement, 284,369
SET POINTER statement, 324
SET RECORD statement, 326,331
SET RECSIZE statement, 327,329,334
SET WINDOW statement, 261,262,266
SET ZONEWIDTH statement, 203,324
Sin function, 122
Size function, 240
Skeleton program, 162,163
SOUND statement, 305-308
Source program, 8
SPLIT command, 211,390
Sqr function, 121,122
Statement number, 387, 409,410
Stored program concept, 6,7
String array, 224,239,292
String constant, 22,24,292
String function, 122,292, 304,305
String manipulation, 292-305
String operations, 292
String variable, 24,292, 301,327
Str$ function, 303,304
Stub subroutine, 163
SUB statement, 141,142, 245,246,334
Subroutine, 118,119, 136-145,152,156,170, 244-246,411
Subroutine, graphic (PICTURE), 279-283
Subroutine name, 141,142
Subscript, 226,229-231, 233,240

Substring, 292,299,300,301, 303,304,327,329
Syntax error, 400,401
System disk drive, 9,360

Tab function, 203,204,324
Table manipulation, 235,243,244
Telecommunication, 414
Test data, 171,172,200, 260,405
Text editor, 371-390
Text file, 319-325
Text file, access, 321-323
Text file, creation, 319-321
TEXT option, 317,319,320,321
Text, plotting, 264
THEN, 56,59,62,68
Time function, 305
Time$ function, 305
TO command, 389
Trace feature, 406
Transformation, picture, 279-280
Trim function, 305
True BASIC, 7,8,362-366, 407-414
True BASIC disk, 8,13
TRY command, 389

Ubound function, 240
Ucase function, 305
Unpack, 327,331
UNSAVE statement (or command), 323,324,334, 368,384
Utility program, 350,351

Val function, 303,304
Variable, 22-26,33,129, 223,224
Variable name, 24-26
Volatility, 314,315

WHEN ERROR IN structure, 304,403
Window, 9,203,209-214, 276,283
WINDOW statement, 283
Write-protect, 364,365
WRITE statement, 326, 329,334

x-y coordinate, 255,256, 257,261,264

Zero divide, 401,402
Zone width, 202,203